*Key Issues*

# POPULATION
Contemporary Responses to Thomas Malthus

*Key Issues*

# POPULATION

## Contemporary Responses to Thomas Malthus

Series Editor

### ANDREW PYLE

University of Bristol

THOEMMES PRESS

© Thoemmes Press 1994

Published in 1994 by
Thoemmes Press
11 Great George Street
Bristol BS1 5RR
England

ISBN
Paper : 1 85506 345 X
Cloth : 1 85506 344 1

*Population: Contemporary Responses to Thomas Malthus*
Key Issues No. 2

*British Library Cataloguing-in-Publication Data*

A catalogue record of this title is available
from the British Library

All rights reserved. No part of this publication may be reproduced, stored in a retrieval system, or transmitted in any way or by any means, electronic, mechanical, photocopying, recording or otherwise, without the written permission of the publisher.

Printed in Great Britain by Antony Rowe Ltd., Chippenham

# CONTENTS

INTRODUCTION
*by Andrew Pyle* .................................. ix

1. THE ANALYTICAL REVIEW
   Vol. XXVIII, August, 1798, pp. 119–125.
   *Anonymous* ..................................... 1

2. THE MONTHLY REVIEW
   Vol. XXVII, September, 1798, pp. 1–9.
   *Anonymous* .................................... 10

3. THE MONTHLY REVIEW
   Vol. XLII, December, 1803, pp. 337–357.
   *Anonymous* .................................... 21

4. THE MONTHLY REVIEW (*continued from above*)
   Vol. XLIII, January, 1804, pp. 56–70.
   *Anonymous* .................................... 46

5. THE GENTLEMAN'S MAGAZINE
   Vol. LXXIV, April, 1804, pp. 335–341.
   *Anonymous* .................................... 65

6. THE BRITISH CRITIC
   Vol. XXIII, January, 1804, pp. 59–69.
   *Anonymous* .................................... 77

7. THE BRITISH CRITIC (*continued from above*)
   Vol. XXIII, March, 1804, pp. 233–245.
   *Anonymous* .................................... 89

8. ANNALS OF AGRICULTURE
Vol. XLI, 1804, pp. 208–231.
by Arthur Young . . . . . . . . . . . . . . . . . . . . . . . . . . . . . 103

9. ANNUAL REVIEW
January, 1804, pp. 292–301.
by Robert Southey . . . . . . . . . . . . . . . . . . . . . . . . . . . 116

10. APPENDIX 1806
by T. R. Malthus . . . . . . . . . . . . . . . . . . . . . . . . . . . . . 138

11. AN EXAMINATION OF MR MALTHUS'S DOCTRINES
by William Hazlitt . . . . . . . . . . . . . . . . . . . . . . . . . . . . 170

12. ON THE PRINCIPLE OF POPULATION
by William Hazlitt . . . . . . . . . . . . . . . . . . . . . . . . . . . . 176

13. ON THE APPLICATION OF MR MALTHUS'S PRINCIPLE TO THE POOR LAWS
by William Hazlitt . . . . . . . . . . . . . . . . . . . . . . . . . . . . 184

14. THE EDINBURGH REVIEW
Vol. XI, October, 1807, pp. 100–115.
Anonymous . . . . . . . . . . . . . . . . . . . . . . . . . . . . . . . . . 193

15. THE EDINBURGH REVIEW
Vol. XVI, August, 1810, pp. 464–476.
by Francis Jeffrey . . . . . . . . . . . . . . . . . . . . . . . . . . . . . 211

16. APPENDIX 1817
by T. R. Malthus . . . . . . . . . . . . . . . . . . . . . . . . . . . . . 224

17. THE QUARTERLY REVIEW
Vol. XVII, July 1817, pp. 360–403.
by J. B. Sumner . . . . . . . . . . . . . . . . . . . . . . . . . . . . . . 246

18. THE LONDON MAGAZINE
    1823, [pp. 465–477 of de Quincey's *Works*].
    *by Thomas de Quincey* . . . . . . . . . . . . . . . . . . . . . . .  286

19. THE VALLEY OF THE AVON
    From *Rural Rides*, 1826, pp. 296–322.
    *by William Cobbett* . . . . . . . . . . . . . . . . . . . . . . . . . .  295

The reviews reprinted in this book have been taken from original copies and the different grammatical and stylistic arrangement of each has been preserved.

# INTRODUCTION

For most of human history, there has been a general assumption that population growth is a good thing.[1] Statesmen have asked themselves what measures they could take to encourage marriages, not to delay or prevent them. In the Christian world, priests have reminded their congregations of the biblical injunction to increase and multiply, and of Saint Paul's maxim that it is better to marry than to burn. Increasing population was supposed to bring both power and prosperity to a state: there would be more young men for the army and navy in times of war, and more productive power for agriculture and industry in times of peace. Such assumptions provide the background for Malthus' *Essay on the Principle of Population* and help to explain its impact.

The dangers of increasing population had not, of course, gone completely unnoticed. Both Plato and Aristotle had noted that too high a birth rate could ruin an otherwise stable city-state and either reduce it to poverty or force it into an unwanted war against its neighbours. Where the land just can't support any more people, drastic measures such as infanticide may become necessary. These warnings were, however, clearly limited in their application to the situation of the Greek city-states; no attempt was made to use them as the basis for generalization.

In the eighteenth century too, there were warning voices, men who, in retrospect, have been labelled 'precursors of Malthus'. In her biography of Malthus, Patricia James discusses three such men: Sir James Steuart (1713-1780), Benjamin Franklin (1706-1790), and the Revd Joseph Townsend (1739-1816).[2] To describe these men as precursors

---

[1] For valuable background on ideas about population before Malthus, see James Bonar, *Theories of Population from Raleigh to Arthur Young*, London, Allen and Unwin, 1931 (reprinted Thoemmes, Bristol, 1992), and D. E. C. Eversley, *Social Theories of Fertility and the Malthusian Debate*, Oxford, Clarendon, 1959.

[2] Patricia James, *Population Malthus, His Life and Times*, London, R.K.P., 1979, pp. 103-8.

of Malthus is however, as James insists, an exaggeration. None of them had Malthus' grasp of general principles; none of them saw population pressing *immediately* on the means of subsistence. They saw population pressure as posing long-term dangers rather than as helping to shape present trends. Nor did they anticipate Malthus' explicit use of the principle of population to refute Utopian schemes for human improvement.

One writer who did anticipate this Malthusian argument was the Revd Robert Wallace (1697-1771). In his *Various Prospects of Mankind, Nature, and Providence* (1761), Wallace posed the following problem to the advocates of human 'improvement'. The diffusion of the principles of the Enlightenment, we are told, will make men wiser and better. This should bring peace and prosperity. But peace and prosperity will result in more marriages – and more children. Within a few generations, population growth will give rise to competition and eventually strife, as too many men fight for too little food. There is no reason to endorse the malicious charge of Hazlitt – that Malthus simply plagiarized from Wallace – but the resemblance is sufficiently strong to be worth noting.

The two chief targets of Malthus' first *Essay on Population* were the Utopian schemes of William Godwin (1756-1836) and the Marquis de Condorcet (1743-94). In his *Enquiry Concerning Political Justice* (1793),[3] Godwin had argued for the perfectibility of man – meaning thereby, not that the individuals of any generation would become absolutely perfect, but that the individuals of each succeeding generation would be superior, physically, intellectually, and morally, to their parents. As we progress in benevolence, he thought, the old distinctions of 'mine' and 'thine' will gradually disappear, and every object will be seen to belong by right to whoever has most *need* of it. On Godwin's theory of justice, the poor may have a moral right to the goods and properties of the rich. It does not follow, he insists, that they would be justified in appropriating those goods by force. A Godwinian social revolution must occur by universal consent.

Godwin takes note of Wallace's objection to the belief in human perfectibility, but insists that to reason in this way is to

[3] William Godwin, *Enquiry Concerning Political Justice* (1793), London, Penguin, 1976.

foresee difficulties at a great distance. 'Myriads of centuries of still increasing population may pass away, and the earth be yet found sufficient for the support of its inhabitants.'[4] And who is to say how much human character itself will change during those centuries? Perhaps, Godwin suggests, sexual desire itself will fade away. After all, he insists, 'one tendency of a cultivated and virtuous mind is to diminish our eagerness for the gratifications of the senses'.[5] Our enlightened descendants, then, may simply give up breeding because they have more interesting things to do. (In his later replies to Malthus, Godwin retracted these fanciful claims and admitted abortion and infanticide into his Utopia.)

Condorcet's *Esquisse Historique des Progres de L'Esprit Humain*,[6] written in hiding during 1794 and published in 1795, a year after his death in prison, is a remarkable document, a sort of *credo* of Enlightenment principles. Although the Revolution had given way to the Terror, and his only realistic prospect was of imprisonment and execution, not a trace of his personal pain and peril appear in the work, which paints a serene picture of the inevitability of human progress. Once humanity has rid itself at last of kings and priests, he insists, a glorious future awaits it.

Condorcet too realizes that over-population might pose a threat to his rosy picture of human progress. The danger, he insists, is not imminent: given the rise in production that will result from our increasing mastery over nature, it may be many centuries before over-population threatens real scarcity. In the meantime, he insists, our moral principles will have altered. We will have abandoned those 'ridicules préjugés de la superstition' which currently degrade our conceptions of ethics.[7] If we have any obligations to beings that do not yet exist, it is not to give them existence but to give them *happiness*. To suppose that it is morally right to burden the earth with 'êtres inutiles et malheureux' is just puerile. What

[4] *ibid.*, p. 769.

[5] *ibid.*, p. 776.

[6] Marie Jean Antoine Nicolas de Caritat, Marquis de Condorcet, *Esquisse d'un Tableau Historique des Progres de L'Esprit Humain* (1795), in Condorcet's *Oeuvres*, Volume 6, Friedrich Frommann Verlag, Stuttgart, 1968.

[7] *ibid.*, pp. 257-8.

precisely Condorcet had in mind is not clear, but it is usually assumed that he was advocating artificial methods of birth control.

The first edition of Malthus' great *Essay* is, primarily, an attack on Godwin and Condorcet.[8] It is largely discursive, and presents the outlines of its case without great reliance on exact facts and figures. To the modern reader, it comes as a surprise: we expect an argument solidly based on statistical evidence, full of tables of births, deaths, and marriages; we find instead a contribution to contemporary political and theological controversy. It is, in fact, an integral part of the backlash, the British reaction against the philosophy of the Enlightenment, now blamed for the Revolution and the Terror.

Malthus' crucial claim is that the principle of population, far from posing a remote threat to Utopian schemes, is actually exerting its influence here and now. In the European colonies in North America, he notes, the population is doubling every twenty-five years. This is due to the special circumstances of unlimited space and food: every man and wife who want to raise a family need only clear another patch of bush. But if population 'naturally' tends to double every generation, why is it that population growth in Europe, Asia, and Africa is so much slower? The answer is simple: population presses upon the available means of subsistence, and is checked by misery and vice. (Only in the second edition of 1803 does the third check, 'moral restraint', come to prominence.)

It follows, Malthus insists, that many of the evils of human life are natural and inevitable, the results of natural law (that is, of Divine ordinance) rather than human mismanagement. Any redistribution of wealth from rich to poor would be self-defeating: it would merely allow the poor to raise more children and thus produce even more misery in the next generation. The Poor Laws are therefore misguided and counter-productive, merely serving to maintain many thousands who consume but do not produce.

Godwin's suggestion that the sexual instinct itself will fade away as men become more enlightened is dismissed with scorn – there is no reason to believe that a well-educated and cultivated gentleman is less subject to the sexual passion than a

---

[8] See T. R. Malthus, *First Essay on Population* (1798), London, Macmillan, 1966.

common labourer. As for Condorcet's veiled hints, they merely reek of *vice*: Malthus always insisted that he was *not* a supporter of artificial means of birth control.

The last two chapters of the first *Essay* present a curious, and extremely heterodox, theodicy. Why, Malthus asks, has God made us as we are, i.e. subject to a passion that has such terrible consequences? The traditional notion that this life is a state of trial is dismissed as inconsistent with the notion of an omniscient being. Our world is rather a 'manufactory of mind', a sort of divine workshop for raising matter to the level of mind. (Failures are not punished but merely recycled.) It is only under conditions of struggle and suffering that the higher mental powers are called forth; if an animal can satisfy its desires too easily, it will never need to reason and exert its powers of will at all. So the principle of population created conditions of scarcity, of competition among men for limited resources; this in turn stimulates effort and encourages intelligent planning; thus are men distinguished from the beasts. The young Darwin may have owed more than one key idea to Malthus' *Essay*.

The early reviewers of the *Essay* clearly saw it as, first and foremost, a hatchet-job on Godwin and Condorcet, and praised it as such. Even then, however, doubts were expressed. The *Analytical Review* is disturbed by the work's extremely gloomy picture of the human condition, with its apparent implication that strife and suffering are simply inevitable. It also notes that the author had, doubtless unintentionally, provided 'the best apology for prostitution ever written'. The *Monthly Review* also praises the demolition of Utopian fantasies, but points disapprovingly to the unorthodox theology of the *Essay*'s final chapters, which seems to do away with the notion of Hell. In the subsequent editions of the *Essay*, the heterodox theology was quietly excised.

Between 1798 and 1803, Malthus spent a great deal of time and labour revising the *Essay*. The result, the 'great quarto' of 1803, is in many respects a completely new work.[9] It is very much more scholarly than its predecessor, making far more use of the existing literature and acknowledging more debts to earlier writers. It is also more 'scientific' in the sense that it rests

---

[9] For a scholarly modern edition of the *Essay*, see T. R. Malthus, *An Essay on the Principle of Population*, ed. Donald Winch, Cambridge, C.U.P., 1992.

its case less on intuitive argument and more on tables of statistics. If the first edition is primarily a work of political philosophy, the second is closer to the modern notion of a social science. It also modifies the argument in one vitally important respect: in addition to 'vice' and 'misery' as checks to population, Malthus now emphasizes the possibility of 'moral restraint' through delayed marriage.

Checks to population are now divided into 'positive' (infant mortality) and 'preventive' (delayed marriage and smaller families). The sexual instinct is no longer represented as a mere blind force of nature but as something that we can in principle restrain and govern. But if it is both prudent and moral to delay marriage, why are artificial methods of birth control denounced as evil? Why not marry early, but just postpone having a family until later? Malthus answers that, for the young man, the *prospect* of the joys of marriage provides a stimulus to industry and achievement which would be quite taken away if one could have the pleasures of sex without the ensuing burden of a family to support. One must add in his defence here that he knew what he was talking about: he delayed marrying his beloved Harriet until he knew he could support a family, and toiled incessantly to achieve the required financial security. One might even argue that we owe the *Essay* itself to repressed sexual energy.

If celibacy in the single state is possible, it can under certain circumstances be morally required. (Let us assume that Malthus accepted the usual moral maxim that 'ought implies can'.) It follows that God or Nature is not directly to blame for human poverty and its resulting miseries. The poor man who has difficulty raising a family must blame not Providence, nor the government, but *himself*:

> When the wages of labour are hardly sufficient to maintain two children, a man marries and has five or six. He of course finds himself miserably distressed. He accuses the insufficiency of the price of labour to maintain a family. He accuses his parish for their tardy and sparing fulfilment of their obligation to assist him. He accuses the avarice of the rich, who suffer him to want what they can so well spare. He accuses the partial and unjust institutions of society, which have awarded him an inadequate share of the produce of the earth. He accuses perhaps the dispensations of Providence,

which have assigned to him a place in society so beset with unavoidable distress and dependence. In searching for objects of accusation, he never adverts to the quarter from which all his misfortunes originate. The last person he would think of accusing is himself, on whom, in fact, the whole of the blame lies, except in so far as he has been deceived by the higher classes of society.[10]

The last clause here is important. The man is not *wholly* to blame for his misfortune if he is simply following the advice of statesmen who mistakenly believe that a large population is a national strength and thus advocate measures to encourage marriage, or of clergymen who recommend young people to marry on the basis of the famous maxim of Saint Paul, i.e. for fear of their otherwise falling into sin. However well-meaning such clergymen may be, Malthus insists, they do a great deal of harm. To marry without a realistic prospect of raising a family is not just imprudent but immoral; to assume that 'God will provide' is to tempt Providence. Far from encouraging young people to marry, clergymen should thus warn them against it:

> To this end, I should propose a regulation to be made, declaring that no child born from any marriage taking place after the expiration of a year from the date of the law [the repeal of the Poor Law], and no illegitimate child born two years from the same date, should ever be entitled to parish assistance. And to give a more general knowledge of this law, and to enforce it more strongly on the minds of the lower classes of people, the clergyman of each parish should, previously to the solemnization of a marriage, read a short address to the parties, stating the strong obligation on every man to support his own children; the impropriety, and even immorality, of marrying without a fair prospect of being able to do this; the evils which have resulted to the poor themselves, from the attempt which had been made to assist, by public institutions, in a duty which ought to be exclusively appropriated to parents; and the absolute necessity which had at length appeared, of abandoning all such institutions, on account of their producing effects totally opposite to those which were intended.[11]

[10] *ibid.*, p. 227.
[11] *ibid.*, p. 261.

This was one of the passages which aroused the most violent protests from Malthus' opponents. To a man like Cobbett, for example, the thought of 'Parson Malthus' preaching a sermon against marriage was just an abomination; other critics poured scorn on the idea of expecting prudence and foresight from the poorest sections of the populace.

In addition to the statesmen and clergymen who recommend early marriage, there is another class of well-meaning but muddled theorists who come in for Malthus' fire. These are the advocates of the so-called 'Rights of Man', who mislead the poor into thinking that they have a moral right to the support of the rich. If Godwin and Condorcet are Malthus' primary targets, Tom Paine is not far behind. In what was perhaps the most savage – and certainly the most hated – passage in the whole *Essay*, Malthus writes:

> A man who is born into a world already possessed, if he cannot get subsistence from his parents on whom he has a just demand, and if the society do not want his labour, has no claim of *right* to the smallest portion of food, and, in fact, has no business to be where he is. At nature's mighty feast there is no vacant cover for him. She tells him to be gone, and will quickly execute her own orders, if he do not work upon the compassion of some of her guests. If these guests get up and make room for him, other intruders immediately appear demanding the same favour. The report of a provision for all that come fills the hall with numerous claimants. The order and harmony of the feast is disturbed, the plenty that before reigned is changed into scarcity; and the happiness of the guests is destroyed by the spectacle of misery and dependence in every part of the hall, and by the clamorous importunity of those who are justly enraged at not finding the provision which they had been taught to expect. The guests learn too late their error, in counteracting those strict orders to all intruders, issued by the great mistress of the feast, who, wishing that all her guests should have plenty, and knowing that she could not provide for unlimited numbers, humanely refused to admit fresh comers when her table was already full.[12]

---

[12] *ibid.*, p. 249.

This famous paragraph was omitted in the 1806 edition, but not because Malthus had changed his mind about the much-vaunted 'Rights of Man'. It is more probable that he withdrew it either because the harshness of its language gave unnecessary offence to tender-minded readers, or because it might be read not merely as denying the poor any *right* to the support of the rich, but as advising the rich even against the promptings of *charity*.

We include in this volume three anonymous reviews of the 1803 edition of the *Essay*. The *British Critic* praises Malthus for his demolition of Godwin and endorses, albeit with some hesitation, Malthus' principles, but goes on to express two deep causes of concern. One is that delayed marriages will inevitably lead to an increase in vice; the other is that the abolition of the Poor Laws would be politically dangerous, 'a measure much too violent' to be acceptable. The *Monthly Review* gives a rough sketch of Malthus' theory, defends his originality, and praises his refutation of the 'sophisms' of Godwin and Condorcet. More importantly, it defends Malthus as a *moral* teacher, activated by enlightened benevolence rather than gloomy misanthropy, and preaching that reason and restraint are ultimately rewarded with happiness. This reviewer even takes it upon himself to defend Malthus' claim that the children of the poor have no right to State support. The *Gentleman's Magazine* reviewer gives us not so much an account of Malthus as of an anonymous pamphlet entitled *Remarks on a Late Publication*.[13] According to the author of the *Remarks*, we are told, Malthus' fundamental principles are sound, but his view of their implications is 'gloomy' and 'exaggerated'. The Poor Laws, in particular, should be reformed but not abolished.

So far, the reviewers have all been anonymous, and most of them have been strongly favourable. Where they have ventured to dissent from Malthus' conclusions, it has always been with caution and respect. In 1804, however, appeared two major attacks on Malthus and his doctrines. Writing in his own *Annals of Agriculture*, Arthur Young (1741–1820) attacked the Malthusian diagnosis of rural poverty as due to population pressure. We could solve the problem of rural poverty, Young

---

[13] Anon., *Remarks on the Essay on the Principle of Population*, London, 1803. Reprinted by Routledge/Thoemmes Press, 1994.

claims, by allocating cottages to poor families, each with a small plot of land attached. The cottage would be leased to a couple on condition that no member of their family demanded assistance from the parish; if they did so, the grant would lapse. By such means, Young argues, population could continue to grow without immediately generating poverty and dependence. It is easy to see why Malthus was not impressed.

The attack by the poet Robert Southey (1774–1843) in the *Annual Review* marks a major shift in Tory attitudes towards Malthus. Hitherto praised for his demolition job on the Utopian fantasies of the Left, he is now denounced as a bad Christian and an unsound moralist. He seeks, says Southey, to represent the sexual urge as something inevitable and ungovernable, thus degrading men and women to the condition of beasts. He seems to think, says Southey, that 'the gratification of lust is a thing of physical necessity, equally with the gratification of hunger', a monstrously immoral proposition. But also, and equally clearly, a *false* proposition, as Malthus himself is obliged to admit.

What is most objectionable in the *Essay*, according to Southey, is its suggestion that the evils which afflict human life are the result of Nature, and hence ultimately of God. Although a Christian minister, Malthus has effectively denied the existence of a benevolent Providence. Population growth, Southey argues, is not a problem, so long as increased production can keep pace with it, as is surely the case at present. When that is no longer possible, celibacy will indeed be morally required. But in the 1803 edition of the *Essay*, Malthus admits that celibacy is possible. His argument against Godwin over the perfectibility of man thus collapses. Malthus can't have it both ways: either *lust* is physically necessary, in which case we can't help having children and God really is to blame for most human suffering; or celibacy is possible, in which case the refutation of Godwin collapses.

As for the celebrated *feast* passage, Southey clearly finds it revolting. Malthus is simply advising the rich to harden their hearts and let the poor starve. Yet he comes before his readers in the garb of a Christian minister! His book is a mixture of truisms (like the fact that man cannot live without food) and sophisms (like the attempt to blame God for all our ills), full of 'folly and wickedness'; his fame will merely be fleeting.

The claim that Malthus had denied Providence is repeated in

Thomas Jarrold's *Dissertations on Man* of 1806.[14] Jarrold, a Manchester physician, found the idea that God would bring more children into the world than He provided nourishment for morally repugnant. The very notion, he insisted, contradicts our conception of a Being that is both wise and benevolent. 'Of Providence', writes Jarrold, 'Mr Malthus seems to have a very vague and imperfect idea.'[15] As for the notorious 'feast' passage, it 'might have been applauded in the councils of Nero, or in the camps of Attila or of Cortez,'[16] but it surely has no place in an enlightened and Christian age. God provides places for all at the feast; latecomers can always go and cultivate the waste lands. (Malthus will retort, of course, that this can only postpone the problem.)

For the 1806 edition of the *Essay*, Malthus made numerous changes. He not only deleted the 'feast' passage but added an appendix (reprinted here) in which he replied to the chief objections made against him. His main points can be listed as follows:

(1) He rejects the allegation that he has denied Providence and contradicted the Biblical injunction to increase and multiply. I am, Malthus insists, not a foe to population as such, but merely to such excess population as causes vice and misery. The only way to increase population without breeding vice and misery is to increase production.

(2) He defends prudence and self-love against the Godwinian theory of justice. The power of self-love is a gift of Providential wisdom; if we were all purely benevolent and no more concerned for our own interests than for those of our neighbours, the consequences would be disastrous.

(3) He replies to Arthur Young over the proposal to allot cottages to poor families. Young is charged with inconsistency for recommending in England the very form of rural economy which – on his own account – has proved so ruinous in France. What would become of the sons and daughters of the cottage-holders?

---

[14] Thomas Jarrold, *Dissertation on Man ... in Answer to Mr Malthus*, London, 1806. Reprinted by Thoemmes, Bristol, 1993.

[15] *ibid.*, p. 327.

[16] *ibid.*, p. 20.

(4) He defends his own consistency against accusations of self-contradiction. As a moralist, one may preach the duty (under certain circumstances) of chastity; as a student of human nature, one may expect one's moral teaching to be largely ignored. One can thus continue to advise the poor against early marriage, while expecting them to ignore one's advice and painting a black picture of the *probable* (not inevitable) consequences.

(5) He vigorously rejects the allegation, made in Cobbett's *Political Register*,[17] that his principles lend support to the slave trade.

The year 1807 saw the appearance of William Hazlitt's substantial *Reply to the Essay on Population*.[18] Hazlitt (1778–1830) was a critic and essayist, and a brilliant polemical writer. In his politics he was a thorough radical, an admirer of Godwin and a firm believer in the ideals of the French Revolution. We reprint here three of Hazlitt's shorter attacks on Malthus, in which the following points are made in a typically forceful manner:

(1) Malthus' originality is denied, and the accusation made that he plagiarized from Wallace.

(2) Malthus' famous geometrical and arithmetical ratios are derided as pseudo-scientific nonsense, an essentially bogus attempt to hide bad politics behind a smokescreen of supposed science.

(3) Malthus' 'refutation' of Godwin is dismissed. As soon as Malthus admits 'moral restraint' in the second edition of the *Essay*, all his arguments against perfectibility collapse.

(4) Malthus is accused of pandering to the political interests of the rich. Why has his book been so successful, Hazlitt asks, when its actual arguments are so weak? The answer is that Malthus has provided a justification for callous indifference among the upper classes to the suffering of the poor. In short, Malthus provides pseudo-science in the service of sinister political interests. 'This will never do.'

---

[17] See Patricia James, pp. 124–6.

[18] William Hazlitt, *Reply to the Essay on Population*, London, 1807, reprinted by Routledge/Thoemmes Press, 1994.

(5) Poverty and hunger are the product of bad – and remediable – human institutions, not ordained by God or Nature. To recommend abolishing the Poor Laws and letting the poor starve is bad enough; to pretend to be doing so in a spirit of enlightened benevolence reeks of hypocrisy.

The prestigious *Edinburgh Review* never actually devoted a review to the *Essay*, although it published numerous articles (some by Malthus himself) on the ensuing debate. Of these articles, we have included two in this volume. In October 1807 there appeared an article by a Justice of the Peace defending Malthus' views of the Poor Laws. Malthus, the anonymous author insists, is not a monster but a man of wide views and generous spirit.

Our other selection dates from 1810, when Francis Jeffrey decided to review two of Malthus' fiercest critics, Ingram and the anonymous Hazlitt. The *Disquisitions on Population* of Robert Acklom Ingram (1763-1809) had appeared in 1808.[19] Like Jarrold, Ingram found that Malthus' views offended against our conception of Divine Providence:

> The religious mind revolts at the apparent want of intelligence and contrivance in the Author of the creation, in infusing a principle into the nature of man, which it required the utmost exertion of human prudence and ingenuity to counteract.[20]

In his 1810 article, Jeffrey accuses the critics of a host of misunderstandings. The *Essay*, he insists, has been far more widely discussed than read; and far more widely read than understood. Malthus has simply gathered together some manifest and undeniable *facts*, and drawn some fairly plain inferences from those facts. Yet for this he is denounced as a malefactor and a hater of mankind!

Something, Jeffrey reasons, must check the tendency of population to increase in a geometrical ratio. All that Malthus insists is that the preventive check is better (and more fitting for a rational and moral being), than the positive check of high infant mortality. As for Ingram's objections, does not the

---

[19] Robert Acklom Ingram, *Disquisitions on Population*, London, 1808.

[20] *ibid.*, p. 5.

Christian religion teach that this life is a state of trial and preparation for the life that is to come? And are not Malthus' principles well suited to such a state?

In his *Appendix* to the 1817 edition of the *Essay* Malthus included replies to recent works by James Grahame and John Weyland. Grahame's *Inquiry into the Principles of Population*[21] (1816) accused Malthus of regarding disease, famine, and war as 'benevolent remedies' ordained by God to offset the evils caused by the principle of population. An exasperated Malthus felt obliged to reply that this was a complete and utter misunderstanding of his position. War, famine, and disease are evils which population growth will occasion, if we permit it. To prevent these evils in the future, we should take steps now to limit family size.

This leads us in turn into Grahame's second charge, that Malthus favoured artificial methods of birth control. This suggestion is indignantly rejected: the only method of limiting family size that I have proposed, Malthus insists, is delayed marriage. It must have galled him to find outspoken advocates of contraception such as Francis Place[22] being labelled 'Malthusians' in the press.

John Weyland's *Principles of Production and Population*[23] (1816) challenged Malthus' assumption of a 'tendency' of human populations to double every twenty-five years unless checked. Here Malthus is on much more shaky ground. The ideal limit to human reproduction might be around one child per couple per year for thirty years – if the mother could survive it. This would give a 'tendency' to reproduce much faster than Malthus postulates. So why does he settle on a 'tendency' to double in twenty-five years, and seek for explanations ('checks') for rates slower than that? Here Malthus replies at some length, without really clearing up the fundamental difficulty.

---

[21] James Grahame, *An Inquiry into the Principle of Population*, London, 1816. Reprinted by Routledge/Thoemmes Press, 1994.

[22] Francis Place, *Illustrations and Proofs of the Principle of Population Including an Examination of the Proposed Remedies of Mr Malthus*, London, 1822. Reprinted by Routledge/Thoemmes Press, 1994.

[23] John Weyland, *Principles of Production and Population as they are affected by the Progress of Society with a View to Moral and Political Consequences*, London, 1816. Reprinted by Routledge/Thoemmes Press, 1994.

Weyland also thought that Britain's cities were *so* unhealthy that they served as vast 'sinks' draining off excessive population. To compensate for such losses, he thought, rural couples should be encouraged to marry early and raise large families. Even if Weyland's facts were correct, Malthus retorts, they would pose no threat to my principles; but it seems likely that he is simply confused on many points.

The conservative *Quarterly* waited for a long time to review the *Essay*, but then provided its readers with a long and very thorough review by J. B. Sumner, which takes up the debate at the stage of Malthus' 1817 *Appendix*. John Bird Sumner (1780–1862) was an Evangelical clergyman, later to become Bishop of Chester (1828) and Archbishop of Canterbury (1848). He was also the author of the *Records of the Creation* (1816), which gave a strongly Malthusian tone to orthodox Christian doctrine.

Sumner takes up the chorus begun by the earliest reviewers, praising Malthus for his demolition-job on the Utopias of the political left. (Robert Owen now takes his place alongside Godwin and Condorcet among the targets.) He goes on to defend Malthus against a host of misconceptions, and to defend his Christian credentials. Malthus' theory, Sumner insists, is compatible with the spirit of Christian charity, and with the Christian notion that this life is a state of trial. It is a pity, Sumner suggests, that Malthus' unfortunate *manner* of expressing his views has given rise to so much outrage and offence. One wonders if he had the 'feast' passage in mind.

We close our volume with two sharply contrasted pieces, both by well-known writers. Thomas de Quincey (1785–1859) was an eccentric but brilliant essayist who clearly took a certain pride in his keen analytical intellect. In his article, 'Malthus', written for the *London Magazine* of 1823, he pours scorn on Malthus' famous geometrical and arithmetical ratios, and dismisses the refutation of Godwin as a mere paralogism. One might expect him then to align himself with the anti-Malthusian camp. Far from it – he then proceeds to turn his critical fire on Malthus' foes, and to point out their misunderstandings and fallacies. What are we meant to conclude from this even-handed double demolition job? De Quincey's conclusion is that, although the arguments on both sides are largely sophisms or confusions, the *Essay* still contains a preponderance of truth over error.

Our final extract is taken from the *Rural Rides* of the radical journalist and politician William Cobbett (1763–1835).[24] Our choice of an extract from the *Rides* may seem eccentric. Since Cobbett wrote extensively against Malthus, it might be asked, why not choose a more explicitly anti-Malthusian polemic? The answer is twofold. In the first place, the *Rides* show Cobbett at his best, speaking of what he knows, i.e. the conditions of rural England. Secondly, the extract chosen is in fact, from first to last, a sustained anti-Malthusian argument.

Cobbett presents to his readers two independent chains of reasoning in support of the conclusion that rural England can comfortably support more than its present population. The churches and manor houses of the valley of the Avon in Wiltshire provide eloquent testimony, he argues, of a once greater population. Yet the valley is no less fertile now than it was in the past. Indeed, a simple calculation reveals that the land can support, in relative comfort, a much greater population than it does at present.

So why is there such desperate rural poverty, if not for reasons of over-population? It is the economic system, Cobbett argues, and in particular the National Debt, which sucks the country's wealth from the rural producers to the mere parasites – politicians, tax men, and of course parsons – in the 'Great Wen' (London). Why is Malthus so widely read and admired? Here Cobbett finds himself largely in agreement with Hazlitt. It is because Malthus' *false* analysis of the cause of poverty (i.e. as due to over-population) is used to support a sinister political programme, and to prop up a monstrous regime. It is simply *bad government* that is responsible for rural poverty. Malthus is popular among the governing classes because he diverts attention from the true cause of poverty and encourages the poor to blame Nature, God, or even themselves for their woes, rather than Pitt and his successors.

*A Note on Editorial Policy*

The aim of this volume is to present a selection of the literature on Malthus' *Essay* from its first edition in 1798 until Malthus' death in 1834. Our emphasis is primarily on the moral and political philosophy rather than on the economics, and on questions of theory rather than of practical application. The

[24] William Cobbett, *Rural Rides*, London, Penguin, 1967.

literature generated by the *Essay* was vast and extremely diverse; no attempt has been made to cover all aspects of it. (The application of Malthus' principles to Irish affairs, for example, is entirely omitted.) We have tried to provide a fair selection of the following types of literature:

(1) The *early* reviews of the 1798 and 1803 editions of the *Essay*, which show how the work was first received by its contemporaries, and set the scene for the subsequent polemics.

(2) The *major* contributors to the controversy – Young, Southey, Hazlitt, Cobbett.

(3) The views expressed in the most prestigious reviews, the *Edinburgh* and the *Quarterly*.

(4) Malthus' own replies, as given in his appendices to the 1806 and 1817 editions of the *Essay*.

No selection policy will please all readers. All we can hope is that this selection does not appear wildly arbitrary and eccentric, and that it will help to provide some insight into the historical context of a classic work.

> Andrew Pyle
> *University of Bristol*
> *June 1994*

# THE ANALYTICAL REVIEW
## Vol. XXVIII, August 1798

Art. II. *An Essay on the Principle of Population, as it affects the future Improvement of Society. With Remarks on the Speculations of Mr. Godwin, M. Condorcet, and other Writers.* 8vo, 396 p. Price 6s. in boards. Johnson. 1798.

The french revolution, which has broken up the established forms of society, and destroyed the distinctions which generations had held in veneration, has very naturally called the attention of all men to the study of the social relations of life, and to the investigation of the powers and expectations of man. The imaginations of men, which are ever soaring above the reality of things, and prepared to take wing upon every remarkable occasion, have conceived, that a new era is about to commence, and that the future history of our species will resemble the past in nothing. Mr. Condorcet, Mr. Godwin, and Mr. Brothers have, indeed, been differently affected by the astonishing events which have lately occurred; but it would be difficult to say of the three which has reasoned and prophesied with most extravagance. It appears to us more probable, that Brothers is the appointed king of the jews, commissioned to collect that extraordinary people from the four winds of Heaven, and to replace them in their father's land, than that every man upon this globe shall be able to sustain himself and the helpless, who depend upon him, by the labour of half an hour in every day; that intellectual vigour shall destroy the sexual appetite; or that man shall no longer be subject to death, but live for ever, without suffering from the wastings of age, or the ravages of disease. Such are the pleasing dreams of Condorcet and Godwin.

The author of the essay before us undertakes to examine the reasons which have been adduced by these gentlemen in favour of their opinions, and he has well performed his task, for he has met them with infinite acuteness, and in the true spirit of candour and philosophy. He is not one of those who rail when they should reason, and laugh when they should refute their antagonists. He is not one of those unfeeling enemies of mankind, who ridicule all ideas of the melioration of the condition of man. He thinks the condition of mankind may be improved, and that an improvement of it ought to be attempted. The question, therefore, between the family of the visionaries and this philosopher is, to *what extent* this improvement can be carried, and *what degree of felicity* man has reason to expect in this world. 'He has read', he says, 'the fanciful speculations of Condorcet and Godwin, with a wish to find them true; but to him does not belong the power of concluding all he wishes to be fact, and of thus subduing the understanding to the will.' We are glad to see a refutation of the new philosophy, if it, indeed, merit the name of philosophy, and more especially by such a man, by a man inclined to admit whatever is admissible in it's favour, and to embrace with eagerness whatever promises benefit to mankind. The speculations of Condorcet, in one sense, belong to another country, and we have a right to look to France for a refutation of them. Mr. Godwin belongs to us, and we have long expected some english philosopher to examine critically what he has so confidently advanced. Whether his hypotheses were esteemed too visionary even to deserve animadversion, or whether his acknowledged acuteness deterred our countrymen from the undertaking, we know not; but the fact is, that the essay before us is the first performance, which professedly treats upon the fundamental principles of his book, and touches the inquiries, which are the basis of all his superstructure, concerning the perfectibility of man. It is not now necessary, that other labourers should enter the field, for we are much mistaken, if this essay will not be considered as a full and fair confutation of this extravagant philosophy.

Our author makes two postulata, on which he bottoms all the observations he offers in refutation of Mr. Godwin's hypotheses. They are the following:

First, That food is necessary to the existence of man.

Secondly, That the passion between the sexes is necessary, and will remain nearly in it's present state.

Mr. Godwin has not attempted to prove, neither has he suggested, that it is probable, that food will not continue to be necessary to the existence of man: yet, as he has ranged so far in the field of conjecture, we wonder he has not told us, that the vigour of improving intellect will, in time, overcome the desire for food, and be, of itself, without the vulgar aid of ordinary diet, equal to the support and the health of the human being. He has found it more easy, however, to dispose of the sexual appetite; yet, as far as facts are concerned, we have as little reason to think, that man will cease to marry and to be given in marriage, like the angels of heaven, as that he will cease to need, for the support of life, the bread which perisheth. Men, the most intellectual, as our author has well observed, have hitherto been much disposed to sexual indulgences; and, we find by daily observation, that the pressure of no difficulties, the experience of no want, deter men from gratifying this impetuous and imperious appetite. Our author is therefore warranted in making this second postulum by the currency of all experience, which establishes his second, as firmly as it does his first, postulatum. It is really astonishing, that Mr. Godwin did not attempt to show the probability of the extinction of the desire and the necessity of food, when he wanted to prove that half an hour, of every day, devoted to labour, by every human being, would be equal to the supply of the wants of all that live.

The postulata of our author being admitted, let us now attempt to analyse his deductions. He observes, that the increase of mankind, when all obstructions to population are removed, would be in a geometrical ratio; whereas the ratio of the increase of the produce of the earth, upon the most romantic supposition, can be only arithmetical. Taking the population of the world at any number, the human species would increase in the ratio of 1. 2. 4. 8. 16. 32. 64. 128, &c. whilst subsistence would only increase as 1. 2. 3. 4. 5. 6. 7. 8, &c. In two centuries and a quarter the population would be, to the means of subsistence, as 512 to 10: in three centuries, as 4096 to 13. This calculation is founded upon the supposition, that no country, England for instance, could be supposed, by the most sanguine, to more than double it's present produce in 25 years, or more than yield, in addition to that double quantity, an increase equal to the present produce of the next 25 years, and so on *ad infinitum*; whereas, if the population doubled itself in 25 years, the next 25 years it would again double itself, or be increased, from the present stock, *four fold*. We confess, that we have not accustomed ourselves to range so far into the world of possibilities, as to think this statement concerning the increase of subsistence to be too timid. We think it very bold, and it much exceeds what we think the reason of the case admits of; on the contrary, we think the statement concerning the increase of population very moderate. If newly settled colonies have *been known* to double their population in 25 years, surely, were all obstructions to this increase, from the difficulty of obtaining subsistence, or, in other words, supporting a family, done away, it is surely reasonable to conclude, that population would be doubled in half that time, and, it is obvious, that it must increase in a geometrical ratio. Our author gives his opponent every advantage, and bottoms his calculations upon indisputable data, that his conclusions may admit of no doubt. Mr. Godwin, admits that there is a principle, which proportions the population to the means of subsistence; but seems not at all to comprehend what that principle is, or how it operates. He will find this well illustrated in the following paragraph:-

P. 29.- 'The way in which these effects are produced seems to be this:

We will suppose the means of subsistence in any country just equal to the easy support of it's inhabitants. The constant effort towards population, which is found to act even in the most vicious societies, increases the number of people before the means of subsistence are increased. The food, therefore, which before supported seven millions, must now be divided among seven millions and a half, or eight millions. The poor, consequently, must live much worse, and many of them be reduced to severe distress. The number of labourers also being above the proportion of the work in the market, the price of labour must tend toward a decrease; while the price of provisions would, at the same time, tend to rise. The labourer therefore must work harder to earn the same as he did before. During this season of distress, the discouragements to marriage, and the difficulty of rearing a family, are so great, that population is at a stand. In the mean time, the cheapness of labour, the plenty of labourers, and the necessity of an increased industry amongst them, encourage cultivators to employ more labour upon their land; to turn up fresh soil, and to manure and improve more completely what is already in tillage; till ultimately the means of subsistence become in the same proportion to the population as at the period from which we set out. The situation of the labourer being then again tolerably comfortable, the restraints to population are in some degree loosened; and the same retrograde and progressive movements with respect to happiness are repeated.'

Our author has expressed, in three propositions, the whole theory, which he means to establish and illustrate:

P. 37. 1. 'That population cannot increase without the means of subsistence, is a proposition so evident, that it needs no illustration.

2. 'That population does invariably increase, where there are the means of subsistence, the history of every people that have ever existed will abundantly prove.

3. 'And, that the superior power of population cannot be checked, without producing misery or vice, the ample portion of these too bitter ingredients in the cup of human life, and the continuance of the physical causes that seem to have produced them, bear too convincing a testimony.'

In order to establish these propositions, our author takes a cursory review of the different states in which mankind have been known to exist, beginning at the most rude, and ending in the most polished. This review occupies the third and fourth chapters. In the fifth chapter we find some very acute, and, we think, original observations on the inefficiency of the poor laws in this country; were we to omit the following paragraph, we should pay no compliment to our readers.

P. 75. 'Suppose, that by a subscription of the rich, the eighteen pence a day which men earn now, was made up five shillings, it might be imagined, perhaps, that they would then be able to live comfortably, and have a piece of meat every day for their dinners. But this would be a very false conclusion. The transfer of three shillings and sixpence a day to every labourer, would not increase the quantity of meat in the country. There is not at present enough for all to have a decent share. What would then be the consequence? The competition among the buyers in the market of meat, would rapidly raise the price from six-pence or seven-pence, to two or three shillings in the pound; and the commodity would not be divided among more than it is at present. When an article is scarce, and cannot be distributed to all, he that can shew the most valid patent, that is, he that offers most money becomes the possessor. If we can suppose the competition among the buyers of meat to continue long enough for a greater number of cattle to be reared annually, this could only be done at the expence of the corn, which would be a very disadvantageous exchange; for it is well known, that the country could not then support the same population; and when subsistence is scarce in proportion to the number of people, it is of little consequence whether the lowest members of the society possess eighteen pence or five shillings. They must at all events be reduced to live upon the hardest fare, and in the smallest quantity.'

We cannot forbear transcribing another paragraph from this valuable chapter.

P. 79. 'It may at first appear strange, but I believe it is true, that I cannot, by means of money, raise a poor man, and enable him to live much better than he did before, without proportionably depressing others in the same class. If I retrench the quantity of food consumed in my house, and give him what I cut off, I then benefit him, without depressing any but myself and family, who, perhaps, may be well able to bear it. If I turn up a piece of uncultivated land, and give him the produce, I then benefit both him and all the members of the society, because what he before consumed is thrown into the common stock, and probably some of the new produce with it. But if I only give him money, supposing the produce of the country to remain the same, I give him a title to a larger share of that produce than formerly, which share he cannot receive without diminishing the shares of others. It is evident that this effect, in individual instances, must be so small as to be totally imperceptible; but still it must exist, as many other effects do, which, like some of the insects that people the air, elude our grosser perceptions.'

Admitting the validity of the argument, from the principle of population, against the practicability of Godwin's scheme of equality, and the perfectibility and happiness of men in society, Mr. Godwin thinks the objection contemplates a very distant evil. Myriads of centuries of still increasing population may pass away, says he, and the earth be still found sufficient for the subsistence of it's inhabitants. This, which is the common reply to this overwhelming argument, of all the family of the visionaries, our author has very seriously considered, and, we think we may add, very satisfactorily refuted.

He supposes Mr. Godwin's system realized, and every obstruction to population removed; on the ability of the soil to meet the wants of the increasing population we have the following observations:

P. 186.-'There can be little doubt, that the equalization of property which we have supposed, added to the circumstance of the labour of the whole community being directed chiefly to agriculture, would tend greatly to augment the produce of the country. But to answer the demands of a population increasing so rapidly, Mr. Godwin's calculation of half an hour a day for each man, would certainly not be sufficient. It is probable that the half of every man's time must be employed for this purpose. Yet with such, or much greater exertions, a person who is acquainted with the nature of the soil in this country, and who reflects on the fertility of the lands already in cultivation, and the barrenness of those that are not cultivated, will be very much disposed to doubt, whether the whole average produce could possibly be doubled in twenty-five years from the present period. The only chance of success would be the ploughing up of the grazing countries, and putting an end almost entirely to the use of animal food. Yet a part of this scheme might defeat itself. The soil of England will not produce much without dressing; and cattle seem to be necessary to make that species of manure, which best suits the land. In China, it is said, that the soil in some of the provinces is so fertile, as to produce two crops of rice in the year without dressing. None of the lands in England will answer to this description.

'Difficult, however, as it might be, to double the average produce of the island in twenty-five years, let us suppose it effected. At the expiration of the first period, therefore, the food, though almost entirely vegetable, would be sufficient to support in health, the doubled population of fourteen millions.

'During the next period of doubling, where will the food be found to satisfy the importunate demands of the increasing numbers. Where is the fresh land to turn up? where is the dressing necessary to improve that which is already in cultivation? There is no person with the smallest knowledge of land, but would say, that it was impossible that the average produce of the country could be increased during the second twenty-five years by a quantity equal to what it at present yields. Yet we will suppose this increase, however improbable, to take place. The exuberant strength of the argument allows of almost any concession. Even with this concession, however, there would be seven millions at the expiration of the second term, unprovided for. A quantity of food equal to the frugal support of twenty-one millions, would be divided among twenty-eight millions.

'Alas! what becomes of the picture where men lived in the midst of plenty: where no man was obliged to provide with anxiety and pain for his restless wants: where the narrow principle of selfishness did not exist: where mind was delivered from her perpetual anxiety about corporal support, and free to expatiate in the field of thought which is congenial to her. This beautiful fabric of imagination vanishes at the severe touch of truth. The spirit of benevolence, cherished and invigorated by plenty, is repressed by the chilling breath of want. The hateful passions that had vanished, re-appear. The mighty law of self-preservation, expels all the softer and more exalted emotions of the foul. The temptations to evil are too strong for human nature to resist. The corn is plucked before it is ripe, or secreted in unfair proportions; and the whole black train of vices that belong to falsehood are immediately generated. Provisions no longer flow in for the support of the mother with a large family. The children are sickly from insufficient food. The rosy flush of health gives place to the pallid cheek and hollow eye of misery. Benevolence yet lingering in a few bosoms, makes some faint expiring struggles, till at length self-love resumes his wonted empire, and lords it triumphant over the world.'

Our author then draws the picture of society after it's attempt to realize the scheme of benevolence and equality, returning again, from dire necessity, to the scheme of private property, monopoly, and selfishness. No hope now is left for man, and we have not yet disposed of one hundred years, much less of myriads of centuries, but what arises from the energy of mind extinguishing the sexual passion. This our author fully examines in the eleventh chapter, and shows, that no experience or probability exists to encourage any such hope.

The sixteenth chapter examines an important part of Dr. Adam Smith's work on the Wealth of Nations; and shows, that every increase of wealth does not better the condition of the labouring poor. We think much of this chapter worthy to be quoted; but the nature of our work forbids us to indulge too freely our feelings on this very important and elaborate essay.

The latter part of this essay is spent in an attempt to show the probability, that man is not placed here in a state of trial, according to the vulgar notion of that term, but for the purpose of awakening and forming his mind; or, to speak more generally, for the purpose of working matter into mind. This view leads the author to conclude in favour of a future state, adapted for the residence of great and noble minds; and that minds, not formed by this process to excellence, will be again extinguished in their parent clay, and lose all conscious existence. Such is the essay to which we invite the reader's attention. It is written with great animation and eloquence, and although we have remarked some instances of inattention and carelessness in the style, yet, in this respect, upon the whole, it is entitled to great praise. Perhaps, too, it might have been compressed into a narrower compass, and we think the arrangement is not always happy; but we have received so much pleasure from the perusal of it, that we are ready to pardon the faults we have mentioned, for they are, indeed, venial. The view it gives us of human life is not the most flattering; neither is it such as affords any pleasure to the author, who appears to feel warmly for the interests of humanity. But, if it be a true view, we must submit to the painful necessity of receiving it. Without intending it, however, we think the author, in this essay, has furnished the best apology for prostitution, that has every been written. Miserable man seems, according to this system, to be doomed to make his choice between prostitution and infanticide; and the philosophy of Hobbes thus appears to be established, which states the natural state of man to be a state of warfare. We cannot doubt that this essay will receive much of the public attention. The subjects on which it treats are not so important, and it is written with so much ability, that we need not invite the metaphysician and philosopher to consider it attentively.

# THE MONTHLY REVIEW
## Vol. XXVII, September 1798

Art. I. *An Essay on the Principle of Population*, as it affects the future Improvement of Society. With Remarks on the Speculations of Mr. Godwin, M. Condorcet, and other Writers. 8vo, pp. 400. 6s. Boards. Johnson. 1798.

Almost half a century has now elapsed, since certain strong spirits in France scattered the seeds of a new species of philosophy, that has already raised its head to heaven and overshadowed the earth. Regarding with fastidious contempt all the established systems of policy, of morals, and of religion, by which the conduct and the opinions of mankind had hitherto been regulated, they laboured with unremitted industry, supported by great talents, to give a new bias to the human mind; and to eradicate from it that principle which had contributed so powerfully to facilitate government; – that principle which impels the many to submit their opinions to the real or supposed superior wisdom of the few. Their labours were successful. Having sapped the foundation on which the superstructure of opinion rested, it was not very difficult to subvert those opinions themselves. Men began to look at the existing establishments of government, and at received systems of religious faith and morals, with a degree of suspicion proportioned to their antiquity; and unfortunately the abuses in the one and the errors in the other, which were but too obvious, served to confirm the favourite dogma of those new apostles, – that they were all founded in tyranny, in hypocrisy, and in fraud. That *unique* phænomenon in the history of man, the French revolution, with the little good and all the evil which it has produced, is one of the consequences of this change. That revolution, which was itself an effect of the new philosophy, gave increased efficacy to its cause; and it imparted new energy to those principles which had already been found so powerful in unsettling the human mind. The new teachers of the world did not neglect to avail themselves of the advantage. They persisted in the attack on the old establishments, moral and political; until, as they supposed, they left not one stone on another of that edifice which it had been the labor of so many centuries to raise, to strengthen, and to embellish.

It is not in the nature of the human mind to rest without a system. No sooner, therefore, had the philosophers demolished the old systems, which, combining perhaps some falsehood with much truth, had the sanction at least of the common-sense of mankind, than they applied themselves to the fabrication of new theories; in which imagination supplied the place of experience, and man was considered as they wished him to be rather than as he is.

Of some of those system-builders, Fancy itself was unable to follow the rapid flights. They conceived man in a state not only such as has never yet existed, but such an one that even a strong imagination cannot conceive it possible for him to exist in it. His present circumstances they describe in the language of opprobrium and contempt; and those to which they suppose he will one day reach, they adorn with poetical panegyric: but of the means by which the transition is to be effected they are silent; and the obvious difficulties, which impede the desired change, they affect to undervalue, or totally overlook.

In this class of men, the late M. Cordorcet and the present Mr. Godwin hold a conspicuous place: – the one inculcating the possibility, if not probability, that the nature of man may be improved to absolute perfection in body and in mind, and his existence in this world protracted to immortality; the other recommending a system of equality which should banish vice and misery from the earth, and sublimate the passions of man into the qualities and dispositions of pure, perfect, and benevolent intellect.

Speculations so fantastic, systems so unfounded in the experience of mankind, and so contrary to those opinions which common sense suggests, and which the experience of several thousand years has corroborated, most men would think fit subjects rather for ridicule than refutation. The author of the volume now before us, however, who seems to possess a very candid mind as well as a sound understanding, believes that more good may result from a fair discussion even of such hypotheses, when advanced by able men, than from affecting to annihilate them by neglect. Such men, he thinks, neglect has no tendency to convince of their mistakes; 'on the contrary, a candid investigation of these subjects, accompanied with a perfect readiness to adopt any theory warranted by sound philosophy, may tend to convince them that in forming improbable and unfounded hypotheses, so far from enlarging the bounds of human science, they are contracting it, throwing us back into the very infancy of knowledge, and weakening the foundations of that mode of philosophising, under the auspices of which science has of late made such rapid advances.' He moreover thinks that a complete and satisfactory answer to them is not difficult to be given. It is involved, he conceives, in a few simple and indubitable propositions, which it is his object in this essay to develope. They are briefly these:

*The power of population is indefinitely greater than the power in the earth to produce subsistence for man.*

*By the law of our nature which makes food necessary to the life of man, the effects of these two unequal powers must be kept equal.*

*Therefore a strong check on population must be kept continually in operation, which check can be found only in vice or in misery, and which therefore will always constitute an insuperable obstacle to the perfectibility of man.*

In illustrating these propositions, the author proves that the difference between the power of population in man, and the power of the earth in producing sustenance, is the difference between a geometrical and an arithmetical series; each generation of man, when not under the influence of any check to population, producing double their own numbers; while the produce of the earth, under the highest degree of cultivation, increases in any determinate period, only by the repeated addition of a fixed quantity. The excess of this power of population, beyond the power of produce, creates what he calls the preventive check on marriage, – which, he says, operates at this day in full force in all the European countries; and he instances its efficacy and manner of operation on the different classes of the community in England.

The second positive check to population is that which represses an increase already begun, and is confined chiefly, though not solely, to the lowest orders of society.

'This check (he says) is not so obvious to common view as the other I have mentioned; and, to prove distinctly the force and extent of its operation, would require, perhaps, more data than we are in possession of. But I believe it has been very generally remarked by those who have attended to bills of mortality, that of the number of children who die annually, much too great a proportion belongs to those, who may be supposed unable to give their offspring proper food and attention; exposed as they are occasionally to severe distress, and confined, perhaps, to unwholesome habitations and hard labour. This mortality among the children of the poor has been constantly taken notice of in all towns. It certainly does not prevail in an equal degree in the country; but the subject has not hitherto received sufficient attention to enable any one to say, that there are not more deaths in proportion, among the children of the poor, even in the country, than among those of the middling and higher classes. Indeed, it seems difficult to suppose that a labourer's wife who has six children, and who is sometimes in absolute want of bread, should be able always to give them the food and attention necessary to support life. The sons and daughters of peasants will not be found such rosy cherubs in real life, as they are described to be in romances. It cannot fail to be remarked by those who live much in the country, that the sons of labourers are very apt to be stunted in their growth, and are a long while arriving at maturity. Boys that you would guess to be fourteen or fifteen, are upon inquiry, frequently found to be eighteen or nineteen. And the lads who drive plough, which must certainly be a healthy exercise, are very rarely seen with any appearance of calves to their legs; a circumstance, which can only be attributed to a want either of proper, or of sufficient nourishment.'

To these obstacles to increase of population in all long-occupied countries, he adds the vicious customs with respect to women, great cities, unwholesome manufactures, luxury, pestilence, and war; all of which, he thinks, may be fairly resolved into MISERY and VICE.

Having established the existence of these checks on population, which, originating in vice or misery, must for ever impede the progress of man towards perfection, he applies them to expose the futility of M. Condorcet's system, as delivered in his Essay on the Progress of the Human Mind. Condorcet, indeed, had in some measure anticipated the objection: for he says, as quoted by our author:

'But in this progress of industry and happiness, each generation will be called to more extended enjoyments, and in consequence, by the physical constitution of the human frame, to an increase in the number of individuals. Must not there arrive a period then, when these laws, equally necessary, shall counteract each other? When the increase in the number of men surpassing their means of subsistence, the necessary result must be, either a continual diminution of happiness and population, a movement truly retrograde, or at least, a kind of oscillation between good and evil? In societies arrived at this term, will not this oscillation be a constantly subsisting cause of periodical misery? Will it not mark the limit when all further amelioration will become impossible, and point out that term to the perfectibility of the human race, which it may reach in the course of ages, but can never pass?'

He then adds,

'There is no person who does not see how very distant such a period is from us; but shall we ever arrive at it? It is equally impossible to pronounce for or against the future realization of an event, which cannot take place, but at an æra, when the human race will have attained improvements, of which we can at present scarcely form a conception.'

'Mr. Condorcet's picture of what may be expected to happen when the number of men shall surpass the means of their subsistence, is justly drawn. The oscillation which he describes, will certainly take place, and will, without doubt, be a constantly subsisting cause of periodical misery. The only point in which I differ from Mr. Condorcet with regard to this picture, is, the period, when it may be applied to the human race. Mr. Condorcet thinks, that it cannot possibly be applicable, but at an æra extremely distant. If the proportion between the natural increase of population and food, which I have given, be in any degree near the truth, it will appear, on the contrary, that the period when the number of men surpass their means of subsistence, has long since arrived; and that this necessary oscillation, this constantly subsisting cause of periodical misery, has existed ever since we have had any histories of mankind, does exist at present, and will for ever continue to exist, unless some decided change take place, in the physical constitution of our nature.

'Mr. Condorcet, however, goes on to say, that should the period, which he conceives to be so distant, ever arrive, the human race, and the advocates for the perfectibility of man, need not be alarmed at it. He then proceeds to remove the difficulty in a manner, which I profess not to understand. Having observed, that the ridiculous prejudices of superstition, would by that time have ceased to throw over morals, a corrupt and degrading austerity, he alludes, either to a promiscuous concubinage, which would prevent breeding, or to something else as unnatural. To remove the difficulty in this way, will, surely, in the opinion of most men, be, to destroy that virtue, and purity of manners, which the advocates of equality, and of the perfectibility of man, profess to be the end and object of their views.'

The author now proceeds to examine the other conjectures of Condorcet, concerning the organic perfectibility of man, and the indefinite prolongation of human life; and these he refutes in an ingenious and satisfactory manner, by arguments for which we must refer the reader to the work itself.

Mr. Godwin's system next comes under consideration:– a system, says our author, the most beautiful and engaging that has ever appeared, but yet only a beautiful and engaging phantom, which vanishes when we awaken to real life, and contemplate the true and genuine situation of man on earth.

'Let us suppose,' says our author, 'all the causes of misery and vice in this island removed. War and contention cease. Unwholesome trades and manufactories do not exist. Crowds no longer collect together in great and pestilent cities for purposes of court intrigue, of commerce, and vicious gratifications. Simple, healthy, and rational amusements take place of drinking, gaming and debauchery. There are no towns sufficiently large to have any prejudicial effects on the human constitution. The greater part of the happy inhabitants of this terrestrial paradise live in hamlets and farm-houses scattered over the face of the country. Every house is clean, airy, sufficiently roomy, and in a healthy situation. All men are equal. The labours of luxury are at end. And the necessary labours of agriculture are shared amicably among all. The number of persons, and the produce of the island, we suppose to be the same as at present. The spirit of benevolence, guided by impartial justice, will divide this produce among all the members of the society according to their wants. Though it would be impossible that they should all have animal food, every day, yet vegetable food, with meat occasionally, would satisfy the desires of a frugal people, and would be sufficient to present them in health, strength and spirits.' –

'With these extraordinary encouragements to population, and every cause of depopulation, as we have supposed, removed, the numbers would necessarily increase faster than in any society that has ever yet been known. But to be quite sure that we do not go beyond the truth, we will only suppose the period of doubling to be twenty-five years, a ratio of increase, which is well known to have taken place throughout all the Northern States of America.

'To answer the demands of a population increasing so rapidly, Mr. Godwin's calculation of half an hour a day for each man, would certainly not be sufficient. It is probably that the half of every man's time must be employed for this purpose. Yet with such, or much greater exertions, a person who is acquainted with the nature of the soil in this country, and who reflects on the fertility of the lands already in cultivation, and the barrenness of those that are not cultivated, will be very much disposed to doubt, whether the whole average produce could possibly be doubled in twenty-five years from the present period. The only chance of success would be the ploughing up all the grazing countries, and putting an end almost entirely to the use of animal food. Yet a part of this scheme might defeat itself. The soil of England will not produce much without dressing; and cattle seem to be necessary to make that species of manure, which best suits the land. In China, it is said, that the soil in some of the provinces is so fertile, as to produce two crops of rice in the year without dressing. None of the lands in England will answer to this description.

'Difficult, however, as it might be, to double the average produce of the island in twenty-five years, let us suppose it effected. At the expiration of the first period therefore the food, though almost entirely vegetable, would be sufficient to support in health, the doubled population of fourteen millions.

'During the next period of doubling, where will the food be found to satisfy the importunate demands of the increasing numbers. Where is the fresh land to turn up? where is the dressing necessary to improve that which is already in cultivation? There is no person with the smallest knowledge of land, but would say, that it was impossible that the average produce of the country could be increased during the second twenty-five years by a quantity equal to what it at present yields. Yet we will suppose this increase, however improbable, to take place. The exuberant strength of the argument allows of almost any concession. Even with this concession, however, there would be seven millions at the expiration of the second term, unprovided for. A quantity of food equal to the frugal support of twenty-one millions, would be to be divided among twenty-eight millions.'

Reasoning in this way, the author proves that, before the end of the first century, there would exist several millions for whom there would be no provision; though, all this time, the yearly increase of the produce of the earth is supposed to be greater than the boldest speculator can imagine. Want, rapine, and murder, he infers, would be paramount through the world; or Mr. Godwin's system must be given up, and an administration of property established, not very different from that which prevails in civilized states at present; as the best, though inadequate, remedy for the evils which would press on the society.

Having thus given a general view of the author's reasoning against the systems of Condorcet and Godwin, our limits will not permit us to enter into a detail of the arguments by which he refutes their subordinate parts, the supposed extinction of the passion between the sexes – mental stimulants, &c. &c. We cannot, however, take our leave of this ingenious and respectable writer, and pass in silence some very interesting positions which he offers, with great modesty, in the conclusion of his work. They relate to the moral situation of man in this life with respect to a future existence; and he endeavours to prove that it is inconsistent with our ideas of the foreknowledge of God, that man should here be in a state of trial. It is more probable, he thinks, that this life is but a mighty process for awakening matter into mind, and that moral evil is probably necessary to the production of moral excellence. The agents of moral evil, he conceives to be instruments in the hands of the Deity, for the production of moral good; and the future and eternal punishments denounced against them by revelation, he believes to mean nothing more than a simple annihilation by death, while the agents of moral good shall flourish in immortality for ever. We shall give two extracts, in which these opinions are exactly stated (pp. 351–354 and 388–391):

'Infinite power is so vast and incomprehensible an idea, that the mind of man must necessarily be bewildered in the contemplation of it. With the crude and puerile conceptions which we sometimes form of this attribute of the Deity, we might imagine that God could call into being myriads, and myriads of existences; all free from pain and imperfection; all eminent in goodness and wisdom; all capable of the highest enjoyments; and unnumbered as the points throughout infinite space. But when from these vain and extravagant dreams of fancy, we turn our eyes to the book of nature, where alone we can read God as he is, we see a constant succession of sentient beings, rising apparently from so many specks of matter, going through a long and sometimes painful process in this world; but many of them attaining, ere the termination of it, such high qualities and powers, as seem to indicate their fitness for some superior state. Ought we not then to correct our crude and puerile ideas of Infinite Power from the contemplation of what we actually see existing? Can we judge of the Creator but from his creation? And, unless we wish to exalt the power of God at the expence of his goodness, ought we not to conclude, that even to the Great Creator, Almighty as he is, a certain process may be necessary, a certain time, (or at least what appears to us as time) may be requisite, in order to form beings with those exalted qualities of mind which will fit them for his high purposes?

'A state of trial seems to imply a previously formed existence, that does not agree with the appearance of man in infancy, and indicates something like suspicion and want of foreknowledge, inconsistent with those ideas which we wish to cherish of the Supreme Being. I should be inclined, therefore, as I have hinted before in a note, to consider the world, and this life, as the mighty process of God, not for the trial, but for the creation and formation of mind; a process necessary, to awaken inert, chaotic matter, into spirit; to sublimate the dust of the earth into soul; to elicit an æthereal spark from the clod of clay. And in this view of the subject, the various impressions and excitements which man receives through life, may be considered as the forming hand of his Creator, acting by general laws, and awakening his sluggish existence, by the animating touches of the Divinity, into a capacity of superior enjoyment. The original sin of man, is the torpor and corruption of the chaotic matter, in which he may be said to be born' –

'When we reflect on the temptations to which man must necessarily be exposed in this world, from the structure of his frame, and the operation of the laws of nature; and the consequent moral certainty, that many vessels will come out of this mighty creative furnace in wrong shapes; it is perfectly impossible to conceive, that any of these creatures of God's hand can be condemned to eternal suffering. Could we once admit such an idea, all our natural conceptions of goodness and justice would be completely overthrown; and we could no longer look up to God as a merciful and righteous Being. But the doctrine of life and immortality which was brought to light by the gospel, the doctrine that the end of righteousness is everlasting life, but that the wages of sin are death, is in every respect just and merciful, and worthy of the Great Creator. Nothing can appear more consonant to our reason, than that those beings which come out of the creative process of the world in lovely and beautiful forms, should be crowned with immortality; while those which come out mis-shapen, those whose minds are not suited to a purer and happier state of existence, should perish, and be condemned to mix again with their original clay. Eternal condemnation of this kind may be considered as a species of eternal punishment; and it is not wonderful that it should be represented, sometimes, under images of suffering. But life and death, salvation and destruction, are more frequently opposed to each other in the New Testament, than happiness and misery. The Supreme Being would appear to us in a very different view, if we were to consider him as pursuing the creatures that had offended him with eternal hate and torture, instead of merely condemning to their original insensibility those beings, that, by the operation of general laws, had not been formed with qualities suited to a purer state of happiness.

'Life is, generally speaking, a blessing independent of a future state. It is a gift which the vicious would not always be ready to throw away, even if they had no fear of death. The partial pain, therefore, that is inflicted by the Supreme Creator, while he is forming numberless beings to a capacity of the highest enjoyments, is but as the dust of the balance in comparison of the happiness that is communicated; and we have every reason to think, that there is no more evil in the world, than what is *absolutely necessary* as one of the ingredients in the mighty process.'

With respect to the first of these propositions, it is obvious that it leads to difficulties as great as those which it is adopted to evade; for is it not as difficult to conceive an Almighty Being bound to a certain process and a certain time in his work of creation or production, as to conceive a just and beneficent Being creating existences embittered by pain and debased by imperfection? – The question between the two opinions seems only to be which attribute shall be sacrificed.

On the theory respecting the punishment of moral evil, we leave the decision to the divines. We are not inclined to think, however, that the general adoption of such an idea would much diminish the quantity of moral evil in the world.

# THE MONTHLY REVIEW
## Vol. XLII, December 1803

Art. 1. *An Essay on the Principle of Population*, or a View of its past and present Effects on Human Happiness; with an Enquiry into our Prospects respecting the future Removal or Mitigation of the Evils which it occasions. A new Edition, very much enlarged. By T. R. Malthus, A.M., Fellow of Jesus College, Cambridge. 4to. pp. 610. 1l. 11s. 6d. Boards. Johnson. 1803.

The fearless spirit of investigation, the inflexible adherence to truth, the sober and liberal turn of mind, and the able manner of discussing nice and intricate points, which were so conspicuous in the *Essay on the Principle of Population*, induced us to speak of it, on its first appearance, in the language of warm commendation;[1] and they equally characterize this production of Mr. Malthus, who now avows himself as its author, in its more finished and systematic form. The principles and views on which it proceeds remain unchanged: but so material are the alterations in its plan and structure, that they intitle it to be considered as a distinct work; and in the shape in which it now presents itself, it stands very much disentangled from the visionary philosophy which it was its primary object to expose: for if at first it only professed to be a refutation of a false hypothesis, it now seeks the same end by exhibiting itself in the more dignified garb of a new and opposite system. As the subject which it embraces is, in many of its parts, of high importance, and of not less novelty, we feel ourselves required to bestow on it more than ordinary attention.

It was an observation of Dr. Franklin, that, on any new discovery being published, the jealousy of philosophers led them first to question its reality; and then, when that point could no longer be disputed, to endeavour to find a prior

---

[1] See Rev. Vol. xxvii. N.S. p. 1.

author, to whom it might be ascribed. Mr. Malthus must not be surprized if his claims, in the same way, should experience the common fate. If, however, the proposition that population must be kept down to the level of subsistence was too obvious to be matter of discovery at this time of day, yet to treat of it professedly, and to follow it to all its consequences, – consequences truly momentous, and never before contemplated, – was a novel course, which it was the good fortune of Mr. Malthus first to tread. For him it was reserved to determine the proportion between the increase of population and that of food, and to ascertain the various modes by which, in different countries and ages, the balance between both has been maintained; to find in it a medium, which exhibits under new aspects the laws and manners of nations; and to establish a test by which to try institutions of the most weighty public concern. He was destined to introduce, by these systems, the light of day into many parts of political economy, and of political arithmetic; to render it a ground furnishing new questions of vast importance to society, to civil government, and to domestic happiness; to make it the means of causing the history of every country, antient and modern, to be perused with new interest; and by its application, to shew the fallacy of captivating theories, and to correct important errors in legislation and in the administration of government:– errors sanctioned by such high names as those of Montesquieu, Hume, Smith, Price, and Robertson.

Perceiving that equality between the population of a country, and the means of subsistence furnished by its territory, is a law of nature, Mr. M. observes that it follows that the sole method of increasing the former is to render the latter more plentiful. He shews also that in regions the most unfavourable, in climates the most ungenial, and among tribes the most rude, the one will press on the limits of the other; that population requires no incitement beyond adequate subsistence; that to attempt to increase it in any other way is not only ineffectual, but highly pernicious; and that, the quantum of the means of subsistence remaining the same, to multiply marriages, and to render births more numerous, would be to accumulate misery, to increase mortality, and to subject the miserable race to the fatal inroads of disease and famine. He therefore cannot regard celibacy, in a certain degree, as a political evil, nor hold that late and less frequent marriages are injurious to the well-being of society; and consequently he cannot deem that policy, which has been known to favour the one and the other, liable to unqualified censure.

We should not wonder if a system, which originated, we are convinced, in an upright and enlightened mind, and which is now submitted to the public with the best intentions and purest views, should call forth clamour, and subject its author to controversy. The censorious may say, and the superficial may be induced to believe, that it exhibits qualities resembling those which have cast odium on the hypotheses of Hobbes and Mandeville; that it has a direct tendency to deaden our choicest sympathies, to extinguish our most refined sentiments, and to damp our most pleasurable aspirations; that it furnishes apologies for the most inhuman practices, and, by implication, countenances institutions hitherto deemed not less impolitic than monstrous; and that it lessens our sorrow on the view of those calamities which sweep away the species, and our horror at usages which are destructive of human life. It should, however, be the object of every honest and considerate inquirer, to discover whether this theory is founded in truth; to ascertain what are the practical hints, and the useful lessons which it furnishes; and to set himself on his guard against the ill effects to which its abuse, or misconceptions with regard to it, may give rise.

The author thus states the propositions on which he builds his system:

> '1. Population is necessarily limited by the means of subsistence.
> '2. Population invariably increases, where the means of subsistence increase, unless prevented by some very powerful and obvious checks.
> '3. These checks, and the checks which repress the superior power of population, and keep its effects on a level with the means of subsistence, are all resolvable into moral restraint, vice, and misery.
>
> 'The first of these propositions scarcely needs illustration. The second and third will be sufficiently established by a review of the past and present state of society.'

He afterward denominates moral restraint, the *preventive* check on population; and vice and misery, the *positive*. The review of these points occupies the greater half of the volume, and includes the cases of the savage nations, of those who at present inhabit Asia and Africa, of the antient Greeks and Romans, and of several of the states of modern Europe. Mr. M. shews that the difference between the power of population in man, and the power of the earth in producing sustenance, is the difference between a geometrical and an arithmetical series; as it is found that each generation of man, when not under the influence of any check on population, doubles its own numbers, while the produce of the earth, under the highest degree of cultivation in any determinate period, only increases by the repeated addition of a fixed quantity. The excess of this power of population creates the preventive check to its progress, namely, moral restraint; or calls forth the operation of the positive, viz. vice and misery. In New Holland, the singularly brutal treatment of the women, the impossibility of rearing many children, the profligacy of manners, wars, secret murders, highly fatal epidemics, and the recurrence of family, keep down the population; which is, however, so much on a level with the miserable food to which these ill-fated beings are habituated, that when any event occasions a deficiency of the usual quantity, scarcity and distress ensue.

It is a very just remark of the author, with regard to Savages, 'that, from their extreme ignorance, the dirt of their persons, and the closeness and filth of their cabins, they lose the advantage which usually attends a thinly peopled country, that of being more exempt from pestilential diseases than those which are fully inhabited;' and equally well founded is that which is supported in the following passage:

'It is not, therefore, as Lord Kaimes imagines, that the American tribes have never increased sufficiently to render the pastoral or agricultural state necessary to them; but, from some cause or other, they have not adopted in any great degree these more plentiful modes of procuring subsistence, and therefore cannot have increased so as to become populous. If hunger alone could have prompted the savage tribes of America to such a change in their habits, I do not conceive that there would have been a single nation of hunters and fishers remaining; but it is evident, that some fortunate train of circumstances, in addition to this stimulus, is necessary for this purpose; and it is undoubtedly probable, that these arts of obtaining food will be first invented and improved in those spots that are best suited to them, and where the natural fertility of the situation, by allowing a greater number of people to subsist together, would give the fairest chance to the inventive powers of the human mind.'

Foreseeing an objection which may be raised to his theory, Mr. Malthus observes:

'The very extraordinary depopulation that has taken place among the American Indians, may appear to some to contradict the theory which is intended to be established; but it will be found that the causes of this rapid diminution may all be resolved into the three great checks to population that have been stated; and it is not asserted, that these checks, operating from particular circumstances with unusual force, may not in some instances be more powerful even than the principle of increase.

'The insatiable fondness of the Indians for spirituous liquors, which, according to Charlevoix, is a rage that passes all expression, by producing among them perpetual quarrels and contests, which often terminate fatally, by exposing them to a new train of disorders which their mode of life unfits them to contend with, and, by deadening and destroying the generative faculty in its very source, may alone be considered as a vice adequate to produce the present depopulation. In addition to this, it should be observed, that almost every where the connexion of the Indians with Europeans, has tended to break their spirit, to weaken or to give a wrong direction to their industry, and in consequence to diminish the sources of subsistence. In St. Domingo, the Indians neglected purposely to cultivate their lands in order to starve out their cruel oppressors. In Peru and Chili, the forced industry of the natives was fatally directed to the digging into the bowels of the earth, instead of cultivating its surface; and among the northern nations, the extreme desire to purchase European spirits, directed the industry of the greatest part of them, almost exclusively, to the procuring of peltry for the purpose of this exchange, which would prevent their attention to the more fruitful sources of subsistence, and at the same time tend rapidly to destroy the produce of the chace. The number of wild animals, in all the known parts of America, is probably even more diminished than the number of people. The attention to agriculture has every where slackened, rather than increased, as might at first have been expected, from European connexion. In no part of America, either North or South, do we hear of any of the Indian nations living in great plenty, in consequence of their diminished numbers. It may not, therefore, be very far from the truth to say, that even now, in spite of all the powerful causes of destruction that have been mentioned, the average population of the American nations is, with few exceptions, on a level with the average quantity of food, which in the present state of their industry they can obtain.'

The chief object of the work may be distinctly understood from this passage:

'The Abbé Raynal, speaking of the ancient state of the British isles, and of islanders in general, says of them: "It is among these people that we trace the origin of that multitude of singular institutions that retard the progress of population. Anthropophagy, the castration of males, the infibulation of females, late marriages, the consecration of virginity, the approbation of celibacy, the punishments exercised against girls who become mothers at too early an age." &c. These customs, caused by a superabundance of population in islands, have been carried, he says, to the continents, where philosophers of our days are still employed to investigate the reason of them. The Abbé does not seem to be aware, that a savage tribe in America, surrounded by enemies, or a civilized and populous nation, hemmed in by others in the same state, is in many respects in a similar situation. Though the barriers to a further increase of population be not so well defined, and so open to common observation on continents, as on islands, yet they still present obstacles that are nearly as insurmountable: and the emigrant, impatient of the distresses which he felt in his own country, is by no means secure of finding relief in another. There is probably no island yet known, the produce of which could not be further increased. This is all that can be said of the whole earth. Both are peopled up to their actual produce. And the whole earth is in this respect like an island. But as the bounds to the number of people on islands, particularly when they are of small extent, are so narrow, and so distinctly marked, that every person must see and acknowledge them; and inquiry into the checks to population on those of which we have the most authentic accounts may perhaps tend considerably to illustrate the present subject. The question that is asked in captain Cook's first voyage, with respect to the thinly scattered savages of New Holland, "By what means the inhabitants of this country are reduced to such a number as it can subsist?" may be asked with equal propriety of the most populous islands in the South Sea, or of the best peopled countries in Europe and Asia. The question, applied generally, appears to me to be highly curious, and to lead to the elucidation of some of the most obscure, yet important points, in the history of human society. I cannot so clearly and concisely describe the precise aim of the first part of the present work, as by saying, that it is an endeavour to answer this question so applied.'

In the South Sea islands, the Eareeoie societies among the higher classes, (noticed by Captain Cook,) the promiscuous intercourse among the lower, infanticide, and war, form the principal restraints on population.

Comparing the state of the inferior classes among civilized nations, with that of the savages who live by hunting or fishing, Mr. M. says that, in regard to bodily labour, their lot may be much the same, but that their privations and sufferings will admit of no comparison.

'Nothing appears to me to place this in so striking a point of view, as the whole tenor of education among the ruder tribes of savages in America. Every thing that can contribute to teach the most unmoved patience under the severest pains and misfortunes, every thing that tends to harden the heart, and narrow all the sources of sympathy, is most sedulously inculcated in the savage. The civilized man, on the contrary, though he may be advised to bear evil with patience when it comes, is not instructed to be always expecting it. Other virtues are to be called into action besides fortitude. He is taught to feel for his neighbour, or even his enemy in distress; to encourage and expand his social affections; and in general, to enlarge the sphere of pleasurable emotions. The obvious inference from these two different modes of education is, that the civilized man hopes to enjoy, the savage expects only to suffer.

'The preposterous system of Spartan discipline, and that unnatural absorption of every private feeling in concern for the public, which has sometimes been so absurdly admired, could never have existed but among a people, exposed to perpetual hardships and privations from incessant war, and in a state under the constant fear of dreadful reverses of fortune. Instead of considering these phenomena as indicating any peculiar tendency to fortitude and patriotism in the disposition of the Spartans, I should merely consider them as a strong indication of the miserable and almost savage state of Sparta, and of Greece in general at that time. Like the commodities in a market, those virtues will be produced in the greatest quantity for which there is the greatest demand; and where patience, under pain and privations, and extravagant patriotic sacrifices, are the most called for, it is a melancholy indication of the misery of the people, and the insecurity of the state.'

Montesquieu seems not a little satisfied with himself, when he states his determination of the question respecting the origin of that excessive population, which supplied the various hordes that at different periods over-ran the Roman empire. This Colossal power, he says, had occasioned a pressure of population towards what he calls the limits of the universe, when the force impelling in this direction grew weak, and at length wholly ceased; and the inundations in the contrary direction followed in course. Mr. Malthus treats this idea as a conceit unworthy of its distinguished author; and he finds the true answer in that power, which population possesses, of doubling itself in the course of each generation, when allowed full scope: which scope it must be conceived to have had among the northern nations, from the inimitable sketch of their manners drawn by Tacitus.

Among the Tartars, and other modern pastoral nations, Mr. Malthus thinks, 'the principal checks which keep the population down to the level of the means of subsistence, are, restraint, from inability to obtain a wife, vicious customs with respect to women, epidemics, wars, famine, and the diseases arising from extreme poverty. The three first checks and the last appear to have operated with much less force among the shepherds of the north of Europe.'

The causes of depopulation in Turkey are ascribed to scantiness of subsistence, occasioned by the enormous vices of the government.

The checks to population in Persia 'seem to be nearly similar to those in the Turkish dominions. The superior destruction of the plague in Turkey, is, perhaps, nearly balanced by the greater frequency of internal commotions in Persia.'

Epidemics and frequent famines produce the same effect in Hindostan; and in Tibet, the regulations of the ecclesiastics, and the prevailing manners of the laity, combine to repress all increase of population.

Mr. M. discards the fanciful hypothesis by which Montesquieu accounts for the crowded population of China; the principal cause of which he thinks to be the habit prevalent among the lower classes of contenting themselves with spare food: but frequent epidemics, famines, and the practice of exposing children, contribute to impose some restraint on its increase. The same causes operate in Japan, with the exception of infanticide: the absence of which is counterbalanced by the wars and commotions by which the latter country is almost constantly distracted.

With regard to ancient Greece,

'The frequent colonizations which issued out of that country, joined to the smallness of the states, which brought the subject immediately home to every thinking person, could not fail to point out to the legislators and philosophers of these times, the strong tendency of population to increase beyond the means of subsistence; and they did not, like the statesmen and projectors of modern days, overlook the consideration of a question which so deeply affects the happiness and tranquillity of society. However we may justly execrate the barbarous expedients which they adopted to remove the difficulty, we cannot but give them some credit for their penetration in seeing it; and in being fully aware, that, if not considered and obviated, it would be sufficient of itself to destroy their best planned schemes of republican equality and happiness.' -

'The legislator of Crete, as well as Solon, Pheidon, Plato, and Aristotle, saw the necessity of checking population in order to prevent general poverty; and, as we must suppose that the opinions of such men, and the laws founded upon them, would have considerable influence, it is probable, that the preventive check to increase, from late marriages and other causes, operated to a considerable degree among the free citizens of Greece.

'For the positive checks to population, we need not look beyond the wars in which these small states were almost continually engaged, though we have an account of one wasting plague at least, in Athens; and Plato supposes the case of his republic being greatly reduced by disease. Their wars were not only almost constant, but extremely bloody. In a small army, the whole of which would probably be engaged in close fight, a much greater number in proportion would be slain, than in the large modern armies, a considerable part of which often remains untouched; and as all the free citizens of these republicks were generally employed as soldiers in every war, losses would be felt very severely, and would not appear to be very easily repaired.'

Among the chief causes which kept the population in antient Rome on a level with the means of subsistence, may be enumerated its wars, the inactivity and poverty of the lower citizens, the employment of slaves, the prevalence of celibacy, and infanticide.

The results of the preceding researches are thus stated:

'All the checks to population which have been hitherto considered in the course of this review of human society, are clearly resolvable into moral restraint, vice, and misery.

'Of moral restraint, though it might be rash to affirm that it has not had some share in repressing the natural power of population, yet it must be allowed to have operated very feebly indeed, compared to the others. Of the preventive check, considered generally, and without reference to its producing vice, though its effect appears to have been very considerable in the later periods of Roman History, and in some few other countries; yet upon the whole, its operation seems to have been inferior to the positive checks. A large portion of the procreative power appears to have been called into action, the redundancy from which was checked by violent causes. Among these, war is the most prominent and striking feature; and after this, may be ranked famines and violent diseases. In most of the countries considered, the population seems to have been seldom measured accurately according to the average and permanent means of subsistence, but generally to have vibrated between the two extremes, and consequently the oscillations between want and plenty are strongly marked, as we should naturally expect among less civilized nations.'

Proceeding to investigate the restraints which depress the population in several of the states of modern Europe, Mr. Malthus mentions Norway as one which furnishes a remarkable instance of the prevalence of the preventive check. The annual deaths in that country are as 1 to 48, and the marriages as 1 to 130.

> 'The peculiar state of Norway throws very strong obstacles in the way of early marriages. There are no large manufacturing towns to take off the overflowing population of the country; and as each village naturally furnishes from itself a supply of hands more than equal to the demand, a change of place in search of work seldom promises any success. Unless, therefore, an opportunity of foreign emigration offer, the Norwegian peasant generally remains in the village in which he was born; and as the vacancies in houses and employments must occur very slowly, owing to the small mortality that takes place, he will often see himself compelled to wait a considerable time, before he can attain a situation which will enable him to rear a family.
>
> 'The Norway farms have in general a certain number of married labourers employed upon them, in proportion to their size, who are called house-men. They receive from the farmer a house and a quantity of land nearly sufficient to maintain a family; in return for which, they are under the obligation of working for him at a low and fixed price whenever they are called upon. Except in the immediate neighbourhood of the towns, and on the sea coast, the vacancy of a place of this kind is the only prospect which presents itself of providing for a family. From the small number of people, and the little variety of employment, the subject is brought distinctly within the view of each individual; and he must feel the absolute necessity of repressing his inclinations to marriage, till some such vacancy offer.'

In the interior of the country, where the preventive check is little obstructed in its operation, the inhabitants live in ease and abundance; while on the coast, where its influence is less, the people are more numerous, and proportionably poor and miserable. The court of Denmark has lately introduced regulations to favour the increase of population, the ill effects of which are dreaded by the sensible Norwegians.

'Norway (says the author,) is, I believe, almost the only country in Europe where a traveller will hear any apprehensions expressed of a redundant population, and where the danger to the happiness of the lower classes of people, from this cause, is, in some degree, seen and understood. This obviously arises from the smallness of the population altogether, and the consequent narrowness of the subject. If our attention were confined to one parish, and there were no power of emigrating from it, the most careless observer could not fail to remark that if all married at twenty, it would be perfectly impossible for the farmers, however carefully they might improve their land, to find employment and food for those that would grow up; but, when a great number of these parishes are added together in a populous kingdom, the largeness of the subject, and the power of moving from place to place, obscure and confuse our view. We lose sight of a truth which before appeared completely obvious; and, in a most unaccountable manner, attribute to the aggregate quantity of land a power of supporting people beyond comparison greater than the sum of all its parts.' –

'Sweden is, in many respects, in a state similar to that of Norway. A very large proportion of its population is, in the same manner, employed in agriculture; and in most parts of the country the married labourers who work for the farmers, like the housemen of Norway, have a certain portion of land for their principal maintenance, while the young men and women that are unmarried, live as servants in the farmers' families. This state of things, however, is not so complete and general, as in Norway; and from this cause, added to the greater extent and population of the country, the superior size of the towns, and the greater variety of employment, it has not occasioned, in the same degree, the prevalence of the preventive check to population, and consequently the positive check has operated with more force, or the mortality has been greater.'

The proportion of the deaths to the population in this country is that of 1 to 34¾. The healthiness of Sweden and Norway is considered as much the same; and hence, the author observes, 'it is difficult entirely to account for the mortality of Sweden, without supposing that the habits of the people, and the continual cry of the government for an increase of subjects, tend to press the population too hard against the limits of subsistence, and, consequently, to produce diseases which are the necessary effect of poverty and bad nourishment; and this, from observation, appears to be really the case.' – The influence of the preventive check, though considerable in Sweden, is not so great as it is in Norway; which occasions the positive checks to operate more in the former country.

A bad rural economy obstructs population in Russia, where it is not the interest of the boor to improve his portion of land, since, if it should produce more than is sufficient to support his family, it is curtailed, while the capitation tax charged on the remainder is the same with that which was paid for the whole. The two *Maisons des Enfans trouvés*, the one situated in Petersburgh, the other in Moscow, form another check on population: alluding to these, the author says:

> 'The surprising mortality which takes place at these two foundling hospitals of Petersburgh and Moscow, which are managed in the best possible manner, as all who have seen them with one consent, assert, appears to me incontrovertibly to prove, that the nature of these institutions is not calculated to answer the immediate end that they have in view, which I conceive to be, the preservation of a certain number of citizens to the state, which might otherwise, perhaps, perish from poverty or false shame. It is not to be doubted, that if the children received into these hospitals had been left to the management of their parents, taking the chance of all the difficulties in which they might be involved, a much greater proportion of them would have reached the age of manhood, and have become useful members of the state.
> 
> 'When we look a little deeper into this subject, it will appear, that these institutions not only fail in their immediate object, but by encouraging, in the most marked manner, habits of licentiousness, discourage marriage, and thus weaken the main spring of population. All the well-informed men with whom I conversed on this subject at Petersburgh, agreed invariably, that the institution had

produced this effect in a surprising degree. To have a child, was considered as one of the most trifling faults which a girl could commit. An English merchant at Petersburgh told me, that a Russian girl living in his family, under a mistress, who was considered as very strict, had sent six children to the foundling hospital without the loss of her place.

'It should be observed, however, that generally speaking, six children are not common in this kind of intercourse. Where habits of licentiousness prevail the births are never in the same proportion to the number of people, as in the married state; and therefore the discouragement to marriage, arising from this licentiousness, and the diminished number of births which is the consequence of it, will much more than counterbalance any encouragement to marriage, from the prospect held out to parents of disposing of the children which they cannot support.

'Considering the extraordinary mortality which occurs in these institutions, and the habits of licentiousness which they have an evident tendency to create, it may be said, perhaps, with truth, that if a person wished to check population, and were not solicitous about the means, he could not propose a more effectual measure, than the establishment of a sufficient number of foundling hospitals, unlimited in their reception of children. And with regard to the moral feelings of a nation, it is difficult to conceive that they must not be very sensibly impaired by encouraging mothers to desert their offspring, and endeavouring to teach them, that their love for their new-born infants is a prejudice, which it is the interest of their country to eradicate. An occasional child murder, from false shame, is saved at a very high price, if it can only be done by the sacrifice of some of the best and most useful feelings of the human heart in a great part of the nation.' –

'The true encouragement to marriage is, the high price of labour, and an increase of employments, which require to be supplied with proper hands; but if the principal part of these employments, apprenticeships, &c. be filled up by foundlings, the demand for labour among the legitimate part of the society must be proportionally diminished, the difficulty of supporting a family be increased, and the best encouragement to marriage removed.'

Notwithstanding the obstacles already mentioned, population advances rapidly in Russia, the births being to the deaths as 2¼ to 1, the deaths to the population as 1 to 52, and the marriages as 1 to 92.

In treating of the checks to population in Holland, the author says:

'A very curious and striking contrast to the Dutch villages, tending to illustrate the present subject, will be recollected in what was said respecting the state of Norway. In Norway, the mortality is 1 in 48, and the marriages 1 in 130. In the Dutch villages, the mortality 1 in 23, and the marriages 1 in 64. The difference both in the marriages and deaths is above double. They maintain their relative proportions in a very exact manner, and shew how much the deaths and marriages mutually depend upon each other, and that, except where some sudden start in the agriculture of a country enlarges the means of subsistence, an increase of marriages will only produce an increase of mortality, and *vice versa*.'

In general, after a great mortality, the number of marriages increases: but it may happen that

'The sudden improvement of the condition of the survivors might give them more of a decent and proper pride; and the consequence would be, that the proportional number of marriages might remain nearly the same, but they would all rear more of their children, and the additional population that was wanted, would be supplied by a diminished mortality, instead of an increased number of births.

'In the same manner, if the population of any country had been long stationary, and would not easily admit of an increase, it is possible that a change in the habits of the people, from improved education, or any other cause, might diminish the proportional number of marriages; but as fewer children would be lost in infancy, from the diseases consequent on poverty, the diminution in the number of marriages would be balanced by the diminished mortality, and the population would be kept up to its proper level by a smaller number of births.

'Such changes, therefore, in the habits of a people should evidently be taken into consideration.

'The most general rule that can be laid down on this

subject is, perhaps, that any *direct* encouragements to marriage must be accompanied by an increased mortality. The natural tendency to marriage is, in every country, so great, that, without any encouragements whatever, a proper place for a marriage will always be filled up. Such encouragements, therefore, must be either perfectly futile, or produce a marriage where there is not a proper place for one, and the consequence must necessarily be, increased poverty and mortality. Montesquieu, in his Lettres Persanes, says, that in the past wars of France, the fear of being inrolled in the militia, tempted a great number of young men to marry, without the proper means of supporting a family, and the effect was, the birth of a crowd of children, "que l'on cherche encore en France, et que la misère, la famine, et les maladies en ont fait disparoître."

Respecting the effects of *towns* on population, the opinion of Mr. Malthus is thus given:

'There is one leading circumstance affecting the mortality of countries, which may be considered as very general, and which is, at the same time, completely open to observation. This is the number of towns in any state, which has been before alluded to, and the proportion of town to country inhabitants. The unfavourable effects of close habitations and sedentary employments on the health are universal; and therefore, on the number of people living in this manner, compared with the number employed in agriculture, will much depend the general mortality of the state. Upon this principle it has been calculated, that when the proportion of the people in the towns, to those in the country, is as 1 to 3, then the mortality is about 1 in 36, which rises to 1 in 35, or 1 in 33, when the proportion of townsmen to villagers is 2 to 5, or 3 to 7; and falls below 1 in 36, when this proportion is 2 to 7, or 1 to 4. On these grounds the mortality in Prussia is 1 in 38; in Pomerania, 1 in 37½; in the Neumark, 1 in 37; in the Churmark, 1 in 35; according to the lists for 1756.'

It has been shewn by a German publicist,

'That the states of Europe may be divided into three classes, to which a different measure of mortality ought to be applied. In the richest and most populous states, where the inhabitants of towns are to the inhabitants of the country, in so high a proportion as 1 to 3, the mortality may be taken as 1 in 30. In those countries which are in a middle state, with regard to population and cultivation, the mortality may be considered as 1 in 32: And in the thinly-peopled northern states, Susmilch's proportion of 1 in 36 may be applied.

'These proportions seem to make the general mortality rather too great, even after allowing epidemick years to have their full effect in the calculations.'

In Swisserland, the author finds the chief prevalence of the preventive check: half the adults in the Pays de Vaud live single, and a still greater proportion in Berne: in which canton, the peasants are not permitted to marry till they are furnished with the arms and accoutrements of the militia. This rule, it is justly observed, induces an economical habit; which, when formed, will dispose the individual to provide something more than what will barely entitle him to enter into the state of wedlock.

The positive checks which, in France and England, obstruct the population, are so well known that they need not be detailed. By comparing the calculations of Messrs. Peuchet and Necker, Mr. M. finds that nearly one third of those who annually reach the age of puberty remain single, and that nearly a million and a half of males between the ages of eighteen and fifty are unmarried.

The following causes are stated as diminishing the proportion of marriages in England. In this, as in all countries of great refinement and luxury, numbers of the wealthy give the preference to a life of celibacy. Many of those who belong to the labouring class are aware that their earnings are too scanty to support a family. The domestics of the great are sensible of the sacrifices to which matrimony would oblige them to submit. The youth engaged in agriculture, or in trade, cannot marry till a farm or some business can be procured. The number of those also is great, who, while single, are able to make a genteel appearance, but who, if they married, would be forced to mix with persons of inferior condition. It is calculated that, in this kingdom, not above half the prolific power of nature is called into action; and that each marriage yields, on an average, upwards of five births.

Availing himself of the various facts which the industry of German writers has collected, the author undertakes to refute many received notions on the subject of political economy, and to point out the fallacy and insufficiency of some very important rules of political arithmetic, hitherto universally received. He thinks that there is one very serious mistake, into which all the writers without exception, who have exercised themselves in calculations of this sort, have fallen; viz. that of regarding the proportion of annual births to annual marriages, as expressing the average number of births produced by each marriage in the course of its duration; whereas that proportion is not in any degree affected by such produce, but is determined by the number of the born who live to be married, for it only expresses what is the number of births which supplies a pair for marriage. It furnishes no clue whatever to ascertain the average fruitfulness of marriages; and it is impossible hence to determine whether a marriage yields two, four, or a hundred births, because, in each case, the proportion of annual births to annual marriages may be the same. This proportion, we are told, expresses the average number of births produced by each marriage, solely in the case of population being completely stationary; if it in any degree fluctuates, it is not worthy of reliance for that purpose. It is this false assumption, that gave rise to all the fears respecting depopulation; which, had the rule been a just one, would have been well grounded: since, on an average taken throughout Europe, the births are to the marriages not so high as four to one, while more than half of the born died before they marry. The author, however, is enabled to shew that, where the births have been to the marriages annually below 4 to 1, population has advanced rapidly, while its progress has been slow where this proportion has been so high as $4^{1}/_{10}$ to 1. Mr. Malthus states that the average number of births produced by each marriage, in the course of its duration, depends on the proportion of births to deaths, and on that of births to marriages; and he is of opinion that, taking the average of Europe, more than half of the born live to the age of puberty, and that each marriage yields more than five children.

In order to illustrate his doctrine as to the superior power of population, he tells us that Prussia and Lithuania, in the year following the great plague which raged in those countries in 1709 and 10, the marriages were nearly double the average of those of the six years preceding that calamity; being to the population as 1 to 26, while that of the births was as 1 to 10, and that of the births to the deaths as $3\frac{1}{5}$ to 1: by which state of things, if it had continued, the population must have doubled in less than ten years. The births were at this time to the marriages as $2\frac{7}{10}$ to 1: but when, from the time of the plague, seven or eight years had elapsed, and the effect of that visitation in diminishing the marriages had been felt, the births were to the marriages as 5 to 1: whence, agreeably to the common notion, was inferred the greater fruitfulness of the marriages, but the proportion of the births to the deaths did not support the conclusion.

Upwards of fifty years ago, there prevailed in Swisserland an apprehension that the population was in a progressive state of decay; and M. Muret, desirous of investigating the causes of such a fact, first set himself to work to ascertain whether it was the fact. On an examination of the registers during three equal periods of seventy years, ending in 1620, 1690, and 1760, he satisfied himself that the annual number of births had been in a course of diminution. Mr. Malthus, without quarrelling with the facts of this writer, disputes his conclusions. A diminution of births, he observes, is no proof of a declining population; nay, he says, the number of births may decrease, while the population increases; which will be the case if the mortality, in the class below marriageable age, diminishes faster than the number of births does. He supposed that, in the periods included by M. Muret, towns became less close, and houses more cleanly; that the mode of living improved; that a greater healthiness prevailed; and that a diminished mortality rendered fewer births necessary to keep up the population. He also adds that, during the first and second of the above periods, the frequent recurrence of the plague rendered necessary an extra number of births, in order to repair its ravages. He shews that, if a district, owing to any cause whatever, becomes more salubrious than it had been, marriages and births must diminish, in order that the population may remain stationary; on the contrary, where the mortality is great, marriages are more frequent, and contracted earlier, whence a greater fecundity arises; and thus it appears that where the proportion of births to the population is great, that is, when the births are comparatively few, we may infer that ease, comfort, and healthiness prevail in a superior degree. To adopt the common mode of regarding numerous births as a favourable symptom, is therefore an evident and a grave error. England, he says, is an instance of the number of births decreasing, while the population has increased.

It appears from the materials collected for the great statistical work, now preparing for publication in France, that the population of the old territory of that country has rather augmented than diminished during the revolution; and Mr. M. is disposed to admit this conclusion, regardless of the authority and reasonings of Sir Francis D'Ivernois. He quotes M. Peuchet as stating, in his *Essai d'une Statistique Générale*, Paris, 1800, that in France 600,000 persons annually arrive at the age of 18, while it is laid down by M. Necker that 440,000 annually contract marriage; which gives a surplus of 80,000 males, who are not necessary to carry on the population. It is also found that there were 1,451,063 of unmarried males, between the ages of 18 and 50. Suppose, then, that of the unmarried males 600,000 were taken to form armies; and that, in order to preserve entire this establishment, 150,000 recruits were annually necessary; the number of males every year attaining the age of puberty, and the stock of the unmarried above mentioned, would furnish this supply. This process might continue for ten years, and allow the average number of marriages of former years to be increased by 10,000. Each year would, indeed, diminish the above class of unmarried by several passing the age of 50: but then, though they might cease to be fit for war, they would still be able to contribute to the population; and, in this respect, would supply the places of younger persons who had been taken to the armies. – The war, he thinks, would rather favour than be prejudicial to population in the interior.

It is generally admitted that agriculture did not decline in France during the late war; and that, on the contrary, the dominion of the plough was extended, land was more subdivided, and consequently the gross produce increased: which is all that relates to mere population. The thinness of the towns, and the higher price of labour, would diminish the mortality, where violence did not operate; while the great increase of illegitimate children, the temporary effect of the immoral and impolitic law of divorce, and the additional marriages, would occasion the births to increase in the proportion of $1/7$th of the whole. Mr. M. allows that the *Analyse des Procès Verbaux der Conseils Généraux de Département* describes the population and agriculture of France in a manner far less favourable, than is consistent with the facts and calculations on which he has founded his conclusions. It is also an admission of the author, and certainly an important one,

> 'That though the numerical population of France may not have suffered by the revolution; yet, that if her losses have been in any degree equal to the conjectures on the subject, her military strength cannot be unimpaired. Her population at present must consist of a much greater proportion than usual of women and children; and the body of unmarried persons of a military age, must be diminished in a very striking manner. This, indeed, is known to be the case, from the returns of the Prefects which have already been received.
>
> 'It has appeared, that the point at which the drains of men will begin essentially to affect the population of a country, is, when the original body of unmarried persons is exhausted, and the annual demands are greater than the excess of the number of males rising annually to the age of puberty, above the number wanted to complete the usual proportion of annual marriages. France was probably at some distance from this point, at the conclusion of the war; but, in the present state of her population, with an increased proportion of women and children, and a great diminution of males of a military age, she could not make the same gigantic exertions which were made at one period, without trenching on the sources of her population.'

With the view of farther corroborating the doctrine which ascribes so wonderful a spring to population, and which regards the checks to it as principally caused by the necessary limits of subsistence, Mr. M. states that

> 'The fertile province of Flanders, which has been so often the seat of the most destructive wars, after a respite of a few years, has always appeared as rich and as populous as ever. The undiminished population of France, which has before been noticed, is an instance very strongly in point. The tables of Susmilch afford continual proofs of a very rapid increase, after great mortalities; and the table for Prussia and Lithuania, which I have inserted, is particularly striking in this respect. The effects of the dreadful plague in London, in 1666, were not perceptible 15 or 20 years afterwards. It may even be doubted, whether Turkey and Egypt are, upon an

average, much less populous for the plagues which periodically lay them waste. If the number of people which they contain be considerably less now than formerly, it is rather to be attributed to the tyranny and oppression of the governments under which they groan, and the consequent discouragements to agriculture, than to the losses which they sustain by the plague. The traces of the most destructive famines in China, Indostan, Egypt, and other countries, are by all accounts very soon obliterated; and the most tremendous convulsions of nature, such as volcanic eruptions and earthquakes, if they do not happen so frequently as to drive away the inhabitants, or destroy their spirit of industry, have been found to produce but a trifling effect on the average population of any state.'

The following passages are highly just, and happily elucidate the theory maintained in this work:

'The highest average proportion of births to deaths in England may be considered as about 12 to 10, or 120 to 100. The proportion in France for ten years, ending in 1780, was about 115 to 100. Though these proportions have undoubtedly varied, at different periods, during the last century, yet we have reason to think that they have not varied in any very considerable degree; and it will appear, therefore, that the population of France and England has accommodated itself more nearly to the average produce of each country than many other states. The operation of the preventive check, vicious manners, wars, the silent, though certain, destruction of life in large towns and manufactories, and the close habitations and insufficient food of many of the poor, prevent population from outrunning the means of subsistence; and if I may use an expression, which certainly at first appears strange, supersede the necessity of great and ravaging epidemicks to destroy what is redundant. If a wasting plague were to sweep off two millions in England, and six millions in France, it cannot be doubted, that after the inhabitants had recovered from the dreadful shock, the proportion of births to deaths would rise much above the usual average in either country during the last century.[2]

---

[2] 'This remark has been, to a certain degree, verified of late in France, by the increase of births which has taken place since the revolution.'

In New Jersey the proportion of births to deaths, on an average of 7 years, ending 1743, was 300 to 100. In France and England, the highest average proportion cannot be reckoned at more than 120 to 100. Great and astonishing as this difference is, we ought not to be so wonder-struck at it, as to attribute it to the miraculous interposition of heaven. The causes of it are not remote, latent, and mysterious, but near us, round about us, and open to the investigation of every inquiring mind. It accords with the most liberal spirit of philosophy to believe, that not a stone can fall, or plant rise, without the immediate agency of divine power. But we know, from experience, that these operations of what we call nature, have been conducted almost invariably according to fixed laws. And since the world began, the causes of population and depopulation have been probably as constant as any of the laws of nature with which we are acquainted.

'The passion between the sexes has appeared in every age to be so nearly the same, that it may always be considered, in algebraic language, as a given quantity. The great law of necessity, which prevents population from increasing in any country beyond the food which it can either produce or acquire, is a law, so open to our view, so obvious and evident to our understandings, that we cannot for a moment doubt it. The different modes which nature takes to repress a redundant population, do not appear indeed to us so certain and regular; but though we cannot always predict the mode, we may with certainty predict the fact. If the proportion of the births to the deaths for a few years, indicate an increase of numbers much beyond the proportional increased or acquired food of the country, we may be perfectly certain, that unless an emigration take place, the deaths will shortly exceed the births, and that the increase that had been observed for a few years, cannot be the real average increase of the population of the country. If there were no other depopulating causes, and if the preventive check did not operate very strongly, every country would, without doubt, be subject to periodical plagues or famines.

'The only true criterion of a real and permanent increase in the population of any country, is the increase of the means of subsistence. But even this criterion is subject to some slight variations, which however are completely open to our observation. In some countries population seems to have been forced; that is, the people have been habituated, by degrees, to live almost upon the smallest possible quantity of food. There must have been periods in such countries when population increased permanently without an increase in the means of subsistence. China, India, and the countries possessed by the Bedoween Arabs, as we have seen in the former part of this work, appear to answer to this description. The average produce of these countries seems to be but barely sufficient to support the lives of the inhabitants, and of course any deficiency from the badness of the seasons must be fatal. Nations in this state must necessarily be subject to famines.

'In America, where the reward of labour is at present so liberal, the lower classes might retrench very considerably in a year of scarcity, without materially distressing themselves. A famine, therefore, seems to be almost impossible. It may be expected, that in the progress of the population of America, the labourers will in time be much less liberally rewarded. The numbers will in this case permanently increase without a proportional increase in the means of subsistence.

'In the different countries of Europe, there must be some variations in the proportion of the number of inhabitants, and the quantity of food consumed, arising from the different habits of living which prevail in each state. The labourers of the South of England are so accustomed to eat fine wheaten bread, that they will suffer themselves to be half starved, before they will submit to live like the Scotch peasants. They might, perhaps, in time, by the constant operation of the hard law of necessity, be reduced to live, even like the lower classes of the Chinese, and the country would then, with the same quantity of food, support a greater population. But to effect this, must always be a difficult, and every friend to humanity will hope, an abortive attempt.' –

'Other circumstances being the same, it may be affirmed, that countries are populous according to the quantity of human food which they produce, or can acquire; and happy, according to the liberality with which this food is divided, or the quantity which a day's labour will purchase. Corn countries are more populous than pasture countries; and rice countries more populous than corn countries. But their happiness does not depend either upon their being thinly or fully inhabited, upon their poverty or their riches, their youth or their age; but on the proportion which the population and the food bear to each other. This proportion is generally the most favourable in new colonies, where the knowledge and industry of an old state, operate on the fertile unappropriated land of a new one. In other cases the youth, or the age, of a state is not, in this respect, of great importance. It is probable that the food of Great Britain is divided in more liberal shares to her inhabitants at the present period, than it was, two thousand, three thousand, or four thousand years ago. And it has appeared that the poor and thinly-inhabited tracts of the Scotch Highlands are more distressed by a redundant population, than the most populous parts of Europe.' –

'Famine seems to be the last, the most dreadful resource of nature. The power of population is so superior to the power in the earth to produce subsistence for man, that, unless arrested by the preventive check, premature death must in some shape or other visit the human race. The vices of mankind are active and able ministers of depopulation. They are the precursors in the great army of destruction, and often finish the dreadful work themselves. But should they fail in this war of extermination, sickly seasons, epidemicks, pestilence, and plague, advance in terrifick array, and sweep off their thousands and ten thousands. Should success be still incomplete, gigantick inevitable famine stalks in the rear, and, with one mighty blow, levels the population with the food of the world.

'Must it not then be acknowledged, by an attentive examiner of the histories of mankind, that, in every age, and in every state, in which man has existed, or does now exist,

'The increase of population is necessarily limited by the means of subsistence.

'Population invariably increases when the means of subsistence increase, unless prevented by powerful and obvious checks.

'These checks, and the checks which keep the population down to the level of the means of subsistence, are, moral restraint, vice, and misery.'

Mr. M. concludes this part of the work with these remarks:

'In comparing the state of society which has been considered in this second book with that which formed the subject of the first, I think it appears that in modern Europe the positive checks to population prevail less, and the preventive checks more, than in past times, and in more uncivilized parts of the world.

'War, the predominant check to the population of savage nations, has certainly abated, even including the late unhappy revolutionary contests: and since the prevalence of a greater degree of personal cleanliness, of better modes of clearing and building towns, and of a more equable distribution of the products of the soil from improving knowledge in political economy, plagues, violent diseases, and famines, have been certainly mitigated, and have become less frequent.

'With regard to the preventive checks to population, though it must be acknowledged, that moral restraint does not at present prevail much among the male part of society; yet I am strongly disposed to believe that it prevails more than in those states which were first considered; and it can scarcely be doubted, that in modern Europe, a much larger proportion of women pass a considerable part of their lives in the exercise of this virtue, than in past times and among uncivilized nations. But however this may be, taking the preventive check in its general acceptation, as implying an infrequency of the marriage union from the fear of a family, without reference to its producing vice, it may be considered, in this light, as the most powerful of the checks, which in modern Europe keep down the population to the level of the means of subsistence.'

[*To be continued.*]

Art. VI. *Mr. Malthus's Essay on the Principle of Population.*

In the preceding part of this article, we endeavoured to shew how the author stated and illustrated his doctrine, and what were the proofs which he brought forwards to support it: we are now to follow him in considering it as it relates to various theories and institutions, which have more or less prevailed in the world. He first takes notice of some extraordinary positions which occur in the famous posthumous publication of M. Condorcet, intitled *Esquisse d'un tableau historique des progrès de l'Esprit humain*, on which he comments with great acuteness and force. He happily exposes the weak parts of that philosopher's system, ably unravels the sophisms by which he defended the visionary expectations there thrown out, and manifests that the principle of population destroys the very foundations on which they were built.

Mr. Malthus does not, like some others of Mr. Godwin's adversaries, (whose silence, however, may be more the effect of prudence than of forbearance,) deem him an antagonist unworthy of his notice; nor does he arraign him in vehement and loose declamation, nor oppose to him pompous inanities dragging after them ponderous comments: but he brings his arguments to bear on that gentleman's system with singular effect, and contrives to make it confute itself. Without being startled by its extravagance, he assumes the supposition of Mr. Godwin's state of society being realized, points out the evils which it would generate, and then demonstrates that antidotes would be sought in the very institutions which Mr. G. has endeavoured to vilify.

The author regards emigration as furnishing a very inadequate remedy for redundant population; and he thinks that it more frequently prevails in consequence of a thirst of gain, or of a spirit of enterprize and religious enthusiasm, than with any view to mere subsistence. He expatiates on the numerous inconveniences attending first settlements, and on that paramount one which is occasioned by the absence of habits suited to the situation. In concluding his chapter on this subject, he observes:

'It is evident, that the reason why the resource of emigration has so long continued to be held out as a remedy to redundant population, is, because, from the natural unwillingness of people to desert their native country, and the difficulty of clearing and cultivating fresh soil, it never is, nor can be adequately adopted. If this remedy were indeed really effectual, and had power so far to relieve the disorders of vice and misery in old states, as to place them in the condition of the most prosperous new colonies, we should soon see the phial exhausted, and when the disorders returned with increased virulence, every hope from that quarter would be for ever closed.

'It is clear, therefore, that with any view of making room for an unrestricted increase of population, emigration is perfectly inadequate; but as a partial and temporary expedient, and with a view to the more general cultivation of the earth, and the wider spread of civilization, it seems to be both useful and proper; and if it cannot be proved that governments are bound actively to encourage it, it is not only strikingly unjust, but in the highest degree impolitick, in them to prevent it. There are no fears so totally ill-grounded, as the fears of depopulation from emigration. The *vis inertiæ* of people in general, and their attachment to their homes, are qualities so strong, and general, that we may rest assured that they will not emigrate, unless, from political discontents, or extreme poverty, they are in such a state, as will make it as much for the advantage of their country as of themselves that they should go out of it.'

In matters of political economy, Mr. M. thinks, the public should be taught to look beyond first appearances: thus, instead of confining the attention to price, it should be directed to contemplate the relation between commodities and the consumer; whence it may be deduced that abstinence from any given article of food arises from the limited quantity of it, and that any advance in the wages of labour will not enable the poor man to procure it, but will increase its price so as to exceed his new gains. In the case of a scarcity of corn, the object should be to husband it as much as possible, and not to furnish the consumer with money, or credit; which would produce only a momentary benefit to the individual, while it augments the permanent general evil:

'No person (says Mr. M.) I believe, will venture to doubt, that, if we were to give three shillings a day to every labouring man in the kingdom, in order that he might have meat for his dinner, the price of meat would rise in the most rapid and unexampled manner. But surely, in a deficiency of corn, which renders it impossible for every man to have his usual share, if we still continue to furnish each person with the means of purchasing the same quantity as before, the effect must be in every respect similar.

'It seems in great measure to have escaped observation,

that the price of corn in a scarcity, will depend much more upon the obstinacy with which the same degree of consumption is persevered in, than on the degree of the actual deficiency. A deficiency of one half of a crop, if the people could immediately consent to consume only one half of what they did before, would produce little or no effect on the price of corn. A deficiency of one twelfth, if exactly the same consumption were to continue for ten or eleven months, might raise the price of corn to almost any height. The more is given in parish assistance, the more power is furnished of persevering in the same consumption, and of course the higher will the price rise before the necessary diminution of consumption is effected.'

Mr. M. is of opinion that 'the very great issue of country bank paper during the years 1800 and 1801 was evidently in its origin rather a consequence than a cause of the high price of provisions; but being once absorbed into the circulation, it must necessarily affect the price of all commodities, and throw very great obstacles in the way of returning cheapness. This is the great mischief of the system.' – He farther observes:

'After the publication, and general circulation of such a work as Dr. Smith's, I confess, that it appears to me strange, that so many men who would yet aspire to be thought political economists, should still think, that it is in the power of the justices of the peace, or even of the omnipotence of parliament, to alter by a *fiat* the whole circumstances of the country; and when the demand for provisions is greater than the supply, by publishing a particular edict, to make the supply at once equal to, or greater, than the demand. Many men who would shrink at the proposal of a maximum, would propose themselves, that the price of labour should be proportioned to the price of provisions, and do not seem to be aware, that the two proposals are very nearly of the same nature, and that both tend directly to famine. It matters not, whether we enable the labourer to purchase the same quantity of provisions which he did before, by fixing their price, or by raising in proportion the price of labour. The only advantage on the side of raising the price of labour, is, that the rise in the price of provisions which necessarily follows it, encourages importation: but putting importation out of the question, which might possibly be prevented by war, or other circumstances, a universal rise of wages in proportion to the price of provisions, aided by adequate parish allowances to those who were thrown out of work, would, by preventing any kind of saving, in the same manner as a maximum, cause the whole crop to be consumed in nine months, which ought to have lasted twelve, and thus produce a famine.'

The poor laws are considered by the author as coming within that class of measures, the ill tendency of which he had before exposed; and the effect of which is to promote population without increasing the means of subsistence, and to create a body of improvident paupers, who are to share with the industrious and thrifty that quantity of food which the country is capable of yielding. He also objects to these laws because they take away a necessary stimulus to exertion, raise the price of provisions while they lower that of labour, generate carelessness and a negligence of the future, remove the checks to idleness and dissipation, constitute a code which is a burthen on the industrious, and excite those harsh and unfeeling dispositions which are so much reprobated in magistrates and parish officers. He likewise remarks that manufactures, set up to employ relieved paupers, intrench on the fair claims of the industrious poor, as they may be the means of throwing them out of work. The common observation that the price of labour ought to be such as to enable the labourer decently to maintain a family, he pronounces to be most erroneous, because it proceeds on the idea that full scope may be allowed to the principle of population.

Allowing Dr. Smith's definition of the wealth of a state to be just, namely, that it is the annual produce of its land and of its labour, Mr. M. says that it hence follows that Dr. S. was in an error when he inferred that every addition to the stock of society is an addition to the funds for the maintenance of labourers; while it is only so when it is convertible into a proportional quantity of provisions; and it will not be so if it has arisen from the produce of labour, instead of the produce of land. A mere increase, of the existing price of labour, if the stock of provisions remain the same, will be only nominal, and will not increase the command of the poor over the necessaries of life; – its sole effect will be, to take a number of hands from an healthy to an unwholeseme occupation, from agriculture to manufactures, and to cause luxuries to be imported. It may be alleged that a country, in which the produce of labour annually increases, may import the produce of land from other states: but this the author considers as impracticable in any considerable degree in large territorial communities, while it cannot be carried into effect to any great extent in a country so favourably formed for it as Great Britain. When the funds for the maintenance of labour become stationary, that is, when the stock of the annual produce of land cannot be farther increased, then (he remarks) commercial states reach the natural limit of their population. – We are inclined to think that our able author has rather magnified the difficulty of importing provisions, and overlooked the effect of importing luxuries; for what are luxuries but more costly articles of sustenance and dress, which leave a greater abundance of those of the ordinary kind for the accommodation of the poor? His objections arising from the dependence and the dangers occasioned by the practice of relying on foreign provisions are incapable of being obviated. The proposition in the *Wealth of Nations*, it would seem, is rather to be qualified, than denied *in toto*; and so this author seems to think, when he says, 'an increase of wealth, though generally, is not necessarily and invariably accompanied by an increase of the funds for the maintenance of labour; and consequently, by the power of supporting a greater number of people, or of enabling the former number to live in greater plenty and happiness.'

If the English reader should be distressed by being told that 'in the history of the world, the nations, whose wealth has been derived principally from manufactures and commerce, have been perfectly ephemeral beings compared with those, the basis of whose wealth has been agriculture; – since it is in the nature of things, that a state which subsists upon a revenue furnished by other countries, must be infinitely more exposed to all the accidents of time and chance, than one which produces its own;' – he will be relieved by perusing what the author immediately subjoins:

> 'We are so blinded by the shewiness of commerce and manufactures, as to believe that they are almost the sole cause of the wealth, power, and prosperity of England. But perhaps, they may be more justly considered as the consequences, than the cause of this wealth. According to

the definition of the Economists, which considers only the produce of land, England is the richest country in Europe in proportion to her size. Her system of agriculture is beyond comparison better, and consequently her surplus produce is more considerable. France is very greatly superior to England in extent of territory and population; but when the surplus produce, or disposeable revenue of the two nations are compared, the superiority of France almost vanishes. And it is this great surplus produce in England, arising from her agriculture, which enables her to support such a vast body of manufacturers, such formidable fleets and armies, such a crowd of persons engaged in the liberal professions, and a proportion of the society living on money rents, very far beyond what has ever been known in any other country of the world.'

The difference between Dr. Smith and the economists, on the subject of productive labour, Mr. M. considers as a question relating to definitions, namely, which of two is the most just? Dr. S., he argues, does not use them fairly, when he applies to their definition reasonings founded on his own; and while he gives the preference to that of Dr. Smith, he admits that theirs, though practically erroneous, is in the abstract correct. When, says he, we find manufacturing capital, by judicious management, have the effect of rendering manufactures cheaper, so that less of revenue (that is, of surplus produce) will command an equal quantity of them, it is difficult not to consider it as productive. He thinks that it cannot be denied to the economists, that generally the surplus produce of the land is the fund which pays every thing: but their error, he conceives, lies in regarding the owners of the land as the sole holders of this fund, while capitalists share in it with them, they being a sort of mortgagees of the land. The rents do not amount to more than a fifth of the gross produce; and the other four fifths are paid by the cultivator in taxes, for the instruments of agriculture, and for manufactures for the use of himself and his family. In this view of the matter, all taxes may be said to fall on the land; and he is disposed to concede to this celebrated sect, that, in an infant state of things, where no national debts have been incurred, nor capitals accumulated, a territorial tax would be the most proper and most fair:

'A tax on net rent (he says) has little or no effect in discouraging the improvement of land, as many have supposed. It is only a tithe, or a tax, in proportion to the gross produce, which does this. No man in his senses will be deterred from getting a clear profit of 20l. instead of 10l. because he is always to pay a fourth or fifth of his clear gains; but when he is to pay a tax in proportion to his gross produce, which, in the case of capital laid out in improvements, is scarcely ever accompanied with a proportional increase of his clear gains, it is a very different thing, and must necessarily impede, in a great degree, the progress of cultivation. I am astonished that so obvious and easy a commutation for tithes, as a land tax on improved rents, has not been adopted. Such a tax would be paid by the same persons as before, only in a better form: and the change would not be felt, except in the advantage that would accrue to all the parties concerned, the landlord, the tenant, and the clergyman. Tithes undoubtedly operate as a high bounty on pasture, and a great discouragement to tillage, which in the present peculiar circumstances of the country is a very great disadvantage.'

This admission, on the part of an author so intelligent, and whose own profession appears to be that of a clergyman, is intitled to serious consideration. If the measure be as safe with respect to the church as the author seems to think, it cannot be doubted that its adoption is ardently to be desired.

Mr. M. is apprehensive that, at present, commerce and manufactures predominate too much in this country; for it is, in his judgment, an error to regard them as invariable and uniform incitements to extract the surplus produce of the earth. On the contrary, he supposes, with Dr. Smith, that the navigation act and the colonial trade, as well as all our commercial monopolies, have forced a great proportion of the capital of the country from agriculture. Government loans, also, by keeping high the interest of money, prevent its being applied to improve the land; for while this interest is 5 or 6 per cent., capital will not be employed to animate husbandry.

As introductory to what the author advances in favour of the laws which gave premiums for the exportation of corn, he says:

'If things had been left to take their natural course, there is no reason to think that the commercial part of the society would have increased beyond the surplus produce of the cultivators; but the high profits of commerce from monopolies, and other peculiar encouragements, have altered this natural course of things; and the body politick is in an artificial, and in some degree, diseased state, with one of its principal members out of proportion to the rest. Almost all medicine is in itself bad; and one of the great evils of illness is, the necessity of taking it. No person can well be more averse to medicine in the animal enconomy, or a system of expedients in political economy, than myself; but in the present state of the country, something of the kind may be necessary to prevent greater evils. It is a matter of very little comparative importance, whether we are fully supplied with broadcloth, linens, and muslins, or even with tea, sugar, and coffee; and no rational politician, therefore, would think of proposing a bounty upon such commodities. But it is certainly a matter of the very highest importance, whether we are fully supplied with food; and if a bounty would produce such a supply, the most liberal political economist might be justified in proposing it; considering food as a commodity distinct from all others, and pre-eminently valuable.'

Dr. Smith maintains that the encouragement given to the industry of towns has drained agriculture of a portion of its capital; and it may be asked whether the corn laws of 1688 and 1700 had not a salutary tendency, as counteracting the above effect; or, if premiums exist which check the produce of corn, is it an evil that there should be others which encourage it? The present author observes that, in the years of abundance, the cultivator seldom reserves any great store of its produce for a future period; since he either wants the inclination or the requisite capital, or he will not encounter the risque of its being damaged. There is, he concludes, no sure way of providing for years of scarcity, except that of encouraging exportation in years of plenty. Where agriculture bears the burthen of high rents and taxes, some means must be taken to set it on a level with that of those countries which are subject to little or none. The exportation of this article yields clear gain; and the more of it is sent abroad, the more additional hands must be employed; while the quantity, so transferred, brings a clear profit to the country, as well as to the adventurer. In the case of other manufactures, part of the net profit is consumed in preparing them, and the gain of the exporter is founded on a loss to the country: but facts tell more than a volume of the ablest reasoning in favour of the laws which encouraged by premiums the exportation of corn, when it was below a certain price:

> 'During the seventeenth century, and indeed the whole period of our history previous to it, the prices of wheat were subject to great fluctuations, and the average price was very high. For fifty years before the year 1700, the average price of wheat per quarter was 3l. 11d. and before 1650 it was 6l. 8s. 10d. From the time of the completion of the corn laws in 1700 and 1706, the prices became extraordinarily steady; and the average price for forty years previous to the year 1750, sunk so low as 1l. 16s. per quarter. This was the period of our greatest exportations. In the year 1757, the laws were suspended, and in the year 1773, they were totally altered. The exports of corn have since been regularly decreasing, and the imports increasing. The average price of wheat for the forty years ending in 1800, was 2l. 9s. 5d; and for the last five years of this period, 3l. 6s. 6d. During this last term, the balance of the imports of all sorts of grain is estimated at 2,938,357, and the dreadful fluctuations of price which have occurred of late years, we are but too well acquainted with.'

A number of acute remarks on the positions of Dr. Smith, and many forcible observations, occur in the discussion of this subject: but we are reluctantly obliged to omit them.

The author refutes several vulgar notions on the subject of cultivating waste lands; and he observes, after our most experienced writers, that these can only be brought into use in proportion to the surplus manure which is yielded by those that are already in tillage. If we rob the cultivated ground of its due portion, in order to lay it on wastes, we become great losers. The extension of tillage depends much on the situation and circumstances of a country; barren heaths are sometimes seen even in China; while the value of territory and the singular constitutions of monastic fraternities in Flanders, would convert a sandy Pontine into a fertilized district.

In the last division of his work, Mr. M. proceeds to state what would be the effect on the condition of society, if his doctrine were adopted and put into practice. It follows directly, he observes, from the superior force of the principle of population, and from its relation to the means of subsistence, that in every old society checks must be applied to keep it under, unless reliance be placed on the harsh methods of which nature makes use, viz. diseases, and want in its various degrees. In these days, no one will propose infanticide, nor recommend a system of perpetual warfare; it cannot, therefore, be well disputed that, of all the checks to accomplish this end, the preventive one, or moral restraint, is the most eligible. It is surely better than it should arise from a foresight of the difficulties attending a family, and the fears of dependent poverty, than from the sweeping effects of extreme wretchedness and misery. Parents, by the laws of nature, as well as by all wise positive laws, are under a moral obligation to provide for their offspring; and this is not less the case, because our poor-code proceeds on a contrary and a false principle; a principle equally injurious to those whom it apparently favours, and burdensome to society at large. If marriages are contracted, and children are begotten, beyond the numbers which the territory can subsist, (or, to use the words of the author, if the population presses on the limits of subsistence,) labourers being too numerous, or the market of labour being overstocked, the commodity will sink in value; those who furnish it will be unable to subsist themselves; and misery must come in to reduce the population to the level of the food. The question then is, how is this misery to be prevented, and how is labour to be kept up to a price which will enable the labourer to command the necessaries and comforts of life? The price of labour, like that of any other commodity, can only be kept high by reducing the number of those who are engaged in it; that is, by checking population: but the question recurs, how is this to be done with the least injury to the virtue and happiness of society? It is answered, by strengthening the preventive check; by giving every aid to the principle of moral restraint; by inculcating it both by precept and example; and by making public opinion, the laws and institutions, the manners and usages of the country, harmonize with it. The simple and obvious, as well as the only efficacious method of diffusing comfort and plenty through a society, is for every individual to refrain from matrimony till he has the means of providing for children. This, which is an act of prudence, is also an indispensible duty; which, like other moral obligations, requires that the passions should be controuled and guided by reason; and which is founded in utility, while its violation is accompanied by its own punishment. In proportion, says Mr. M., as this rule is observed, will the state of society be advanced. – His scheme of improvement differs from most of those ameliorations which other speculatists hold out; it is more moderate, and it proceeds from different causes:

> 'The improvement here supposed, if we ever should make approaches towards it, is to be effected in the way in which we have been in the habit of seeing all the greatest improvements effected, by a direct application to the interest and happiness of each individual. It is not required of us to act from motives, to which we are unaccustomed; to pursue a general good, which we may not distinctly comprehend, or the effect of which may be weakened by distance and diffusion. The happiness of the whole is to be the result of the happiness of individuals, and to begin first with them. No co-operation is required. Every step tells. He who performs his duty faithfully will reap the full fruits of it, whatever may be the number of others who fail. This duty is express, and intelligible to the humblest capacity. It is merely that he is not to bring beings into the world for whom he cannot find the means of support. When once this subject is cleared from the obscurity thrown over it by parochial laws and private benevolence, every man must feel the strongest conviction of such an obligation. If he cannot support his children, they must starve; and if he marry in the face of a fair probability that he shall not be able to support his children, he is guilty of all the evils which he thus brings upon himself, his wife, and his offspring. It is clearly his interest, and will tend greatly to promote his happiness, to defer marrying, till, by industry and economy, he is in a capacity to support the children that he may reasonably expect from his marriage; and as he cannot in the mean time gratify his passions, without violating an express command of God, and running a great risk of injuring himself, or some of his fellow creatures, considerations of his own interest and happiness will dictate to him the strong obligation to moral restraint.'

Mr. M. is aware that it may be objected to this doctrine, that it has a tendency to increase vice among the lower classes; a consequence which he exceedingly deprecates, and which induces him to admit that it is improper to enforce by compulsory methods this principle of moral restraint, salutary as it is, while by every indirect mode he would encourage and sanction it.

The portion that each individual has a right to the means of subsistence; and, if he chuses to marry, that of requiring the society in which he lives to furnish him with labour, and so to recompense him for it that he may be able to provide for his family; is here controverted, and we think unanswerably refuted. It is considered as founded on the notion before demonstrated to be erroneous, that the means of subsistence may be made to keep pace with the uncontrouled progress of population. The author then states the grounds of the law of nature according to which population increases; which was intended as well to people uninhabited districts, as to keep up or slowly to increase the population of old states. He shews that, while the purposes of nature would remain unanswered, we should be losers on the score of enjoyment, if the passions were weaker and more blunt; whereas, allowing them their present strength, we have only to controul them in order to obtain a very considerable sum of happiness, a sum probably greater than we should secure if their indulgence were less restricted. This natural law is not distinguished from others; it holds out rewards in exchange for sacrifices, it offers permanent happiness in lieu of momentary gratification, and reason cannot dispute its obligation, while revelation enforces its observance by the most awful sanctions. It is in vain to argue on it; it is one of the conditions of the feast to which we have been invited; stern necessity commands obedience, and punishes its infringements with the most afflicting visitations.

If states would favour such a limited population as the produce of the territory would support in plenty and comfort, – if each individual would feel convinced that he was not to give existence to beings whom he had no prospect of being able to maintain, – offensive war must cease, because there would be no surplus population; and internal tumult and internal tyranny, which mutually create each other, would terminate, because the incentives to the former would not exist. It should be the aim of a wise state to preserve the population and the means of subsistence on a level, and to ensure as great an actual population as is consistent with the absence of poverty and dependence.

Agreeing to the propriety of the strong words used by the *Comité de Mendicité* of the Constituent Assembly, when speaking of the English poor laws, that they are "*la plaie politique de l'Angleterre la plus devorante*;" and sensible, at the same time, that they cannot be all at once abolished, but convinced that it is a measure which the safety of the country imperiously demands; Mr. M. says that it should be commenced with the view of being gradually accomplished:

> 'To this end, I should propose a regulation to be made declaring, that no child born from any marriage, taking place after the expiration of a year from the date of the law, and no illegitimate child born two years from the same date, should ever be entitled to parish assistance. And to give a more general knowledge of this law, and to enforce it more strongly on the minds of the lower classes of people, the clergyman of each parish should, previously to the solemnization of a marriage, read a short address to the parties, stating the strong obligation on every man to support his own children; the impropriety, and even immorality, of marrying without a fair prospect of being able to do this; the evils which had resulted to the poor themselves, from the attempt which had been made to assist, by publick institutions, in a duty which ought to be exclusively appropriated to parents; and the absolute necessity which had at length appeared, of abandoning all such institutions, on account of their producing effects totally opposite to those which were intended.
> 
> 'This would operate as a fair, distinct, and precise notice, which no man could well mistake; and, without pressing hard on any particular individuals, would at once throw off the rising generation from that miserable and helpless dependence upon the government and the rich, the moral as well as physical consequences of which are almost incalculable. When the poor are in the habit of constantly looking to these sources, for all the good or evil they enjoy or suffer, their minds must almost necessarily be under a continual state of irritation against the higher classes of society, whenever they feel distressed from the pressure of circumstances.'

He then adds;

> 'After the publick notice which I have proposed had been given, and the system of poor laws had ceased with regard to the rising generation, if any man chose to marry, without a prospect of being able to support a family, he should have the most perfect liberty so to do. Though to marry, in this case, is in my opinion clearly an immoral act, yet it is not one, which society can justly take upon itself to prevent or punish; because the punishment provided for it by the laws of nature, falls directly and most severely upon the individual who commits the act, and, through him, only more remotely and feebly on the society. When nature will govern and punish for us, it is a very miserable ambition, to which to snatch the rod from her hands, and draw upon ourselves the odium of executioner. To the punishment, therefore, of nature he should be left, the punishment of severe want. He has erred in the face of a most clear and precise warning, and can have no just reason to complain of any person but himself, when he feels the consequences of his error. All parish assistance should be most rigidly denied him; and if the hand of private charity be stretched forth in his relief, the interests of humanity imperiously require that it should be administered very sparingly. He should be taught to know that the laws of nature, which are the laws of God, had doomed him and his family to starve for disobeying their repeated admonitions; that he had no claim of right on society for the smallest portion of food, beyond that which his labour would fairly purchase; and that, if he and his family were saved from suffering the utmost extremities of hunger, he would owe it to the pity of some kind benefactor, to whom therefore, he ought to be bound by the strongest ties of gratitude.'

Having urged not only the expediency but the absolute necessity of gradually abolishing the present plans of parochial relief; and of guarding against every thing in our institutions, usages, and manners, which misleads on this subject, and which is inconsistent with a just estimate of the principle of population; the author suggests a general national system of education for the poor. He proposes that part of their instruction should consist of an explanation of their real situation, and of their obligations not to entail misery on society, nor to plunge themselves in distress, by contracting marriages when they have not the means of supporting a family. In recommending this extensive plan of education, he comments on the insufficiency of Sunday schools for the purpose, and refers the friends of popular vandalism to the benefits arising from the scheme which he proposes, as exemplified in the practice of Scotland and Swisserland.

Mr. M. submits to examination a variety of plans which have been offered with a view to the amelioration of the poor. When, like that brought forwards by Mr. Gourlay, they happen to be founded on facts, he inquires whether their success does not depend on their being partial; and whether the benefits would not disappear, if they were universally adopted. He also considers them as they bear on the principle of population, and thus makes it clearly manifest that it is proper to dismiss various proposals which wear an inviting aspect.

Though the author has been called to combat theories which hold out visionary prospects of the future amelioration of the state of man, and to counteract the suggestions of the most powerful passions of our nature, still it is evident that his ideas proceed from no gloomy views nor morose disposition, but that he is actuated by the purest philanthropy and the most genuine benevolence. In proof of this statement, we might appeal to the whole tenour of his meritorious and important researches: but, for this purpose, we shall only adduce the admirable paragraph which closes them:

> 'On the whole, though our future prospects respecting the emigration of the evils arising from the principle of population, may not be so bright as we could wish, yet they are far from being entirely disheartening, and by no means preclude that gradual and progressive improvement in human society, which, before the late wild speculations on the subject, was the object of rational expectation. To the laws of property and marriage, and to the apparently narrow principle of self-love, which prompts each individual to exert himself in bettering his condition, we are indebted for all the noblest exertions of human genius, for every thing that distinguishes the civilized from the savage state. A strict inquiry into the principle of population leads us strongly to the conclusion, that we shall never be able to throw down the ladder by which we have risen to this eminence; but it by

no means proves that we may not rise higher by the same means. The structure of society, in its great features, will probably always remain unchanged. We have every reason to believe that it will always consist of a class of proprietors, and a class of labourers; but the condition of each, and the proportion which they bear to each other, may be so altered as greatly to improve the harmony and beauty of the whole. It would, indeed, be a melancholy reflection, that, while the views of physical science are daily enlarging, so as scarcely to be bounded by the most distant horizon, the science of moral and political philosophy should be confined within such narrow limits, or at best be so feeble in its influence, as to be unable to counteract the increasing obstacles to human happiness arising from the progress of population. But however formidable these obstacles may have appeared in some parts of this work, it is hoped that the general result of the inquiry is such, as not to make us give up the cause of the improvement of human society in despair. The partial good which seems to be attainable, is worthy of all our exertions; is sufficient to direct our efforts and animate our prospects. And although we cannot expect that the virtue and happiness of mankind will keep pace with the brilliant career of physical discovery, yet if we are not wanting to ourselves, we may confidently indulge the hope, that, to no unimportant extent, they will be influenced by its progress, and will partake in its success.'

From the elaborate view which we have taken of this performance it will appear how highly we estimate its value. In the pursuit of a not less intricate than important branch of knowledge, the author has earned honourable distinction; and wherever, in future, any positions in political economy are discussed, his name will be associated with those of Montesquieu and Turgot, of Hume and Smith. If he has taken a less wide range and if he elucidates fewer questions than the last mentioned author, he claims the merit of being the first to place on a proper basis, to ascertain the force, and to set forth the vast influence of one of the most essential principles which affect the well being of society; a principle which, elucidated as it has been by him, throws broad day-light on various abstract theories, and on sundry grave institutions; a principle which he has made the ground-work of speculations that deeply interest the whole human race, and which hold out to posterity the prospect of better days. If this volume inculcates lessons little grateful to the ardour of youth, – if it enjoins a controul of difficult acquisition over our passions and propensities, – if it requires that the choicest cup of human enjoyment should not be tasted till a late period, – if it demands that what, according to the historian, formed part of the manners of some barbarous nations should prevail among those that are enlightened, namely *sera venus, inexhaustaque pubertas*, – if it constrains us to bend our necks under this galling yoke, let us not forget that it has been borne before by rude tribes; that religion, that intellectual pursuits, the regular toils of honest industry, innocent amusements, the discipline of the thoughts, and discreet conduct, will greatly lighten it, and in time so reduce its pressure as to render it hardly perceptible. Let it also be recollected that this probation ensures an ample share of enjoyment to the individual; while, in proportion as it is generally practised, it will effect a state of society free from the visitations of infections and disease, of famine, of wars, of tyranny, or of anarchy; a state in which the blessings of comfort, abundance, health, freedom, and good order, will be shared by all ranks. The difficulty with which any law, that militates against our strongest natural inclinations, becomes established, must render this happy æra a distant one; while the infirmities inseparable from all, and so prevalent in some, will ever prevent its being completely realized: yet any gradual progress towards it will amply reward the utmost exertions that we can command. If persons imagine that a state of society, in any degree resembling that which has been here sketched, by the price of aught else than of a strict and severe discipline, they have little studied the constitution under which we live; or, if they think that the happiness of early marriages is not purchased at too high a price, when that price is a greater mortality, arising out of want, out of poor and scanty sustenance, out of wars, epidemics, and plagues, and out of the rest of misery's long train; such may protest against the doctrine of the author, or may ridicule his reasonings: but, in the eyes of the judicious and the intelligent, his system will appear in harmony with the other laws of nature, and his conclusions will be marked by each badge of truth.

When, from the matter of this work, we direct our attention to its execution, we must qualify our commendation. It cannot escape the reader that Mr. Malthus is a scholar, conversant with the fine models of antiquity, capable of appreciating their excellencies, and of relishing their beauties: but if, with the Stagirite, he be an indefatigable searcher after truth, with him also he seems to disdain the graces of style, and the charms of composition. If he often reminds us of the same philosophers' forcible combinations and apposite terms, it cannot be denied that numerous exceptions occur in his pages; while it is clear that, on the score of brevity and method, he must have had in view a far less perfect model, if he had *any* in contemplation. The criticisms of this kind, to which the immortal labours of Dr. Smith are liable, apply in like manner to the valuable production which we now dismiss; and which, we would gladly hope, will receive from the public a degree of attention corresponding with its very substantial merits.

# THE GENTLEMAN'S MAGAZINE
## Vol. LXXIV, April 1804

*An Essay on the Principle of Population; or, A View of its past and present Effects on Human Happiness; with an Enquiry into our Prospects respecting the future Removal or Mitigation of the Evils which it occasions. A new Edition, very much enlarged. By T. R. Malthus, M.A., Fellow of Jesus College, Cambridge.*

The first edition was published anonymously in 1798; but, on its appearing in its present enlarged state, it has produced "*Remarks*" on it, in an 8vo pamphlet, by an anonymous writer, who observes, "Mr. Malthus has certainly no inconsiderable claim to the praise of originality, both in the establishment and elucidation of a definite principle of population, and in the positions and conclusions which he has laboured to deduce from it. Many political writers have indeed been fully aware of the incalculably prolific sources of the multiplication of the species; and speculators, from the days of Plato to those of Mr. Godwin, have had an eye to its probable consequences in their sweeping systems of universal greatness and felicity. But these circumstances, so far from diminishing the author's merit as an original, elevate his powers and his composition to a higher rank, as having attained that reach which others had surveyed but dimly at a distance. The chief point, and a very material one it is, upon which Mr. Malthus differs from all who have written before him, is, that the latter have always been of opinion, that the evils arising from too numerous population, or, in other terms, from the unrestrained agency of the *principle* of population, were remote, and could not be experienced by society, until the whole earth were cultivated like a garden, and the produce forced to the utmost limit of its powers. An event so improbable, or if possible, necessarily placed at so great a distance, might fairly be considered as a cypher in the calculation of human happiness, and as forming no objection to any hypothesis that might terminate in the expectation of it. This great obstacle being removed, the speculators on the perfectibility of human nature and human society have soared with unshackled pinions into regions far beyond the ken of ordinary observers, and there erected their "gorgeous palaces," and indulged their golden dreams. And had Mr. Malthus proposed no other object, and attained no other end, than the fundamental refutation of these systems, this alone would have entitled him to the praise and gratitude of the genuine supporters of inductive philosophy. It is a great purport of his argument and detail to shew that the principle of population has for ages back, in almost every stage of society, been checked and repressed by a great law of nature, the ratio which animated life bears to the means of subsistence: and that this check, with all its consequences, which have been referred to some future, distant, unattainable period, has in fact existed, almost from the first creation of the world, in the very form in which it was conjectured that it might then exist. He has clearly established, that it is the actual and not the possible improvement of the earth which circumscribes its population; and that, as the ratio of increase in the fruits of the land is much more slow than the possible ratio of multiplication of the species, this multiplication is necessarily restrained by the want of subsistence. But at the same time, with regard to the progress of population, it is not whether the land be poor or rich, but whether it be rapidly thriving or stationary? But (in states once fully peopled) the most rapid possible increase in fertility would not by any means suffice for a concomitant unlimited increase of the species. This doctrine is stated by Mr. Malthus, in the two following propositions placed at the beginning of his work: I. 'Population is necessarily limited by the means of subsistence.' II. 'Population invariably increases, where the means of subsistence increase, unless prevented by the operation of some very powerful and obvious checks'. This doctrine is not only readily demonstrable, but simply intelligible. It is one of those fundamental laws of nature which history and observation, as well as reasoning, point out. But, for a clear and definitive view of the subject, and for its extension and illustration, we are indebted to the author of the "Essay." The important enquiry, however, is, how far the operation of this principle affects the happiness of man, or tends to advance or retard the progress of society; and of this part of the subject the author has given the most gloomy and exaggerated view. Proceeding upon principles which the following pages may perhaps demonstrate to be unjust, he has represented one of the wisest and most beautiful provisions of nature as the direst instrument of vice and misery. The novelty of his speculations appears to have drawn him into the great error of all system-formers; and, by confining his attention to one object solely, he has neglected the operation of all the other wheels in the great machine of society. Pursuing his hypothesis, I had almost said with the ardour of discovery, he endeavours to establish the principle of population as the master-spring in this social and political machine; and to its favourable or unfavourable action attributes at least one half of the goods or ills of society. The third proposition which it is the principal object of the "Essay" to establish, and which the author endeavours to illustrate by copious statistical documents, from antient and modern history, is, that 'the checks which repress the superior power of population are all resolvable into *moral restraint*, VICE and MISERY.' An error of some importance, which prevails in this work, consists in the author's confounding together these three checks, without discriminating the peculiar operation of each. He seems to consider all of them as necessary agents, in regulating the population of a country, or, if not necessary in the nature of things, at least rendered so by the present condition of society. And, too little inclined to represent the government of Providence in a favourable point of view, he ascribes to *vice* and *misery* tenfold the agency which he allows to *moral restraint*: but a developement of the natural order of things will tend best to evince the fallacy of this distorted view of man in his social state, and to shew the true and obvious check which nature has provided for redundant population. Another error into which the author has fallen is that he has not sufficiently explained and defined the mode in which vice and misery check the progress of population. He sometimes describes vice and misery as the direct *consequence* of excessive population; at other times he endeavours to establish that the prevalence of vice and misery constitutes the chief check upon the *production* of that excessive population; and of an argument thus conveniently varying its form, he does not neglect to avail himself. But a principal error, which is diffused throughout the work, and disfigures the whole tenor of his reasonings, is, that the *principle* of population, and population simply considered, or the actual existence and perhaps increase of given numbers, are most unaccountably confounded together, and the checks upon both blended into one mass of argument, as though they arose from similar sources, or tended to similar ends. The author denominates moral restraint the preventive, and vice and misery the positive, checks upon the *principle* of population, whereas the former almost solely refers to the principle, as prevention can constitute its only restraint. Vice and misery may be causes of mortality, but, except in very peculiar cases, they can in no way affect the *principle* of population; and it may perhaps be demonstrated, in the following pages, that they have little or no influence upon population simply considered." (p. 1-6.)

"It is one of the primary objects of Mr. M's reasonings to prove that moral restraint is an insufficient check to population; and that vice and misery have hitherto, in all countries, been the chief agents in 'keeping down the number of inhabitants upon a level with the food of the earth.' (p. 9.)

Mr. M. calculates, that, at the highest estimation, not more than half of the prolific power of this country is called forth in preserving the population at its present level. What then are we to conclude forms the restraint upon the other half of the populating power? Mr. M. asserts, of moral restraint, that, "whatever hopes we may entertain of its prevalence in future, it has undoubtedly operated, in past ages, with very inconsiderable force." Vice and misery, the other two causes that he enumerates, are, therefore, according to him, the chief and almost sole repressing powers. It follows, then, as a direct consequence from the preceding position, that nearly half of the adults in this country are incapacitated, by vice and misery, for the purposes of contributing to the population of the country; or, what is as palpably absurd, that nearly all those who do not marry, or have not children, are restrained, by vice and misery, from becoming husbands and fathers. When the doctrine of Mr. M. is thus immediately brought home to our understandings, by its application to a single and comprehensible case, its fallacy, and, indeed, absurdity, are clearly demonstrated, and his reasonings, which are frequently plausible enough in speculation, set to flight when they come at issue with fact. But, with regard to the check repressing population, England is very much in the same predicament with every other civilized country of modern Europe; and therefore the inference just mentioned, drawn from Mr. M's reasoning, may be applied to all the civilized parts of that continent. No one, however, can be so blind or outrageous as to maintain that a proportion of the inhabitants of Europe, by any means equal or comparable to that just stated of England, are incapacitated, by vice or misery, for the propagation and support of the species. But it is true, at the same time, that the population of Europe is repressed, by some cause or other, within its present limits: vice and misery, therefore, are not causes of sufficient magnitude to come up to the point at which population is checked by a previous principle, and, consequently, cannot, in strict propriety, be denominated checks. They may, and, unfortunately for mankind, actually do, occasion much mortality, by inducing disease in every various form. But I need not hesitate in asserting that the present condition of society in this island, and every civilized country, possesses energies for a momentum of population that would resist ten times the vice and misery which prevailed in any one of them." (p. 15.)

The Remarker observes, that neither promiscuous intercourse nor drinking prevent population. "The population of France has increased since the Revolution. The proportion of illegitimate children during the old government was enormous, $\frac{1}{47}$th of the whole annual births, now $\frac{1}{11}$th; and the practice of every other vicious custom that can obstruct increase has been increased with similar latitude; yet, in opposition to the combined influence of all these preventive causes, the population of France has even augmented under the losses and desolation which she has experienced in her armies abroad and her citizens at home. The vice of drinking to excess does not so much strike at the root of population as at the ruin of families; being a prolific source of that constant influx of wretchedly poor and unemployed persons who abound in great towns, and not only consume the subsistence which might maintain a more virtuous population, but become the scourge of society, thieves, robbers, and assassins. But, granting that drunkenness does prevent the birth of great numbers, and occasions premature death: add to this the preventions and mortality occasioned by this vice; and to their agency join the influence of every other vice in the long and black catalogue; then enquire whether England or any other country of Europe has ever complained of a deficiency in population from these causes, and whether, if these countries were suddenly, by some supernatural power, to be doubled in fertility, the population would not, almost as suddenly, experience a proportionate increase, in spite of a resisting power fifty times stronger than the limited prevalence of these vices in any country could possibly effect. The case is indeed difficult to conceive, because a general plenty would diminish the mortality occasioned by these vices. But let the plenty be confined to those only who incapacitate neither themselves nor others for extending the population of the country by the practice of vice, and the increase will be made with a rapidity little retarded by the deduction. The truth is, that the great source of Mr. M's errors, in treating of the fundamental part of this hypothesis, consists in this, that he has confounded together the principle of population, population simply considered, and mortality, and has adopted these terms vaguely and promiscuously, as convenience suggested." (p. 20.)

That the principle of population has been, and still continues to be, much impaired by the effects of vice and misery, may be matter of speculation; but the result will in no way affect the happiness or increase of our species. All that concerns the practical philosopher and politician is this consideration, that an increase of the species, from a small stock lately planted in a distant part of the world, has been rapid and extensive enough to establish that the *principle* is sufficiently prolific for any state, and for any of the purposes of society, with very few casual exceptions, not invalidating the general rule. The world, perhaps, never had to deplore a diminution in her population from licentiousness or slavery alone. The population of Russia, and of every other country, is much more prone to excess than deficiency. (p. 22.) "There is a passage, rather unguarded, in one of the latter chapters of the Essay, which is clearly and explicitly of the very same doctrine that I am contending for. 'No cause,' says the author, 'physical or moral, unless it operate in an excessive and unusual manner, can have any considerable effects on the population, except in as far as it influences the produce and the distribution of the means of subsistence.' In this opinion I entirely coincide; but must confess that it appears to be totally inconsistent with the doctrines that I have been endeavouring to refute; viz. that *vice* and *misery* are the great checks to population." (p. 23.)

*The fear of misery*, which Mr. M. makes synonymous with *misery*, is only another expression for moral restraint, which is the only remaining check on population, and of very powerful and very general agency, notwithstanding Mr. M's observations to the contrary. The artificial habits and notions of large classes most powerfully aid and promote the operation of the preventive check, and a considerable part of the prolific power of society suspended or wasted by the love of indolence, self-indulgence, and luxury. The influence of moral restraint is thus very highly and unduly aggravated in all the upper ranks of polished life, and in a numerous class just raised above the lowest, such as domestic servants, commercial clerks, apprentices, and upper servants, who are maintained by their masters, and are without any stock for the purposes of entering upon matrimonial life, or employed in functions for which marriage would incapacitate and remove them. Fellows of colleges, professional men of sound emoluments, and almost all men whose literary education is their only fortune, are obliged to spend the early, often a considerable, part of their lives in celibacy. With the lowest ranks of society, the labouring poor, though almost every circumstance in their condition is inimical to it, moral restraint, has very considerable and universal influence. The general equalization of the wages of labour, the amount of these wages being on an average a sufficient provision for marriage, the universal ignorance, want of foresight, and unbridled passion, which enter into the condition of the poor, are circumstances peculiarly unfavourable to the opening of this check; but, besides an opinion, which is prevalent among many in this class, that celibacy is the fate to which belong the fewest cares and the most enjoyments, it is invariably observable, that, in all the countries of Europe, where parish-registers are kept, or accurate observation has been made, from the rude territory of the Laplanders to the polished countries of France, Italy, and England, years of scarcity are attended and followed by few marriages, while years of plenty and prosperity witness a numerous lift of alliances. And this fact places beyond controversy the truth, that foresight and moral restraint are virtues practised by the very lowest, as well as by the middle and higher ranks of society; while the circumstance in their condition just now mentioned, the general equalization of the wages of labour, is so peculiarly adverse to the practice of this virtue, as to evince the great strength of other motives to moral restraint. (pp. 29, 30.)

There is a singular obscurity and uncertainty in Mr. M's use of the term *moral restraint*. Most commonly he uses it in the general but definite signification; at other times, where he is disposed to heap blame and vice and misery upon mankind, he confines it to the virtue of chastity in single life, a construction most decidedly improper and inapplicable. "Moral restraint," he says, "must be allowed to produce a certain degree of temporary unhappiness." Now this restraint, being not an act but a habit of the mind, this temporary unhappiness must at least be of frequent recurrence, and thus the cup of life be materially embittered by it. (p. 34.)

The Remarker is of opinion, that the evils which Mr. M. conceives it possible to mitigate or remove, have from the beginning of time, been mitigated and removed; and that this country, or any in Europe, is over-peopled, may very reasonably be doubted. That poverty and neglect, which has not its origin in idleness and profligacy, is of rare occurrence, even in the most crowded cities (pp. 40-42.) "Late marriages, which Mr. M. proposes as the great remedy for the removal of vice and misery is a very unpromising scheme at least." (p. 43.) "To the accomplishment of which, there is less an objection than the direct repugnance of human nature and universal feeling." (p. 46.) – 'The first obvious tendency of the English poor-laws,' says Mr. M. 'is, to increase population without increasing the food for its support. A poor man (he continued) may marry without any prospect of being able to support a family without parish assistance. They may be said, therefore, to create the poor which they maintain; and as the provisions of the country must, in consequence of the increased population, be distributed to every man in smaller proportions, it is evident that the labour of those who are not supported by parish assistance, will purchase a smaller quantity of provisions than before, and, consequently, more of them must be driven to apply to parish assistance.' "The premises of this argument," says the Remarker, "are just, and furnish much important matter of enquiry. But the conclusion does not appear to me by any means sound or satisfactory. Such a self-increasing system, proceeding in the geometrical series described by the author, must long ago have swallowed up at least nine-tenths of the population of this country. The second objection to the poor-laws of England, adduced by Mr. Malthus, is, that 'the quantity of provisions confirmed in workhouses upon a part of society that cannot be considered as the most valuable part, diminishes the shares that would otherwise belong to more industrious and more worthy members, and thus forces more to become dependent.' The inference drawn in this latter argument is precisely the same as in the former, and liable to the same objection, *reductio ad absurdum*. But the position itself indicates very narrow views of policy; for, the greater part of those who are subsisted in parish-workhouses are the old, the infirm, and the absolutely indigent, who must be maintained by some funds either drawn directly from their poor relations, which would increase the very evil complained of by Mr. Malthus, or from the wealthier part of society, by regular contributions. But I shall not dwell upon the futility of the latter position. Thus far the author's doctrine appears to be just, that the parish-workhouses of England do, in a very great measure, create their own poor. The easy and universal access to those charities tends to diminish the influence of moral restraint; they act as a bounty upon marriage, and weaken the spring to exertion and parsimony. They may be said, therefore, with justice, to encourage those very marriages which they are obliged to support, and the production of those very children which they are obliged to maintain; and it is only because the sources of poor-law revenue are limited, that the numbers supported by it have limits also. But the operation of these laws is worse than nagatory; it is positively bad; and in the author's sentiments I entirely agree, that they directly tend to encourage idleness, to reward want, and to cherish a spirit of prodigality and dependence. Mr. Malthus may therefore be justly of opinion, that, as they at present stand, nothing short of entire abolition can ever remove the evils which originate in them. But I am very far from coinciding with him in opinion, that the poor in a flourishing, and more especially in a commercial, country should be left altogether to nature and chance for subsistence in all the vicissitudes of life and of fortune. It may, I think, be demonstrated, that provisionary laws for the relief of the poor, under very strict limitations, are very important objects of political legislation. And in a manufacturing country, where the demand for labour is always very precarious, where the wages of labour are perpetually varying, and where a full complement of inhabitants renders these variations dreadful instruments of misery, the duty of provision is decided and imperious. And this provision ought to be either legislative or parochial. If the affair be left to private and spontaneous charity, the contribution will be either too great or too little: it must of necessity be variable in its amount, precarious in the supply, and, generally speaking, ill applied. Private benefactors are neither willing nor able to make the proper enquiries, nor to observe the due medium between liberality and profusion, between satisfying the absolute demands, and gratifying the inclinations, of those whom they relieve. The funds for the assistance of the poor must be levied upon the rich according to a certain rate, and distributed by appropriate persons. And let us not despair of being able to establish parochial or other fixed institutions for the relief of certain classes of indigent poor, upon principles neither remote from our conceptions, nor far removed from our abilities to comprehend." (pp. 50–53.) That comparatively very small body of society, the aged and infirm poor, require constant maintenance, and are, of all others, best entitled to the relief of a parish, as such relief encourages industry by diminishing the oppression of unproductive idleness. (p. 53.) The last scarcities in this country have given rise to much argument and speculation. "Much has been said, unnecessarily, to prove that where the stock of corn or potatoes is too small for all to have their accustomed quota, some, and perhaps very large numbers, must submit to curtail their shares of consumption. But that this diminution ought to fall entirely, or very nearly so, upon the rich, and that in proportion to their riches, is a position that does not seem even yet to have been satisfactorily established, though the principle upon which it is founded seems to be plain and unqualified. The community of labouring people are, generally speaking, obliged to maintain themselves upon the smallest quantity of food, and that consisting of the absolute necessaries of life. This circumstance in their condition naturally arises out of the nature of society. If the wages of labour were very considerably above this lowest point, equal, suppose to the master's profits, these labourers themselves would turn masters; and, unless a fresh supply of hands were constantly flowing to the offices of daily labour, these offices would remain unperformed; an impossible supposition. But bad seasons and deficient crops affect only the necessaries of life, corn, potatoes, &c.; a scarcity in these articles, therefore, if not remedied by law, or voluntary compact, must fall upon the whole consumption of the lowest orders, and famine, partial or universal, must be the consequence. The food of the middle and higher orders consists only in part of corn and potatoes; and scarcity in the supply of these articles has a comparatively trifling effect upon their whole consumption. And, as a certain number of labourers must be maintained in every state, and the existing numbers are seldom more than is required, it becomes a national concern to continue these numbers, which in times of dearth can only be done by making the evil of scarcity fall where its weight will least be felt, upon the higher classes of society." (pp. 54, 55.) "The great evil of our parish institutions is, that they do not discriminate the proper objects of assistance. A healthy labourer, however poor, ought not to be supported by the publick; nor ought his wife, if she be healthy; nor her children, except in case of scarcity of provisions. Our workhouses, though they do not profess to support these objects, actually do to a great extent; and whatever they consume is unjustly drawn from the common flock of provision destined for the maintenance of that class to which they belong." (pp. 59, 60.) "In a commercial and manufacturing country like this, though the demand for labour may, upon an average, keep pace with the supply of labouring hands, yet as great numbers are often suddenly thrown out of employ, and remain so for some days, or even weeks, some public institutions for the purpose of affording employment in these seasons of emergency, and which would furnish low wages, adequate to temporary relief, and at the same time oblige the labourer to regular habits of industry, would assuredly have the happiest effects upon their morals and prosperity. Were a small part of the work required by the publick, such, for example, as the repair of highways, the furnishing supplies for the army or navy, and other public occupations that require little skill or education, be taken from the rapacious hands of contractors, and annually supplied from institutions that employ labourers out of work, the interests of the country, both moral and political, would be advanced more than is generally conceived. The rate of wages should be low, otherwise the institution would soon become a trade itself, and subject to competition and precarious employment, as much as any other trade. But the work done at this low rate should be sold to government, or the public, at the ordinary price which similar work done by regular labourers will fetch. The surplus money might be appropriated to the support of the institution itself, and might, perhaps, abundantly suffice for that purpose.

All general truths must be made up of particulars; and surely no truth is better established than that, in the manufacturing towns of Birmingham, Manchester, Leeds, &c. the injury done to the morals, the industry, and the prosperity of the lower orders, by the precarious demand for labour in the different manufactories, is an evil incalculably great and pressing. Every new war, every continental disturbance, every suspicion upon foreign or domestic credit, the abolition of old manufactories, the introduction of new ones, improvements in machinery, and, finally, the unbounded spirit of speculation, alternating the acquisition and loss of immense capitals, are dreadful instruments constantly to impede the motions of the great commercial machine. They are considerations that astonish and confound the speculator; and they are real and prolific sources of vice, misery, and ruin. Very much, therefore, of the good morals and happiness of a people depends upon the wisdom and the exertion of its governors, the establishment of salutary laws and useful institutions; and it has been my chief object, in these "Remarks" upon the Essay on Population, to demonstrate that it is in the power of public institutions, aided by private virtue, very greatly to diminish the *vice* and *misery* that now exist in the world." (pp. 60–62.)

# THE BRITISH CRITIC
## Vol. XXIII, January 1804

Art VIII. *An Essay on the Principle of Population. By T. R. Malthus, A.M. Fellow of Jesus College, Cambridge. Second Edition, greatly enlarged.* 4to. 1l. 11s. 6d. Johnson. 1803.

Among the various subjects of politics, there does not exist one that is more important to the welfare of the state, or to the happiness of individuals, than the theory and principle of population: nor is there any one that has been so erroneously treated, or so much misunderstood, even by modern writers. Opinions, which would have vanished on investigation, have been repeated from author to author; and we have seen the wildest and crudest theories proposed for the amelioration of the human race, which, from the irresistible operations of nature, were totally impracticable.

Mr. Malthus was first led to direct his attention to this point, by a paper in Godwin's Inquirer; and he published, in 1798, the first edition of this Essay, a small tract, which, by some accident, escaped our notice. The facts collected by Mr. Malthus, and the just reasoning deduced from them, completely refuted all the visionary theories of Godwin, and demonstrated their futility. The latter, indeed, attempted to reply, but with little success.

In his former work, the author supposed, that vice and misery were the principal causes which kept the population of the earth within the actual limits to which we find it is confined; he now allows, that the virtuous celibacy of a considerable portion of the human race is also, more or less, concerned in this depression of the numbers of the species; and it cannot be asserted, that this restraint can positively be considered either as vice or misery.

The present work is divided into four Books. In the first, Mr. Malthus considers the checks to population in past times, and in the less civilized parts of the world; and he commences by an inquiry into the different ratios between the increase of the human race, and the production of food. The views of nature, in providing for a constant succession of beings, necessarily caused the principle of increase in organized bodies to be peculiarly active, that it might be able to replenish the world, and surmount the continual action of the several causes of destruction: hence, irrational beings often propagate faster than the food prepared for them; and their increase is checked by other tribes seizing either them or their subsistence. In man, another check takes place, from the fears his reason suggests to him, that his offspring may want food, or may lose their relative rank in society; these fears lead him to abstain from propagating his species.

From observations made on the progress of population in America, it appears that the numerical population of some parts of that state has doubled, by procreation alone, in twenty-five years; and, from particular facts, it is even probable, that this might take place in the short space of ten years. To this increase, there is no other limit in theory, than the inability to procure food for such excessive multitudes, as would quickly be produced, if the increase continued unrestrained. The impossibility of causing the other productions of the earth to keep pace with such an increase, must be obvious upon the least reflection, although Mr. Malthus enters largely upon that subject.

The author then proceeds to show, that even this want of food, or famine, is not the only check which population receives; but that it is almost constantly kept down to the limits of subsistence by other checks. These are, either preventive, which have for their foundation the above-mentioned fears; or positive, which includes every cause tending in any degree to shorten human life, as war, diseases, want, vices, &c. All these species of obstacles to population, are ultimately resolvable into moral restraint, vice, or misery.

Notwithstanding some of these checks are constantly operating in every country, yet Mr. Malthus thinks that there exists, in most states, a continual effort in the population, to increase beyond the means of subsistence; and, from the alternate reaction of these two causes upon each other, retrograde and progressive movements, with respect to the happiness of the species, arise at different times.

"This sort of oscillation will not probably be obvious to common view; and it may be difficult even for the most attentive observer to calculate its periods. – One principal reason why this oscillation has been less remarked, and less decidedly confirmed by experience than might naturally be expected, is, that the histories of mankind which we possess, are, in general, histories only of the higher classes. We have not many accounts, that can be depended upon, of the manners and customs of that part of mankind where these retrograde and progressive movements chiefly take place.

"A circumstance which has perhaps more than any other contributed to conceal this oscillation from common view, is, the difference between the nominal and real price of labour. It very rarely happens, that the nominal price of labour universally falls; but we well know that it frequently remains the same, while the nominal price of provisions has been gradually rising. This is, in effect, a real fall in the price of labour; and, during this period, the condition of the lower classes of the community must be gradually growing worse. But the farmers and capitalists are growing rich from the real cheapness of labour. Their encreasing capitals enable them to employ a greater number of men; and, as the population had probably suffered some check from the greater difficulty of supporting a family, the demand for labour, after a certain period, would be great in proportion to the supply, and its price would of course rise, if left to find its natural level; and thus the wages of labour, and consequently the condition of the lower classes of society, might have progressive and retrograde movements, though the price of labour might never nominally fall. In savage life, where there is no regular price of labour, it is little to be doubted that similar oscillations take place." P. 15.

This oscillation has been admitted by several of the most able political writers, and of its existence, no doubt can reasonably be entertained; yet, that Mr. Malthus may not appear too much inclined to speculative opinions of which we have no accurate relations, he waves the subject, and proceeds in his enquiry, by a careful examination of the existing histories of mankind, passing in a regular order, from the lowest state of human society to the Roman empire in the plenitude of its glory.

It does not appear, that in the state of society usually distinguished by the appellation of savage, the preventive check is much in force; the thoughtlessness of that state, and the constant habit observed in savages of indulging their passions on every opportunity, are well known. The positive checks to population, act however with increased force; want in all its various forms, vicious habits with respect to the female sex, the difficulty of rearing children, and the nearly continual state of warfare in which uncivilized society is plunged, all contribute to repress the population within the limits of subsistence. Mr. Malthus is, in our opinion very judiciously, not inclined to join with certain philosophical writers, in highly extolling the advantages of savage life. The sole advantage is leisure, from want of employment; but this leisure is counterbalanced in plentiful countries, by the slight value attached to the life of the lower classes. The characteristic habits of uncivilized and civilized life are, as is well observed by the author, strongly marked in their respective modes of education. The young savage is taught to suffer with fortitude; the citizen, to enjoy with prudence. The one is constantly presented with the picture of distress in every possible form, and hence his mind is filled with gloomy ideas, and tortured with revenge; the other is taught, among Christians at least, to love even his enemy, and to look forward to a calm enjoyment of prosperity, rather than to acquire a sullen indifference to adversity. The rigid discipline of Sparta, analogous to that of savage life, and which has been so frequently extolled by political writers, is considered by Mr. Malthus as a strong proof of the savage state of Sparta, and indeed of Greece in general. As commodities are usually produced in proportion to the demand, so are also political virtues; and, proceeding upon this principle, he observes, that when fortitude and patience are sedulously cultivated, we may be certain that the state is miserable and insecure.

The ancient inhabitants of the north of Europe, next engage the author's attention. Shepherd nations have, he observes, a confidence in attempting colonization, from their mobility; and, to this they are more strongly impelled, because their women, living more at their ease than in hunting nations, are more prolific; and also because their stock of cattle naturally requires a large extent of territory. In fact, the whole north of Europe and of Asia, was at one time possessed by the Tartars, who poured forth continual colonies to the south. That a want of subsistence was the cause of these emigrations, there can be no doubt; although, in the pages of history, they appear only as the ambitious projects of the northern chiefs; but, as Mr. Malthus again observes, it is the great misfortune of history to detail with precision the motives of the leaders, and so overlook the causes which often crowd their standards with willing followers.

Of the continual attacks on the Roman empire by the Scandinavian and German tribes, in which immense numbers fell, and of their final success, a long detail is given from Gibbon. That author agrees with Hume and Robertson, in supposing, that the north was not more populous formerly, notwithstanding their spirit of military emigration. Mr. Malthus very properly exposes the ridiculous solution of Montesquieu to the question, why the north does not pour forth the same colonies at present as it did formerly? and, very justly distinguishing between a redundant population and one actually great, is of opinion, that the north was probably ill peopled. The state of manners being simple, and analogous to those of America, they probably increased very rapidly; and the superabundant inhabitants were obliged to emigrate in search of new habitations. That this spirit might not be checked, by the inhabitants becoming attached to the land, the laws allowed them to retain their farms for a single year only; and this habit of emigration was the more necessary, because poor, cold, and thinly inhabited countries are not disposed to generate epidemic disorders; while, in warmer or more populous states, continued want produces diseases which carry off great numbers, and, of course, make room for the survivors. A check being given to the emigration, by the neighbouring countries having been conquered and possessed by the bravest and strongest of their tribes, the more northern ones were obliged to turn their attention to maritime affairs, that they might discharge their superfluous hands. The maritime nations of the south falling into the possession of these adventurers, an entire check was put to the population of the north, by want of room to extend themselves; and this probably gave rise to the prevalence of the preventive check which is, at present, so observable in the north.

We are rather surprized, that Mr. Malthus should not have noticed the polygamy allowed to the northern females, the relics of which custom are still to be traced in the countries conquered by the Scandinavian nations. It would be curious to enquire, whether this polygamy was adopted after the fall of the Roman empire, as a remedy against an excessive population, for which no vent could then be found, agreeably to his ideas on this custom in Thibet, or whether it was derived from their progenitors.

From the consideration of the manner in which the population was kept down among the ancient inhabitants of the north of Europe, Mr. Malthus proceeds to those checks which take place in the modern pastoral nations of Tartary and Arabia. These are still more disposed to emigrate, from their habits of living in tents, and of constantly wandering from place to place. They are dispersed over the countries possessed by them, in an exact proportion to the means of subsistence: a distribution which is indeed universal, although commerce renders it less obvious in civilized countries. Pastoral nations are given to rapine, and have continual quarrels with their neighbours, respecting their lands; this state of warfare is the principal cause which represses the population within the limits of subsistence. If the population was not checked by this constant drain, it appears probable that they would (as does indeed actually take place in the more peaceable tribes) become miserably poor; and their numbers would be diminished by the severe pressure of want.

The depopulation of the western coast of Africa, by the operation of the slave trade, has been the subject of much declamation; but the author is of opinion, that the numerical population of this coast has not been diminished in the least, by this transportation of his inhabitants. That the number of inhabitants is still redundant, the frequent famines that take place, although the country is thinly peopled, are evident proofs. This small actual population arises from the multiplicity of independent states; the narrow extent and constant quarrels of which, produce a general insecurity of property, and do not allow the inhabitants to exert their industry. The same insecurity of property, and consequent diminution of industry, is, he thinks, the cause of the decline of population of Egypt.

Siberia, to which Mr. Malthus next advances (in consequence of his general method of proceeding according to the relative rank of nations in civilization, rather than according to their contiguity) affords him an opportunity of showing how useless it is to attempt forcing the population of a country, by any other means of procuring a vent for its produce, even though its natural fertility would support a greater number of inhabitants.

"Man, though he may often be produced without a sufficient demand for him, cannot really multiply and prosper unless his labour be wanted; and the reason the population goes on so slowly in these countries, is, that there is very little demand for men. The mode of agriculture is described to be extremely simple, and to require very few labourers.

"With such a system of agriculture, and with few or no manufactures, the demand for men must be very easily satisfied. Corn will undoubtedly be very cheap, but labour will be in proportion still cheaper. Though the farmer may be able to provide an ample quantity of food for his own children, yet the wages of his labourer will not be sufficient to enable him to rear up a family with ease.

"If, from observing the deficiency of population, compared with the fertility of the soil, we were to endeavour to remedy it by giving a bounty upon children and thus enabling the labourer to rear up a greater number, what would be the consequence? Nobody would want the work of these supernumerary labourers that were thus brought into the market. It might be supposed, perhaps, that if there were much good land unused, the redundant population would naturally betake itself to the cultivation of it, and raise its own food: but, though there are many countries where good land remains uncultivated, there are very few where it may be obtained by the first person who chuses to occupy it. Even were this the case, there would be still some obstacles remaining. The supernumerary labourer, whom I have described, has no funds whatever that can enable him to build a house, to purchase stock and utensils, and to subsist till he has brought his new land into proper order, and obtained an adequate return. Even the children of the farmer, when they grow up would find it very difficult to obtain these necessary funds. In a state of society, where the market for corn is extremely narrow, and the price very low, the cultivators are always poor; and though they may be able amply to provide for their family in the simple article of food, yet they cannot realise a capital to divide among their children, and enable them to undertake the cultivation of fresh land. Though the necessary capital might be very small, yet even this small sum the farmer perhaps cannot acquire; for, when he grows a greater quantity of corn than usual, he finds no purchaser for it, and cannot convert it into any permanent article, which will enable any of his children to command an equivalent portion of subsistence or labour in future. In general, therefore, he contents himself with growing only what is sufficient for the immediate demands of his family, and the narrow market to which he is accustomed.

"It is not therefore a direct encouragement to the procreation and rearing of children that is wanting in these countries, in order to increase their population; but the creation of an effectual demand for the produce of the soil, by promoting the means of its distribution." P. 122.

The general tenor of this reasoning must be allowed to be perfectly just; but, when Mr. Malthus proceeds as follows, we find some cause to dissent from him.

"This can only be effected, either by the introduction of manufactures, and by inspiring the cultivator with a taste for them, which must necessarily be a work of time; or by assisting new colonists, and the children of the old cultivators, with capital to enable them to occupy successively, and bring into cultivation, all the land that is fit for it. The late Empress of Russia adopted both these means of increasing the population in her dominions." Ibid.

As the want of a market is the principal reason that the Russian colonies in Siberia have not increased with the same celerity as the colonies in America, the supply of capital does not seem the proper means to remove the defect, because this want must be the more severely felt in proportion as the supply becomes more abundant.

When a nation is seated amidst other agricultural states, its consumption must, of course, be confined to its own population. The introduction of manufactures certainly augments that consumption, and thus enlarges the market; but, unless these manufactures can be exported, or a luxury is encouraged, which will be detrimental to the military force of the nation, the increased demand produced by them will be trifling. The true means of calling forth the energies of a state, whose situation or laws do not allow of exportation, seems to be, in the establishment of a complicated system of magistracy, of a numerous clergy, or of a large standing army, or in undertaking great public works, as roads, canals, &c. which may employ nearly as many consumers, as the surplus produce of the country will allow of maintaining. In nations which can export their commodities, the absence of these consumers can be dispensed with, from the facility with which such nations can sell their surplus produce to their improvident neighbours, and convert it into disposeable revenue.

The great discouragement to agriculture, by the law of the maximum which obtains in the Eastern empire, is stated by Mr. Malthus to be among the principal causes of its declining population. He very properly exposes the extreme absurdity of Mr. Eton, in prophecying the total extinction of the Turkish population in another century, if things should continue in their present course. The plague also has a considerable effect in depressing the numbers of the people. The absence of this disorder in Persia, is probably balanced by the continual convulsions which for so long a period have agitated that empire, and by the late marriages of its inhabitants, in consequence of the expence attendant on a family in that country.

Although the religion of Hindustan bestows, like most others, much praise on marriage, yet it considers absolute chastity as equally meritorious, and even seems to confine its attention, as to the propagation of the species, to the production of an heir only. Hence Mr. Malthus is of opinion, that the preventive check has a considerable share in repressing the numbers of the Hindus. Female polygamy is likewise used in some parts of the east, and particular in Thibet, in which last country a great number of monastic institutions are also to be found.

The attention of the Chinese to agriculture enables them to counteract, in some degree, the consequence of their propensity to the married state. The number, however, of the people is so immense, that the greater part live in extreme misery. Mr. Malthus agrees with Hume, that the permission of infanticide tends to increase this population, which is only kept down by epidemic diseases and famine, both frequent in China. The dissoluteness and turbulence of the Japanese afford an ample source of destruction.

The checks to population among the Greeks are those to which Mr. Malthus next adverts, and they furnish him with much important matter, as their political writers appear to have understood the subject better than any of the moderns. The turbulent politics of Greece, divided into several little states, engaged in continual quarrels, occasioned a constant drain of people by war; yet, notwithstanding this check, and the colonies they sent off at all convenient times, the population was not sufficiently repressed to allow of all the free citizens living in a comfortable manner; and the distress of the lower classes of them gave rise to many propositions for their relief. Pheidon of Corinth proposed to limit the population of the state, without equalizing property. Phaleas of Chalcedon, to equalize the citizens. Plato adopted the idea of a limited number of late marriages, the destruction of the children of the poorer classes, and of those which were weakly or deformed. Aristotle, to late marriages added the limitation of the children of each marriage to a certain number, and the destruction of the rest. This celebrated philosopher was of opinion, that an equality among the citizens could not be kept up by any other means than by restraining population within determinate limits. Mr. Malthus, with great propriety, considers the horrid expedients proposed by these philosophers to effect an equality, as a conclusive argument against a system which would require such extraordinary and inhuman sacrifices.

Among the Romans, war and the use of slaves appear to be the principal checks to population; that infanticide moreover prevailed to a considerable degree, Mr. Malthus makes no doubt. The laws for encouraging marriage, and the little effect they produced, are a convincing proof of the vicious habits of the higher classes; while the inferior citizens (or middle class) were, in consequence of the slaves filling up every employment, reduced to live on charity, and were of course unable to bring up a family. The author acknowledges the justice of Hume's observation, respecting the unfavourableness of slavery to the propagation of the species in rich countries, on account of the expence of rearing the offspring. He shows, however, at the same time, the errors respecting the relative population of ancient and modern times, into which that writer and Wallace have fallen.

In the second Book, he considers the checks to population in the states of modern Europe, commencing with Norway, and ending with Scotland and Ireland, but omitting the southern countries. It would take up too much room to follow the author through such a copious subject; of which, however, an idea may be formed, by the analysis we have given of the preceding Book and it would be in some measure unnecessary, as these states are more generally known. We shall therefore only notice a few miscellaneous remarks, which appear new, or otherwise important.

According to Mr. Malthus, the subject of population seems better understood in Norway than in any other country; and fears are very generally entertained, that a redundant population, in consequence of some late alterations in the law, will diminish the present comfortable situation of the peasantry. Of the bad effects of foundling hospitals, if carried to any extent, Russia affords an irrefragable instance; they not only diminish the actual population of a country, but also produce a general dissoluteness of manners; and increase the difficulty of rearing a family, by filling up those apprenticeships for services which would otherwise be filled by the children of the poor. From conversations with some of the Swiss peasantry, he conjectures, that the poor might soon be taught the theory of a superabundant population lowering the price of labour.

The recent events in France render that country an object of importance; as, notwithstanding the blood shed in the convulsive movements of that state, it appears, from the most authentic accounts, that its population is in fact increased. Its military force must be nevertheless impaired, from the loss of so many adult males, whose place is now supplied by a greater proportion of females and children; and France must feel this the more sensibly, as it was at all times weak in adult males, from the general habit of early marriages, and consequent number of children.

On the checks to population in the British islands, Mr. Malthus treats at great length. The preventive check operates with great force in England, partly from the facility of an illicit connection with the sex, and partly from a love of independence and of the comforts of life. It has been usual to consider a great proportion of births as the surest sign of the prosperity of a state: the author, however, is of the contrary opinion and, after stating, from various data, that the annual average proportion of births in England and Wales is to the whole population as 1 to 30, he thus proceeds.

> "Sir Francis D'Ivernois very justly observes, that if the various states of Europe kept and published annually an exact account of their population, noting carefully, in a second column, the exact age at which the children die, the second column would show the relative merits of the governments, and the comparative happiness of their subjects. A simple arithmetical statement would then, perhaps, be more conclusive than all the arguments that could be adduced. In the importance of the inferences to be drawn from such tables, I fully agree with him: and to make these inferences, it is evident that we should attend less to the column expressing the number of children born, than to the column expressing the number which survived the age of infancy and reached manhood; and this number will almost invariably be the greatest, where the proportion of births to the whole population is the least. In this point we rank next after Norway and Switzerland, which, considering the number of our great towns and manufactories, is certainly a very extraordinary fact. As nothing can be more clear, than that all our demands for population are fully supplied; if this be done with a small proportion of births, it is a decided proof of a very small mortality; a distinction on which we may justly pride ourselves. Should it appear from future investigations, that I have made too great an allowance for omissions, both in the births and in the burials, I shall be extremely happy to find, that this distinction, which, all other circumstances being the same, I consider as the surest test of happiness and good government, is even greater than I have supposed it to be. In despotic, miserable, or naturally unhealthy countries, the proportion of births to the whole population will generally be found very great." P. 314.

In the general tenor of this reasoning, we agree with Mr. Malthus; and most earnestly hope, that further investigation will corroborate such a favourable statement of the superior happiness we enjoy above the other states of Europe. In Scotland, the condition of the poorer classes is rapidly ameliorating; yet, notwithstanding dreadful epidemics, and a very extensive emigration, which takes off half the surplus births, its population is still redundant, and it is of course subject to frequent famines; but, in consequence of improvements in its agriculture, it is not so much overheaped as it was formerly, when it contained much fewer inhabitants. The extended use of potatoes in Ireland has occasioned an increase of its population, much beyond the demand for labour, and has, of course, sunk the lower classes into the most abject poverty. The misery thus produced, and the political disorders which arise out of it, are, however, some kind of check to the further increase of its population.

*(To be concluded in our next.)*

[March, 1804]

From the ample investigation the author has thus bestowed on the subject, he draws several important conclusions, all tending to show, that the absolute population of any country depends upon the quantity of food it can produce or acquire; and that, in general, countries may be said to be happy, according to the quantity of food which a day's labour will purchase. Millions of human beings have had their existence repressed, from want of this food; although, in many places, an absolute famine may never have been experienced; the other checks having sufficed to restrain the population within the limits of subsistence. If these checks fail of their effect, famine may then be apprehended, to level the population to the food produced. This dreadful scourge cannot be produced simply by population, as the progress of the latter is gradual, though rapid; but, by obliging the lower classes of mankind to subsist on the smallest possible quantity of food, an overgreat population turns even the slightest deficiency of the supply into a severe dearth.

In the third Book, Mr. Malthus treats of the different systems of politics, which have been proposed, or have prevailed, in society, as to their effect on the evils arising from the principle of population. In this part of the work, he differs from Wallace and Condorcet, who, in their speculations, did not apprehend that the population of the world would be redundant till the whole earth was cultivated to the utmost; an event which they both conceived to be at an immense distance. The former of these writers admitted, that this redundancy would destroy his whole system of equality; and the latter, that a distinct limit being thus put to the increase of the human species, an oscillation between happiness and misery would take place. Mr. Malthus, on the contrary, thinks this oscillation is in continual action; and that a redundancy of population has occurred in most states, ever since any history of mankind has been recorded.

Of the visionary system of Godwin, Mr. Malthus observes, that as this scheme would call forth all the powers of procreation, the mere redundancy of people, in consequence of such unlimited increase, would, in a very few years, oblige the system to be abandoned, even allowing every possible improvement in agriculture. Godwin seemed disposed to admit the truth of this remark, in a reply which, as we have above stated, he published to the first edition of Mr. Malthus's Essay. As a check, however, to this redundancy, Godwin hints at limiting the number of children from each marriage; observing that infanticide, to be effectual, must be committed to the magistrate, and not left to the parents. This expedient, although sanctioned by the names of Plato and Aristotle, Mr. Malthus very properly reprobates, in the strongest terms. As to the sufficiency of that prudential sentiment, which causes persons to abstain from marriage, proposed also by Godwin, it must be observed, that on his theory it could have but little force.

The author is decidedly against the English system of poor-laws. He does not deny, that they were instituted for a benevolent purpose; but thinks, that they have failed in attaining their end; and that, if they had been executed in a more complete manner, they would have been still more injurious than at present. He explains how much the classes immediately above the parish poor were injured, in the late scarcities, by the relief granted being proportioned to the price of corn; which, by enabling the dependents on the parish to persist in the usual consumption, threw all the distress upon those above them, and contributed more to heighten the price than the deficiency of the crop. In respect to the price of labour, the most important subject in political œconomy, he observes as follows.

"There is no one that more ardently desires to see a real advance in the price of labour than myself; but the attempt to effect this object, by forcibly raising the nominal price, which was practised to a certain degree, and recommended almost universally during the late scarcities, every thinking man must reprobate, as puerile and ineffectual.

"The price of labour, when left to find its natural level, is a most important political barometer, expressing the relation between the supply of provisions and the demand for them; between the quantity to be consumed and the number of consumers; and, taken on the average, independently of accidental circumstances, it further expresses clearly, the wants of the society respecting population; that is whatever may be the number of children to a marriage, necessary to maintain exactly the present population, the price of labour will be just sufficient to support this number, or be above it, or below it, according to the state of the real funds for the maintenance of labour, whether stationary, progressive, or retrograde. Instead, however, of considering it in this light, we consider it as something which we can raise or depress at pleasure, something which depends principally upon his Majesty's Justices of the Peace. When an advance in the price of provisions already expresses, that the demand is too great for the supply, in order to put the labourer in the same condition as before, we raise the price of labour, that is, we increase the demand; and are then much surprised, that the price of provisions continues rising. In this, we act much in the same manner as if, when the quicksilver in the common weatherglass stood at *stormy*, we were to raise it, by some forcible pressure, to *settled fair*, and then be astonished that it continued raining." P. 406.

After observing, that Dr. S. Smith has clearly shown how a scarcity tends to throw labourers out of employment, or to force them to work for smaller wages, from the inability of the masters to give the same wages, and that a scarcity must, in the natural course of things, tend to lower, instead of raising, the price of labour, he proceeds thus.

"After the publication, and general circulation of such a work as Dr. Smith's, I confess, that it appears to be strange, that so many men, who would yet aspire to be thought political œconomists, should still think, that it is in the power of the justices of the peace, or even of the omnipotence of Parliament, to alter, by a *fiat*, the whole circumstances of the country; and, when the demand for provisions is greater than the supply, by publishing a particular edict, to make the supply at once equal to, or greater than, the demand. Many men, who would shrink at the proposal of a maximum, would propose themselves, that the price of labour should be proportioned to the price of provisions; and do not seem to be aware, that the two proposals are very nearly of the same nature, and that both tend directly to famine. It matters not, whether we enable the labourer to purchase the same quantity of provisions which he did before, by fixing the price, or by raising in proportion the price of labour. The only advantage on the side of raising the price of labour is, that the rise in the price of provisions, which necessarily follows it, encourages importation; but, putting importation out of the question, which might possibly be prevented by war, or other circumstances, a universal rise of wages, in proportions, aided by adequate parish allowances to those who were thrown out of work, would, by preventing any kind of saving, in the same manner as a maximum, cause the whole crop to be consumed in nine months, which ought to have lasted twelve, and thus produce a famine." P. 408.

The arguments here adduced appear conclusive against some of the measures proposed, and even practised, in the late dearths. Indeed, the present system of the poor-laws, and the subordinate matters connected with them, are by many persons considered as open to numerous objections. Mr. Malthus is of opinion, that if they had never existed, there might have occurred a few instances of more severe distress; but the aggregate happiness of the poor would have been greater. The independent spirit of the English peasantry, he thinks, has operated as a powerful check to the pernicious tendency of those laws to raise the price of provisions, and to overstock the market with labour. He agrees with Sir F. M. Eden, in condemning the practice of parishes employing their poor in manufactures; considering this step, not only as a cruel robbery of the industrious poor, who are thus made sometimes to contribute to the ruin of their own trade, but also as a practice which tends ultimately to increase, more rapidly than usual, the number of dependents on the parishes.

Mr. Malthus employs much ingenious disquisition respecting the comparative merits of the agricultural and commercial systems; and declares decidedly in favour of the former, as the foundation, at least, of the whole system of national prosperity. He is, however, perfectly aware of the advantages derived from commerce and manufactures, and regards them as calculated to enlarge our enjoyments and increase our happiness; but contends, that they ought to be considered as accessories only to agriculture. He observes, that a capital employed on the land, even if the speculation is unsuccessful, as to the profit of the individual, can scarcely fail of being highly productive to society. On the contrary, a capital employed in trade may be profitable to the individual, and yet almost totally unproductive to society. A surplus produce of land has a real value, in being capable of supporting a number of persons exempted from the labours of agriculture, who may be otherwise employed in the service of society; this being indeed the fund that maintains the proprietors, manufacturers, and other consumers. Manufactures may indeed yield the same revenue, yet it is accidental, and must depend upon circumstances; for, if purchasers could not be found, the labour would have been totally useless.

"In this history of the world, the nations, whose wealth has been derived principally from manufactures and commerce, have been perfectly ephemeral beings, compared with those, the basis of whose wealth has been agriculture. It is in the nature of things, that a state which subsists upon a revenue furnished by other countries, must be infinitely more exposed to all the accidents of time and chance, than one which produces its own.

"No error is more frequent, than that of mistaking effects for causes. We are so blinded by the shewiness of commerce and manufactures, as to believe that they are almost the sole cause of the wealth, power, and prosperity of England. But perhaps, they may be more justly considered as the consequences, than the cause of this wealth. According to the definitions of the economists, which consider only the produce of land, England is the richest country in Europe in proportion to her size. Her system of agriculture is beyond comparison better, and consequently her surplus produce is more considerable. France is very greatly superior to England in extent of territory and population, but when the surplus produce, or disposeable revenue of the two nations are compared, the superiority of France almost vanishes. And it is this great surplus produce in England, arising from her agriculture, which enables her to support such a vast body of manufactures, such formidable fleets and armies, such a crowd of persons engaged in the liberal professions, and a proportion of the society living on money rents, very far beyond what has ever been known in any other country of the world. – Of late years indeed, the part of the society, not connected with agriculture, has unfortunately increased beyond this produce; but the average importation of corn, as yet bears but a small proportion to that which is grown in the country, and consequently the power which England possesses of supporting so vast a body of idle consumers, must be attributed principally to the greatness of her surplus produce.

"It will be said, that it was her commerce and manufactures which encouraged her cultivators to obtain this great surplus produce, and therefore indirectly, if not directly, created it. That commerce and manufactures produce this effect in a certain degree, is true; but that they sometimes, produce a contrary effect, and generally so, when carried to excess, is equally true. Undoubtedly agriculture cannot flourish without a vent for its commodities, either at home or abroad; but when this want has been adequately supplied, the interests of agriculture demand nothing more. When too great a part of a nation is engaged in commerce and manufactures, it is a clear proof, that, either from undue encouragement, or from other particular causes, a capital is employed in this way to much greater advantage than on land; and under such circumstances, it is impossible, that the land should not be robbed of much of the capital which would naturally have fallen to its share." P. 437.

"And the experience of the last twenty years seems to warrant us in concluding, that the high price of provisions, arising from the abundance of commercial wealth, accompanied, as it has been, by very great variations, and by a great rise in the price of labour, does not operate as an encouragement to agriculture, sufficient to make it keep pace with the rapid strides of commerce." P. 439.

Hence, although Mr. Malthus does not approve of the different expedients of encouragement and restraint which pervade the whole of the commercial system, he thinks it necessary to give the same encouragement to agriculture as to manufactures, by a bounty on the exportation of corn; that being the only means of enabling the agricultural population to keep pace with the commercial. The predominance of the latter in any state, in such a degree as to render the importation of corn necessary, which is the case at present in England, is, in his opinion, an evil fraught with the most dangerous consequences.

The prevailing errors on the subject of population are treated by Mr. M. in a masterly manner. Most nations have been desirous of increasing the number of their inhabitants, and have vainly hoped, by bounties on marriage and children, to augment their population, without previously augmenting their resources.

"The prejudices on the subject of population, bear a very striking resemblance to the old prejudices about specie, and we know how slowly, and with what difficulty, these last have yielded to juster conceptions. Politicians, observing that states which were powerful and prosperous were almost invariably populous, have mistaken an effect for a cause, and concluded that their population was the cause of their prosperity, instead of their prosperity being the cause of their population, as the old political economists concluded, that the abundance of specie was the cause of national wealth, instead of the effect of it. The annual produce of the land and labour, in both these instances, became, in consequence, a secondary consideration, and its increase, it was conceived, would naturally follow the increase of specie in the one case, or of population in the other. The folly of endeavouring, by forcible means, to increase the quantity of specie in any country, and the absolute impossibility of accumulating it beyond a certain level, by any human laws that can be devised, are now fully established, and have been completely exemplified in the instances of Spain and Portugal; but the illusion still remains concerning population; and, under this impression, almost every political treatise has abounded in proposals to encourage population, with little or no comparative reference to the means of its support. Yet, surely, the folly of endeavouring to increase the quantity of specie in any country, without an increase of the commodities which it is to circulate, is not greater than that of endeavouring to increase the number of people, without an increase of the food which is to maintain them; and it will be found, that the level above which no human laws can raise the population of a country, is a limit more fixed and impassable, than the limit to the accumulation of specie. However improbable, in fact, it is possible to conceive, that means might be invented of retaining a quantity of specie in a state, greatly beyond what was demanded by the produce of its land and labour; but when, by great encouragement, population has been raised to such a height, that this produce is meted out to each individual in the smallest portions that can support life, no stretch of ingenuity can even conceive the possibility of going further." P. 474.

Both Sir James Steuart, and the author of *L'ami des hommes*, had fallen into the error of considering population as the efficient cause of prosperity; but further consideration convinced them of their error; and the preceding observations of Mr. Malthus appear perfectly just. He also shows, that the superfluities of the higher classes, and the number of animals kept for pleasure, as well as the lands not cultivated, do not affect the average pressure of distress on the poor, but only lessen the actual population of the country.

In the fourth Book, the author treats "of our future prospects respecting the removal or mitigation of the evils arising from the principle of population," and shows, that as it is necessary some check, either natural or moral, should be applied to prevent an excessive population, there can be no hesitation, respecting the superiority of moral restraint. To this, however, mankind have been little attentive; because the poverty and contagious diseases, which are the natural consequences of increasing too fast, do not immediately follow the conduct which leads to them.

By a general practice of moral restraint, and late marriages, the author apprehends that very beneficial effects, in respect to the general happiness of society, would be produced, in a method perfectly consonant both to natural religion and the Christian revelation. He considers the sentiments hitherto entertained respecting marriage, and offspring, as having had their origin in the political view of rearing soldiers for the defence of the state; but; if these sentiments were no longer entertained, war might perhaps cease from a want of combatants. This expectation, however, seems to us chimerical. Nothing can be more absurd, in his opinion, than to encourage marriage among the poor; as it tends to overstock the market with labourers, and, of course, depresses their condition.

The principal objection to his system, Mr. Malthus acknowledges to be, the fear of increasing the quantity of vice. The temptations, however, to a breach of chastity, which arise from continued restraint, he considers as by no means comparable to those which arise from poverty. On account, however, of this contingent increase of vice from restraint, he only contends for leaving every man to his free choice in regard to marriage or celibacy. This, he thinks, is not the case at present; our poor laws afford, he observes, a systematic encouragement to marriage; private benevolence tends constantly to equalize, as much as possible, the circumstances of the single and the married man; and, in the higher classes of society, superior respect always attends the married woman.

Mr Malthus, as we have seen, is of opinion, that the principal cause of poverty is to be sought in the redundancy of population, and is totally unconnected with human institutions. This doctrine may perhaps seem unfavourable to liberty, by enabling governments to lay the blame of the miseries produced by their oppressions, upon nature, and the subjects' own imprudence. He offers, however, many arguments against such an application; and shows that the lower classes, by being made acquainted with the true cause of the poverty and distress under which they labour, would become more tractable, and of course the executive government would not require the same strength.

The poor laws ought, according to this author, to be abolished; but, for the sake of humanity and justice, gradually: the personal consequence of single women so increased, that they may, in that respect, be on a level with married ones; and a national system of education adopted for the poorer classes. The first and last of these means have been frequently recommended. He observes, that there exists in every country a certain standard of wretchedness, below which men cease to marry; and that we ought to raise this standard point as high as possible. Our private charities should therefore, he thinks, be restrained, and every thing avoided that tends to encourage marriage among the poor; or to remove that inequality which ought always to subsist between the single man, and him that has a family. Upon these grounds, he objects to the systems of Sir James Steuart, Mr. Townsend, and A. Young, Esq. On the cow-system of the latter, he remarks, that at first much good would appear to be produced; but that, as soon as the commons had been allotted, and land began to be scarce, difficulties still greater than the present would occur, from the extended population, which a habit of early marriage, fostered by this system, would produce.

We consider Mr. Malthus's observations respecting the use of potatoes, or the cheap soups of Count Rumford, as perfectly just, and dictated by a spirit of liberality. If these were adopted for the food of the poor, the price of labour would, as he observes, be regulated by the price of those articles, as it is now, in some measure, by the price of wheat. This lowering the price of labour might be proposed by a commercial politician, with a view of underselling foreigners in the market; but the policy of condemning our poor to rags and wretchedness, with the view of increasing our exports, is detestable, and must be abhorred by every friend of mankind. Under that system also, if the average consumption of potatoes should at any time equal the average growth, and a scarcity of that article should ensue, it would occasion a more dreadful dearth than a scarcity of wheat; because the poor, having been habituated to live on the cheapest and most productive food, would be without any substitute, except the bark of trees, and a great part of them must of necessity be starved. The question is not, as Mr. Young seems to have stated it, how to provide in the best and cheapest manner for a given number of people; this involves no difficulty; but the true consideration is, how to provide for those who are in want, so as to prevent a constant accumulation of their number; and this is no easy task.

Unless the marriage of the poor can be restrained, Mr. Malthus imagines no permanent improvement of their condition can take place; a diminution of mortality (by the introduction of the cow-pox or otherwise) will only produce a greater mortality in future; and, if their condition is ameliorated in one place, it will be depressed in another. Luxury, which tends to raise the standard at which marriage ceases, he considers as advantageous, because it tends to prevent that union. By thus diminishing the numbers of the lower classes of society, the industrious, he observes, would have a greater chance of rising into the middling station. The price of labour ought to allow subsistence for a family of six children; if a labourer had more than that number, some allowance might be made, so as to raise his condition to that standard, which might be done without encouraging marriage. This advance in the price of labour would not be such as to put a stop to our manufactures; because, the price of provisions would be more equal, the poor-rates would be abolished, a great saving of what is at present expended upon young children who die prematurely would take place, and œconomical and industrious habits would generally prevail.

In the conclusion of his work, Mr. Malthus observes, that as civilized society requires manufactures and large towns, this would diminish, in some degree, the necessity of a very great extension of the preventive check; and, although it would be absurd to suppose, that more chastity would be found in the single state than at present, the duration of that state might certainly be prolonged as far as is necessary, without any great restraint. He is of opinion, that if the prudential check to marriage could be increased, without a very great increase of the illicit intercourse of the sexes, the happiness of society would be highly promoted; that this might be done is evident, he thinks, from the example of Norway, Switzerland, England, and Scotland, where, although that check operates with greater force than in the neighbouring states, those countries rank higher in point of chastity. At any rate, allowing an increase of vicious intercourse between the sexes, the diminution of the vices arising from indigence would, he thinks, fully counterbalance that evil; and the cause of happiness would have, in addition, the advantage of diminished mortality, and superior comforts.

The author even imagines, that although it would be highly advantageous that positive institutions should co-operate with prudential restraints, yet much good would be done, by merely laying aside the institutions which encourage marriage, and no longer circulating opinions and doctrines which favour it. Nay, even the mere knowledge of the effects produced by the tendency of the species to increase, would, in his judgment, be beneficial; as it would prevent the rich from exerting their benevolence in a wrong direction, by showing them the physical impossibility of assisting the poor, so as to enable them to marry early, and bring up a large family with decency; and it would teach the poor, that the causes of poverty have no connexion with forms of government, or the unequal distribution of property; which would tend to render them more contented and peaceable.

The importance of this work, to the general interests of society, has led us to be rather copious in our account of it. The lights which the author has thrown upon the subject, are of the most interesting nature. All the former systems are, indeed, in a manner, overturned by his principles, and the important deductions he has drawn from them; and yet, such appears to be the general correctness of his remarks, that we must more frequently give than withhold our assent. Legislators and politicians have been constantly in the habit of endeavouring to increase, by positive laws, the number of the people, as if their number were the efficient cause of prosperity; with the same views, they have deplored, and attempted to stop, the occasional emigrations of the natives. This conduct, we are now told, is absurd in the extreme; an increase of the people will immediately follow any improvement of the country, merely from the course of nature, and independent of positive institutions. If this improvement however is not made, to stop the emigration of the superfluous hands is, in fact, only condemning them to want and misery at home. On the same principles, nations have encouraged the importation of foreigners, which, abstracted from the view of introducing new arts, equally militates against the just principles of policy; as their introduction can only tend to impoverish the natives, and hinder their increase at any favourable time. This importation of foreigners has been carried to the utmost excess in the West-Indies, where a strange race has been introduced, whose condition renders them disloyal, and whose numbers makes them formidable. The fear, least the mother country should be unable to afford the necessary supply of hands, and should be depopulated in the endeavour, was undoubtedly the original cause of this step; a fear, however, which now appears perfectly groundless. Mr. Malthus notices a fact strongly in point, namely, that the two provinces of Spain from which the greatest emigration took place to America, became, in consequence of an extended demand for people, more populous.

At the same time that we give Mr. Malthus praise for his industry in collecting facts, and for his ingenuity in applying them, to show the remote cause of the misery and distress of the lower classes of society, we dissent from him, in the means he proposes for avoiding those evils in future. The total abolition of the poor laws, even though gradual, is a measure much too violent. Nor are we for introducing actual changes hastily, upon any theory, however specious. We do not object to a national system of education, if directed by wholesome views, and on sound principles: but we cannot agree with his ideas of extending the period, and even the habit, of celibacy. That, by such conduct, much poverty and distress in families might be occasionally avoided, we do not deny; but, unless monastic institutions for the female sex were revived (an event neither likely to occur, nor fit to be recommended) this would be accompanied with a very great increase of vice. An increase which we are taught, by every principle of religion, natural or revealed, to consider as of much greater consequence than any temporary pressure of circumstances.

Independently of religion and morality, even political reasons stand in the way of a great extension of Mr. Malthus's system. A district formed with such habits, if it were capable of discharging its superfluous members upon its neighbours, and of drawing from them the necessary supply of domestic servants, might perhaps be looked up to, in theory, as the model of a perfect state; when applied, however, to an entire nation, and still more to the European republic, we cannot assent to it as eligible. The countries in which the preventive check to population is most prevalent, and its concomitant effects most visible, seem to be the only countries in which it can be adopted. The inhospitable climate of Norway, whatever happiness its peasantry may enjoy, offers too uninviting a prospect to tempt the cupidity of the more powerful monarchies of the south. The insular situation of Great Britain protects it from invasion; and the large disposeable revenue which is yielded by its commerce, enables it to hire others to fight its battles. It consequently does not require so much attention to absolute population; and its inhabitants are enabled to enjoy their advantages, without any great danger of falling under the dominion of nations richer in men, and moved by a single mind.

Upon the continent, however, the case is different. A state which should adopt such prudential maxims, must be weak in its admiration, from the independency of the inhabitants, and their jealous restrictions on the executive power; and it must have the reputation of being rich. With two such powerful incentives to rouse the passions of the surrounding nations, and with a restrained population, insufficient to supply defensive armies, nothing but the mutual jealousies of its neighbours could save it from falling at once under their dominion. At all times, notwithstanding its wishes to be neutral, it would be drawn into the disputes of its neighbours, if it were only that it might serve as the theatre of war, as well to keep the distresses incident to war from their own dominions, as because the abundance of its surplus produce would be well adapted for the subsistence of the contending armies: this has been the fate of Flanders, Italy, and Poland. In such a state, to the misery of having armies of foreigners ranging through its territories, would be added the still greater misery of foreign factions, arising out of the relations springing up between individuals and the contending powers; until at length, exhausted by faction, it would sink under the dominion of the most fortunate of its neighbours, or be divided among them, as soon as they could agree respecting the partition.

The general adoption of such habits by all the European states, supposing for a moment such an event possible, would only tend to hasten the period when Russia will attempt to overwhelm the northern and midland states with her numerous forces; or, to encourage the followers of some new prophet, or other adventurer, from the sandy plains of Arabia, again to overrun the southern parts, and to wash away the crimes or errors of the inhabitants in their blood.

It is but justice to this author to declare, that in this edition of his Essay, we do not find any trace of what we conceived to be intimated in the former; a notion that human minds were framed, by some natural process, from inert matter. On the contrary, he seems here to write as impressed with a due sense of religious as well as moral truths.

Respecting the style of this work, as we have given several extracts, we have, of course, little to say. A desire to leave nothing unsaid upon a subject of so much importance, has certainly led Mr. Malthus to be rather diffuse. A more concise view might have been more pleasing to some persons, and better adapted for general reading. For ourselves, we can truly say, that we found every part of the work so curious, and so ably treated, that it did not appear to us too long.

# ANNALS OF AGRICULTURE
Vol. XLI, 1804
[Arthur Young]

On the application of the principles of population, to the question of assigning land to cottages.
*By the Editor*

In the whole circle of political oeconomy, there is not a more important question, than the enquiry which involves in it the legislation of the poor. After 200 years experience in England, we seem to have grown old in policy, without the benefit of experience; and a multiplicity of publications have appeared, proceeding in almost all their discussions, so much on theory and reasoning, that the writers seem to have thought it a question that could never be experimentally decided. A very ingenious writer, the Rev. Mr. Malthus; has just published, a 4to. volume, on the *Principles of Population*, in which he has added to the number; but still moving in the same circle of enquiry, that of *theory* alone. In this work he has taken occasion to contrast my representation of the state of the poor of France, inserted in my Travels through that kingdom, with later representations of a cottage system in England, found chiefly in the counties of Lincoln and Rutland; in which he contends, that I am entirely at variance with what I printed on the state of France. In this observation, I think he has been led into a considerable error; and that there really is a marked, and essential distinction, between the result of property in land in France; and that mode of giving it which I have recommended for England, not theoretically, but in direct conclusion from many facts.

The reader will, however, permit me to make one previous observation. It is this: that a writer like myself, who has employed not a short life in the acquisition of facts, which he has been in the progressive habit of laying before the public, is not bound to reconcile such facts, or to withhold any, because they militate with others, that he has before communicated. He is rather bound in candour, to the directly contrary conduct: his business is to search for important facts for public use; and though he may adduce his own conclusions and reflections, as they strike him at the moment, it ought not to be expected from him, that his ideas are to remain stationary, while he is advancing in inquiries. He knows that the main object is facts; to comment on them is an inferior business, and it would be a pernicious one, more futile even then mere theory, were his attention first given to former opinions, drawn from very different premises, and thus became solicitous, not to illustrate and apply his new information, without a caution first given to reconciling it with former circumstances. Were I in a future tour at home, or on the continent, to meet with a system of supporting the poor very different from any hitherto known, I should publish the particulars with the reflections that occurred in my mind at the time; and if my former opinions drawn from very different sources, were obliterated from my mind, I do not assert that I would not recur to them; but assuredly the less they were attended to the better, for such attention would be apt to lead much more to a care of avoiding seeming contradictions, from a merely selfish motive, than to a full elucidation of the new question then started. The one conduct is, that of a man who considers only his own reputation: the other, of one who looks only at conveying fully to his readers the facts he has gained, and the impression they make at the moment on his mind. Supposing, therefore, Mr. Malthus, had found me at different periods, and speaking from very different facts, recommending directly contrary systems; he ought not, therefore, to have condemned me, but rather have deemed it a proof that I gave the public the information I possessed *fully* and without those reserves which a timid caution would have been careful to retain. But in the present question I think it will not be difficult to prove, that the system described in France, and that recommended in England, are materially different.

I found population in France, by means of small properties in land, carried to an excess, that produced great misery and wretchedness; and as a conclusion, I declare against the system.

In England, I found districts, where cottagers *renting*, (and possessing) land, gave them such comfort, that even in the scarcity, they neither received nor applied for any parochial relief; and as a conclusion I declare FOR the system.

Mr. Malthus condemns me for inconsistency.

Were the opinions really inconsistent, this would give me small concern; the facts remain for him and others to work upon. But let us enquire how this case stands?

In France, the landed property in question, is possessed by the cottagers in full right, and disposeable at his pleasure; and the general custom is to leave it by will in equal division among the children. It is not a plot of ground surrounding the cottage as in England; in most instances, the residence is in a village or town, the land at a distance: and I expressly declare, the subdivision goes to such an extent, that a single cherry-tree, with the spot it covers, has been the whole of the property, yet a possessor kept at home by the charms of this property. How Mr. Malthus, can compare such facts with the system partially adopted in England, or with the proposition founded on it, I am utterly at a loss to conceive, for they have not one single point in common.

The mischiefs resulting from our system of poor rates is well understood by that gentleman, and it was to get rid of them that the practice of Rutland and Lincoln, was recommended. It would have been more satisfactory, had Mr. Malthus stated this at his 573d, page, for in the *Question of Scarcity*, p. 70. I state it as the result in those counties; and at p. 79, my proposal, expressly as an ease to poor rates; but, if his extracts be merely read, this part of the effect, is omitted altogether: and the following passage, contains all Mr. M. has given in reply to the memoir inserted in the Annals. Vol. xxxvi. p. 497.

"Mr. Young, has since pursued his idea more in detail, in a pamphlet, entitled *An Inquiry into the propriety of applying Wastes to the better Maintenance and support of the Poor.* But the impression on my mind is still the same; and it appears to me calculated to assimilate the condition of the labourers of this country, to that of the lower classes of the Irish. Mr. Young seems in a most unaccountable manner, to have forgotten all his general principles on this subject. He has treated the question of a provision for the poor, as if it was merely how to provide in the cheapest and best manner for a *given number* of people. If this had been the sole question, it would never have taken so many hundred years to resolve. But the real question is, how to provide for those who are in want, in such a manner, as to prevent a continual accumulation of their numbers? and it will readily occur to the reader, that a plan of giving them land and cows cannot promise much success in this respect. If after all the commons had been divided, the poor laws were still to continue in force; no good reason can be assigned, why the rates should not in a few years be as high as they are at present, independently of all that had been expended in the purchase of land and stock".

Writers who have such confidence in their theoretical reasonings as to give a desultory attention to facts, are too apt to venture their conclusions without due care of the foundation "calculated to assimilate the condition of the labourers of this country to that of the lower classes of the Irish." It would be marvellous indeed, if that system which in Lincoln and Rutland, produces probably the most comfortable peasantry in the British dominions should assimilate the condition of our poor to those of a country become the most miserable in Europe, because there is none of that *facility* of getting land of which Mr. M. repeatedly speaks. - On the contrary, the Irish now hire it with the utmost difficulty, and at rents the most exorbitant: and their increased misery may for what he or I know to the contrary, arise from this circumstance.

In regard to the distinction between providing for a given number of people, and preventing a continual accumulation of numbers, I consider Mr. Malthus' remark as inapplicable. The proposal of annexing land to cottages, provides comfortably for the families that have it; and were the system to be pursued to all the people thus bred, the objection would have great weight, because multiplication would be endless. But this is expressly provided against; as these words will shew, viz. "The allotments to remain the property of the poor to whom assigned, so long as all the family living at the time of the assignment or born to the father afterwards, shall not be chargeable to the parish; to descend to his family, subject to the same conditions." *Annals*, Vol, 36. p. 641. - Supposing the fact, which is nearly the truth, that a house will every where have a family in it: here is one taken from the parish, the inhabitant in a state of comfort instead of misery; under the encouragement to be industrious instead of idle and dependant: and the population increasing TAKEN FROM parochial relief, instead of being ADDED TO the poor list. Numbers might, and probably would remain the same or nearly the same; but in the present case the progressive population remains under the poor laws; in the proposition this population is cut off from their influence, and the encouragement to marry would remain exactly in that proportion less than at present. They marry now from dependance on the parish; they would not marry then unless by industry and saving they had made a much better provision than that dependance. The system therefore, tends directly to lessen a vicious accumulation of numbers. Give the fee of the land to the possessor and he might divide it in the French system: but that being in the parish all the evils flowing in France, from landed property, are prevented.

As to the supposition of the poor laws continuing in force, it is idle: for the supposition is directly the reverse; it would be insanity indeed, to give land with the immediate intention of arresting the progress of those laws, and yet to leave them in force upon the population thus provided for. Whatever the plan may be that leaves those laws to their present operation must prove abortive.

*Mr. Malthus has the following observation*

> "A farmer or gentleman living in a grazing country, has, we will suppose, a certain number of cottages on his farm; being a liberal man, and liking to see all the people about him comfortable, he may join a piece of land to his cottages, sufficient to keep one or two cows, and give, besides, high wages. His labourers will, of course, live in plenty, and be able to rear up large families; but a grazing farm requires few hands; and though the master may choose to pay those that he employs well, he will not probably wish to have more labourers on his farm than his work requires. He does not therefore, build more houses, and the children of the labourers whom he employs must evidently emigrate and settle in other countries. While such a system continues peculiar to certain families, or certain districts, no great inconveniences arise from it to the community in general; and it cannot be doubted, that the individual labourers employed on these farms are in an enviable situation, and such as we might naturally wish was the lot of all our labourers. But it is perfectly clear that such a system could

not in the nature of things, possess the same advantages, if it were made general; because there would then be no countries to which the children could emigrate with any prospect of finding work. Population would evidently encrease beyond the demand of towns and manufactories, and universal poverty must necessarily ensue."

If this writer imagines that the cottage system alluded to, be found only in grazing districts, he is in an error: it is found rarely in the grazing district, but in a country not peculiar for fertility, as he might have seen from the rents annexed to Mr. Gourlay's enquiry; so far therefore, as his objection is founded, on this circumstance, it falls to the ground. The remark that the children must emigrate and settle in other countries is true, to the same amount that would take place were no land annexed to the cottages. Mr. Malthus certainly knows that young men and women in the country do not marry with a view to the demand of the farmers, but are impelled by very different feelings. Were political reasonings to influence them, this might, in prudence, take place; but such reasonings have nothing to do in the question, and our inquiry ought to go solely to the restraint or check on propagation: here opinions must vary; some thing may be alledged on both sides. Possessing land the families are better fed and more at their ease, and therefore would be led more to *marriage*; but being brought up in habits of regular industry far beyond the children of the poor, having no property, they would be led to delay marrying till they had saved enough to do it under the expectation of comfortable circumstances, but especially waiting till they could get a cottage; this is material, whereas when the dependance is on mere labour, and the parish support eventually, marriages are very often the result of illicit connections; but still they marry, as every vicinity can testify. The less industrious and frugal, and the more profligate the people are, the promiscuous intercourse of the sexes is more common, and this certainly is attended with a small increase of numbers. But this circumstance, Mr. Malthus will not avail himself of, or he would not have agreed with Mr. Bernard, p. 585, in commending virtue, prudence, and industry; for a profligate handsome girl will prevent the increase deprecated so much by Mr. M. more than the virtue of half a dozen parishes will promote it.

But still Mr. M. contends that the system could not be general, in answer to this we must agree to some common date whereon to reason. I ask what cannot be denied, that in this inquiry *cottage* and *family* be accepted as synonymous terms. In the preceding passage, this gentleman seems most unaccountably to forget that every cottage without land has a family in it already, from which what he calls emigration *must* take place. This is the state of things at present throughout the kingdom, and if towns, manufactures regiments, &c. do not take off the superfluity of both sexes, it must regorge in the village, and produce misery: there can be no doubt of this, and we see it more or less every where; if new houses are not built to keep this increased population at home, it emigrates to towns, &c. and I contend that cottages ought not to be built without land, to render the inhabitants comfortable. Mr.M. says, that *with land* they will increase, who doubts it? they certainly will, though perhaps not more than without it. The superfluity must emigrate: so they must in every case, and if there is not a demand for this superfluity, misery is the consequence. Unquestionably, this is exactly the same in both cases; there may be half a million of these cottages in England and Wales: and the question between Mr. Malthus, and myself is, shall their inhabitants be in a comfortable state, cut off from parish relief, or shall they remain miserably poor, and dependant on increasing rates? this enquiry is confined to the cottagers: we have no more to do with the increase of their population, in one case than in the other; the ease and comfort of that increase will depend on the demand of flourishing or declining fabrics. But will any man contend that you shall not render 500,000 families comfortable because they will increase? seeming to assume the false supposition that if they are *not* comfortable they will not increase; though the proofs to the contrary are to be seen by millions.

The collateral circumstance provided for in my proposition of cutting off the increase from becoming burthensome to the parish, would prove a means, and probably, a very effective means of lessening poor rates in proportion to the extension of the plan, and as this would, on the part of the poor, be a condition voluntarily submitted to, it would be free from the objections that bear against so violent and absolutely arbitrary a measure as that proposed by this gentleman, of declaring every child born in future to be cut off from all parochial relief:

a law which from its violence would probably never be executed, but were it strictly executed as he proposes, would blow up mischief and insurrection in every part of the kingdom. To attain the same end, or nearly the same end, by lenient means, and with the consent of the poor themselves, would surely be a more safe and humane measure.

In truth this project of Mr. Malthus, combined, as he has combined it, with the prophecy of repeated scarcities, (p. 444) which he considers as unavoidable, and with a progressive rise in the price of provisions, would, in the extent of the plan, and in the severity of the execution, he proposes, be a most iniquitous proceeding, and open on all sides, such scenes of distress as would be a more cruel tax on every heart that could feel, than the poor rate itself with all its defects. The rising generation would be reared and educated by the assistance and under the influence of these old laws, consequently without that due preparation which should precede so great a change, and numerous families of orphans would speedily be left cut off from every resource but one to which Mr. Malthus does not allude: the immediate hand of God to feed or take them. Though in some respects this horrible plan would be gradual in operation, yet it would in most others, and in its general operation, be a sudden, (for a few years do not exclude the term in so great a measure) violent, and dangerous revolution in the policy of a great empire. And on what is the success of this revolution made to depend? why on young men and women avoiding matrimony and keeping themselves chaste without it!!! How so very sensible a man could bring himself to speculate and reason as he has done on this topic, is to me wonderful: he sees the absolute necessity of this prodigy to his plan, and therefore labours to shew the probability of it, as he contends that man as such, has no right to existence,[1] he will

---

[1] "A man who is born into a world already possessed, if he cannot get subsistence from his parents, on whom he has a just demand, and if the society do not want his labour, has no claims of *right* to the smallest portion of food; and, in fact, has no business to be where he is. At nature's mighty feast there is no vacant cover for him." p. 531. Were the providence of the Almighty, no better dependance for such a man, than the speculations of such philosophical politicians, sad, indeed, would it be for the human race; better be a *young Raven*, than a man!

"I should propose a regulation to be made, declaring, that no child born from any marriage, taking place after the expiration of a year from the date of the law; and no illegitimate child born two years from the same date,

certainly contend that he has no right to a woman – that he has not that right which God and nature and a revelation preached *to the poor,* had positively given to him. A system that runs counter to the strongest passions in the heart of man must be built upon sand, would tumble about the ears of the projectors *and great would be the fall thereof.*

Mr. Malthus has, with considerable ability, analysed the consequence of increasing numbers, and he has pointed out the tendency of checks to population – but he does not seem fully to apprehend (though in one or two passages he touches lightly on the subject, apparently to guard himself from the imputation) the moral conclusion which must be drawn from his work: it is this, that nothing could render his plan successful but profligacy of manners – his great project demands a restraint on marriage; his next step that of preserving chastity in the single state is so perfectly visionary when applied to a great nation, that he must know what would be the consequence, and what alone would be likely to answer his purpose – a general and promiscuous intercourse of the sexes. This would give him *the check* he searches for; and this would be the infallible result of such a system. The sentiments of this able writer in the 2d chapt. of his 4th book, are excellent, and were the system generally possibly, his conclusions are well founded: but they appear to be utterly repugnant to the nature and state of man. – Suppose virtues which he does not nor ever did possess: and depend on contingencies which, however they may be wished, are never to be expected; and consequently a most inadequate foundation for so daring a measure as a sudden and violent change in a system that has been progressive for 200 years.

"When the wages of labour are hardly sufficient to maintain two children, a man marries and has five or six, he of course

> should ever be entitled to parish assistance; – all such assistance should be most rigidly denied him. He should be taught to know, that the laws of nature, which are the laws of God, had doomed him and his family to starve, for disobeying their repeated admonitions; that he had no claim of right on society, for the smallest portion, beyond *that which his* labour would fairly purchase. With regard to illegitimate children, they should on no account whatever, be allowed to have any claim to parish assistance. If the parents desert their child, they ought to be made answerable for the crime. The infant is, comparatively speaking, of no value to the society, as others will immediately supply its place"!!! – that is, it is to be starved to death, if private charity does not take it. Were such as system really

finds himself miserably distressed, he accuses the insufficiency of the price of labour to maintain a family, he accuses his parish for their tardy and sparing fulfilment of their obligation to assist him; he accuses the avarice of the rich who suffer him to want what they can so well spare. He accuses the partial and unjust institutions of society, which have awarded him an inadequate share of the produce of the earth. He accuses perhaps, the dispensations of Providence which have assigned to him a place in society so beset with unavoidable distress and dependance. In searching for objects of accusation he never adverts to the quarter from which all his misfortunes originate. The last person that he would think of accusing is himself, on whom, in fact, the whole of the blame lies, except in as far as he has been deceived by the higher classes of society. He may perhaps, wish that he had not married, because he now feels the inconveniences of it: but it never enters into his head that he can have done any thing wrong. He has always been told that to raise up subjects for his king and country, is a very meritorious act; he has done this act, and yet is suffering for it: he naturally thinks that he is suffering for righteousness sake; and it cannot but strike him as most extremely unjust and cruel in his king and country, to allow him thus to suffer, in return for giving them what they are continually declaring that they particularly want." – "they are themselves the cause of their own poverty (*by marrying*;) the society in which they live, and the government which presides over it, are totally without power in this respect," p. 506.

In this passage the author has stated a set of accusations, in order to confute the whole by one bold assertion. To me it appears that the poor fellow is justified in every one of these complaints, that of Providence alone excepted. The price of labour is insufficient to maintain a large family: the parish, in all probability, is tardy and sparing; the rich landowner is (relative to him) avaricious of the land which would support him: he HAS AN INADEQUATE SHARE of the produce of the earth: his complaints ARE founded: he has NOT done wrong, and he ought NOT to accuse himself for following the dictates of God, of nature, and of revelation. He may see other

executed *in all its parts*, what would it prove, but a premium to profligacy, whoredom, abortion, and murder.

cottagers with 3 or 4 acres of land, for which perhaps, they pay as large a rent as any farmer in the neighbourhood, living comfortably and independent of the parish, and has he not cause to accuse institutions which deny him that which the rich could well spare, and which would give him all that he wants? to tell such a man while in health and vigour that, *he is not to marry but to burn*; that like the fellow of a college, waiting some 20 years for a fat living, that he is to do the same, thus *burning*; remaining chaste is a cruel insult: – to be chaste until what happens: until he has saved enough to support a family without a house to put them in, or land to feed them! his prospect, supposing him both patient and chaste, is absolutely hopeless: after waiting 20 years to save money, he may wait 20 more for a cottage! – What then *must* be his conduct? assuredly to marry the moment he can secure a habitation, which if he misses he may never see the opportunity return. Never let it be forgotten that *house* and *family* are synonymous terms. Mr. Malthus describes the patience, forbearance, and chastity, but after all have been exerted, where is the house? what do you offer to his hope but patience, that is to attain no object – burning without the remedy of marriage – chastity without the hope of a wife – prudence to save for the possession of what can never be possessed – to wait 10 years for a wife without a bed, and children without house, land, or cow! An idea more visionary never issued from the heated imagination of a poet than an able, cool, and philosophic head has wrought with all its reasoning powers into a policy for legislative adoption.

It does not appear that Mr. Malthus in his considerations on the state of our poor, has sufficiently adverted to the circumstance, universal in the country parishes with which I am acquainted, that *house* and *family* are synonymous terms. In the state wherein England has been for many years, every cottage has a family: and when marriages do not take place, it is for want of more habitations. I do not know a parish where if a land proprietor were to build more cottages, they would not be immediately inhabited, at any rent he could with the smallest degree of reason demand. This is a circumstance which presents an obvious check to population, that at present acts powerfully in England; and it is with me a question whether it does not act too powerfully as seems to be manifest in the very great rise of labour in all the districts with which I am well acquainted; not a rise of the moment only, but of several years standing: and this circumstance bears so strongly on the inquiry, that I cannot but recommend it to the attention of so very able a writer. The times of actual scarcity are not to be reasoned upon when any average is our guide – for what at 4 or 5l. a quarter, must create great distress to those who consume wheat only, whatever the price of labour may be; but without excluding such years, it particularly deserves enquiry, how many families were able to support themselves through the late scarcities by means of certain small portions of property which could not in the nature of things produce a *profit* nearly equal to what they would have received from their parishes, had they not possessed such property, seeming to prove that the lowness of the wages of labour, are not so inadequate as may have been thought: *provided* the reliance on the parish were cut off. Where an improvident spirit and a want of economy, nursed up by the poor laws, are found, no price of labour would be adequate; and if the possession or occupation of a small space of land be the effective means of exciting this sober, industrious and saving spirit, then the means are in our hands for placing the lower classes in their best possible situation: the cottage poor in a state of comfort and independence on rates: and their superlucration of numbers taken off by towns, &c. &c. In this latter class, a declension of manufactures would produce misery; – but, it might be prudent to consider this evil as absolutely and physically impossible to present. Proportioned to the appearance of this evil should be a restriction on *new* cottages; which, on the contrary, would, at any time, by their multiplication, give a power of increasing the manufacturing classes. This may possibly be the utmost means of insuring as large a portion of happiness amongst the poor, as human institutions permit.

In comparing the price of labour with the expenses of living, one circumstance deserves attention: a poor family's expenses in winter, are greater than they are in summer, by at least the amount (whatever that may be) of fire and candle: and a more expensive attention is necessary to cloathing. The winter wages must therefore, be equal to their support; but the wages of summer, much exceed those of winter: in many districts, to a considerable degree; and I conceive, that it is saving in this season, which enables some among the poor, to raise themselves much above the average state of comfort, without applying for the parish for assistance. I do not from this conclude that the price of labour is as high as it ought to be, had poor rates no existence; but, I merely wish that the question were fully discussed, not by reasoning, but in reference to multiplied facts. To excite general industry and frugality, while poor rates remain, is utterly impossible.

*General Corollaries*

I. The present poor laws, cure few evils which they did not first create: but, the extent, duration, and force of their operation, are too great to allow of any sudden or arbitrary change.

II. They prevent industry, sobriety, and frugality.

III. They increase mouths, without a proportional increase of labour.

IV. The number of marriages will chiefly depend on the number of cottages: and population will depend entirely on that number.

V. Population depends but little on the ease of the people. A house will contain a family, whether the family be comfortable, or in misery.

VI. It is impossible to prevent increase by any laws, policy, or system, but such as morals forbid. It is possible to restrain the people from marriage, for any given number of years, without they shall be certain at the end of the period of being able to marry, that is, sure of a habitation: and with such certainty, the restraint would be a premium on licentious intercourse.

VII. The possession (indivisibly) or the occupation of a small space of land, will keep the poor from the parish even in scarcities: and, might be made the means of gradually extinguishing most of the present system.

VIII. Land thus annexed to cottages, places the inhabitants in a superior state of comfort; encourages industry, increases the quantity of labour from a given number of people; promotes sobriety, and creates frugality. And the children thus bred make better labourers, servants, workmen, and soldiers, than others educated in poverty and vice.[2]

---

[2] It would take too much time at present, to reply to Mr. Malthus's opinions on potatoes, and to shew that he has mistaken my reasoning, I have only one observation to make; that the population of Ireland, had depended fully as much on the extreme ease, with which (according to their manners) cabbins are raised, as on potatoes being their food. On the effect of that root on population, I may enlarge hereafter.

# ANNUAL REVIEW
January 1804
[Robert Southey]

Art. XVII. *An Essay on the Principles of Population; or, a View of its past and present Effects on human Happiness.* By T. R. MALTHUS, *Fellow of Jesus College, Cambridge.* 4to. pp. 610.

The public opinion has already been pronounced upon the merits of this Essay. Mr. Malthus embarked upon the tide just at the happy moment, at the flood when it leads on to fortune, and such was the unnatural and unwholesome state of our moral and political atmosphere, that he appeared like a philosopher, as he would have appeared like a giant had he walked abroad in a *mirage*.

No wise man had ever doubted, and no christian had ever disbelieved, that the general condition of mankind could be improved, till the unhappy consequences of the French revolution shook the liberties and morals of Europe. This amelioration was rendered probable to the good by reason, and certain by faith; they religiously expected what they benevolently desired. For these rational and righteous hopes, men who had no faith and little reason, substituted wild speculations how men might live for ever; and these speculations were combated by those who had just reason enough to expose the absurdity of their antagonists, and just faith enough to raise an outcry against their infidelity.

Mr. Malthus's object is to refute the opinion of the perfectibility of man, in other words, to prove that no material improvement can ever be expected in the state of society.

"In an inquiry concerning the future improvement of society, the mode of conducting the subject which naturally presents itself, is

"1. An investigation of the causes that have hitherto impeded the progress of mankind towards happiness; and

"2. An examination into the probability of the total or partial removal of these causes in future.

"To enter fully into this question, and to enumerate all the causes that have hitherto influenced human improvement, would be much beyond the power of an individual. The principal object of the present essay is to examine the effects of one great cause intimately united with the very nature of man, which, though it has been constantly and powerfully operating since the commencement of society, has been little noticed by the writers who have treated this subject. The facts which establish the existence of this cause have, indeed, been repeatedly stated and acknowledged; but its natural and necessary effects have been almost totally overlooked; though probably among these effects may be reckoned a very considerable portion of that vice and misery, and of that unequal distribution of the bounties of nature, which it has been the unceasing object of the enlightened philanthropist in all ages to correct.

"The cause to which I allude, is the constant tendency in all animated life to increase beyond the nourishment prepared for it."

"Taking the whole earth instead of this island, emigration would of course be excluded; and supposing the present population equal to a thousand millions, the human species would increase as the numbers 1, 2, 4, 8, 16, 32, 64, 128, 256, and subsistence as 1, 2, 3, 4, 5, 6, 7, 8, 9. In two centuries the population would be to the means of subsistence as 256 to 9; in three centuries as 4096 to 13, and in two thousand years the difference would be almost incalculable."

This last paragraph is the sum and substance of eight quarto pages; and in fact, the whole work is written in the same ratio: viz. eight lines of sense and substance to $8 \times 30 = 240$ lines of verbiage and senseless repetition; and even of these eight lines, all the pomp of numerals and ratios might have been cashiered by substituting a proposition which no one in his senses would consider as other than axiomatic. Suppose a married couple to have six children, (not half the number which they would have if you suppose *all* checks to population removed) and suppose all their posterity to marry, and each couple to increase in the same proportion; and it is evident on the slightest reflection, that in a given number of generations, their posterity would want standing room. (That it must be so, the role of multiplication would enable a child to demonstrate, and a school-boy who has advanced in arithmetic as far as compound interest, may astonish his younger sister both by the fact, and by the exact number of years in which it would take place.) On the other hand, let the productiveness of the earth be increased beyond the hopes of the most visionary agriculturist, still the productions take up room; if the present crop of turnips occupy one-fifth of the space of the turnip field, the increase can never be more than quintuple; and if you suppose two harvests for one, the increase still cannot exceed ten: so that supposing a little island of a single acre, and its productions occupying one-fifth of its absolute space, and sufficient to maintain two men and two women, four generations would outrun its possible power of furnishing them with food. We may boldly affirm that a truth so self-evident as this, was never overlooked, or even by implication contradicted. What proof has Mr. Malthus brought, what proof can he bring, that every writer or theorist has overlooked this fact, which would not apply (with reverence be it spoken) to the Almighty himself, when he pronounced the awful command, 'Increase and multiply?'

From page 17 to page 355, Mr. Malthus retails and details from others' travels, and from his own, facts of all nations and all ages, in all states of society, to prove that men have suffered, and are suffering, from ignorance, filth, famine, diseases, large cities, unwholesome employment, superstition, bad passions, bad habits, bad laws, and bad government; that all these have made men wicked, and poor, and miserable; and that men in wickedness, and misery, and dearth of subsistence, do not rear, even if they beget, as large families as happy and good people would do. Now we put it seriously to Mr. Malthus's good sense, whether or no, if he had simply stated this in one sentence of half-a-dozen, or half-a-score lines, any one individual in Europe would have felt the least inclination to contradict the statement? The whole of these pages would make a sensible first sentence of an essay in a newspaper on the subject of population; (for it is right to begin with a statement which no one can, or can wish to controvert,) but 355 quarto pages to say it out in! – The Minerva press, and his Majesty's law-printers are not more merciless to paper and printers' ink.

This mighty discovery Mr. Malthus opposes to all good

feelings and all good hopes, with this he triumphantly destroys all arguments for all amelioration of the state of the human race. It is brought in its full force against Mr. Godwin. This was the original mark and object of the work, and it is to this that Mr. Malthus owes his present high reputation: long as the passage is we shall therefore give it at length.

"Let us imagine for a moment, Mr. Godwin's system of equality realised in its utmost extent, and see how soon this difficulty might be expected to press, under so perfect a form of society. A theory that will not admit of application cannot possibly be just.

"Let us suppose all the causes of vice and misery in this island removed. War and contention cease. Unwholesome trades and manufactories do not exist. Crowds no longer collect together in great and pestilent cities, for purposes of court intrigue, of commerce, and vicious gratification. Simple, healthy, and rational amusements, take place of drinking, gaming, and debauchery. There are no towns sufficiently large, to have any prejudicial effects on the human constitution. The greater part of the happy inhabitants of this terrestrial paradise live in hamlets and farm houses, scattered over the face of the country. All men are equal. The labours of luxury are at an end; and the necessary labours of agriculture are shared amicably among all. The number of persons and the produce of the island we suppose to be the same as at present. The spirit of benevolence guided by impartial justice, will divide this produce among all the members of society according to their wants. Though it would be impossible that they should all have animal food every day, yet vegetable food, with meat occasionally, would satisfy the desires of a frugal people, and would be sufficient to preserve them in health, strength, and spirits.

"Mr. Godwin considers marriage as a fraud, and a monopoly.[1] Let us suppose the commerce of the sexes established upon principles of the most perfect freedom. Mr. Godwin does not think himself, that this freedom would lead to a promiscuous intercourse; and in this, I perfectly agree with him. The love of variety is a vicious, corrupt, and

---

[1] Political Justice, b. viii. c. viii. p. 498. et seq.

unnatural taste, and could not prevail, in any great degree, in a simple and virtuous state of society. Each man would probably select for himself a partner, to whom he would adhere, as long as that adherence continued to be the choice of both parties. It would be of little consequence, according to Mr. Godwin, how many children a woman had, or to whom they belonged. Provisions and assistance would spontaneously flow from the quarter in which they abounded, to the quarter in which they were deficient.[2] And every man, according to his capacity, would be ready to furnish instruction to the rising generation.

"I cannot conceive a form of society so favourable, upon the whole, to population. The irremediableness of marriage, as it is at present constituted, undoubtedly deters many from entering into this state. An unshackled intercourse, on the contrary, would be a most powerful incitement to early attachments: and as we are supposing no anxiety about the future support of children to exist, I do not conceive there would be one woman in a hundred, of twenty-three years of age, without a family.

"With these extraordinary encouragements to population, and every cause of depopulation, as we have supposed, removed, the numbers would necessarily increase faster than in any society that has ever yet been known. I have before mentioned, that the inhabitants of the back settlements of America appear to double their numbers in fifteen years. England is certainly a more healthy country than the back settlements of America; and as we have supposed every house in the island to be airy and wholesome, and the encouragements to have a family, greater even than in America, no probable reason can be assigned, why the population should not double itself, in less, if possible, than fifteen years. But to be quite sure that we do not go beyond the truth, we will only suppose the period of doubling to be twenty-five years; a ratio of increase which is well known to have taken place throughout all the northern states of America.

"There can be little doubt that the equalization of property which we have supposed, added to the circumstance of the labour of the whole community being directed chiefly to

---

2 Political Justice, b. viii. c. viii. p. 504.

agriculture, would tend greatly to augment the produce of the country. But to answer the demands of a population increasing so rapidly, Mr. Godwin's calculation of half an hour a day would certainly not be sufficient. It is probable, that the half of every man's time must be employed for this purpose. Yet with such, or much greater exertions, a person who is acquainted with the nature of the soil in this country, and who reflects on the fertility of the lands already in cultivation, and the barrenness of those that are not cultivated, will be very much disposed to doubt, whether the whole average produce could possibly be doubled in twenty-five years from the present period. The only chance of success would be from the ploughing up most of the grazing countries, and putting an end almost entirely to animal food. Yet this scheme would probably defeat itself. The soil of England will not produce much without dressing; and cattle seem to be necessary to make that species of manure which best suits the land.

"Difficult, however, as it might be, to double the average produce of the island in twenty-five years, let us suppose it effected. At the expiration of the first period, therefore, the food, though almost entirely vegetable, would be sufficient to support in health the doubled population of 22 millions.

"During the next period, where will the food be found to satisfy the importunate demands of the increasing numbers? Where is the fresh land to turn up? Where is the dressing necessary to improve that which is already in cultivation? There is no person with the smallest knowledge of land, but would say, that it was impossible that the average produce of the country could be increased during the second twenty-five years, by a quantity equal to what it at present yields. Yet we will suppose this increase, however improbable, to take place. The exuberant strength of the argument allows of almost any concession. Even with this concession, however, there would be eleven millions at the expiration of the second term unprovided for. A quantity equal to the frugal support of 33 millions would be to be divided among 44 millions.

"Alas! what becomes of the picture, where men lived in the midst of plenty, where no man was obliged to provide with anxiety and pain for his restless wants; where the narrow principles of selfishness did not exist; where the mind was delivered from her perpetual anxiety about corporeal support, and free to expatiate in the field of thought which is congenial to her. This beautiful fabrick of the imagination vanishes at the severe touch of truth. The spirit of benevolence, cherished and invigorated by plenty, is repressed by the chilling breath of want. The hateful passions that had vanished reappear. The mighty law of self-preservation expels all the softer, and more exalted emotions of the soul. The temptations to evil are too strong for human nature to resist. The corn is plucked before it is ripe, or secreted in unfair proportions; and the whole black train of vices that belong to falsehood are immediately generated. Provisions no longer flow in for the support of a mother with a large family. The children are sickly from insufficient food. The rosy flush of health gives place to the pallid cheek, and hollow eye of misery. Benevolence, yet lingering in a few bosoms, makes some faint expiring struggles, till at length self-love resumes his wonted empire, and lords it triumphant over the world.

"No human institutions here existed, to the perverseness of which Mr. Godwin ascribes the original sin of the worst men.[3] No opposition had been produced by them between publick and private good. No monopoly had been created of those advantages which reason directs to be left in common. No man had been goaded to the breach or order by unjust laws. Benevolence had established her reign in all hearts. And yet in so short a period as fifty years, violence, oppression, falsehood, misery, every hateful vice, and every form of distress, which degrade and sadden the present state of society, seem to have been generated by the most imperious circumstances, by laws inherent in the nature of man, and absolutely independent of all human regulations.

"If we be not yet too well convinced of the reality of this melancholy picture, let us but look for a moment into the next period of twenty-five years, and we shall see 44 millions of human beings without the means of support: and at the conclusion of the first century, the population would be 176 millions, and the food only sufficient for 55 millions, leaving 121 millions unprovided for. In these ages, want, indeed, would be triumphant, and rapine and murder must reign at large: and yet all this time we are supposing the produce of

---

[3] Ib. c. iii. p. 340.

the earth absolutely unlimited, and the yearly increase greater than the boldest speculator can imagine.'

The pop-gun made a loud report in the world, and effectually smote down the champion against whom it was levelled. Mr. Malthus could not have obtained more credit in the eighth century for laying the devil, than he has in the eighteenth for laying Mr. Godwin. The question contended was, whether or not there were any hopes of mankind; whether wisdom would be progressive with knowledge, and virtue with wisdom, and happiness with virtue. Shame on the age we live in that this question should be disputed! Shame on the country we live in, that such a question should be debated by no better advocates than Messrs. Godwin and Malthus! Menelaus and Paris were not more unworthy representatives of the collected heroism of Greece and Troy, than these men of the knowledge and intellect of England. To Mr. Godwin's presumption his antagonist is indebted for his victory; only such a Goliath could have called forth such a David. Mr. Godwin had confounded together all principles pure and impure; he had attempted to amalgamate stoicism and sensuality; he had diluted the wisdom of the antients with his own folly; he had kneaded up their wheat, and barley, and millet, with his own *album græcum*, and this precious wafer was to be swallowed as the bread of life – the sacrament of philosophy! What wonder that this should inspire equal talents with the hope of equal success? If the Nervous Cordial sells, so also may the Balm of Gilead. Dr. Solomon is perfectly justifiable in calling Dr. Brodum a quack; and in the country where one of these worthies can ride in his carriage, it must be the other's own fault if he continues to walk a-foot. "Mr. Malthus appeared, and we heard no more of Mr. Godwin." – so it was said in that style of panegyric which may be called the brief sublime. And indeed Mr. Godwin himself has admitted the whole force of his antagonist's argument.

In animals, the benevolent system of destruction keeps down their numbers to a due proportion with their food. Wisely did the Hindoos unite the creator, the preserver, and the destroyer, in their triunal God, – and what better proof of wisdom and benevolence than that death should be made subservient to life? No such check exists to the multiplication of the human race, but among them moral and physical evil (each producing the other in alternation) supply its place, till wisdom having perfected virtue, shall destroy all evil by rendering it no longer necessary. An optimist might thus express the substance of his creed. Mr. Malthus also is an optimist, but of the Pangloss school, holding that the present state of society is, with all its evils, the best of all possible states, and that it never can be better. To some such point of attainable perfection, for arguments sake, he supposes the human race to have attained, and then attempting the *reductio ad absurdum*, he argues against the blessing from its excess. The principle of population, he says, would in one generation disturb, and in a second, destroy this state of happiness, and mankind must then revert to the present system. Mr. Godwin yields, proposing, however, exposure and abortion as remedies; but these, says his victorious rival, "clearly come under the head of vice."

It is to the last degree idle to write in this way without having stated the meaning of the words vice and virtue. That these are vices in the present state of society, who doubts? so was celibacy in the patriarchal ages. Vice and virtue subsist in the agreement of the habits of a man with his reason and conscience, and these can have but one moral guide – utility, or the virtue and happiness of rational beings. We mention this, not under the miserable notion that any state of society will render these actions capable of being performed with conscience and virtue, but to expose the utter ungroundedness of the writer's speculation: adding, however, that if we believed with Mr. Malthus's *warmest* partizans, that men never will in general be capable of regulating the sexual appetite by the law of reason, and that the gratification of lust is a thing of physical necessity, equally with the gratification of hunger, (a faith which we should laugh at for its silliness, if its wickedness had not pre-excited abhorrence) nothing would be more easy than to demonstrate that abortion, or the exposure of children, or artificial sterility on the part of the male, would become virtues: – a thought which we turn from with loathing, but not with greater loathing than we do from the degrading theory of which it would be a legitimate consequence. By a yet stronger inconsequence, this theory (so far as it is aimed against the hopes of the progressive improvement of mankind) pleads for the existence, not only of these vices, but of a thousand others, and of the brutal ignorance and misery, the production of which does alone render those actions crimes: it pleads for the continuance of all this misery whereof these very vices form a part, in order to prevent that state of society, in which, admitting one or other of these actions after the birth of every second or third child, the whole earth might be imagined filled to its utmost extent with enlightened and happy beings.

If then Mr. Malthus's reasoning were just, the application would be absurd, for what can be more absurd than to abandon all hope of this attainable state of happiness because certain evils would exist in it, and therefore to remain contented with the continuance of those very evils, and of all the other evils which, upon the admitted hypothesis, would be removed? What should we say to the physician who should object to the cow-pox, and to all remedies for scrofula and syphilis, for fear that when these diseases were annihilated, men should become plethoric and subject to apoplexy from excess of health?

But the reasoning is as absurd as the application: the whole proceeds upon the assumption, that lust and hunger are alike passions of physical necessity, and the one equally with the other independent of the reason and the will. If this were true, chastity could not exist; fornication would be as indispensable as food, every single man must be a brotheller, every single woman a strumpet. There lives not a wretch corrupt enough of heart, and shameless enough of front to say that this is so: there lives not a man who can look upon his wife and his daughter, who can think upon his sister, and remember her who bore him, without feeling indignation and resentment that he should be insulted by so infamous an assertion. But if the possibility of chastity be admitted (and it will be seen that Mr. Malthus does hereafter fully admit it) the whole argument against the system of equality, against the perfectibility, or to use a more accurate and less obnoxious term, the improveability of man, falls to the ground. Mr. Godwin has been knocked down by the wind of the pop-gun, the pellet has missed him. Drawcansir is driven off the stage, and his enemies may get up and dance.

Having thus rescued the philosopher from the Philistines, let us try the truth of Mr. Malthus's principle as applied against all those who hope for any reformation in the state of society.

"The power of population is so superior to the power in the earth to produce subsistence for man, that, unless arrested by the preventive check, premature death must in some shape or other visit the human race. The vices of mankind are active and able ministers of depopulation. They are the precursors in the great army of destruction, and often finish the dreadful work themselves. But should they fail in this war of extermination, sickly seasons, epidemics, pestilence, and plague, advance in terrific array, and sweep off their thousands and ten thousands. Should success be still incomplete, gigantic inevitable famine stalks in the rear, and, with one mighty blow, levels the population with the food of the world.

"Must it not then be acknowledged, by an attentive examiner of the histories of mankind, that, in every age, and in every state in which man has existed, or does now exist, "The increase of population is necessarily limited by the means of subsistence?

"Population invariably increases when the means of subsistence increase, unless prevented by powerful and obvious checks.

"These checks, and the checks which keep the population down to the level of the means of subsistence, are, moral restraint, vice, and misery."

"The great error under which Mr. Godwin labours, throughout his whole work, is, the attributing of almost all the vices and misery that prevail in civil society to human institutions. Political regulations, and the established administration of property, are, with him, the fruitful sources of all evil, the hotbeds of all the crimes that degrade mankind. Were this really a true state of the case, it would not seem an absolutely hopeless task, to remove evil completely from the world; and reason seems to be the proper and adequate instrument, for effecting so great a purpose. But the truth is, that, though human institutions appear to be the obvious and obtrusive causes of much mischief to mankind, they are, in reality, light and superficial, in comparison with those deeper-seated causes of evil which result from the laws of nature."

"The circulation of Paine's Rights of Man, it is supposed, has done great mischief among the lower and middling classes of people in this country. This is probably true; but not because man is without rights, or that these rights ought not to be known; but because Mr. Paine has fallen into some fundamental errors respecting the principles of government, and in many important points has shewn himself totally unacquainted with the structure of society, and the different moral effects to be expected from the physical difference between this country and America. Mobs, of the same description as those collections of people known by this name in Europe, could not exist in America. The number of people without property, is, there, from the physical state of the country, comparatively small; and therefore the civil power which is to protect property, cannot require the same degree of strength. Mr. Paine very justly observes, that whatever the apparent cause of any riots may be, the real one is always want of happiness; but when he goes on to say, it shews that something is wrong in the system of government, that injures the felicity by which society is to be preserved, he falls into the common error of attributing all want of happiness to government. It is evident, that this want of happiness might have existed, and from ignorance might have been the principal cause of the riots, and yet be almost wholly unconnected with any of the proceedings of government."

Mr. Malthus has ravelled together his truisms and his sophisms with some intricacy, but it is not so difficult as he may suppose to disentangle them. We admit the whole extent of the vice and misery in the world; he has not in the slightest point exaggerated it. It remains to be seen whether human institutions, or the laws of nature be in fault; it remains to be seen (we speak with reverence and not without indignation) whether we are to complain of the folly of man, or of the will of God, for this is the alternative. Let not the impiety of the question be imputed to us!

It has been amply shewn by this author, and it never was denied or doubted, that in all ages and in all states of society, men have suffered, and are suffering, from ignorance, filth, famine, diseases, large cities, unwholesome employment, superstition, bad passions, bad habits, bad laws, and bad governments, and that some or other of these causes have everywhere, and at all times, checked population, and do still continue to check it. "The period," says he, "when the number of men surpass their means of subsistence has long since arrived, and this constantly subsisting cause of periodical misery has existed ever since we have had any histories of mankind, does exist at present, and will for ever continue to exist, unless some decided change take place in the *physical constitution of our nature.*" If for these last words we substitute the *existing systems of society*, we shall convert the sentence into truth.

In New Holland, where there does not exist a man to a square mile, the number of men exceeds their means of subsistence. What is required to remedy the evil here, and to make the natives increase as rapidly as the Anglo-Americans – a change in their physical or in their moral nature? In England the inhabitants might be trebled, and the island still produce enough for the comfortable subsistence of all; yet in England population is checked, a great part of the people are in want, and every profession, trade, calling, whereby man or woman can earn support, is overstocked. Where lies the fault if New Holland be not as fully peopled in proportion as England, if England be not as fully peopled in proportion as China, if China be not peopled in the fullest proportion, not to its actual, but to its possible powers of production? Is it in human institutions, or in the laws of nature? Is it in man or in God? *Wilt thou condemn me that thou mayest be righteous*, said the Lord: who is he that will dare answer the question in Mr. Malthus's behalf? If a country be over-peopled, and crowded, and distressed, in regard to its system of society, before it be half peopled in proportion to its size and power of production; the fault lies in that system of society, not in the system of nature. If, while not a tenth, nay not an hundredth part of the habitable world be cultivated, mankind be every where in want, the fault is their own. All that Mr. Malthus has done is to prove that radical evil in society which his whole work is designed to palliate.

Till the whole earth be peopled to its utmost capacity, it is the fault of man if any check to population exist, except such as are dispensed by the elements and the operations of physical nature: his moral nature is in his own power, and it hath been said, "Be ye perfect, even as your father in heaven is perfect."

So much for Mr. Malthus's argument against the hopes of the human race! It has been demonstrated that all checks to population, till the power of production can be pushed no farther, and actual room for farther increase be wanting, must be attributed to error and ignorance in man, not to unerring nature and omniscient goodness. When that point has been reached, it has been demonstrated that the practice of one virtue will secure the happiness of mankind and render it permanent. Either chastity is possible, or it is not; in the one case his argument has been shown to be groundless, in the other inapplicable: one of the horns of this dilemma must wound him, and either wound must be mortal. He has played off his positive check and his preventive check, but they have not saved him from this check-mate.

By these miserable sophisms Mr. Malthus has obtained the high reputation which he at present enjoys; his book having become the political bible of the rich, the selfish, and the sensual; nor need we wonder that so contemptible a book should have produced so much mischief: if the body be corrupt and predisposed to mortification, a scratch will occasion death. But to our utter astonishment we find that, though in this present edition the author has retained and enlarged all these arguments, and insisted upon their application; at the end of the volume he admits every thing which he has controverted in the beginning, and is clearly and confessedly a convert to the doctrine of the perfectibility of man! He draws a picture of christian society, in which the well being of all is founded upon this very virtue of chastity, the non-existence of which was to destroy all the theories of Godwin and Condorcet.

> "The difficulty of moral restraint, will perhaps be objected to this doctrine. To him who does not acknowledge the authority of the christian religion, I have only to say, that, after the most careful investigation, this virtue appears to be absolutely necessary, in order to avoid certain evils which would otherwise result from the general laws of nature. According to his own principles, it is his duty to pursue the greatest good consistent with these laws; and not to fail in this important end, and produce an over-balance of misery, by a partial obedience to some of the dictates of nature while he neglects others. The path of virtue, though it be the only path which leads to permanent happiness, has always been represented by the heathen moralists, as of difficult ascent.
>
> "To the christian I would say, that the scriptures most clearly and precisely point it out to us as our duty, to restrain our passions within the bounds of reason; and it is a palpable disobedience of this law, to indulge our desires in such a manner, as reason tells us, will unavoidably end in misery. The christian cannot consider the difficulty of moral

restraint as any argument against its being his duty; since in almost every page of the sacred writings, man is described as encompassed on all sides by temptations, which it is extremely difficult to resist; and though no duties are enjoined, which do not contribute to his happiness on earth as well as in a future state, yet an undeviating obedience is never represented as an easy task."

"In a society, such as I have supposed, all the members of which endeavour to attain happiness by obedience to the moral code, derived from the light of nature, and enforced by strong sanctions in revealed religion, it is evident that no such marriages could take place; and the prevention of a redundant population, in this way, would remove one of the principal causes, and certainly the principal means of offensive war; and at the same time tend powerfully to eradicate those two fatal political disorders, internal tyranny and internal tumult, which mutually produce each other.

"Weak in offensive war, in a war of defence, such a society would be strong as a rock of adamant. Where every family possessed the necessaries of life in plenty, and a decent portion of its comforts and conveniences, there could not exist that hope of change, or at best that melancholy and disheartening indifference to it, which sometimes prompts the lower classes of people to say, 'let what will come, we cannot be worse off than we are now.' Every heart and hand would be united to repel an invader, when each individual felt the value of the solid advantages which he enjoyed, and a prospect of change presented only a prospect of being deprived of them.

"As it appears, therefore, that it is in the power of each individual to avoid all the evil consequences to himself and society resulting from the principle of population, by the practice of a virtue clearly dictated to him by the light of nature, and expressly enjoined in revealed religion; and as we have reason to think that the exercise of this virtue to a certain degree, would rather tend to increase than diminish individual happiness; we can have no reason to impeach the justice of the Deity, because his general laws make this virtue necessary, and punish our offences against it by the evils attendant upon vice, and the pains that accompany the various forms of premature death. A really virtuous society such as I have supposed, would avoid these evils. It is the apparent object of the Creator to deter us from vice by the pains which accompany it, and to lead us to virtue by the happiness that it produces. This object appears to our conceptions to be worthy of a benevolent Creator. The laws of nature respecting population, tend to promote this object. No imputation, therefore, on the benevolence of the Deity, can be founded on these laws, which is not equally applicable to any of the evils necessarily incidental to an imperfect state of existence."

Wherein then does Mr. Malthus differ from those who maintain the perfectibility of man? that is, who believe a state of society to be possible, in which every man shall enjoy as much happiness as his physical and moral powers are capable of enjoying; that happiness being regulated by and subservient to the general welfare? If man can retain his passions in a conceivable state of knowledge, what is to stop his improvement? The latter part of his book therefore palpably confutes the former, and he perishes by a stupid suicide, like the scorpion who strikes his tail into his own head.

We are now then to rank Mr. Malthus among the political reformers: he has discovered that moral restraint is practicable, and that it is a remedy equivalent to the evil of a redundant population. Let us see how he applies this principle.

"When the wages of labour are hardly sufficient to maintain two children, a man marries and has five or six. He of course finds himself miserably distressed. He accuses the insufficiency of the price of labour to maintain a family. He accuses his parish for their tardy and sparing fulfilment of their obligation to assist him. He accuses the avarice of the rich, who suffer him to want what they can so well spare. He accuses the partial and unjust institutions of society, which have awarded him an inadequate share of the produce of the earth. He accuses perhaps the dispensations of Providence, which have assigned to him a place in society so beset with unavoidable distress and dependance. In searching for objects of accusation, he never adverts to the quarter from which all his misfortunes originate. The last person that he would think of accusing is himself, on whom, in fact, the whole of the blame lies, except in as far as he has been deceived by the higher classes of society. He may perhaps wish that he had not married, because he now feels the inconveniences of it; but it never enters into his head that he can have done any thing wrong. He has always been told that to raise up subjects for his king and country is a very meritorious act. He has done this act, and yet is suffering for it. He naturally thinks that he is suffering for righteousness sake; and it cannot but strike him as most extremely unjust and cruel in his king and country, to allow him thus to suffer, in return, for giving them what they are continually declaring that they particularly want.

"Till these erroneous ideas have been corrected, and the language of nature and reason has been generally heard on the subject of population, instead of the language of error and prejudice, it cannot be said that any fair experiment has been made with the understandings of the common people; and we cannot justly accuse them of improvidence and want of industry till they act as they do now, after it has been brought home to their comprehensions, that they are themselves the cause of their own poverty; that the means of redress are in their own hands, and in the hands of no other persons whatever; that the society in which they live, and the government which presides over it, are totally without power in this respect; and however ardently they may desire to relieve them, and whatever attempts they may make to do so, they are really and truly unable to execute what they benevolently wish, but unjustly promise; that when the wages of labour will not maintain a family, it is an incontrovertible sign that their king and country do not want more subjects, or at least that they cannot support them; that if they marry in this case, so far from fulfilling a duty to society, they are throwing a useless burden on it, at the same time that they are plunging themselves into distress; and that they are acting directly contrary to the will of God, and bringing down upon themselves various diseases, which might all, or in a great part, have been avoided, if they had attended to the repeated admonitions which he gives, by the general laws of nature, to every being capable of reason."

"I have reflected much on the subject of the poor laws, and hope, therefore, that I shall be excused, in venturing to suggest a mode of their gradual abolition, to which, I confess, that at present I can see no material objection. Of this, indeed, I feel nearly convinced, that, should we ever become sufficiently sensible of the wide-spreading tyranny, dependence, indolence, and unhappiness, which they create, as seriously to make an effort to abolish them, we shall be compelled to adopt the principle if not the plan, which I shall mention. It seems impossible to get rid of so extensive a system of support, consistently with humanity, without applying ourselves directly to its vital principle and endeavouring to counteract that deeply-seated cause, which occasions the rapid growth of all such establishments, and invariably renders them inadequate to their object.

"To this end, I should propose a regulation to be made, declaring, that no child born from any marriage, taking place after the expiration of a year from the date of the law; and no illegitimate child born two years from the same date, should ever be entitled to parish assistance. And to give a more general knowledge of this law, and to enforce it more strongly on the minds of the lower classes of people, the clergyman of each parish should, previously to the solemnization of a marriage, read a short address to the parties, stating the strong obligation on every man to support his own children; the impropriety, and even immorality, of marrying without a fair prospect of being able to do this; the evils which had resulted to the poor themselves, from the attempt which had been made to assist, by public institutions, in a duty which ought to be exclusively appropriated to parents; and the absolute necessity which had at length appeared, of abandoning all such institutions, on account of their producing effects totally opposite to those which were intended."

"After the public notice which I have proposed had been given, and the system of poor laws had ceased with regard to the rising generation, if any man chose to marry, without a prospect of being able to support a family, he should have the most perfect liberty so to do. Though to marry, in this case, is in my opinion clearly an immoral act, yet it is not one, which society can justly take upon itself to prevent or punish; because the punishment provided for it by the laws of nature, falls directly and most severely upon the individual who commits the act, and, through him, only more remotely and feebly on the society. When nature will govern and punish for us, it is a very miserable ambition, to wish to snatch the rod from her hands, and draw upon ourselves the odium of executioner. To the punishment, therefore, of nature he should be left, the punishment of severe want. He has erred in the face of a most clear and precise warning and can have no just reason to complain of any person but himself, when he feels the consequences of his error. All parish assistance should be most rigidly denied him: and if the hand of private charity be stretched forth in his relief, the interests of humanity imperiously require that it should be administered very sparingly. He should be taught to know that the laws of nature, which are the laws of God, had doomed him and his family to starve for disobeying their repeated admonitions; and that he had no claim of right on society for the smallest portion of food, beyond that which his labour would fairly purchase; and that, if he and his family were saved from suffering the utmost extremities of hunger, he would owe it to the pity of some kind benefactor, to whom, therefore, he ought to be bound by the strongest ties of gratitude.

"If this system were pursued, we need be under no apprehensions whatever, that the number of persons in extreme want would be beyond the power and the will of the benevolent to supply. The sphere for the exercise of private charity would, I am confident, be less than it is at present; and the only difficulty would be, to restrain the hand of benevolence from assisting those in distress in so liberal a manner as to encourage indolence and want of foresight in others.

"With regard to illegitimate children, after the proper notice had been given, they should on no account whatever be allowed to have any claim to parish assistance. If the parents desert their child, they ought to be made answerable for the crime. The infant is, comparatively speaking, of no value to the society, as others will immediately supply its place. Its principal value is on account of its being the object of one of the most delightful passions in human nature – parental affection. But if this value be disregarded, by those who are alone in a capacity to feel it, the society cannot be called upon to put itself in their place; and has no further business in its protection, than in the case of its murder or intentional ill-treatment to follow the general rules in punishing such crimes; which rules, for the interests of morality, it is bound to pursue, whether the object, in the particular instance, be of value to the state or not."

The remedy then which this profound politician proposes for the existing evils of society in England, is simply to abolish the poor rates, and starve the poor into celibacy. That moral restraint, that chastity which, according to his own argument, is all that is wanting to render possible and permanent the system of equality, he expects and demands now from the poor. The exercise of that virtue, which as he had reasoned, could only exist in men highly enlightened and highly virtuous, he expects and demands from the ignorant, degraded, brutalized, miserable, poor people of England! If you beget children, he says to them, they must perish for want. No public relief is to be given to the starving infant, society is not to interfere, except that it is to hang the mother, if she shorten the sufferings of her babe by destroying it! This reformer calls for no sacrifice from the rich; on the contrary, he proposes to relieve them from their parish rates: he recommends nothing to them but that they should harden their hearts. They have found a place at the table of nature; and why should they be disturbed at their feast? It is Mr. Malthus's own metaphor!

"A man who is born into a world already possessed, if he cannot get subsistence from his parents, on whom he has a just demand, and if the society do not want his labour, has no claim of right to the smallest portion of food, and, in fact, has no business to be where he is. At nature's mighty feast there is no vacant cover for him. She tells him to be gone, and will quickly execute her own orders, if he do not work upon the compassion of some of her guests. If these guests get up and make room for him, other intruders immediately appear demanding the same favour. The report of a provision for all that come, fills the hall with numerous claimants. The order and harmony of the feast is disturbed, the plenty that before reigned is changed into scarcity; and the happiness of the guests is destroyed by the spectacle of misery and dependence in every part of the hall, and by the clamorous importunity of those, who are justly enraged at not finding the provision which they had been taught to expect. The guests learn too late their error, in counteracting those strict orders to all intruders, issued by the great mistress of the feast, who, wishing that all her guests should have plenty, and knowing that she could not provide for unlimited numbers, humanely refused to admit fresh comers when her table was already full."

It is easy to see what, upon Mr. Malthus's view of society, would become the perfect system of policy, when the English constitution shall have expired by that *euthanasia* which Hume foretold, or rather by that atrophy which daily wastes away its vital powers, that slow poison which has been year after year administered. The first step would be to commute the miseries of poverty for the comforts of servitude: for this, the frequent argument that the negro-slaves are happier than the poor people of England, has prepared our legislators; and the poor might be brought to it, as they are to be brought to celibacy, – by starving. It having been found that slaves are more manageable than servants, the next discovery would be the great fitness of considering them as cattle, for which the whole system of our slave-laws has also prepared us. Having adopted the wisdom of Oriental monarchies, we should then readily adopt the magnificence of Oriental manners; and introduce into England the wise invention of Semiramis for counteracting the principle of population. The advantages are obvious: the people would be happier, because poverty would be annihilated; the fine arts would be improved, inasmuch as we should rear our own opera-singers, and reform our church-music according to Italian taste; and the proceedings of government would be wonderfully facilitated, for John Bull has been at times a refractory animal, but John Ox would certainly be tractable.

What then is the purport of this quarto volume? To teach us, first, that great misery and great vice arise from poverty; and that there must be poverty in its worst shapes, wherever there are more mouths than loaves, and more heads than brains. Secondly, that the only remedy is, that the poor should not be encouraged to breed. There is not a man in England who was ignorant of the first fact, nor a mistress of a family who does not advise her servants not to marry. No wonder that Mr. Malthus should be a fashionable philosopher! He writes advice to the poor for the rich to read; they of course will approve his opinions, and, understanding with perfect facility the whole of his profound reasonings, will of course admit them with perfect satisfaction.

The folly and the wickedness of this book have provoked us into a tone of contemptuous indignation: in affixing these terms to the book, let it not be supposed that any general condemnation of the author is implied, grievously as he has erred in this particular instance. – Mr. Malthus is said to be a man of mild and unoffending manners, patient research, and exemplary conduct. This character he may still maintain; but as a political philosopher, the farthing candle of his fame must stink and go out.

# APPENDIX 1806
[T. R. Malthus]

*Reply to the Chief Objections which have been urged against the Essay on the Principle of Population.*

In the preface to the last edition of the Essay, I expressed a hope that the detailed manner in which I had treated the subject and pursued it to its consequences, though it might open the doors to many objections, and expose me to much severity of criticism, might be subservient to the important end of bringing a subject so nearly connected with the happiness of society into more general notice. Conformably to the same views I should always have felt willing to enter into the discussion of any serious objections that were made to my principles or conclusions, to abandon those which appeared to be false, and to throw further lights, if I could, on those which appeared to be true. But though the work has excited a degree of public attention much greater than I could have presumed to expect, yet very little has been written to controvert it; and of that little, the greatest part is so full of illiberal declamation, and so entirely destitute of argument, as to be evidently beneath notice. What I have to say therefore at present, will be directly rather more to the objections which have been urged in conversation, than to those which have appeared in print. My object is to correct some of the misrepresentations which have gone abroad respecting two or three of the most important points of the Essay; and I should feel greatly obliged to those who have not had leisure to read the whole work, if they would cast their eyes over the few following pages, that they may not, from the partial and incorrect statements which they have heard, mistake the import of some of my opinions, and attribute to me others which I have never held.

The first grand objection that has been made to my principles is that they contradict the original command of the Creator, to increase and multiply and replenish the earth. But those who have urged this objection have certainly either not read the work, or have directed their attention solely to a few detached passages, and have been unable to seize the bent and spirit of the whole. I am fully of opinion, that it is the duty of man to obey this command of his Creator, nor is there in my recollection a single passage in the work which, taken with the context, can to any reader of intelligence warrant the contrary inference.

Every express command given to man by his Creator is given in subordination to those great and uniform laws of nature which he had previously established; and we are forbidden both by reason and religion to expect that these laws will be changed in order to enable us to execute more readily any particular precept. It is undoubtedly true that, if man were enabled miraculously to live without food, the earth would be very rapidly replenished; but as we have not the slightest ground of hope that such a miracle will be worked for this purpose, it becomes our positive duty as reasonable creatures, and with a view of executing the commands of our Creator, to inquire into the laws which he has established for the multiplication of the species. And when we find, not only from the speculative contemplation of these laws, but from the far more powerful and imperious suggestions of our senses, that man cannot live without food, it is a folly exactly of the same *kind* to attempt to obey the will of our Creator by increasing population without reference to the means of its support, as to attempt to obtain an abundant crop of corn by sowing it on the wayside and in hedges, where it cannot receive its proper nourishment. Which is it, I would ask, that best seconds the benevolent intentions of the Creator in covering the earth with esculent vegetables, he who with care and foresight duly ploughs and prepares a piece of ground, and sows no more seed than he expects will grow up to maturity, or he who scatters a profusion of seed indifferently over the land, without reference to the soil on which it falls, or any previously preparation for its reception?

It is an utter misconception of my argument to infer that I am an enemy to population. I am only an enemy to vice and misery, and consequently to that unfavourable proportion between population and food which produces these evils. But this unfavourable proportion has no necessary connection with the quantity of absolute population which a country may contain. On the contrary, it is more frequently found in countries which are very thinly peopled than in those which are populous.

The bent of my argument on the subject of population may be illustrated by the instance of a pasture farm. If a young grazier were told to stock his land well, as on his stock would depend his profits, and the ultimate success of his undertaking, he would certainly have been told nothing but what was strictly true. And he would have to accuse himself, not his advisers, if in pursuance of these instructions he were to push the breeding of his cattle till they became lean and half-starved. His instructor, when he talked of the advantages of a large stock, meant undoubtedly stock in proper condition, and not such a stock as, though it might be numerically greater, was in value much less. The expression of stocking a farm well does not refer to particular numbers, but merely to that proportion which is best adapted to the farm, whether it be a poor or a rich one, whether it will carry fifty head of cattle or five hundred. It is undoubtedly extremely desirable that it should carry the greater number, and every effort should be made to effect this object; but surely that farmer could not be considered as an enemy to a large quantity of stock, who should insist upon the folly and impropriety of attempting to breed such a quantity, before the land was put into a condition to bear it.

The arguments which I have used respecting the increase of population are exactly of the same nature as these just mentioned. I believe that it is the intention of the Creator that the earth should be replenished;[1] but certainly with a healthy, virtuous, and happy population, not an unhealthy vicious, and miserable one. And if in endeavouring to obey the command to increase and multiply, we people it only with beings of this latter description, and suffer accordingly, we have no right to impeach the justice of the command, but our irrational mode of executing it.

In the desirableness of a great and efficient population, I do not differ from the warmest advocates of increase. I am perfectly ready to acknowledge with the writers of old, that it is not extent of territory but extent of population that measures the power of states. It is only as to the mode of obtaining a vigorous and efficient population that I differ from them; and

---

[1] This opinion I have expressed.

in thus differing I conceive myself entirely borne out by experience, that great test of all human speculations.

It appears from the undoubted testimony of registers, that a large proportion of marriages and births is by no means necessarily connected with a rapid increase of population, but is often found in countries where it is either stationary or increasing very slowly. The population of such countries is not only comparatively inefficient from the general poverty and misery of the inhabitants, but invariably contains a much larger proportion of persons in those stages of life in which they are unable to contribute their share to the resources or the defence of the state.

This is most strikingly illustrated in an instance which I have quoted from M. Muret, in a chapter on Switzerland, where it appeared that, in proportion to the same population, the Lyonois produced 16 births, the Pays de Vaud 11, and a particular parish in the Alps only 8; but that at the age of 20 these three very different numbers were all reduced to the same. In the Lyonois nearly half of the population was under the age of puberty, in the Pays de Vaud one third, and in the parish of the Alps only one fourth. The inference from such facts is unavoidable, and of the highest importance to society.

The power of a country to increase its resources or defend its possessions must depend principally upon its efficient population, upon that part of the population which is of an age to be employed effectually in agriculture, commerce, or war; but it appears with an evidence little short of demonstration, that in a country, the resources of which do not naturally call for a larger proportion of births, such an increase, so far from tending to increase this efficient population, would tend materially to diminish it. It would undoubtedly at first increase the number of souls in proportion to the means of subsistence, and consequently cruelly increase the pressure of want; but the number of persons rising annually to the age of puberty might not be so great as before, a larger part of the produce would be distributed without return to children who would never reach manhood; and the additional population, instead of giving additional strength to the country, would essentially lessen this strength, and operate as a constant obstacle to the creation of new resources.

We are a little dazzled at present by the population and power of France, and it is known that she has always had a large proportion of births: but if any reliance can be placed on what are considered as the best authorities on this subject, it is quite certain, that the advantages which she enjoys do not arise from any thing peculiar in the structure of her population; but solely from the great absolute quantity of it, derived from her immense extent of fertile territory.

The effective population in this country, compared with the whole, is considerably greater than in France; and England not only can, but does, employ a larger proportion of her population in augmenting and defending her resources than her great rival. According to the *Statistique générale et particulière de la France* lately published, the proportion of the population under twenty is almost $9/20$; in England it is probably not much more than $7/20$. Consequently, out of a population of ten millions, England would have a million more of persons above twenty than France, and would at least have three or four hundred thousand more males of a military age. If our population were of the same description as that of France, it must be increased numerically by more than a million and a half in order to enable us to produce from England and Wales the same number of persons above the age of Twenty as at present, and if we had only an increase of a million, our efficient strength in agriculture, commerce, and war, would be in the most decided manner diminished, while at the same time the distresses of the lower classes would be dreadfully increased. Can any rational man say that an additional population of this description would be desirable, either in a moral or political view? And yet this is the kind of population which invariably results from direct encouragements to marriage, or from that want of personal respectability which is occasioned by ignorance and despotism.

It may perhaps be true that France fills her armies with greater facility and less interruption to the usual labours of her inhabitants than England; and it must be acknowledged that poverty and want of employment are powerful aids to a recruiting serjeant; but it would not be a very humane project, to keep our people always in want for the sake of enlisting them cheaper, nor would it be a very politic project, to diminish our wealth and strength with the same economical view. We cannot attain incompatible objects; if we possess the advantage of being able to keep nearly all our people constantly employed either in agriculture or commerce, we cannot expect to retain the opposite advantage of their being always at leisure, and willing to enlist for a very small sum.[2] But we may rest perfectly assured that, while we have the efficient population, we shall never want men to fill our armies if we propose to them adequate motives.

In many parts of the Essay I have dwelt much on the advantage of rearing the requisite population of any country from the smallest number of births. I have stated expressly that a decrease of mortality at all ages is what we ought chiefly to aim at; and as the best criterion of happiness and good government, instead of the largeness of the proportion of births, which was the usual mode of judging, I have proposed the smallness of the proportion dying under the age of puberty. Conscious that I had never intentionally deviated from these principles, I might well be rather surprised to hear that I had been considered by some as an enemy to the introduction of the vaccine inoculation, which is calculated to attain the very end which I have uniformly considered as so desirable. I have indeed intimated what I still continue most firmly to believe, that if the resources of the country would not permanently admit of a greatly accelerated rate of increase in the population (and whether they would or not, must certainly depend upon other causes besides the number of lives saved by the vaccine inoculation),[3] one of two things would happen, either an increased mortality of some other diseases, or a diminution in the proportion of births. But I have expressed my conviction that the latter effect would take place, and therefore, consistently with the opinions which I have always maintained, I ought to be, and am, one of the warmest friends to the introduction of the cow-pox. In making every exertion which I think likely to be effectual, to increase the comforts and diminish the mortality among the poor, I act in the most exact conformity to my principles. Whether those are equally

---

[2] This subject is strikingly illustrated in Lord Selkirk's lucid and masterly observations 'On the Present State of the Highlands, and on the Causes and Probable Consequences of Emigration', to which I can with confidence refer the reader.

[3] It should be remarked, however, that a young person saved from death is more likely to contribute to the creation of fresh resources than another birth. It is a great loss of labour and food to begin over again. And universally it is true that, under similar circumstances, that article will come the cheapest to market which is accompanied by fewest failures.

consistent who profess to have the same object in view, and yet measure the happiness of nations by the large proportion of marriages and births, is a point which they would do well to consider.

It has been said by some that the natural checks to population will always be sufficient to keep it within bounds, without resorting to any other aids; and one ingenious writer has remarked that I have not deduced a single original fact from real observations to prove the inefficiency of the checks which already prevail.[4] These remarks are correctly true, and are truisms exactly of the same kind as the assertion that man cannot live without food. For undoubtedly, as long as this continues to be a law of his nature, what are here called the natural checks cannot possibly fail of being effectual. Besides the curious truism that these assertions involve, they proceed upon the very strange supposition that the *ultimate* object of my work is to check population, as if anything could be more desirable than the most rapid increase of population unaccompanied by vice and misery. But of course my ultimate object is to diminish vice and misery, and any checks to population which may have been suggested are solely as means to accomplish this end. To a rational being, the prudential check to population ought to be considered as equally natural with the check from poverty and premature mortality, which these gentlemen seem to think so entirely sufficient and satisfactory; and it will readily occur to the intelligent reader, that one class of checks may be substituted for another, not only without essentially diminishing the population of a country, but even under a constantly progressive increase of it.[5]

On the possibility of increasing very considerably the effective population of this country, I have expressed myself in some parts of my work more sanguinely, perhaps, than experience would warrant. I have said that in the course of some centuries it might contain two or three times as many

---

[4] I should like much to know what description of facts this gentleman had in view when he made this observation. If I could have found one of the kind which seems here to be alluded to, it would indeed have been truly original.

[5] Both Norway and Switzerland, where the preventive check prevails the most, are increasing with some rapidity in their population; and in proportion to their means of subsistence, they can produce more males of a military age than any other country of Europe.

inhabitants as at present, and yet every person be both better fed and better clothed.[6] And in the comparison of the increase of population and food at the beginning of the Essay, that the argument might not seem to depend upon a difference of opinion respecting facts, I have allowed the produce of the earth to be unlimited, which is certainly going too far. It is not a little curious therefore, that it should still continue to be urged against me as an argument, that this country might contain two or three times as many inhabitants; and it is still more curious, that some persons, who have allowed the different ratios of increase on which all my principal conclusions are founded, have still asserted that no difficulty or distress could arise from population, till the productions of the earth could not be further increased. I doubt whether a stronger instance could readily be produced of the total absence of the power of reasoning than this assertion, after such a concession, affords. It involves a greater absurdity than the saying that because a farm can, by proper management, be made to carry an additional stock of four head of cattle every year, that therefore no difficulty or inconvenience would arise if an additional forty were placed in it yearly.

The power of the earth to produce subsistence is certainly not unlimited, but it is strictly speaking indefinite; that is, its limits are not defined, and the time will probably never arrive when we shall be able to say, that no farther labour or ingenuity of man could make further additions to it. But the power of obtaining an additional quantity of food from the earth by proper management, and in a certain time, has the most remote relation imaginable to the power of keeping pace with an unrestricted increase of population. The knowledge and industry which would enable the natives of New Holland to make the best use of the natural resources of their country must, without an absolute miracle, come to them gradually and slowly; and even then, as it has amply appeared, would be perfectly ineffectual as to the grand object; but the passions which prompt to the increase of population are always in full vigour, and are ready to produce their full effect even in a state of the most helpless ignorance and barbarism. It will be readily allowed, that the reason why New Holland, in proportion to

[6] P. 512, 4to edit.

its natural powers, is not so populous as China, is the want of those human institutions which protect property and encourage industry; but the misery and vice which prevail almost equally in both countries, from the tendency of population to increase faster than the means of subsistence, form a distinct consideration, and arise from a distinct cause. They arise from the incomplete discipline of the human passions; and no person with the slightest knowledge of mankind has ever had the hardihood to affirm that human institutions could completely discipline all the human passions. But I have already treated this subject so fully in the course of the work, that I am ashamed to add any thing further here.

The next grand objection which has been urged against me, is my denial of the *right* of the poor to support.

Those who would maintain this objection, with any degree of consistency, are bound to show that the different ratios of increase with respect to population and food, which I attempted to establish at the beginning of the Essay, are fundamentally erroneous; since on the supposition of their being true, the conclusion is inevitable. If it appear, as it must appear on these rations being allowed, that it is not possible for the industry of man to produce sufficient food for all that would be born, if every person were to marry at the time when he was first prompted to it by inclination, it follows irresistibly that all cannot have a *right* to support. Let us for a moment suppose an equal division of property in any country. If, under these circumstances, one half of the society were by prudential habits so to regulate their increase that it exactly kept pace with their increasing cultivation, it is evident that they would always remain as at first. If the other half, during the same time, married at the age of puberty, when they would probably feel most inclined to it, it is evident that they would soon become wretchedly poor. But upon what plea of justice or equity could this second half of the society claim a right, in virtue of their poverty, to any of the possessions of the first half? This poverty had arisen entirely from their own ignorance or imprudence; and it would be perfectly clear, from the manner in which it had come upon them, that if their plea were admitted, and they were not suffered to feel the particular evils resulting from their conduct, the whole society would shortly be involved in the same degree of wretchedness. Any voluntary and temporary assistance which might be given as a measure of charity by the richer members of the society to the others, while they were learning to make a better use of the lessons of nature, would be quite a distinct consideration, and without doubt most properly applied; but nothing like a claim of *right* to support can possible be maintained till we deny the premises; till we affirm that the American increase of population is a miracle, and does not arise from the great facility of obtaining the means of subsistence.[7]

In fact, whatever we may say in our declamations on this subject, almost the whole of our *conduct* is founded on the non-existence of this right. If the poor had really a claim of *right* to support, I do not think that any man could justify his wearing broadcloth, or eating as much meat as he likes for dinner, and those who assert this right, and yet are rolling in their carriages, living every day luxuriously, and keeping even their horses on food of which their fellow creatures are in want, must be allowed to act with the greatest inconsistency. Taking an individual instance without reference to consequences, it appears to me that Mr. Godwin's argument is irresistible. Can it be pretended for a moment that a part of the mutton which I expect to eat today would not be much more beneficially employed on some hard-working labourer who has not perhaps tasted animal food for the last week, or on some poor family who cannot command sufficient food of any kind fully to satisfy the cravings of appetite? If these instances were not of a nature to multiply in proportion as such wants were indiscriminately gratified, the gratification of them, as it would be practicable, would be highly beneficial; and in this case I should not have the smallest hesitation in most fully allowing the right. But as it appears clearly both from theory and

---

[7] It has been said that I have written a quarto volume to prove that population increases in a geometrical, and food in an arithmetical ratio; but this is not quite true. The first of these propositions I considered as proved the moment that the American increase was related, and the second proposition as soon as it was enunciated. The chief object of my work was to inquire what effects these laws, which I considered as established in the first six pages, had produced, and were likely to produce, on society: a subject not very readily exhausted. The principal fault of my details is that they are not sufficiently particular; but this was a fault which it was not in my power to remedy. It would be a most curious, and to every philosophical mind a most interesting piece of information, to know the exact share of the full power of increase which each existing check prevents; but at present I see no mode of obtaining such information.

experience, that if the claim were allowed it would soon increase beyond the *possibility* of satisfying it, and that the practical attempt to do so, would involve the human race in the most wretched and universal poverty, it follows necessarily that our conduct, which denies the right, is more suited to the present state of our being, than our declamations which allow it.

The great author of nature, indeed, with that wisdom which is apparent in all his works, has not left this conclusion to the cold and speculative consideration of general consequences. By making the passion of self-love beyond comparison stronger than the passion of benevolence, he has at once impelled us to that line of conduct which is essential to the preservation of the human race. If all that might be born could be adequately supplied, we cannot doubt that he would have made the desire of giving to others as ardent as that of supplying ourselves. But since, under the present constitution of things, this is not so, he has enjoined every man to pursue as his primary object his own safety and happiness, and the safety and happiness of those immediately connected with him; and it is highly instructive to observe that, in proportion as the sphere contracts, and the power of giving effectual assistance increases, the desire increases at the same time. In the case of children, who have certainly a claim of *right* to the support and protection of their parents, we generally find parental affection nearly as strong as self-love; and except in a few anomalous cases, the last morsel will be divided into equal shares.

By this wise provision the most ignorant are led to promote the general happiness, an end which they would have totally failed to attain if the moving principle of their conduct had been benevolence.[8] Benevolence indeed, as the great and constant source of action, would require the most perfect knowledge of causes and effects, and therefore can only be the attribute of the Deity. In a being so short-sighted as man, it would lead into the grossest errors, and soon transform the fair and cultivated soil of civilized society into a dreary scene of want and confusion.

---

[8] In saying this let me not be supposed to give the slightest sanction to the system of morals inculcated in the *Fable of the Bees*, a system which I consider as absolutely false, and directly contrary to the just definition of virtue. The great art of Dr. Mandeville consisted in misnomers.

But though benevolence cannot in the present state of our being be the great moving principle of human actions, yet, as the kind corrector of the evils arising from the other stronger passion, it is essential to human happiness; it is the balm and consolation and grace of human life, the source of our noblest efforts in the cause of virtue, and of our purest and most refined pleasures. Conformably, to that system of general laws, according to which the Supreme Being appears with very few exceptions to act, a passion so strong and general as self-love could not prevail without producing much partial evil; and to prevent this passion from degenerating into the odious vice of selfishness,[9] to make us sympathise in the pains and pleasures of our fellow-creatures, and feel the same *kind* of interest in their happiness and misery as in our own, though diminished in degree, to prompt us often to put ourselves in their place, that we may understand their wants, acknowledge their rights, and do them good as we have opportunity; and to remind us continually, that even the passion which urges us to procure plenty for ourselves was not implanted in us for our own exclusive advantage, but as the means of procuring the greatest plenty for all; these appear to be the objects and offices of benevolence. In every situation of life there is ample room for the exercise of this virtue; and as each individual rises in society, as he advances in knowledge and excellence, as his power of benefiting others becomes greater, and the necessary attention to his own wants less, it will naturally come in for an increasing share among his constant motives of action. In situations of high trust and influence it ought to have a very large share, and in all public institutions be the great moving principle. Though we have often reason to fear that our benevolence may not take the most beneficial direction, we need never apprehend that there will be too much of it in society. The foundations of that passion on which our preservation depends are fixed so deeply in our nature, that no reasonings or addresses to our feelings can essentially disturb it. It is just therefore, and proper, that all the positive precepts

[9] It seems proper to make a decided distinction between self-love and selfishness, between that passion which under proper regulations is the source of all honourable industry, and of all the necessaries and conveniences of life, and the same passion pushed to excess, when it becomes useless and disgusting, and consequently vicious.

should be on the side of the weaker impulse; and we may safely endeavour to increase and extend its influence as much as we are able, if at the same time we are constantly on the watch to prevent the evil which may arise from its misapplication.

The law which in this country entitles the poor to relief is undoubtedly different from a full acknowledgment of the natural right; and from this difference and the many counteracting causes that arise from the mode of its execution, it will not of course be attended with the same consequences. But still it is an approximation to a full acknowledgment, and as such appears to produce much evil, both with regard to the habits and the temper of the poor. I have in consequence ventured to suggest a plan of gradual abolition, which, as might be expected, has not met with universal approbation. I can readily understand any objections that may be made to it, on the plea that the right having been once acknowledged in this country, the revocation of it might at first excite discontents; and should therefore most fully concur in the propriety of proceeding with the greatest caution, and of using all possible means of preventing any sudden shock to the opinions of the poor. But I have never been able to comprehend the grounds of the further assertion which I have sometimes heard made, that if the poor were really convinced that they had no claim of right to relief, they would in general be more inclined to be discontented and seditious. On these occasions the only way I have of judging is to put myself in imagination in the place of the poor man, and consider how I should feel in his situation. If I were told that the rich by the laws of nature and the laws of the land were bound to support me, I could not, in the first place, feel much obligation for such support; and in the next place, if I were given any food of an inferior kind, and could not see the absolute necessity of the change, which would probably be the case, I should think that I had good reason to complain. I should feel that the laws had been violated to my injury, and that I had been unjustly deprived of my right. Under these circumstances, though I might be deterred by the fear of an armed force from committing any overt acts of resistance, yet I should consider myself as perfectly justified in so doing, if this fear were removed; and the injury which I believed that I had suffered might produce the most unfavourable effects on my general dispositions towards the higher classes of society. I cannot indeed conceive anything more irritating to the human feelings, than to experience that degree of distress which, in spite of all our poor laws and benevolence, is not unfrequently felt in this country; and yet to believe that these sufferings were not brought upon me either by my own faults, or by the operation of those general laws which, like the tempest, the blight, or the pestilence, are continually falling hard on particular individuals, while others entirely escape, but were occasioned solely by the avarice and injustice of the higher classes of society.

On the contrary, if I firmly believed that by the laws of nature, which are the laws of God, I had no claim of *right* to support I should, in the first place, feel myself more strongly bound to a life of industry and frugality; but if want, notwithstanding, came upon me, I should consider it in the light of sickness, as an evil incidental to my present state of being, and which, if I could not avoid, it was my duty to bear with fortitude and resignation. I should know from past experience, that the best title I could have to the assistance of the benevolent would be, the not having brought myself into distress by my own idleness or extravagance. What I received would have the best effect on my feelings towards the higher classes. Even if it were much inferior to what I had been accustomed to, it would still, instead of an injury, be an obligation; and conscious that I had no claim of *right*, nothing but the fear of absolute famine, which would overcome all other considerations, could morally justify resistance.

I cannot help believing that if the poor in this country were convinced that they had no claim of *right* to support; and yet in scarcities and all cases of urgent distress were liberally relieved, which I think they would be, the bond which unites the rich with the poor would be drawn much closer than at present, and the lower classes of society, as they would have less real reason for irritation and discontent, would be much less subject to these uneasy sensations.

Among those who have objected to my declaration that the poor have no claim of *right* to support is Mr. Young, who, with a harshness not quite becoming a candid inquirer after truth, has called my proposal for the gradual abolition of the poor laws a horrible plan, and asserted that the execution of it would be a most iniquitous proceeding. Let this plan however be compared for a moment with that which he himself and others have proposed, of fixing the sum of the poor's rates, which on no account is to be increased. Under such a law, if the distresses of the poor were to be aggravated tenfold, either by the increase of numbers or the recurrence of a scarcity, the same sum would invariably be appropriated to their relief. If the statute which gives the poor a right to support were to remain unexpunged, we should add to the cruelty of starving them the extreme injustice of still *professing* to relieve them. If this statute were expunged or altered, we should virtually deny the right of the poor to support, and only retain the absurdity of saying that they had a right to a certain sum; an absurdity on which Mr. Young justly comments with much severity in the case of France.[10] In both cases the hardships which they would suffer would be much more severe, and would come upon them in a much more unprepared state, than upon the plan proposed in the Essay.

According to this plan all that are already married, and even all that are engaged to marry during the course of the year, and all their children, would be relieved as usual; and only those who marry subsequently, and who of course may be supposed to have made better provision for contingencies, would be out of the pale of relief.

Any plan for the abolition of the poor laws must presuppose a general acknowledgment that they are essentially wrong, and that it is necessary to tread back our steps. With this acknowledgment, whatever objections may be made to my plan, in the too frequently short-sighted views of policy, I have no fear of comparing it with any other that has yet been

---

[10] The National Assembly of France, though they disapproved of the English poor laws, still adopted their principle, and declared that the poor had a right to pecuniary assistance; that the Assembly ought to consider such a provision as one of its first and most sacred duties; and that with this view, an expense ought to be incurred to the amount of 50 millions a year. Mr. Young justly observes, that he does not comprehend how it is possible to regard the expenditure of 50 millions a sacred duty, and not extend that 50 to 100 if necessity should demand it, the 100 to 200, the 200 to 300, and so on in the same miserable progression which has taken place in England. Travels in France, c. xv. p. 439.

I should be the last man to quote Mr. Young against himself, if I thought he had left the path of error for the path of truth, as such kind of inconsistency I hold to be highly praiseworthy. But thinking, on the contrary, that he has left truth for error, it is surely justifiable to remind him of his former opinions. We may recall to a vicious man his former virtuous conduct, though it would be useless and indelicate to remind a virtuous man of the vices which he had relinquished.

advanced, in point of justice and humanity; and of course the terms iniquitous and horrible 'pass by me like the idle wind which I regard not'.

Mr. Young it would appear has not given up this plan. He has pleaded for the privilege of being inconsistent, and has given such reasons for it that I am disposed to acquiesce in them, provided he confined the exercise of this privilege to different publications, in the interval between which he may have collected new facts; but I still think it not quite allowable in the same publication; and yet it appears that in the very paper in which he has so severely condemned my scheme, the same arguments which he has used to reprobate it are applicable with equal force against his own proposal, as he has there explained it.

He allows that his plan can only provide for a certain amount of families, and has nothing to do with the increase from them;[11] but in allowing this, he allows that it does not reach the grand difficulty attending a provision for the poor. In this most essential point, after reprobating me for saying that the poor have no claim of *right* to support, he is compelled to adopt the very same conclusion, and to own that 'it might be prudent to consider the misery to which the progressive population might be subject, when there was not a sufficient demand for them in towns and manufactures, as an evil which it was absolutely and physically impossible to prevent'. Now the sole reason why I say that the poor have no claim of *right* to support is the physical impossibility of relieving this progressive population. Mr. Young expressly acknowledges this physical impossibility; yet with an inconsistency scarcely credible still declaims against my declaration.

The power which the society may possess of relieving a certain portion of the poor is a consideration perfectly distinct from the general question; and I am quite sure I have never said that it is not our duty to do all the good that is practicable. But this limited power of assisting individuals cannot possibly establish a general right. If the poor have really a natural right to support, and if our present laws be only a confirmation of this right, it ought certainly to extend unimpaired to all who are in distress, to the increase from the cottagers as well as to the cottagers themselves; and it would be a palpable injustice in

[11] *Annals of Agriculture*, No. 239, p. 219.

the society to adopt Mr. Young's plan, and purchase from the present generation the disfranchisement of their posterity.

Mr. Young objects very strongly to that passage of the Essay,[12] in which I observe that a man who plunges himself into poverty and dependence, by marrying without any prospect of being able to maintain his family, has more reason to accuse himself than the price of labour, the parish, the avarice of the rich, the institutions of society, and the dispensations of Providence; except in as far as he has been deceived by those who ought to have instructed him. In answer to this, Mr. Young says, that the poor fellow is justified in every one of these complaints, that of Providence alone excepted; and that seeing other cottagers living comfortably with three or four acres of land, he has cause to accuse institutions which deny him that which the rich could well spare, and which would give him all he wants.[13] I would beg Mr. Young for a moment to consider how the matter would stand, if his own plan were completely executed. After all the commons had been divided as he has proposed, if a labourer had more than one son, in what respect would this son be in a different situation from the man that I have supposed? Mr. Young cannot possibly mean to say, that if he had the very natural desire of marrying at twenty, he would still have a right to complain that the society did not give him a house and three or four acres of land. He has indeed expressly denied this absurd consequence, though in so doing he has directly contradicted the declaration just quoted.[14] The progressive population, he says, would, according to his system, be cut off from the influence of the poor laws, and the encouragement to marry would remain exactly in that proportion less than at present. Under these circumstances, without land, without the prospect of parish relief, and with the price of labour only sufficient to maintain two children, can Mr. Young seriously think that the poor man, if he be really aware of his situation, does not do wrong in marrying, and ought not to accuse himself for following what Mr. Young calls the dictates of God, of nature, and of revelation? Mr. Young cannot be

---

12   Book iv. c. iii. p. 506, 4to. edit.
13   Annals of Agriculture, No. 239, p. 226.
14   Annals of Agriculture, No. 239, p. 214.

unaware of the wretchedness that must inevitably follow a marriage under such circumstances. His plan makes no provision whatever for altering these circumstances. He must therefore totally disregard all the misery arising from excessive poverty, or if he allows that these supernumerary members must necessarily wait, either till a cottage with land becomes vacant in the country, or that by emigrating to towns they can find the means of providing for a family, all the declamation which he has urged with such pomp against deferring marriage in my system, would be equally applicable in his own. In fact, if Mr. Young's plan really attained the object which it professes to have in view, that of bettering the condition of the poor, and did not defeat its intent by encouraging a too rapid multiplication, and consequently lowering the price of labour, it cannot be doubted that not only the supernumerary members just mentioned, but all the labouring poor, must wait longer before they could marry than they do at present.

The following proposition may be said to be capable of mathematical demonstration. In a country, the resources of which will not permanently admit of an increase of population more rapid than the existing rate, no improvement in the condition of the people which would tend to diminish mortality could *possibly* take place without being accompanied by a smaller proportion of births, supposing of course no particular increase of emigration.[15] To a person who has considered the subject, there is no proposition in Euclid which brings home to the mind a stronger conviction than this, and there is no truth so invariably confirmed by all the registers of births, deaths, and marriages that have ever been collected. In this country it has appeared that, according to the returns of the population

---

[15] With regard to the resource of emigration, I refer the reader to the 4th chapter, Book iii. of the Essay. Nothing is more easy than to say, that three fourths of the habitable globe are yet unpeopled but it is by no means so easy to fill these parts with flourishing colonies. The peculiar circumstances which have caused the spirit of emigration in the Highlands, so clearly explained in the able work of Lord Selkirk before referred to, are not of constant recurrence; not is it by any means to be wished that they should be so. And yet without some such circumstances, people are by no means very ready to leave their native soil, and will bear much distress at home, rather than venture on these distant regions. I am of opinion that it is both the duty and interest of government to facilitate emigration; but it would surely be unjust to oblige people to leave their country and kindred against their inclinations.

act, the proportion of births to deaths is about 4 to 3. This proportion with a mortality of 1 in 40,[16] would double the population in 83 years and a half; and as we cannot suppose that the country could admit of more than a quadrupled population in the next hundred and sixty-six years, we may safely say that its resources will not allow of a permanent rate of increase greater than that which is taking place at present. But if this be granted, it follows as a direct conclusion that if Mr. Young's plan, or any other, really succeeded in bettering the condition of the poor, and enabling them to rear more of their children, the vacancies in cottages in proportion to the number of expectants would happen slower than at present and the age of marriage must inevitably be later. Those, therefore, who propose plans for bettering the condition of the poor, and yet at the same time reprobate later or fewer marriages, are guilty of the most puerile inconsistency; and I cannot but be perfectly astonished that Mr. Young, who once understood the subject, should have indulged himself in such a poor declamation about passions, profligacy, burning, and ravens. It is in fact a silly, not to say impious, declamation against the laws of nature and the dispensations of Providence.

With regard to the expression of later marriages, it should always be recollected that it refers to no particular age, but is entirely comparative. The marriages in England are later than in France, the natural consequence of that prudence and respectability generated by a better government; and can we double that good has been the result? The marriages in this country now are later than they were before the revolution and I feel firmly persuaded that the increased healthiness observed of late years could not possibly have taken place without this accompanying circumstance. Two or three years in the average age of marriage, by lengthening each generation, and tending, in a small degree, both to diminish the prolificness of marriages, and the number of born living to be married, may make a considerable difference in the rate of increase, and be adequate to allow for a considerably diminished mortality. But I would on no account talk of any limits whatever. The only plain and intelligible measure with regard to marriage is the having a fair prospect of being able to maintain a family. If the possession of one of Mr. Young's cottages would give the

---

[16] Table iii. p. 238, 4to. edit.

labourer this prospect, he would be quite right to marry; but if it did not, or if he could only obtain a rented house without land, and the wages of labour were only sufficient to maintain two children, does Mr. Young, who cuts him off from the influence of the poor laws, presume to say that he would still be right in marrying.[17]

Mr. Young has asserted that I have made perfect chastity in the single state absolutely necessary to the success of my plan; but this surely is a misrepresentation. Perfect virtue is indeed absolutely necessary to enable man to avoid *all* the moral and physical evils which depend upon his own conduct; but whoever expected perfect virtue upon earth? I have said what I conceive to be strictly true, that it is our duty to defer marriage till we can feed our children, and that it is also our duty not to indulge ourselves in vicious gratifications; but I have never said that I expected either, much less both, of these duties to be completely fulfilled. In this, and a number of other cases, it may happen, that the violation of one of two duties will enable a man to perform the other with greater facility; but if they be really both duties, and both practicable, no power *on earth* can absolve a man from the guilt of violating either. This can only be done by that God who can weigh the crime against the temptation, and will temper justice with mercy. The moralist is still bound to inculcate the practice of both duties, and each individual must be left to act under the temptations to which he is exposed as his conscience shall dictate. Whatever I may have said in drawing a picture *professedly* visionary, for the sake of illustration, in the practical application of my principles I have taken man as he is, with all his imperfections on his head. And thus viewing him, and knowing that some checks to the population must exist, I have not the slightest hesitation in saying that the prudential check to marriage is better than premature mortality. And in this decision I feel myself completely justified by experience.

In every instance that can be traced, in which an improved government has given to its subjects a greater degree of foresight, industry, and personal dignity, these effects, under

---

[17] The lowest prospect with which a man can be justified in marrying seems to be the power, when in health, of earning such wages as, at the average price of corn, will maintain the average number of living children to a marriage.

similar circumstances of increase, have invariably been accompanied by a diminished proportion of marriages. This is a proof that an increase of moral worth in the general character is not at least *incompatible* with an increase of temptations with respect to one particular vice; and the instances of Norway, Switzerland, England and Scotland, adduced in the last chapter of this Essay, show that, in comparing different countries together, a small proportion of marriages and births does not necessarily imply the greater prevalence even of this particular vice. This is surely quite enough for the legislator. He cannot estimate with tolerable accuracy the degree in which chastity in the single state prevails. His general conclusions must be founded on general results, and these are clearly in his favour.

To much of Mr. Young's plan, as he has at present explained it, I should by no means object. The peculiar evil which I apprehended from it, that of taking the poor from the consumption of wheat, and feeding them on milk and potatoes might certainly be avoided by a limitation of the number of cottages; and I entirely agree with him in thinking that we should not be deterred from making 500 000 families more comfortable, because we cannot extend the same relief to all the rest. I have indeed myself ventured to recommend a general improvement of cottages, and even the cow system on a limited scale; and perhaps, with proper precautions, a certain portion of land might be given to a considerable body of the labouring classes.

If the law which entitles the poor to support were to be repealed, I should most highly approve of any plan which would tend to render such repeal more palatable on its first promulgation; and in this view, some kind of compact with the poor might be very desirable. A plan of letting land to labourers, under certain conditions, has lately been tried in the parish of Long Newnton in Gloucestershire; and the result, with a general proposal founded on it, has been submitted to the public by Mr. Estcourt. The present success has been very striking; but in this, and every other case of the kind, we should always bear in mind that no experiment respecting a provision for the poor can be said to be complete till succeeding generations have arisen.[18] I doubt if there ever has been an

---

[18] In any plan, particularly of a distribution of land, as a compensation for the relief given by the poor laws, the succeeding generations would form

instance of anything like a liberal institution for the poor which did not succeed on its first establishment, however it might have failed afterwards. But this consideration should by no means deter us from making such experiments, when present good is to be obtained by them, and a future overbalance of evil not justly to be apprehended. It should only make us less rash in drawing our inferences.

With regard to the general question of the advantages to the lower classes of possessing land, it should be recollected that such possessions are by no means a novelty. Formerly this system prevailed in almost every country with which we are acquainted, and prevails at present in many countries where the peasants are far from being remarkable for their comforts, but are, on the contrary, very poor, and particularly subject to scarcities. With respect to this latter evil, indeed, it is quite obvious that a peasantry which depends principally on its possessions in land must be more exposed to it than one which depends on the general wages of labour. When a year of deficient crops occurs in a country of any extent and diversity of soil, it is always partial, and some districts are more affected than others. But when a bad crop of grass, corn, or potatoes, or a mortality among cattle, falls on a poor man, whose principal dependence is on two or three acres of land, he is in the most deplorable and helpless situation. He is comparatively without money to purchase supplies, and is not for a moment to be compared with the man who depends on the wages of labour, and who will of course be able to purchase that portion of the general crop, whatever it may be, to which his relative situation in the society entitles him. In Sweden, where the farmers' labourers are paid principally in land, and often keep two or three cows, it is not uncommon for the peasants of one district to be almost starving, while their neighbours at a little distance are living in comparative plenty. It will be found indeed generally that, in almost all the countries which are particularly subject to scarcities and famines, either the farms are very small, or the labourers are paid principally in land.

the grand difficulty. All others would be perfectly trivial in comparison. For a time everything might go on very smoothly, and the rates be much diminished; but afterwards they would either increase again as rapidly as before, or the scheme would be exposed to all the same objections which have been made to mine, without the same justice and consistency to palliate them.

China, Indostan, and the former state of the Highlands of Scotland furnish some proofs among many others of the truth of this observation; and in reference to the small properties of France, Mr. Young himself in his tour particularly notices the distress arising from the least failure of the crops; and observes that such a deficiency as in England passes almost without notice, in France it is attended with dreadful calamities.[19]

Should any plan therefore of assisting the poor by land be adopted in this country, it would be absolutely essential to its ultimate success to prevent them from making it their principal dependence. And this might probably be done by attending strictly to the two following rules. Not to let the divisions of land be so great as to interrupt the cottager essentially in his usual labours; and always to stop in the further distribution of land and cottages when the price of labour, independent of any assistance from land, would not at the average price of corn maintain three, or at least two children. Could the matter be so ordered that the labourer, in working for others, should still continue to earn the same real command over the necessaries of life that he did before, a very great accession of comfort and happiness might accrue to the poor from the possession of land, without any evil that I can foresee at present. But if these points were not attended to, I should certainly fear an approximation to the state of the poor in France, Sweden, and Ireland; nor do I think that any of the partial experiments that have yet taken place afford the slightest presumption to the contrary. The result of these experiments is indeed exactly such as one should have expected. Who could ever have doubted that if, without lowering the price of labour, or taking the labourer off from his usual occupations, you could give him the produce of one or two acres of land and the benefit of a cow, you would decidedly raise his condition? But it by no means follows that he would retain this advantage if the system were so extended as to make the land his principal dependence, to lower the price of labour and, in the language of Mr. Young, to take the poor from the consumption of wheat and feed them on milk and potatoes. It does not appear to me so marvellous as it does to Mr. Young that the very same system, which in

---

[19] Travels in France, vol. i. c. xii. p. 409. That country will probably be the least liable to scarcities, in which agriculture is carried on as the most flourishing *manufacture* of the state.

Lincolnshire and Rutlandshire may produce now the most comfortable peasantry in the British dominions should, in the end, if extended without proper precautions, assimilate the condition of the labourers of this country to that of the lower classes of the Irish.

It is generally dangerous and impolitic in a government to take upon itself to regulate the supply of any commodity in request, and probably the supply of labourers forms no exception to the general rule. I would on no account therefore propose a positive law to regulate their increase; but as any assistance which the society might give them cannot, in the nature of things, be unlimited, the line may fairly be drawn where we please; and with regard to the increase from this point, everything would be left as before to individual exertion and individual speculation.

If any plan of this kind were adopted by the government, I cannot help thinking that it might be made the means of giving the best kind of encouragement and reward to those who are employed in our defence. If the period of enlisting were only for a limited time, and at the expiration of that time every person who had conducted himself well was entitled to a house and a small portion of land, if a country labourer, and to a tenement in a town and a small pension, if an artificer, all inalienable, a very strong motive would be held out to young men, not only to enter into the service of their country, but to behave well in that service; and in a short time there would be such a martial population at home, as the unfortunate state of Europe seems in a most peculiar manner to require. As it is only limited assistance that the society can possibly give, it seems in every respect fair and proper that, in regulating this limit, some important end should be attained.

If the poor laws be allowed to remain exactly in their present state, we ought at least to be aware to what cause it is owing that their effects have not been more pernicious than they are observed to be, that we may not complain of, or alter those parts, without which we should really not have the power of continuing them. The law which obliges each parish to maintain its own poor is open to many objections. It keeps the overseers and churchwardens continually on the watch to prevent new comers, and constantly in a state of dispute with other parishes. It thus prevents the free circulation of labour from place to place, and renders its price very unequal in different parts of the kingdom. It disposes all landlords rather to pull down than to build cottages on their estates; and this scarcity of habitations in the country, by driving more to the towns than would otherwise have gone, gives a relative discouragement to agriculture, and a relative encouragement to manufactures. These, it must be allowed, are no inconsiderable evils; but if the cause which occasions them were removed, evils of much greater magnitude would follow. I agree with Mr. Young in thinking that there is scarcely a parish in the kingdom where, if more cottages were built, and let at any tolerably moderate rents, they would not be immediately filled with new couples. I even agree with him in thinking that, in some places, this want of habitations operates too strongly in preventing marriage. But I have not the least doubt that, considered generally, its operation in the present state of things is most beneficial; and that it is almost exclusively owing to this cause that we have been able to long to continue the poor laws. If any man could build a hovel by the roadside, or on the neighbouring waste, without molestation, and yet were secure that he and his family would always be supplied with work and food by the parish, if they were not readily to be obtained elsewhere, I do not believe that it would be long before the physical impossibility of executing the letter of the poor laws would appear. It is of importance, therefore, to be aware that it is not because this or any other society has really the power of employing and supporting all that might be born, that we have been able to continue the present system; but because by the indirect operation of this system, not adverted to at the time of its establishment, and frequently reprobated since, the number of births is always very greatly limited, and thus reduced within the pale of possible support.

The obvious tendency of the poor laws is certainly to encourage marriage; but a closer attention to all their indirect as well as direct effects, may make it a matter of doubt how far they really do this. They clearly tend, in their general operation, to discourage sobriety and economy, to encourage idleness and the desertion of children, and to put virtue and vice more on a level than they otherwise would be; but I will not presume to say positively that they tend to encourage population. It is certain that the proportion of births in this country compared with others in similar circumstances is very small: but this was to be expected from the superiority of the government, the more respectable state of the people, and the more general spread of a taste for cleanliness and conveniences. And it will readily occur to the reader that, owing to these causes, combined with the twofold operation of the poor laws, it must be extremely difficult to ascertain, with any degree of precision, what has been their effect on population.

The only argument of a general nature against the Essay which strikes me as having any considerable force is the following. It is against the application of its principles, not the principles themselves, and has not, that I know of, been yet advanced in its present form. It may be said that, according to my own reasonings and the facts stated in my work, it appears that the diminished proportion of births, which I consider as absolutely necessary to the permanent improvement of the condition of the poor, invariably follows an improved government, and the greater degree of personal respectability which it gives to the lower classes of society. Consequently, allowing the desirableness of the end, it is not necessary, in order to obtain it, to risk the promulgation of any new opinions which may alarm the prejudices of the poor, and the effect of which we cannot with certainty foresee; but we have only to proceed in improving our civil polity, conferring the benefits of education upon all, and removing every obstacle to the general extension of all those privileges and advantages which may be enjoyed in common, and we may be quite sure that the effect to which I look forward, and which can alone render these advantages permanent, will follow.

I acknowledge the truth and force of this argument, and have only to observe, in answer to it, that it is difficult to conceive that we should not proceed with more celerity and certainty towards the end in view, if the principal causes which tend to promote or retard it were generally known. In particular, I cannot help looking forward to a very decided improvement in the habits and temper of the lower classes, when their real situation has been clearly explained to them; and if this were done gradually and cautiously, and accompanied with proper moral and religious instructions, I should not expect any danger from it. I am always unwilling to believe that the general dissemination of truth is prejudicial. Cases of the kind are undoubtedly conceivable, but they should be admitted with very great caution. If the general presumption in favour of the advantage of truth were once essentially shaken, all ardour in its cause would share the same fate, and the interests of knowledge and virtue most decidedly suffer. It is besides a species of arrogance not lightly to be encouraged, for any man to suppose that he has penetrated further into the laws of nature than the great Author of them intended, further than is consistent with the good of mankind.

Under these impressions I have freely given my opinions to the public. In the truth of the general principles of the Essay I confess that I feel such a confidence that, till something has been advanced against them very different indeed from anything that has hitherto appeared, I cannot help considering them as incontrovertible. With regard to the application of these principles the case is certainly different; and as dangers of opposite kinds are to be guarded against, the subject will of course admit of much latitude of opinion. At all events, however, it must be allowed that, whatever may be our determination respecting the advantages or disadvantages of endeavouring to circulate the truths on this subject among the poor, it must be highly advantageous that they should be known to all those who have it in their power to influence the laws and institutions of society. That the body of an army should not in all cases know the particulars of their situation may possibly be desirable; but that the leaders should be in the same state of ignorance will hardly, I think, be contended.

If it be really true, that without a diminished proportion of births[20] we cannot attain any *permanent* improvement in the health and happiness of the mass of the people, and secure that description of population which, by containing a larger share of adults, is best calculated to create fresh resources, and consequently to encourage a continued increase of efficient population; it is surely of the highest importance that this should be known, that if we take no steps directly to promote this effect, we should not at least, under the influence of the former prejudices on this subject, endeavour to counteract it.[21]

---

[20] It should always be recollected that a diminished *proportion* of births may take place under a constant annual increase of the absolute number. This is, in fact, exactly what has happened in England and Scotland during the last forty years.

[21] We should be aware that a scarcity of men, owing either to great losses, or to some particular and usual demand, is liable to happen in every country; and in no respect invalidates the general principle that has been advanced. Whatever may be the tendency to increase, it is quite clear that an

And if it be thought inadvisable to abolish the poor laws, it cannot be doubted that a knowledge of those general principles, which render them inefficient in their humane intentions, might be applied so far to modify them and regulate their execution, as to remove many of the evils with which they are accompanied, and make them less objectionable.

There is only one subject more which I shall notice, and that is rather a matter of feeling than of argument. Many persons, whose understandings are not of that description that they can regulate their belief or disbelief by their likes or dislikes, have professed their perfect conviction of the truth of the general principles contained in the Essay; but, at the same time, have lamented this conviction, as throwing a darker shade over our views of human nature, and tending particularly to narrow our prospects of future improvement. In these feelings I cannot agree with them. If, from a review of the past, I could not only believe that a fundamental and very extraordinary improvement in human society was possible, but feel a firm confidence

---

extraordinary supply of men cannot be produced either in six months, or six years; but even with a view to a more than usual supply, causes which tend to diminish mortality are not only more certain but more rapid in their effects than direct encouragements to marriage. An increase of births may, and often does, take place, without the ultimate accomplishment of our object; but supposing the births to remain the same, it is impossible for a diminished mortality not to be accompanied by an increase of effective population.

We are very apt to be deceived on this subject by the almost constant demand for labour which prevails in every prosperous country; but we should consider that in countries which can but just keep up their population, as the price of labour must be sufficient to rear a family of a certain number, a single man would have a superfluity, and labour would be in constant demand at the price of the subsistence of an individual. It cannot be doubted that in this country we could soon employ double the number of labourers if we could have them at our own price; because supply will produce demand as well as demand supply. The present great extension of the cotton trade did not originate in an extraordinary increase of demand, at the former prices, but it an increased supply at a much cheaper rate, which of course immediately produced an extended demand. As we cannot, however, obtain men at sixpence a day by improvements in machinery, we must submit to the necessary conditions of their rearing; and there is no man, who has the slightest feeling for the happiness of the most numerous class of society, or has even just views of policy on the subject, who would not rather choose that the requisite population should be obtained by such a price of labour, combined with such habits, as would occasion a very small mortality, than from a great proportion of births, of which comparatively few would reach manhood.

that it would take place, I should undoubtedly be grieved to find that I had overlooked some cause, the operation of which would at once blast my hopes. But if the contemplation of the past history of mankind, from which alone we can judge of the future, renders it almost impossible to feel such a confidence, I confess, that I had much rather believe that some real and deeply-seated difficulty existed, the constant struggle with which was calculated to rouse the natural inactivity of man, to call forth his faculties, and invigorate and improve his mind; a species of difficulty which it must be allowed is most eminently and peculiarly suited to a state of probation; than that nearly all the evils of life might with the most perfect facility be removed, but for the perverseness and wickedness of those who influence human institutions.[22]

A person who held this latter opinion must necessarily live in a constant state of irritation and disappointment. The ardent expectations, with which he might begin life, would soon receive the most cruel check. The regular progress of society, under the most favourable circumstances, would to him appear slow and unsatisfactory; but instead even of this regular progress, his eye would be more frequently presented with retrograde movements and the most disheartening reverses. The changes to which he had looked forward with delight would be found big with new and unlooked-for evils, and the characters on which he had reposed the most confidence would be seen frequently deserting his favourite cause, either from the lessons of experience or the temptation of power. In this state of constant disappointment, he would be but too apt to attribute everything to the worst motives; he would be inclined to give up the cause of improvement in despair; and judging of the whole from a part, nothing but a peculiar goodness of heart and amiableness of disposition could preserve him from that sickly and disgusting misanthropy which is but too frequently the end of such characters.

---

[22] The misery and vice arising from the pressure of the population too hard against the limits of subsistence, and the misery and vice arising from promiscuous intercourse, may be considered as the Scylla and Charybdis of human life. That it is possible for each individual to steer clear of both these rocks is certainly true, and a truth which I have endeavoured strongly to maintain; but that these rocks to not form a difficulty independent of human institutions, no person with any knowledge of the subject can venture to assert.

On the contrary, a person who held the other opinion, as he would set out with more moderate expectations, would of course be less liable to disappointment. A comparison of the best with the worst states of society, and the obvious inference from analogy, that the best were capable of further improvement, would constantly present to his mind a prospect sufficiently animating to warrant his most persevering exertions. But aware of the difficulties with which the subject was surrounded, knowing how often in the attempt to attain one object some other had been lost, and that though society had made rapid advances in some directions, it had been comparatively stationary in others, he would be constantly prepared for failures. These failures, instead of creating despair, would only create knowledge; instead of checking his ardour, would only give it a wiser and more successful direction; and having founded his opinion of mankind on broad and general grounds, the disappointment of any particular views would not change this opinion; but even in declining age he would probable be found believing as firmly in the reality and general prevalence of virtue, as in the existence and frequency of vice; and to the last, looking forward with a just confidence to those improvements in society, which the history of the past, in spite of all the reverses with which it is accompanied, seems clearly to warrant.

It may be true that if ignorance is bliss, 'tis folly to be wise; but if ignorance be not bliss, as in the present instance; if all false views of society must not only impede decidedly the progress of improvement, but necessarily terminate in the most bitter disappointments to the individuals who form them; I shall always think that the feelings and prospects of those who make the justest estimates of our future expectations are the most consolatory; and that the characters of this description are happier themselves, at the same time that they are beyond comparison more likely to contribute to the improvement and happiness of society.[23]

---

[23] While the last sheet of this Appendix was printing, I heard with some surprise that an argument had been drawn from the Principle of Population in favour of the slave trade. As the just conclusion from that principle appears to me to be exactly the contrary, I cannot help saying a few words on the subject.

If the only argument against the slave trade had been that, from the mortality it occasioned, it was likely to unpeople Africa or extinguish the human race, some comfort with regard to these fears might, indeed, be drawn from the principle of Population; but as the necessity of the abolition has never, that I know of, been urged on the ground of these apprehensions, a reference to the laws which regulate the increase of the human species was certainly most unwise in the friends of the slave trade.

The abolition of the slave trade is defended principally by the two following arguments:

1st. That the trade to the coast of Africa for slaves, together with their subsequent treatment in the West Indies, is productive of so much human misery, that its continuance is disgraceful to us as men and as Christians.

2d. That the culture of the West-India islands could go on with equal advantage, and much greater security, if no further importation of slaves were to take place.

With regard to the first argument it appears, in the Essay on the Principle of Population, that so great is the tendency of mankind to increase, that nothing but some physical or moral check operating in an *excessive* and *unusual* degree, can permanently keep the population of a country below the average means of subsistence. In the West India islands a constant recruit of labouring negroes is necessary; and consequently the immediate checks to population must operate with *excessive* and *unusual* force. All the checks to population were found resolvable into moral restraint, vice, and misery. In a state of slavery moral restraint cannot have much influence; nor in any state will it ever continue permanently to diminish the population. The whole effect, therefore, is to be attributed to the *excessive* and *unusual* action of vice and misery; and a reference to the facts contained in the Essay incontrovertibly proves that the condition of the slaves in the West Indies, taken altogether, is most wretched, and that the representations of the friends of the abolition cannot easily be exaggerated.

It will be said that the principal reason why the slaves in the West Indies constantly diminish is that the sexes are not in equal numbers, a considerable majority of males being always imported; but this very circumstance decides at once on the cruelty of their situation, and must necessarily be one powerful cause of their degraded moral condition.

It may be said also, that many towns do not keep up their numbers, and yet the same objection is not made to them on that account. But the cases will admit of no comparison. If, for the sake of better society or higher wages, people are willing to expose themselves to a less pure air, and greater temptations to vice, no hardship is suffered that can reasonably be complained of. The superior mortality of towns falls principally upon children, and is scarcely noticed by people of mature age. The sexes are in equal numbers, and every man after a few years of industry may look forward to the happiness of domestic life. If during the time that he is thus waiting, he acquires various habits which indispose him to marriage, he has nobody to blame except himself. But with the negroes the case is totally different. The unequal number of the sexes shuts out at once the majority of them from all chance of domestic happiness. They have no hope of this kind to sweeten their toils, and animate their exertion; but are necessarily condemned either to unceasing privation, or to the most vicious excesses; and thus shut out from every cheering prospect, we cannot be surprised that they are in general ready to welcome that death which so many meet with in the prime of life.

The second argument is no less powerfully supported by the Principle of

Population than the first. It appears, from a very general survey of different countries, that under every form of government, however unjust and tyrannical, in every climate of the known world, however apparently unfavourable to health, it has been found that population, with the sole exception above alluded to, has been able to keep itself up to the level of the means of subsistence. Consequently if by the abolition of the trade to Africa, the slaves in the West Indies were placed only in a *tolerable* situation, if their civil condition and moral habits were only made to *approach* to those which prevail among the mass of the human race in the worst-governed countries of the world, it is contrary to the general laws of nature to suppose that they would not be able, by procreation, fully to supply the effective demand for labour; and it is difficult to conceive that a population so raised would not be in every point of view preferable to that which exists at present.

It is perfectly clear, therefore, that a consideration of the laws which govern the increase and decrease of the human species tends to strengthen, in the most powerful manner, all the arguments in favour of the abolition.

With regard to the state of society among the African nations, it will readily occur to the reader that, in describing it, the question of the slave trade was foreign to my purpose; and I might naturally fear that if I entered upon it I should be led into too long a digression. But certainly all the facts which I have mentioned, and which are taken principally from Park, if they not absolutely *prove* that the wars in Africa are excited and aggravated by the traffic on the coast, tend powerfully to confirm the *supposition*. The state or Africa, as I have described it, is exactly such as we should expect in a country where the capture of men was considered as a more advantageous employment than agriculture or manufactures. Of the state of these nations some hundred years ago it must be confessed that we have little knowledge that we can depend upon: but allowing that the regular plundering excursions, which Park describes, are of the most ancient date; yet it is impossible to suppose that any circumstance which, like the European traffic, must give additional value to the plunder thus acquired, would not powerfully aggravate them, and effectually prevent all progress towards a happier order of things. As long as the nations of Europe continue barbarous enough to purchase slaves in Africa, we may be quite sure that Africa will continue barbarous enough to supply them.

# AN EXAMINATION OF MR. MALTHUS'S DOCTRINES
[William Hazlitt]

1. Of the Geometrical and Arithmetical Series

Wallace, the author of '*Various Prospects of Mankind, Nature, and Providence*,' was the first person, we believe, who applied the principle of the superior power of increase in population over the means of subsistence, as an insuperable objection to the arguments for the perfectibility of man, for which, in other respects, this author was an advocate. He has devoted a long and elaborate Essay to prove these two points:– 1. That there is a natural and necessary inability in the means of subsistence to go on increasing always in the same ratio as the population, the limits of the earth necessarily limiting the actual increase of the one, and there being no limits to the tendency to increase in the other; 2. That the checks which have hitherto, and which always *must* keep population down to the level of the means of subsistence, are *vice* and *misery*; and consequently, that in a state of perfectibility, as it is called, viz. in a state of perfect wisdom, virtue, and happiness, where these indispensable checks to population, vice and misery, were entirely removed, population would go on increasing to an alarming and most excessive degree, and unavoidably end in the utmost disorder, confusion, vice and misery. – (See *Various Prospects, &c.* p. 113-123.)

The principle laid down by this author, that population could not go on for ever increasing at its natural rate, or free from every restraint, either moral or physical, without ultimately outstripping the utmost possible increase of the means of subsistence, we hold to be unquestionable, if not self-evident: the other principle assumed by the original author, viz. that vice and misery are the only possible checks to population, we hold to be false as a matter of fact, and peculiarly absurd and contradictory, when applied to that state of society contemplated by the author, that is to say, one in which abstract reason and pure virtue, or a regard to the general good, should have got the better of every animal instinct and selfish passion. Of this, perhaps, a word hereafter. But be this as it may, both the principle of the necessary increase of the population beyond the means of subsistence, and the application of that principle as a final obstacle to all Utopian perfectibility schemes, are borrowed (whole) by Mr. Malthus from Wallace's work. This is not very stoutly denied by his admirers; but, say they, Mr. Malthus was the first to reduce the inequality between the possible increase of food and population to a mathematical certainty, to the arithmetical and geometrical ratios. In answer to which, we say, that those ratios are, in a strict and scientific view of the subject, entirely fallacious – a pure fiction. For a grain of corn or of mustard-seed has the same or a greater power of propagating its species than a man, till it has overspread the whole earth, till there is no longer any room for it to grow or to spread farther. A bushel of wheat will sow a whole field: the produce of that field will sow twenty fields, and produce twenty harvests. Till there are no longer fields to sow, that is, till a country or the earth is exhausted, the means of subsistence will go on increasing in more than a geometrical ratio; will more than double itself in every generation or season, and will more than keep pace with the progress of population; for this is supposed only to double itself, where it is unchecked, every twenty years. Therefore it is not true as an abstract proposition, that of itself, or in the nature of the growth of the produce of the earth, food can only increase in the snail-pace progress of an arithmetical ratio, while population goes on at a swinging geometrical rate: for the food keeps pace, or more than keeps pace, with the population, while there is room to grow it in, and after that room is filled up, it does not go on, even in that arithmetical ratio – if does not increase at all, or very little. That is, the ratio, instead of being always true, is never true at all: neither before the soil is fully cultivated, nor afterwards. Food does not increase in an arithmetical series in China, or even in England: it increases in a geometrical series, or as fast as the population, in America. The rates at which one or the other increase naturally, or can be made to increase, have no relation to an arithmetical and geometrical series. They are co-ordinate till the earth, or any given portion of it, is occupied and cultivated, and, after that, they are quite disproportionate: or rather, both stop practically at the same instant; the means of subsistence with the limits of the soil, and the population with the limits of the means of subsistence. All that is true of Mr. Malthus's doctrine, then, is this, that the tendency of population to increase remains after the power of the earth to produce more food is gone; that the one is limited, the other unlimited. This is enough for the morality of the question: his mathematics are altogether spurious. Entirely groundless as they are, they have still been of the greatest use to Mr. Malthus, in alarming the imaginations and confounding the understandings of his readers. For, if the case had been represented as it stands, the increase of population would have seemed, till the limits of the earth were full, a great moral good; and after they were passed, a physical impossibility, the state of society remaining the same. But, by means of the arithmetical and geometrical series, ever present to the mental eye, and overlaying the whole question, whether applicable to it or not, it seems, first, as if this inordinate and unequal pressure of population on the means of subsistence was, at all times, and in all circumstances, equally to be dreaded, and equally inevitable; and again, as if, the more that population advanced, the greater the evil became, the actual excess as well as the tendency to excess. For it appears by looking at the scale, at the 'stop-watch' of the new system of morals and legislation, as if, when the population is at 4, the means of subsistence is at 3; so that there is here only a deficit of 1 in the latter, and a small corresponding quantity of *vice* and *misery*; but that when it gets on to 32, the means of subsistence being only 6, here is a necessary deficiency of food, and all the comforts of life, to 26 persons out of 32, so that life becomes an evil, and the world a wretched lazar-house, a monstrous sink of misery and famine, one foul abortion, in proportion as it is full of human beings enjoying the comforts and necessaries of life. It consequently follows, that the more we can, by the wholesome *preventive* checks of vice and misery, keep back the principle of population to its first stages, and the means of subsistence to as low a level as possible, we keep these two mechanical, and otherwise unmanageable principles, in closer harmony, - hinder the one from pressing excessively on the other, and by producing the least possible quantity of good, prevent the greatest possible quantity of evil. This doctrine is false in fact and theory. Its advocates do not understand it, nor is it intelligible. The actual existence of 26 persons in want, when there is only food for six out of 32, is a chimera which never entered the brains of any one not an adept in Mr. Malthus's mathematical series; the population confessedly never can or does exceed the means of subsistence in a literal sense; and the tendency to exceed it in a moral sense, that is, so as to destroy the comforts and happiness of society, and occasion vice and misery, does not depend on the actual population supported by actual means of subsistence, but solely on the greater or less degree of *moral restraint*, in any number of individuals (ten hundred or ten millions), inducing them to go beyond or stop short of impending vice and misery in the career of population. The instant, however, any increase in population, with or without an increase in the means of subsistence, is hinted, the disciples of Mr. Malthus are struck with horror at the vice and misery which must ensue to keep this double population down; nay, mention any improvement, any reform, any addition to the comforts or necessaries of life, any diminution of vice and misery, and the infallible result in their apprehensive imaginations is only an incalculable increase of vice and misery, from the increased means of subsistence, and the increased population that would follow. They have but this one idea in their heads; it comes in at every turn, and nothing can drive it out. Twice last year did Major Torrens go down to the City Meeting with Mr. Malthus's arithmetical and geometrical ratios in his pocket, as a double and effectual bar to Mr. Owen's plan, or, indeed, if he is consistent, to any other plan of reform. He appeared to consider these ratios as decisive against any philosophical scheme of *perfectibility*, and as proportionably inimical to any subordinate approximation to any such ultimate visionary perfection. He argued that Mr. Owen's 'projected villages,' if realised in all their pauper splendour, and to the projector's heart's content, would, by providing for the support and increased comforts of an additional population, only (by that very means) give a double impetus to the mechanical operation of the ratios in question, and produce a double quantity of crime and misery, by making the principle of population press with extended force on the means of subsistence. This is what we cannot comprehend. Suppose Mr. Owen's plan, or any other, would afford double employment, double comfort and subsistence to the poor throughout the country, where would be the harm of this, where the objection, near or remote, except on the false principles laid down or insinuated in Mr. Malthus's work? For instance, if another island such as England could by an enchanter be conjured up in the middle of the sea, with all the same means of subsistence, arts, trades, agriculture, manufactures, institutions, laws, &c. as this country, we ask whether this new country would not be a good in proportion to the number of beings maintained in such a state of comfort: or, if these gentlemen will have it so, in proportion to the increase of population pressing on the means of subsistence? We say it would be a good, just in the same sense and proportion that it would be an evil, if England as it is, with all its inhabitants, means of subsistence, arts, trades, manufactures, agriculture, institutions, laws, King, Lords and Commons, were sunk in the sea? Who would not weep for England so sunk, – who would not rejoice to see another England so rising up out of the same element? The good would be immense, and the evil would be none: for it is evident, that though the population of both islands would be double that of either singly, it is the height of absurdity to suppose this would increase the tendency of the population to press more upon the means of subsistence, or to produce a greater quantity of vice and misery in either, than if the one or the other did not exist. But the case is precisely the same if we suppose England itself, *our* England, to be doubled in population and the means of subsistence: – if we suppose such an improvement in our arts, trade, manufactures, agriculture, institutions, laws, every thing, possible, as to maintain double the same number of Englishmen, in the same or in a greater degree of comfort and enjoyment, of liberty, virtue, knowledge, happiness, and independence. The population being doubled would not press more unequally on double the means of subsistence, than half that population would press on half those means of subsistence. If this increase would be an evil, the destroying half the present population, and half the present means of subsistence, the laying waste more lands, the destroying arts and the implements of husbandry, the re-barbarising and the re-enslaving the country, would be a good. The sinking the maritime counties with all their inhabitants in the Channel, instead of 'redeeming tracts from the sea.' would be a great good to the community and the State; the flooding the fen districts would do something, in like manner, to prevent the pressure of the principle of population on the level of the means of subsistence; and if thirty-nine out of forty of the counties could be struck off the list of shires, and the whole island reduced to a sand-bank, the King of England would reign, according to these speculatists, over forty or forty thousand times the quantity of liberty, happiness, wisdom, and virtue, that he now does, having no subjects, or only a select few, for the principle of population to commit its ravages upon by overstepping the means of subsistence. The condition of New Zealand must approach nearer to the *beau ideal* of political philosophy contemplated by these persons, than the state of Great Britain in the reign of George III. Such is the logical result of their mode of reasoning, though they do not push it to this length; – they only apply it to the defence of all existing abuses, and the prevention of all timely reform! Its advocates are contented to make us of it as a lucky diversion against all Utopian projects of perfectibility, and against every practical advance in human improvement. But they cannot consistently stop here, for it requires not only a shrinking back from every progressive refinement, but a perpetual deterioration and retrograde movement from the positive advances we have made in civilization, comfort, and population, to the lowest state of barbarism, ignorance, and depopulation – till we come back to the age of acorns and pig-nuts, and reduce this once flourishing, populous, free, industrious, independent, and contented people, to a horde of wandering savages, housing in thickets, and living on dewberries, shell-fish, and crab-apples. *This will never do.*

## ON THE PRINCIPLE OF POPULATION AS AFFECTING THE SCHEMES OF UTOPIAN IMPROVEMENT
[William Hazlitt]

'A swaggering paradox, when once explained, soon sinks into an unmeaning common-place.'

This excellent saying of a great man was never more strictly applicable to any system than it is to Mr. Malthus's paradox, and his explanation of it. It seemed, on the first publication of the Essay on Population, as if the whole world was going to be turned topsy-turvy, all our ideas of moral good and evil, were in a manner confounded, we scarcely knew whether we stood on our head or our heels: but after exciting considerable expectation, giving us a good shake, and making us a little dizzy, Mr. Malthus does as we do when we shew the children *London*, – sets us on our feet again, and every thing goes on as before. The common notions that prevailed on this subject, till our author's first population-scheme tended to weaken them, were that life is a blessing, and that the more people could be maintained in any state in a tolerable degree of health, comfort and decency, the better: that want and misery are not desirable in themselves, that famine is not to be courted for its own sake, that wars, disease and pestilence are not what every friend of his country or his species should pray for in the first place: that vice in its different shapes is a thing that the world could do very well without, and that if it could be got rid of altogether, it would be a great gain. In short, that the object both of the moralist and politician was to diminish as much as possible the quantity of vice and misery existing in the world: without apprehending that by thus effectually introducing more virtue and happiness, more reason and good sense, that by improving the manners of a people, removing pernicious habits and principles of acting, or securing greater plenty, and a greater number of mouths to partake of it, they were doing a disservice to humanity. Then comes Mr. Malthus with his octavo book, and tells us there is another great evil, which had never been found out, or at least not sufficiently attended to till his time, namely, excessive population: that this evil was infinitely greater and more to be dreaded than all others put together; and that its approach could only be checked by vice and misery: that any increase of virtue or happiness was the direct way to hasten it on; and that in proportion as we attempted to improve the condition of mankind, and lessened the restraints of vice and misery, we threw down the only barriers that could protect us from this most formidable scourge of the species, population. Vice and misery were indeed evils, but they were absolutely necessary evils; necessary to prevent the introduction of others in an incalculably and inconceivably greater magnitude; and that every proposal to lessen their actual quantity, on which the measure of our safety depended, might be attended with the most ruinous consequences, and ought to be looked upon with horror. I think that this description of the tendency and complexion of Mr. Malthus's first essay is not in the least exaggerated, but an exact and faithful picture of the impression, which is made on every one's mind.

After taking some time to recover from the surprise and hurry into which so great a discovery would naturally throw him, he comes forward again with a large quarto, in which he is at great pains both to say and unsay all that he has said in his former volume; and upon the whole concludes, that population is in itself a good thing, that it is never likely to do much harm, that virtue and happiness ought to be promoted by every practicable means, and that the most effectual as well as desirable check to excessive population is *moral restraint*. The mighty discovery thus reduced to, and pieced out by common sense, the wonder vanishes, and we breathe a little freely again. Mr. Malthus is, however, by no means willing to give up his old doctrine, or *eat his own words*: he stickles stoutly for it at times. He has his fits of reason and his fits of extravagance, his yielding and his obstinate moments, fluctuating between the two, and vibrating backwards and forwards with a dexterity of self-contradiction which it is wonderful to behold. The following passage is so curious in this respect that I cannot help quoting it in this place. Speaking of the Reply of the author of the Political Justice to his former work, he observes, 'But Mr. Godwin says, that if he looks into the past history of the world, he does not see that increasing population has been controlled and confined by vice and misery *alone. In this observation I cannot agree with him.* I will thank Mr. Godwin to name to me any check, that in past ages has contributed to keep down the population to the level of the means of subsistence, that does not fairly come under some form of vice or misery; except indeed the check of *moral restraint, which I have mentioned in the course of this work*; and which to say the truth, whatever hopes we may entertain of its prevalence in future, has undoubtedly in past ages operated with very inconsiderable force.'[1] When I assure the reader that I give him this passage fairly and fully, I think he will be of opinion with me, that it would be difficult to produce an instance of a more miserable attempt to reconcile a contradiction by childish evasion, to insist upon an argument, and give it up in the same breath. Does Mr. Malthus really think that he has such an absolute right and authority over this subject of population, that provided he mentions a principle, or shews that he is not ignorant of it, and cannot be caught *napping* by the critics, he is at liberty to say that it has or has not had any operation, just as he pleases, and that the state of the fact is a matter of perfect indifference? He contradicts the opinion of Mr. Godwin that vice and misery are not the only checks to population, and gives as a proof of his assertion, that he himself truly has mentioned another check. Thus after flatly denying that moral restraint has any effect at all, he modestly concludes by saying that it has had some, no doubt, but promises that it will never have a great deal. Yet in the very next page, he says, 'On this sentiment, whether virtue, prudence or pride, which I have already noticed under the name of moral restraint, or of the more comprehensive title, the *preventive* check, it will appear, that in the sequel of this work, I shall lay considerable stress.' p. 385. This kind of reasoning is enough to give one the headache.

The most singular thing in this singular performance of our author is, that it should have been originally ushered into the world as the most complete and only satisfactory answer to the speculations of Godwin, Condorcet and others, or to what has been called the modern philosophy. A more complete piece of

---

[1] The prevalence of this check may be estimated *by the general proportion* of virtue and happiness in the world, for if there were no such check, there could be nothing but vice and misery.

wrong-headedness, a more strange perversion of reason could hardly be devised by the wit of man. Whatever we may think of the doctrine of the progressive improvement of the human mind, or of a state of society in which every thing will be subject to the absolute control of reason, however absurd, unnatural, or impracticable we may conceive such a system to be, certainly it cannot without the grossest inconsistency be objected to it, that such a system would necessarily be rendered abortive, because if reason should ever get the mastery over all our actions, we shall then be governed entirely by our physical appetites and passions, without the least regard to consequences. This appears to me a refinement on absurdity. Several philosophers and speculatists had supposed that a certain state of society very different from any that has hitherto existed was in itself practicable; and that if it were realised, it would be productive of a far greater degree of human happiness than is compatible with the present institutions of society. I have nothing to do with either of these points. I will allow to any one who pleases that all such schemes are 'false, sophistical, unfounded in the extreme.' But I cannot agree with Mr. Malthus that they would be *bad*, in proportion as they were *good*; that their excellence would be their ruin; or that the true and only unanswerable objection against all such schemes is that very degree of happiness, virtue, and improvement, to which they are supposed to give rise. And I cannot agree with him in this, because it is contrary to common sense, and leads to the subversion of every principle of moral reasoning. Without perplexing himself with the subtle arguments of his opponents, Mr. Malthus comes boldly forward, and says, 'Gentlemen, I am willing to make you large concessions, I am ready to allow the practicability and the desirableness of your schemes; the more happiness, the more virtue, the more refinement they are productive of, the better; all these will only add to the "exuberant strength of my argument"; I have a short answer to all objections, to be sure I found it in an old political receipt-book, called Prospects, &c. by one Wallace, a man not much known, but no matter for that, *finding is keeping*, you know:' and with one smart stroke of his wand, on which are inscribed certain mystical characters, and algebraic proportions, he levels the fairy enchantment with the ground. For, says Mr. Malthus, though this improved state of society were actually realised, it could not possibly continue, but must soon terminate in a state of things pregnant with evils far more insupportable than any we at present endure, in consequence of the excessive population which would follow, and the impossibility of providing for its support.

This is what I do not understand. It is, in other words, to assert that the doubling the population of a country, for example, after a certain period, will be attended with the most pernicious effects, by want, famine, bloodshed, and a state of general violence and confusion; this will afterwards lead to vices and practices still worse than the physical evils they are designed to prevent, &c. and yet that at this period those who will be the most interested in preventing these consequences, and the best acquainted with the circumstances that lead to them, will neither have the understanding to foresee, nor the heart to feel, nor the will to prevent the sure evils to which they expose themselves and others, though this advanced state of population, which does not admit of any addition without danger is supposed to be the immediate result of a more general diffusion of the comforts and conveniences of life, of more enlarged and liberal views, of a more refined and comprehensive regard to our own permanent interests, as well as those of others, of correspondent habits and manners, and of a state of things, in which our gross animal appetites will be subjected to the practical control of reason. The influence of rational motives, of refined and long-sighted views of things is supposed to have taken the lace of narrow, selfish, and merely sensual motives: this is implied in the very statement of the question. 'What conjuration and what mighty magic' should thus blind our philosophical descendants on this single subject in which they are more interested than in all the rest, so that they should stand with their eyes open on the edge of a precipice, and instead of retreating from it, should throw themselves down headlong, I cannot comprehend; unless indeed we suppose that the impulse to propagate the species is so strong and uncontrolable, that reason has no power over it. This is what Mr. Malthus was at one time strongly disposed to assert, and what he is at present half inclined to retract. Without this foundation to rest on, the whole of his reasoning is unintelligible. It seems to me a most childish way of answering any one, who chooses to assert that mankind are capable of being governed entirely by their reason, and that it would be better for them if they were, to say, No, for if they were governed entirely by it, they would be much less able to attend to its dictates than they are at present: and the evils, which would thus follow from the unrestrained increase of population, would be excessive. – Almost every little Miss, who has had the advantage of a boarding-school education, or been properly tutored by her mamma, whose hair is not of an absolute flame-colour, and who has hopes in time, if she behaves prettily, of getting a good husband, waits patiently year after year, looks about her, rejects or trifles with half a dozen lovers, favouring one, laughing at another, chusing among them 'as one picks pears, saying, this I like, that I loathe,' with the greatest indifference, as if it were no such very pressing affair, and *all the while behaves very prettily*:– why, what an idea does Mr. Malthus give us of the grave, masculine genius of our Utopian philosophers, their sublime attainments and gigantic energy, that they will not be able to manage these matters as decently and cleverly as the silliest woman can do at present! Mr. Malthus indeed endeavours to soften the absurdity by saying that moral restraint at present owes its strength to selfish motives: what is that to the purpose? If Mr. Malthus chooses to say, that men will always be governed by the same gross mechanical motives that they are at present, I have no objection to make to it; but it is shifting the question: it is not arguing against the state of society we are considering from the consequences to which it would give rise, but against the possibility of its ever existing. It is absurd to object to a system on account of the consequences which would follow if we once suppose men to be actuated by entirely different motives and principles from what they are at present, and then to say, that those consequences would necessarily follow, because men would never be what we suppose them. It is very idle to alarm the imagination by deprecating the evils that must follow from the practical adoption of a particular scheme, yet to allow that we have no reason to dread those consequences, but because the scheme itself is impracticable. – But I am ashamed of wasting the reader's time and my own in thus beating the air. It is not however my fault that Mr. Malthus had written nonsense, or that others have admired it. It is not Mr. Malthus's nonsense, but the opinion of the world respecting it, that I would be thought to compliment by this serious refutation of what in itself neither deserves nor admits of any reasoning upon it. If, however, we recollect the source from whence Mr. Malthus borrowed his principle and the application of it to improvements in political philosophy, we must allow that he is merely passive in error. The principle itself would not have been worth a farthing to him without the application, and accordingly he took them as he found them lying snug together; and as Trim having converted the old jackboots into a pair of new mortars immediately planted them against whichever of my uncle Toby's garrisons the allies were then busy in besieging, so the public-spirited gallantry of our modern engineer directed him to bend the whole force of his clumsy discovery against that system of philosophy which was the most talked of at the time, but to which it was the least applicable of all others. Wallace, I have no doubt, took up his idea either as a paradox, or a *jeu d'esprit*, or because any thing, he thought, was of weight enough to overturn what had never existed any where but in the imagination; or he was led into a piece of false logic by an error we are very apt to fall into, of supposing because he had never been struck himself by the difficulty of population in such a state of society, that therefore the people themselves would not find it out, nor make any provision against it. But though I can in some measure excuse a lively paradox, I do not think the same favour is to be shewn to the dull, dogged, voluminous repetition of an absurdity.

I cannot help thinking that our author has been too much influenced in his different feelings on this subject, by the particular purpose he had in view at the time. Mr. Malthus might not improperly have taken for the motto of his first edition, – 'These three bear record on earth, vice, misery, and population.' In his answer to Mr. Godwin, this principle was represented as an evil, for which no remedy could be found but in evil; – that its operation was mechanical, unceasing, necessary; that it went straight forward to its end, unchecked by fear, or reason, or remorse; that the evils, which it drew after it, could only be avoided by other evils, by actual vice and misery. Population was, in fact, the great Devil, the untamed Beelzebub that was only kept chained down by vice and misery, and which, if it were once let loose from these restraints, would go forth, and ravage the earth. That they were, of course, the two main props and pillars of society, and that the lower and weaker they kept this principle, the better able they were to contend with it: that therefore any diminution of that degree of them, which at present prevails, and is found sufficient to keep the world in order, was of all things chiefly to be dreaded. – Mr. Malthus seems fully aware of the importance of the stage-maxim, To elevate and surprise. Having once heated the imaginations of his readers, he knows that he can afterwards mould them into whatever shape he pleases. All this bustle and terror, and stage-effect, and theatrical mummery was only to serve a temporary purpose, for all of a sudden the scene is shifted, and the storm subsides. Having frighted away the boldest champions of modern philosophy, this monstrous appearance, full of strange and inexplicable horrors, is suffered quietly to shrink back to its natural dimensions, and we find it to be nothing more than a common-sized tame looking animal, which however requires a chain and the whip of its keeper to prevent it from becoming mischievous. Mr. Malthus then steps forward and says, 'The evil we were all in danger of was not population, – but philosophy. Nothing is to be done with the latter by mere reasoning. I, therefore, thought it right to make use of a little terror to accomplish the end. As to the principle of population you need be under no alarm; only leave it to me, and I shall be able to manage it very well. All its dreadful consequences may be easily prevented by a proper application of the motives of common prudence and common decency.' If, however, any one should be at a loss to know how it is possible to reconcile such contradictions, I would suggest to Mr. Malthus the answer which Hamlet makes to his friend Guilderstern, "Tis as easy as lying: govern these ventiges (the poor-rates and private charity) with your fingers and thumb, and this same instrument will discourse most excellent music; look you, here are the stops,' (namely, Mr. Malthus's Essay and Mr. Whitbread's Poor Bill).

# ON THE APPLICATION OF MR. MALTHUS'S PRINCIPLE TO THE POOR LAWS
[William Hazlitt]

In speaking of the abolition of the Poor Laws, Mr. Malthus says:–

'To this end, I should propose a regulation to be made, declaring, that no child born from any marriage, taking place after the expiration of a year from the date of the law, and no illegitimate child born two years from the same date, should ever be entitled to parish assistance. And to give a more general knowledge of this law, and to enforce it more strongly on the minds of the lower classes of people, the clergyman of each parish should, after the publication of banns, read a short address, stating the strong obligation on every man to support his own children; the impropriety, and even immorality, of marrying without a prospect of being able to do this; the evils which had resulted to the poor themselves from the attempt which had been made to assist by public institutions in a duty which ought to be exclusively appropriated to parents; and the absolute necessity which had at length appeared of abandoning all such institutions, on account of their producing effects totally opposite to those which were intended.

'This would operate as a fair, distinct, and precise notice, which no man could well mistake, and, without pressing hard on any particular individuals, would at once throw off the rising generation from that miserable and helpless dependence upon the government and the rich, the moral as well as physical consequences of which are almost incalculable.

'After the public notice which I have proposed had been given, and the system of poor-laws had ceased with regard to the rising generation, if any man chose to marry, without a prospect of being able to support a family, he should have the most perfect liberty so to do. Though to marry, in this

## Application of Malthus's Principle to the Poor Laws 185

case, is, in my opinion, clearly an immoral act, yet it is not one which society can justly take upon itself to prevent or punish; because the punishment provided for it by the laws of nature falls directly and most severely upon the individual who commits the act, and through him, only more remotely and feebly, on the society. When Nature will govern and punish for us, it is a very miserable ambition to wish to snatch the rod from her hands, and draw upon ourselves the odium of executioner. To the punishment therefore of Nature he should be left, the punishment of want. He has erred in the face of a most clear and precise warning, and can have no just reason to complain of any persons but himself when he feels the consequences of his error. All parish assistance should be most rigidly denied him; and he should be left to the uncertain support of private charity. He should be taught to know, that the laws of Nature, which are the laws of God, had doomed him and his family to starve,[1] for disobeying their repeated admonitions; that he had no claim of *right* on society for the smallest portion of food, beyond that which his labour would fairly purchase; and that if he and his family were saved from feeling the natural consequences of his imprudence, he would owe it to the pity of some kind benefactor, to whom, therefore, he ought to be bound by the strongest ties of gratitude.'

This passage has been well answered by Mr. Cobbett in one word, 'Parson': – the most expressive apostrophe that ever was made; and it might be answered as effectually by another word, which I shall omit. When Mr. Malthus asserts, that the poor man and his family have been doomed to starve by the laws of nature, which are the laws of God, he means by the laws of God and nature, the physical and necessary inability of the earth to supply food for more than a certain number of human beings; but if he means that the wants of the poor arise from the impossibility of procuring food for them, while the rich roll in abundance, or, we will say, maintain their dogs and horses, &c. out of their ostentatious superfluities, he asserts what he knows not to be true. Mr. Malthus wishes to confound the necessary limits of the produce of the earth with the arbitrary and artificial distribution of the produce according to the institutions of society, or the caprice of individuals, the laws of

---

[1] Altered in the last edition, to 'suffer.'

God and nature with the laws of man. And what proves the fallacy is, that the laws of man in the present case actually afford the relief, which he would wilfully deny; he proposes to repeal those laws, and then to tell the poor man impudently, that 'the laws of God and nature have doomed him and his family to starve, for disobeying their repeated admonitions,' stuck on the church-door for the last twelve months! 'Tis much.

I have in a separate work made the following remarks on the above proposal, which are a little cavalier, not too cavalier; – a little contemptuous, not too contemptuous; a little gross, but not too gross for the subject. –

'I am not sorry that I am at length come to this page. It will I hope decide the reader's opinion of the benevolence, wisdom, piety, candour, and disinterested simplicity of Mr. Malthus's mind. Any comments that I might make upon it to strengthen this impression must be faint and feeble. I give up the task of doing justice to the moral beauties that pervade every line of it, in despair. These are some instances of an heroical contempt for the narrow prejudices of the world, of a perfect refinement from the vulgar feelings of human nature, that must only suffer by a comparison with any thing else.

I shall not myself be so uncandid as not to confess, that I think the poor laws bad things; and that it would be well, if they could be got rid of, consistently with humanity and justice. This I do not think they could in the present state of things, and other circumstances remaining as they are. The reason why I object to Mr. Malthus's plan is, that it does not go to the root of the evil, or attack it in its principle, but its effects. He confounds the cause with the effect. The wide spreading tyranny, dependence, indolence, and unhappiness, of which Mr. Malthus is so sensible, are not occasioned by the increase of the poor-rates, but these are the natural consequence of that increasing tyranny, dependence, indolence, and unhappiness occasioned by other causes.

Mr. Malthus desires his readers to look at the enormous proportion in which the poor-rates have increased within the last ten years. But have they increased in any greater proportion than the other taxes, which rendered them necessary, and, which I think, were employed for much more

# Application of Malthus's Principle to the Poor Laws 187

mischievous purposes? I would ask, what have the poor got by their encroachments for the last ten years? Do they work less hard? Are they better fed? Do they marry oftener, and with better prospects? Are they grown pampered and insolent? Have they changed places with the rich? Have they been cunning enough, by means of the poor-laws, to draw off all their wealth and superfluities from the men of property? Have they got so much as a quarter of an hour's leisure, a farthing candle, or a cheese-paring more than they had? Has not the price of provisions risen enormously? Has not the price of labour almost stood still? Have not the government and the rich had their way in every thing? Have they not gratified their ambition, their pride, their obstinacy, their ruinous extravagance? Have they not squandered the resources of the country as they pleased? Have they not heaped up wealth on themselves, and their dependents? Have they not multiplied sinecures, places, and pensions? Have they not doubled the salaries of those that existed before? Has there been any want of new creations of peers, who would thus be impelled to beget heirs to their titles and estates, and saddle the younger branches of their rising families, by means of their new influence, on the country at large? Has there been any want of contracts, of loans, of monopolies of corn, of a good understanding between the rich and the powerful to assist one another, and to fleece the poor? Have the poor prospered? Have the rich declined? What then have they to complain of? What ground is there for the apprehension, that wealth is secretly changing hands, and that the whole property of the country will shortly be absorbed in the poor's fund? Do not the poor create their own fund? Is not the necessity for such a fund first occasioned by the unequal weight with which the rich press upon the poor; and has not the increase of that fund in the last ten years been occasioned by the additional exorbitant demands, which have been made upon the poor and industrious, which, without some assistance from the public, they could not possibly have answered? Whatever is the increase in the nominal amount of the poor's fund, will not the rich always be able ultimately to throw the burthen of it on the poor themselves? But Mr. Malthus is a man of general principles. He cares little about these circumstantial details, and petty objections. He takes higher ground. He deduces all his conclusions, by an infallible logic, from the laws of God and nature. When our Essayist shall prove to me, that by these paper bullets of the brain, by his ratios of the increase of food, and the increase of mankind, he has prevented one additional tax, or taken off one oppressive duty, that he has made a single rich man retrench one article at his table: that he has made him keep a dog or a horse the less, or part with a single vice, arguing from a mathematical admeasurement of the size of the earth, and the number of inhabitants it can contain, he shall have my perfect leave to disclaim the right of the poor to subsistence, and to tie them down by severe penalties to their good behaviour, on the same profound principles. But why does Mr. Malthus practise his demonstrations on the poor only? Why are they to have a perfect system of rights and duties prescribed to them? I do not see why they alone should be put to live on these metaphysical board-wages, why they should be forced to submit to a course of *abstraction*; or why it should be meat and drink to them, more than to others, to do the will of God. Mr. Malthus's gospel is preached only to the poor! – Even if I approved of our author's plan, I should object to the principle on which it is founded. The parson of the parish, when a poor man comes to be married – No, not so fast. The author does not say, whether the lecture he proposes is to be read to the poor only, or to all ranks of people. Would it not sound oddly, if when the squire, who is himself worth a hundred thousand pounds, is going to be married to the rector's daughter, who is to have fifty, the curate should read them a formal lecture on their obligation to maintain their own children and not turn them on the parish? Would it be necessary to go through the form of the address, when an amorous couple of eighty presented themselves at the altar? If the admonition were left to the parson's own discretion, what affronts would he not subject himself to, from his neglect of old maids, and superannuated widows, and from his applying himself familiarly to the little shop-keeper, or thriving mechanic? Well, then, let us suppose that a very poor hard-working man comes to be married, and that the clergyman can take the liberty with him: he is to warn him first against fornication, and in the next place against matrimony. These are the two greatest sins which a poor man can commit, who can neither be supposed to keep his

## Application of Malthus's Principle to the Poor Laws 189

wife, nor his girl. Mr. Malthus, however, does not think them equal: for he objects strongly to a country fellow's marrying a girl whom he has debauched, or, as the phrase is, making an honest woman of her, as aggravating the crime; because, by this means, the parish will probably have three or four children to maintain instead of one. However, as it seems rather too late to give advice to a man who is actually come to be married, it is most natural to suppose that he would marry the young woman in spite of the lecture. Here then he errs in the fact of a precise warning, and should be left to the punishment of *nature*, the punishment of severe want. When he begins to feel the consequences of his error, all parish assistance is to be rigidly denied him, and the interests of humanity imperiously require that all other assistance should be withheld from him, or most sparingly administered. In the meantime, to reconcile him to this treatment, and let him see that he has nobody to complain of but himself, the parson of the parish comes to him with the certificate of his marriage, and a copy of the warning he had given him at the time, by which he is taught to know that the laws of nature, which are the laws of God, had doomed him and his family to starve for disobeying their repeated admonitions; that he had no claim of right to the smallest portion of food beyond what his labour would actually purchase; and that he ought to kiss the feet and lick the dust off the shoes of him, who gave him a reprieve from the just sentence which the laws of God and nature had passed upon him. To make this clear to him, it would be necessary to put the Essay on Population into his hands, to instruct him in the nature of a geometrical and arithmetical series, in the necessary limits to population from the size of the earth; and here would come in Mr. Malthus's plan of education for the poor, writing, arithmetic, the use of the globes, &c. for the purpose of proving to them the necessity of their being starved. It cannot be supposed that the poor man (what with his poverty and what with being priest-ridden) should be able to resist this body of evidence, he would open his eyes to his error, and "would submit to the sufferings that were absolutely irremediable, with the fortitude of a man, and the resignation of a Christian." He and his family might then be sent round the parish in a starving condition, accompanied by the constables and *quondam* overseers of the poor, to see that no person, blind to "the interests of humanity," practised upon them the abominable deception of attempting to relieve their remediless sufferings; and by the parson of the parish, to point out to the spectators the inevitable consequences of sinning against the laws of God and man. By celebrating a number of these *Auto da fes* yearly in every parish, the greatest publicity would be given to the principle of population, "the strict line of duty would be pointed out to every man," enforced by the most powerful sanctions; justice and humanity would flourish, they would be understood to signify that the poor have no right to live by their labour, and that the feelings of compassion and benevolence are best shewn by denying them charity; the poor would no longer be dependent on the rich, the rich could no longer wish to reduce the poor into a more complete subjection to their will, all causes of contention, of jealousy, and of irritation would have ceased between them, the struggle would be over, each class would fulfil the task assigned by heaven; the rich would oppress the poor without remorse, the poor would submit to oppression with a pious gratitude and resignation; the greatest harmony would prevail between the government and the people; there would be no longer any seditions, tumults, complaints, petitions, partisans of liberty, or tools of power; no grumbling, no repining, no discontented men of talents proposing reforms, and frivolous remedies, but we should all have the same gaiety and lightness of heart, and the same happy spirit of resignation that a man feels when he is seized with the plague, who thinks no more of the physician, but knows that his disorder is without cure. The best-laid schemes are subject, however, to unlucky reverses. Some such seem to lie in the way of that pleasing Euthanasia, and contented submission to the grinding law of necessity, projected by Mr. Malthus. We might never reach the philosophic temper of the inhabitants of modern Greece and Turkey in this respect. Many little things might happen to interrupt our progress, if we were put into ever so fair a train. For instance, the men might perhaps be talked over by the parson, and their understandings being convinced by the geometrical and arithmetical ratios, or at least so far puzzled, that they would have nothing to say for themselves, they might prepare to submit to their fate with a tolerable grace. But I am afraid that the women might prove

## Application of Malthus's Principle to the Poor Laws 191

refractory. They never will hearken to reason, and are much more governed by their feelings than by calculations. While the husband was instructing his wife in the principles of population, she might probably answer that "she did not see why her children should starve, when the squire's lady or the parson's lady kept half a dozen lap-dogs, and that it was but the other day, that being at the hall, or the parsonage-house, she heard Miss declare that not one of the brood that were just littered should be drowned – It was *so inhuman* to kill the poor little things – Surely the children of the poor are as good as puppy-dogs! Was it not a week ago that the rector had a new pack of terriers sent down, and did I not hear the squire swear a tremendous oath, that he would have Mr. Such-a-one's fine hunter, if it cost him a hundred guineas? Half that sum would save us from ruin." – After this curtain-lecture, I conceive that the husband might begin to doubt the force of the demonstrations he had read and heard, and the next time his clerical monitor came, might pluck up courage to question the matter with him; and as we of the male sex, though dull of apprehension, are not slow at taking a hint, and can draw tough inferences from it, it is not impossible but the parson might be *gravelled*. In consequence of these accidents happening more than once, it would be buzzed about that the laws of God and nature, on which so many families had been doomed to starve, were not so clear as had been pretended. This would soon get wind amongst the mob: and at the next grand procession of the Penitents of famine, headed by Mr. Malthus in person, some discontented man of talents, who could not bear the distresses of others with the fortitude of a man and the resignation of a Christian, might undertake to question Mr. Malthus, whether the laws of nature or of God, to which he had piously sacrificed so many victims, signified any thing more than the limited extent of the earth, and the natural impossibility of providing for more than a limited number of human beings; and whether those laws could be justly put in force, to the very letter, while the actual produce of the earth, by being better husbanded, or more equally distributed, or given to men and not to beasts, might maintain in comfort double the number that actually existed, and who, not daring to demand a *fair* proportion of the produce of their labour, humbly crave charity, and are refused out of regard to the interests of justice and humanity. Our philosopher, at this critical juncture not being able to bring into the compass of a few words all the history, metaphysics, morality, and divinity, or all the intricacies, subtleties, and callous equivocations contained in his quarto volume, might hesitate and be confounded – his own feelings and prejudices might add to his perplexity – his interrogator might persist in his question – the mob might become impatient for an answer, and not finding one to their minds, might proceed to extremities. Our unfortunate Essayist (who by that time would have become a bishop) might be ordered to the lamp-post, and his book committed to the flames, – I tremble to think of what would follow: – the poor-laws would be again renewed, and the poor no longer doomed to starve by the laws of God and nature! Some such, I apprehend, might be the consequences of attempting to enforce the abolition of the poor-laws, the extinction of private charity, and of instructing the poor in their metaphysical rights.'

Art. VII. *A short Inquiry into the Policy, Humanity, and past Effects of the Poor Laws.* By one of his Majesty's Justice of the Peace for the Three Inland Counties. 8vo. London. 1807.

Without meaning to derogate from the importance of those political laws by which civil liberty is secured, we may be permitted to observe, that mankind have generally appeared a little too fearful of the tyranny of their rulers, and somewhat too indifferent about their ignorance. With respect to the leading objects of civil liberty, this may, perhaps, be right. It requires no great depth of thought to provide against the undisguised outrages of despotism; and accordingly, where the spirit of freedom has prevailed, legislators have been generally successful in devising effectual securities for the enjoyment of those privileges which are essential to freedom. In the more delicate arrangements of internal policy, however, ignorance may be fully as mischievous as bad intention; it is of little importance that legislators are elected according to the forms of a free constitution, if they do not know how to direct their power to the only proper and rational end, the happiness of the people; and as a statesman, whose mind is enlightened with liberal notions of policy, can have no imaginable motive to withhold from mankind the benefits of his wisdom, the welfare of the people may, in many important points, be more successfully promoted under an absolute government, where the legislators are well instructed, than under a free government, where they are ignorant or incapable. It is a very great mistake to ascribe all the miseries of mankind to malignant abuses of power; a very great portion of the mischief which has resulted from misgovernment, may be referred to the injudicious attempts of their rulers to ameliorate their condition. The schemes of Frederic of Prussia, and of Joseph of Austria, for the encouragement of commerce, were singularly pernicious and absurd, and produced, undoubtedly, a great deal of individual distress; yet, it cannot be doubted, that their intentions were to encourage commerce, although it would have been much for the advantage of their subjects that they had exercised a less watchful superintendance over their concerns. In endeavouring also to provide a decent subsistence for the poor, the English legislature, with the most benevolent anxiety for their welfare, are generally acknowledged to have aggravated their misery, instead of having relieved it. The mischiefs which their ill-judged efforts have brought upon society, clearly show the importance of that science, which professes not so much to benefit mankind by exhibiting for their choice perfect patterns of political constitutions, as by enlightening those who administer the systems that are established. There is no doubt that the authors of the English poor laws were actuated by the purest and most upright intentions; and yet the practical evil which has flowed from their erring benevolence, has scarcely fallen short of what tyrants have contrived to accomplish.

The present publication seems to have originated in the best intentions; and if we had nothing to do but with the design and motives of the work, we should feel it to be our duty to bestow on it unqualified praise. The author frequently displays a very laudable anxiety for the welfare of the poor; he seems to have bestowed no common attention on the subject; and we can only lament, that his zeal (at least as far as this performance is concerted) should have been so unprofitably directed. His views on the poor laws, and on all the great questions connected with that important subject, are wild and impracticable, founded entirely on narrow notions, or exploded errors; and the projects of reformation which he recommends, would infallibly aggravate the evils which they are intended to remedy, by adding to that mass of paltry devices and artificial regulations by which the great arrangements of society are already too much obstructed. Although we must do him the justice to say, that his mind is not tainted with any illiberal antipathy to Mr Malthus, yet he appears to have perused his work with a predetermined resolution to misunderstand his views. We really scarcely can refrain from sympathising with that eminent philosopher, who, though he has enlarged the boundaries of science, and entitled himself to the rare commendation of having added to that class of important truths which have only to be explained in order to command our immediate assent, yet seems destined to be either the sport of misconception or the object of the most indecent and acrimonious abuse. Our author seems also conversant in Dr Smith's writings, and really to understand the plainer doctrines of political economy, when they are brought to bear on a particular case; but he is sure to bewilder himself in general speculation: his delusions are not even plausible: and although he may have made himself familiar with a few elementary principles of the science, he certainly has not imbibed any thing of the spirit of that enlightened philosophy which has dawned upon all his schemes of reformation consist entirely of artificial regulations and restraints; he tears to pieces the natural order of society, without the smallest compunction – as if there could not be a fitter subject for the experiments of thoughtless projectors. Nothing, however, is so amusing as the great affection which this learned justice professes, on all occasions, for penalties. The whole of his complicated machinery is to be kept right by means of penalties; if any of his devices and regulations fail in their intended object, those who are entrusted with carrying them into effect, are to be loaded with heavy penalties; the zeal and vigilance of the many officers, who are created by his plan, are to be stimulated by penalties; if the discretionary power, which makes such a conspicuous figure in all his arrangements, is abused, he has again recourse to penalties, penalties, in short, like the warm water and phlebotomy of the renowned Sangrado, appear to be considered by our author as an infallible specific for the most obstinate disorders that can afflict the body politic. As it appears to us that the absurdity of this work will generally prove an effectual antidote to the errors which it contains, we propose to give but a very brief summary of its contents, pointing out, as we proceed, the various delusions into which the author has been betrayed. We shall then venture to lay before our readers a few general observations on the important subject on which it treats.

The greater part of those reasoners who are in the habit of misunderstanding and misrepresenting Mr Malthus, would have some chance of attaining clearer views on the subject of population, if, instead of indulging themselves in rambling declamation, they would attend to the very simple proposition from which his doctrines are deduced, namely, that the human race have a tendency to increase faster than food can be provided for them. If this proposition be true, then it necessarily follows, that the only effectual encouragement which can be given to population is to increase the agricultural produce of a country; and if population be increased without a corresponding increase of food, they must starve, or, at least, be reduced to the most extreme misery. Our author, however, has found out that Mr Malthus proposes to repress the population by artificial checks; and he set out immediately with declaiming in favour of a *redundant* population, showing how intimately it is connected with national strength, and quoting Bacon and Locke on the subject. He then proceeds to observe, that the population of a country is not limited by the quantity of food which it produces, but that it may support a greater population by *importing* corn; and that a commercial and manufacturing country, by exchanging its manufactures for the produce of an agricultural nation, can easily procure an addition to the quantity of subsistence which its own territory will produce. The number of its inhabitants, therefore, depends, according to our author, not on the quantity of food which it produces, but on the demand for men, and on the high price of labour.

Now, we do not recollect that Mr Malthus has any where ventured to assert, that an additional population cannot be subsisted on imported corn; so that his doctrines are no way affected by this statement of our author's; and as to the quibble about population not depending on the relative quantity of food, but on the demand for labour, it will be sufficient to observe, that if population depends on the demand for labour, the demand for labour depends on the relative quantity of subsistence. It is not money which really constitutes the wages of labour; but it is what money can purchase, namely, the necessaries and conveniences of life. Without a sufficient quantity of corn, therefore, for the food of the labourer, how could there be any demand for labour, when there could not be funds for its payment? Notwithstanding, however, our resources from imported corn, there is another circumstance which fills our author with various alarms for the population. Owing to the favourable state of society which prevails in Britain, the labourer, he observes, will not marry unless his wages are such as to enable him to command a competent quantity of the necessaries and even the luxuries of life. High wages, he appears to imagine, discourage population. He is never at a loss, however, for a scheme, and accordingly proposes, that, to encourage the labourer to marry, a poor rate should be imposed in order to make up his wages to the sum necessary for that purpose, as if an increase of population could be supported by donations of money. Another notable effect which would follow from this device would be, that as high wages raise the price for our manufactures, and thus discourage their exportation, by giving the labourer part of his wages in the form of a poor rate, we would keep wages low; in other words, we would bribe the labourer with high wages to work cheap!

Next follows what the author calls 'A historical deduction of the effects of the poor laws in England.' He informs us, at great length, that England has been increasing, since the days of Elizabeth, in prosperity, in opulence, and in population; all which, we are given to understand, is wholly to be ascribed to the operation of the poor laws. It appears to us to be so extremely absurd to assert that population can be increased by means of the poor laws, that we cannot refrain from submitting the following argument to the attention of our author. Supposing a country able to support, in tolerable comfort, from the produce of its own territory, along with what it can import, a population of 1,000,000, is he prepared to maintain, that by taxing the rich, in order to give to each labourer an addition to his weekly wages of five shillings, the country would be enabled to support a greater number of inhabitants in the same degree of comfort? If he is not prepared to go to this length, his argument, respecting the increase of population derived from the poor laws, falls instantly to the ground.

The humanity of those institutions for the relief of the poor, is also a favourite topic of declamation with this writer; and although we fully acquit him of any design to do injustice to Mr Malthus, he has certainly contrived to exhibit him in a very unfair and unamiable light to his readers. After complimenting him on the openness and boldness with which he avows his doctrines in the face of popular obloquy, he observes, that it is, however, a matter of great joy to those who differ from him in opinion, that 'in indulging the finer feelings of the heart, they are at the same time promoting the best interests of the country; that in encouraging marriage, and, as they believe, happiness and morality among the lower orders, –in assisting women, at a time when they are most of all in need of comfort and support, – and in helping them to rear their children in soundness of body and mind, they are employed in preparing the instruments of their country's welfare and prosperity, and not sowing the seeds of want, vice, and misery; that in *rescuing the trembling limbs of age from cold and wretchedness*, they are not bestowing upon idleness the encouragements due only to virtue and industry.' In what part of the Essay on Population, we beg leave to ask, are men forbid to 'indulge the finer feelings of the heart;' to 'assist women, when they are most of all in need of comfort and support;' or, 'to rescue the trembling limbs of age from cold and wretchedness?' Mr Malthus expressly states, in various parts of his work, that if it were possible to draw, from the resources of the rich, the means of ameliorating the condition of the poor, he should have no objection to impose a very heavy assessment for that purpose. But it is because the poor laws, instead of 'rescuing the trembling limbs of age from cold and wretchedness,' are a most fertile source of misery to the poor, that Mr Malthus wishes them to be gradually abolished. We do not, therefore, see the necessity of such an ostentatious parade of the 'finer feelings of the heart' upon this occasion: to say the least of it, it appears to be quite useless and inapplicable.

As far as the principles of Mr Malthus respect public charity, we do not think they can well be controverted. But it does not appear to us, that they furnish a rule for the exercise of private charity. There is an essential difference between public and private benevolence. All schemes for the general relief of the poor must proceed on views of justice and policy alone. There is a risk, lest profuse liberality should encourage improvidence, or produce other mischiefs, of which we may not be at first aware: we must not only look, therefore, at the particular object to be relieved, but we must consider what may be the effect of our exertions on the general happiness of the community. In the charitable donations of individuals, the case is entirely different; the practice of benevolence is enjoined to those who have neither the capacity nor the means of being informed about the general good; their object, therefore, is to relieve misery; and the principal object of their inquiry will naturally be, the necessities of the object on whom their charity is to be bestowed. There is no danger that the liberality of individuals will ever flow so certainly, or so abundantly, as to draw after it any sort of dependance. Private benevolence, therefore, far from appearing as the stern judge of human frailties, relieves, not those only who have fallen into distress from no fault of their own, but those also who have no plea to offer but that of actual wretchedness: genuine benevolence, in short, visits and relieves distress without any strict inquiry into its cause, wherever it is to be found. We cannot therefore agree with Mr Malthus, that the hand of private benevolence should be very sparingly stretched out, for the relief of those who have involved themselves in difficulties by the imprudence of an early marriage. Whatever bad effects a propensity to early marriages, among the labouring classes of the community, might produce on the general state of society, yet the error (if it be an error) is, with respect to individuals, of the most venial kind; and, even if merit or demerit is to be taken as the scale by which we are to measure out our benevolence, we do not by any means think that they will be placed at the bottom of it. On the other hand, however, we entirely concur with Mr Malthus, that they are not proper objects of public charity, because the certainty of this resource would obviously create the mischief which it is intended to relieve.

Our author, after having recovered from this burst of philanthropy, endeavours to obviate the objections which have been made to the poor laws. For this purpose he extenuates their evils, which he classes with those petty irregularities from which no comprehensive arrangement of policy can be free; and declaims against those, who, in political contrivances, aim at theoretic perfection. Instead of being discouraged by the evils incident to the system, we should *make new laws* (he observes) to counteract these evils. He accordingly proposes a scheme of regulations, for excluding those who have not been provident and saving when they had it in their power, from all participation in the benefits of the poor laws; which has only one fault, namely, that it is utterly impracticable. It would also, he imagines, tend greatly to produce economy among the labouring classes, if offices were erected by government, for receiving such trifling sums as they should have saved from their earnings: parish schools, he thinks, ought also to be established for their instruction, and cottages, with three or four acres of waste land, should be bestowed on those labourers who have brought up three children, or more, to a certain age; provided, however, they have given them such instruction *as should seem good to the legislature*. With respect to offices established by government, it requires no great foresight to perceive, that it would soon turn out to be a most useless and ridiculous job. We know of no labourers who have either the opportunity or the inclination to lay up money: when they save any thing from their wages, they generally deposit it in the fund of a friendly society, as a resource against sickness or old age. If, however, a labourer is determined upon hoarding, he will always find some creditable individual who will pay him interest for the smallest sums; he must, of course, be subjected to all the risks of other lenders, and must, like them, exert his vigilance to avoid them. But, in truth, it is of more consequence to observe, that this watchful superintendance over the poor, – this constant tampering with all their concerns, which seems to have infected the higher orders of society, is calculated to reduce them to a state of the most helpless ignorance and improvidence; and, by dispensing, in their case, with the exercise of all those virtues which steer other men through the hazards of life, to strip them of every energetic and manly quality. The establishment of schools for their instruction might certainly be attended with good effects; but the plan of providing cottages for those who may have brought up three children to a certain age, besides being fantastic in its principle, seems quite impracticable. Men have sufficient motives to bring up their children with decency and propriety without any reward; and if they do not find a sufficient recompense in the feelings of their own minds, we do not think that the prospect of living in an eleemosynary cottage will furnish an effectual inducement. Besides, how is it certain that these cottages would be bestowed on meritorious objects? It appears to us quite as likely that they would be the asylum of indolence, as of industry. The great fault of all complex contrivances is, that they are apt to be perverted from their objects by those who are entrusted with their execution; and they always prove, sooner or later, a receptacle of the most pernicious abuses. On reading all these fine schemes for the benefit of the poor, one would naturally imagine that they must be in a most wretched situation where nothing of that kind is attempted for their relief. In Scotland, however, we have neither government bank offices, nor cottages, nor work-houses, and yet the condition of the labouring part of the community is extremely comfortable. They are provident and economical, – principally, we believe, because they are well educated, and not liable to be debased in their habits by a system of poor laws.

From one hopeless project our author proceeds to another equally hopeless, namely, the employment of the poor. Before the expedience of any plan for this purpose can be admitted, he must prove, first, that the fear of want is not of itself a sufficient stimulus to industry; and, 2dly, that where plenty of work is to be had, those who are in want of it cannot seek it out for themselves, without the assistance of the legislature. The laws for the employment of the poor have, it seems, fallen into almost total neglect; and our author, with his usual sagacity, infers, that their execution must have been placed in improper hands. For amending this defect, he proposes a very complicated scheme, into the details of which, however we really cannot enter particularly. Several parishes are to be erected into a district, over which one officer is to preside, - his diligence and activity to be encouraged by rewards, and enforced by *heavy penalties*. As a centre of general communication for the whole country, a Board of Commissioners is to be established in London, 'consisting of the most *enlightened* and *independent* gentlemen of large fortune, well acquainted with the commercial and agricultural interests of their country; serving without salary; and bound to the strict discharge of their duty *under penalties*.' Any partiality or imposition on the part of the district officer, to be also punished with *very heavy penalties*.

A whole chapter is next devoted to an inquiry into the cause of the augmentation which has taken place in the poor rates, which is in a great measure ascribed to the great rise in the price of all the necessaries of life. Our author then proceeds to inquire, why England, which was formerly an exporting country, is now obliged to import. This he seems to consider as the chief cause of the distresses of the poor; and he accordingly suggests various plans for removing it; all of which have for their object the increase of the agricultural produce of the country. But as we do not believe, that, if the condition of the poor in England be depressed, it is at all owing to the circumstance of our importing corn, neither do we think the evil would be permanently removed, by increasing the quantity of food produced in the country. The condition of the labourer depends on the relation between the supply of food, and the population among whom the food is to be divided. It is a matter of no consequence to him, whether it be produced in the country, or whether it be imported, provided there is an abundant supply. If his situation is depressed, an increase of agricultural produce will no doubt relieve him for a time; but population will soon increase, and the same difficulties will again recur. It is not on the absolute supply of food, but on its relative supply, that the condition of the labourer depends; and this supply will be great or small, according to the degree in which the preventive check to population prevails. As an addition to the agricultural produce of the country will not, however, prevent the recurrence of scarcity, our author has another recipe for that purpose. He proposes to transport 25,000 Chinese to the Cape of Good Hope, for the purpose of raising a surplus supply of food, which is to be in part collected by the governor in payment of taxes, and warehoused, until the state of the supply shall be known in Britain, where it can be imported if required, and, if not, it is to be exported to other countries, even at a loss! It is quite amusing to consider our author's schemes. Before such a projector, all sort of difficulties vanish. Even the ordinary operations of nature are accelerated, if they happen to be too slow (as indeed they generally are) for bringing his projects to maturity. The work concludes with a proposal for rendering every species of income rateable to the poor laws. As the system, however, appears to us to be radically wrong, we should decidedly object to any plan by which a greater sum would be collected. Our author's object is indeed not to increase the burden, but to distribute it more equally. We have no doubt, however, that the consequence would be, the collection of a larger sum, which would only serve to increase beggary and dependance, and, instead of relieving the poor, to render them more wretched. Having now concluded our remarks on the work before us, we shall lay before our readers a general view of the spirit and tendency of all those plans which have been adopted for ameliorating the condition of the poor.

When persons belonging to that class of society by whom the rest are clothed, lodged and fed, fall into misery and poverty, not through any fault of their own, but from the visitation of providence, it appears, at first view, to be exceedingly just and reasonable, that those who have profited by their industry, should, in the day of their calamity, help to mitigate their distress. In order to give effect to this apparently benevolent principle, various schemes have been suggested. It has sometimes been proposed to regulate the wages of labour so as always to ensure to the labourer a competent command over the necessaries and simpler luxuries of life; at other times, large sums of money have been levied on the rich to relieve the sufferings of the poor; or when labour was supposed to be scarce, plans have been set on foot for their support by finding work for the labourer. The impossibility, however, of raising by artificial regulations the wages of those who work, or of relieving their sufferings when their wages are inadequate, either by giving them money or by furnishing them with work when the effectual fund for the support of labour has declined, has been very clearly demonstrated by several writers, particularly by Mr Malthus, whose reasonings have thrown quite a new light on this interesting subject.

In the system of English poor laws, *all* these different expedients are occasionally made use of to relieve the distresses of the poor. By the 43d of Elizabeth, the justices are empowered to levy a general assessment for the relief of the impotent; they are also required to set poor children to work, or those who are able to work and cannot find employment. 'What is this (Mr Malthus observes) but saying that the funds for the maintenance of labour in this country may be increased at will, and without limit, by the *fiat* of government, or an assessment of the overseers? Strictly speaking, this clause is as arrogant, and as absurd, as if it had enacted that two ears of wheat should in future grow, where one only had grown before. Canute, when he commanded the waves not to wet his princely feet, did not in reality assume a greater power over the laws of nature. No directions are given to the overseer how to increase the funds for the maintenance of labour; the necessity of industry, economy, and enlightened exertion, in the management of agricultural capital, is not insisted on, for this purpose; but it is expected that a miraculous increase of these funds should immediately follow an edict of government made at the discretion of some ignorant parish officer.'

The same act gives to the justices an unlimited power of levying whatever assessment they may think necessary for the relief of the poor; it enables them also, to judge who are fit objects of public charity. Nothing is so contrary to the spirit of sound legislation, as the unnecessary creation of discretionary power; and it need excite little surprise, when the legislators of the land, abdicating their own natural functions, have confided the exercise of such a delicate trust to the justice of the peace, that abuse and corruption have been the consequence. To provide a full and certain relief, even for the infirm and the impotent, must tend to render them beggarly and improvident. But in England the objects of parochial relief have been greatly multiplied. It has been thought necessary to offer charity to the labourer in full possession of health and strength. And what is still more revolting to every idea of sound policy and common sense, the *quantum* of relief given to him is proportioned to the high price of corn; which is the same thing as saying, that he shall consume the same quantity of subsistence when it is scarce, as when it is plenty; when it is not to give him, as when it is to give him; in short, that the great majority of the community shall never feel the pressure of scarcity. Agreeably to these notions, a table was published for the information of magistrates and overseers, in which the sum necessary for the support of the labourer was computed according as the price of bread should vary, or as the labourer's family should be either small or large. By this mode of computation, it may easily be conceived, what an enormous assessment would be requisite in a time of scarcity, to give to the labourer the sum necessary for his support according to the price of bread in 1795. Twenty-five shillings in the week was the sum allotted for the support of a labourer with a family of seven children. This principle was acted upon very generally during the scarcity of 1795, and during the scarcities also of 1799 and 1800; and the weekly allowance which the labourer received frequently exceeded his wages. Mr Malthus mentions, that he has known a labourer whose earnings amounted to ten shillings *per* week, receive fourteen shillings from the parish. 'Such instances (he observes) could not possibly have been universal, without raising the price of wheat very much higher than it was during any part of the dearth. But similar instances were by no means infrequent; and the system itself, of measuring the relief given by the price of grain, was general.' After being made acquainted with these facts, it need excite very little surprise, that the poor laws, as they are administered, have succeeded in some measure in debasing the character of the common people in England; and that, in some parishes, every fourth man receives parish relief. The enormous sums which have been squandered away for the vain purpose of enabling the labourer to consume the same quantity of corn when it is scarce as when it is plenty, have an obvious tendency to raise its money price, and thus to depress the condition of all those who do not receive parish relief. The poor laws thus contribute to create the poor whom they maintain.

When there is a scarcity of subsistence, it is perfectly evident, that want must be felt somewhere; and even if it were possible entirely to relieve the labourer, the evil would not be removed; it would be only transferred to another class of the community. The good to be done in a time of scarcity by pecuniary contributions is quite partial: it does not even palliate the general evil; it only relieves one person at the expense of another. The middling classes of the community, were, according to Mr Malthus, visibly depressed by the extravagant largesses which were squandered on the poor in 1799 and 1800. And he shows, clearly indeed, that this must have been the case. The reasonings of that writer on the subject of the poor laws, are truly admirable for their clearness and their originality. The evils which were at that time produced by the inconsiderate profusion with which parochial relief was granted, were too visible to escape the notice of the most superficial observer; but while other writers busied themselves in criticising and in amending paltry details, Mr Malthus went to the bottom of the evil, and showed that the system was so vicious in its principle, that no amendments could render it beneficial. Even if eighteen shillings in the pound were levied for the relief of the poor, Mr Malthus shows, that the poor would not be relieved. 'Great changes (he observes) might indeed be made. The rich might become poor, and some of the poor rich; but, while the present proportion between the population and the food continues, a part of society must necessarily find it difficult to support a family; but this difficulty will necessarily fall on the least fortunate members.' That the poor laws may mitigate cases of severe distress, appears probable. But when it is considered, that they necessarily require a system of harsh and tyrannical restraint – that they obstruct the free circulation of labour – that they are a constant source of tyranny, contention, and legal wrangling, and that they tend to produce alienation between the rich and the poor, rendering the poor thankless and beggarly, and the rich hard-hearted; we may well inquire whether the good which the produce, could not be procured without such a lamentable train of attendant evils.

The mischief produced by the poor laws, seems to have been insisted on by almost every writer on the subject; and Burnet[1] in the excellent remarks with which he closes his history, seems to be decidedly of opinion, that they ought to be abolished. Most writers, however, object to the administration of the poor laws, than to the principles on which they are founded; and they have accordingly suggested various improvements and emendations. They put down the present scheme of regulations, in order to make way for a set of their own, which are no doubt sufficiently plausible in theory, but which could not be reduced to practice, without producing the evils already complained of. In 1796, a plan for reforming the poor laws was brought forward by Mr Pitt, full of device and regulation, provided with work-houses, schools of industry, superintendants, visitors, warehousemen, justices of the peace vested with large discretionary powers, – the whole a most complex contrivance, and leading to every species of abuse. Another plan has been since brought forward by Mr Whitbread, for the avowed purpose of rendering the poor laws obsolete. This desireable object, was to be effected by the establishment of schools, where the lower classes of society might be instructed, and gradually so improved in their habits, as to be set above receiving parish relief. However highly we may approve of this institution, and however much we may have been surprised, that a plan for improving the faculties of rational creatures should have met with any obstruction, we doubt much whether it would have brought about any general change in the manners of the English populace, particularly while such a source of moral depravation as the poor laws was suffered to exist. There were other regulations in this plan, of which we have already expressed our opinion, such as the establishment of banks for receiving the hoardings of the poor, and the erection of cottages for their comfort. The granting of honorary badges as a reward for decent conduct, seems quite fantastical. The great point in all those arrangements ought to be, to free society as much as possible from burdensome restraints. And we cannot help thinking, that legislators would succeed much better in their plans, if their minds could be weaned from that love of device and contrivance with which they seem to have been in all ages too much infected.

---

[1] Burnet, Hist. of his own times, Vol. VI. p. 314.

Mr Malthus has, however, proposed a plan of his own for giving effect to his principles, which seems more simple, and better calculated for answering its purpose, than any of those complicated schemes. He is of opinion, that a regulation should be made, declaring that no child born from any marriage, taking place after the expiration of a year from the date of the law, and that no illegitimate child born two years after the same date, should ever be entitled to parish assistance. To give a more general knowledge of this law, he proposes that the clergyman of the parish should, previous to every marriage, read a short address to the parties, stating the strong obligation on every man to support his own children, and the necessity which had at length appeared, from regard to the poor themselves, of abandoning all public institutions for their relief, as they had produced effects totally opposite to those which were intended.

This plan has been reprobated as iniquitous and cruel; but if the poor laws are to be abolished, it is impossible to conceive in what way this great reformation can be brought about with less hardship to those concerned. Those who had been accustomed to depend upon parochial relief, would have that dependance still left them; so that they could not be said to suffer any injury, and the rising generation would have a plain warning that they had nothing to depend upon for their support but their own exertions. The plan, therefore, seems, in this respect, to be perfectly unexceptionable, and to accord with that enlightened humanity which the writings of Mr Malthus generally display. The scheme appears, however, to be in some respects unsatisfactory and incomplete. It does not seem to be founded on that full and distinct view of the poor laws, on which alone a suitable remedy can be founded. When we consider how much Mr Malthus must have reflected on the poor-laws, and that it is principally to the writings of that eminent philosopher, that we are indebted for any clear views on the subject, it is with the most respectful diffidence that the following observations are offered to the attention of the reader.

It is the opinion of Sir F.M. Eden,[2] and it seems, indeed, extremely probable, that the law passed in the reign of Queen Elizabeth had no relation to the able-bodied labourer, but was

[2] Vol. 9. p. 584.

only meant for the relief of those who either had not work, or who were unable to work. In later years, however, they have been generally extended to the relief of the labourer; and the quantity of that relief has been measured by the high price of provisions. The poor rates have accordingly increased enormously; so that, in the year 1801, they were said to amount to the incredible sum of 10,000,000*l*. Formerly they did not exceed 3,000,000*l*. To add generally to the earnings of the labourer, when his wages are low, or when the price of subsistence is high, is in effect the same thing as forcibly to raise the wages of labour, or to fix a maximum on the price of provisions. In a season of scarcity, such a measure, whatever disorder and mischief it may be attended with, cannot even materially relieve those for whose benefit it is intended. The labourers and their families form by far the greater proportion of every community, and it must be chiefly by their savings that a diminished supply of corn can be made to last, till a fresh supply can be procured. No other order of men can be substituted in their place to bear the burden. Individual labourers may, indeed, be raised; and individuals in a higher situation may be depressed; – but the pressure of scarcity must always be heavily felt by the great body of the people. The same reasoning applies to the low price of labour, which always indicates an increase of population, without a corresponding increase of food. But it is evidently the same thing, whether population is increased in proportion to the food, or whether the food has decreased in proportion to the population. Both evils are exactly the same, and can only be removed by increasing the supply of food.

It may be said, however, that, in a scarcity, the hardship is exclusively borne by the poor, the rich being enabled, by means of money, to consume the same quantity of subsistence as before, and that pecuniary contributions may place the two classes more upon a level, and force the rich to bear their share in the burden. But, even if the rich were forced to abridge their consumption, they bear such a small proportion to the mass of the community, that the poor would be but little benefited; and it is moreover impossible to effect this, except by levelling the rich with the poor. The enormous sums which were lavished for the relief of the indigent during the late scarcities, contributed not so much to affect the rich, as the classes immediately above the poor, whom it depressed, Mr Malthus observes, in the most marked manner. Now, even if the poor were to be relieved in this way, it does not appear, that the general mass of misery would be lessened; – their sufferings would be merely transferred to another class of society equally deserving attention and relief, and the number of those demanding parochial assistance would be increased. The ease, however, which the poor can derive from this miserable resource is so trifling, that it can never be felt. Even if all the forced savings of this class of the community were distributed to them *gratis*, it would furnish a remedy completely insignificant, when compared with such an extensive and deep-rooted malady. During the late scarcities, therefore, seven millions a year appear to have been squandered for no other purpose than to recruit for beggars.

As the object for which this money is raised, – namely, to relieve the great body of the people from the pressure of scarcity, appears to be completely unattainable; as the degree of pressure must be exactly such as to make the diminished supply of corn last out the year; as pecuniary contributions cannot lessen it, and can do very little towards altering the mode of its distribution, the situation of the poor would not be at all affected, if the able-bodied labourer were wholly excluded from parochial relief. If this arrangement were once carried into effect, the expenditure of the poor-laws would be very materially curtailed, as, we believe, the greater part of the relief granted, is given to able-bodied labourers with families.

Mr Malthus, in his plan for the abolition of the poor-laws, does not appear to us to distinguish between the original and genuine objects of parochial relief, and those to whom that charity has been most improperly extended. His reasonings, however, are evidently directed against the practice of giving relief to the labourer; and, so far from thinking his plan either cruel or iniquitous, as it has been most unjustly termed, the evil which Mr Malthus is for doing away by mild and gradual reformation, might, in our apprehension, without producing any bad effects, be much more speedily got quit of. To the common labourer who is able to work, all sort of charity ought, on a warning of six months or a year, to be refused; and this ought not to be left to the justices of the peace, – it ought to be established by law. In the recurrence of a scarcity, the practice of measuring out relief by the price of provisions, should never again be resorted to.

With respect to those who are really destitute, it appears, by experience, that a full and certain relief cannot be provided for them, without producing very melancholy effects on the manners of the people. A better plan for modifying the relief which is given to them, cannot be resorted to, than that proposed by Mr Malthus. Whether the relief ought to be entirely taken away, as in Scotland, or whether it ought to be so far reduced, as either to come in aid of personal exertion or of voluntary charity, is a question which requires very serious consideration. From a very careful examination of this important subject, it clearly appears to us, that it is much safer to fall short than to exceed, in relieving distress by public charity. What may be wanting in public, is generally made up by private benevolence. But there is no way of correcting the evil of profuse donations enforced by the authority of law.

# EDINBURGH REVIEW
## Vol. XVI, August 1810
### [Francis Jeffrey]

Art. XI. *Disquisitions on Population.* By Robert Acklom Ingram, B. D. 1809.

*Reply to the Essay on Population by the Rev. T. R. Malthus In a Series of Letters.* 8vo. London, 1808.

We should scarcely have thought it worth while to take any notice of these disquisitions, which consist, in a great degree, of strange misapprehensions and misrepresentations of the doctrines they profess to discuss, if we had not observed, among many persons, besides Mr Ingram and his anonymous coadjutor, an ignorance of the principles of population, which seems to us nearly unaccountable, considering the careful and detailed manner in which the subject has been lately explained. The excellent work of Mr Malthus, though it has certainly produced a great and salutary impression on the public mind, appears to us to have been much more generally talked of than read, and more generally read than understood. To those who have gone over it with attention, without being able to understand it, we cannot flatter ourselves, that the few observations which we are about to make will be of much use; but there is a class of readers for whom we cannot help feeling considerable affection, who are tempted, we believe, occasionally to turn over our transitory pages, when they would shrink from the perusal of a bound quarto, or two massive octavos. That these judicious persons are in nowise deterred from discussing the merits of the said quartos and octavos merely because they have not read them, every day's experience sufficiently proves; and, indeed, it would be a cruel preventive check on conversation, to insist upon such previous drudgery; but still, if we may judge of the feelings of others from our own under similar circumstances, it is, upon the whole, an advantage to a man to understand something about the subject on which he is going to deliver his opinion. It is a great gratification to us to think, that we have afforded this advantage to our friends, on many important subjects, in morals, politics, and the various branches of science; and we would fain hope, that we may now render them a small service of the same kind, on the no less important subject of population. At all events, we can promise them, that what we are going to say will, in one respect at least, have a much stronger claim on their attention than the work of Mr Malthus, – that of brevity.

This celebrated work may be said to consist of two separate parts. In the first place, of some very important statements in point of *fact*, the truth of which neither is nor can be denied, though the different parts of the statement had never before been brought together, nor the nature of their connexion pointed out: and, in the second place, of certain *reasonings* and practical inferences deduced from these facts. Now, the first part, or the mere statement of indisputable facts, forms by far the largest and the most important part of the work; and, strange as it must appear to every one who is capable of forming an opinion on the subject, it is to this part that the most violent objections have been made. It is for having stated, with inimitable caution and accuracy, facts which cannot possibly be called in question, that Mr Malthus has been assailed with such clamorous reproaches, – that he has been accused of sophistry, of presumption, of blasphemy, inhumanity and love of vice and corruption. Against such charges, we know that he would disdain to be defended; nor would our compassion for those who have advanced them have been quite strong enough to make us undertake the hopeful task of undeceiving them, if their errors did not appear to originate in a few fundamental mistakes, which may probably obstruct the reception of important truths in more dispassionate minds.

The radical proposition, then, which we wish to impress upon our readers is, that throughout the greater part of his invaluable work, Mr Malthus is occupied merely with the statement, detail and illustration, of a few very important and radical *facts*, the truth and certainty of which, none of his detractors have been bold enough to call in question; and that, disclaiming all pretensions to discovery, he has aimed only at fixing the attention of mankind on the true character of certain phenomena that have always been before their eyes. To satisfy the most suspicious of our readers, how very innocent, and, at the same time, how very important this task was, we shall now endeavour to give such a short abstract of the fundamental principles of the work, as, we flatter ourselves, will occasion no perplexity to persons of the most slender capacity.

In the first book of the *Wealth of Nations*, Dr Smith, when explaining the causes which proportion the reward of labour to the extent of the funds for its support, justly observes, 'It is in this manner that the demand for *men*, like that for any other commodity, necessarily regulates the production of men; – quickens it, when it goes on too slowly; and stops it, when it advances too fast. It is this demand which regulates and determines the state of population in all the different countries of the world – in North America, in Europe and in China; which renders it rapidly progressive in the first, slow and gradual in the second, and altogether stationary in the last.' This passage of Dr Smith, which we think we have heard first suggested to Mr Malthus the idea of his essay, is illustrated and confirmed by a crowd of indisputable facts, to whatever country on the globe our view may be directed.

In taking a survey of this kind, it will speedily be discovered to be a fact that admits of no dispute, that the rate of population is by no means the same in all the countries of the world, – and that there is a notable difference in its progress, not only in North America, for instance, compared with Europe or Asia in general, but a similar difference in the different states of Europe, at the same period of time, and in the same state at different periods. As men cannot live without food, it will also be readily admitted to be a fact, that those variations in the rate of population must have been universally preceded and accompanied by variations in the means of maintaining labourers; on which, indeed, the demand before mentioned must necessarily depend. Where these funds are rapidly increasing as in North America, the demand for an increasing number of labourers, makes it easy to provide an ample subsistence for each; and the population of the country is observed to make rapid advances. Where these funds increase only at a moderate rate, as in most of the countries of Europe, there the demand for labourers is moderate; the command of the labourer over the means of subsistence is consequently much diminished; and the population is observed to proceed with a moderate pace, varying in each country, as nearly as may be, according to the variations in the funds for its support. Where these funds are stationary, as we are taught to believe is the case in China, and as has certainly been the case in Spain, Italy, and probably most of the countries of Europe, during certain periods of their history, there the demand for labour being stationary, the command of the labourer over the means of subsistence, is comparatively very scanty, and population is observed to make no perceptible progress, and sometimes to be even diminished.

In the second place, it is a fact equally notorious, that the actual increase of the funds for the maintenance of labour does not depend simply upon the physical capacity of any particular country to produce food and other necessaries, but upon the degree of industry, intelligence and activity, with which these powers are at any particular time called forth. We observe countries, possessing every requisite for producing the necessaries and conveniences of life in abundance, sunk in a state of ignorance and indolence, from the vices of their governments, or the unfortunate constitution of their society, - and slumbering on for ages with scarcely any increase in the means of subsistence, till some fortunate event introduces a better order of things; and then, the industry of the nation being roused, and allowed to exert itself with more freedom, more ample funds for the maintenance of labour are immediately provided, and population is observed to make a sudden start forwards, at a rate quite different from that at which it had before proceeded.

This seems to have been the case with many of the countries of Europe, during some periods of this history; but is more particularly remarkable in Russia, the population of which, though very early inhabited, was so extremely low before the beginning of the last century, and has proceeded with such rapid steps since, particularly since the reign of Catherine II.

It is also a fact that has often attracted observation in a review of the history of different nations, that the waste of people occasioned by the great plagues, famines and other devastations, to which the human race has been occasionally subject, has been repaired in a much shorter time than it would have been, if the population, after these devastations, had only proceeded at the same rate as before. From which it is apparent, that, after the void thus occasioned, it must have increased much faster than usual; and the greater abundance of the funds for the maintenance of labour, which would be left to the survivors under such circumstances, indicates again the usual conjunction of a rapid increase of population with a rapid increase of the funds for its maintenance. Just after the great pestilence in the time of Edward III, a day's labour would purchase a bushel of wheat; while, immediately before, it would hardly have purchased a peck.

With regard to the minor variations in the different countries of Europe, it is an old and familiar observation, that, wherever any new channels of industry, and new sources of wealth, are opened, so as to provide the means of supporting an additional number of labourers, there, almost immediately, a stimulus is given to the population; and it proceeds, for a time, with a vigour and celerity proportionate to the greatness and duration of the funds on which alone it can subsist.

In the third place, it is no less certain and visible, that, in a few countries where the funds for the maintenance of labour are in great abundance, the rate at which population increases is so rapid, that, if it were to continue unabated, the largest and richest territory, nay, the whole globe of the earth, would, in a few centuries, be completely possessed; but, as the great abundance of these funds appears absolutely to depend upon the circumstance of there being an abundance of good land to be had at a very low price, it is quite clear that this state of things cannot possibly continue; and that the funds for the maintenance of labour must, in the progress of cultivation and population, cease to increase with the same rapidity very long before they come to a stop, or before the country can be considered as fully peopled. The impossibility of the continued increase of these funds at the same rate, will be still more evident when applied to the peopled states of Europe and Asia, under any imaginable system of government: and, in reference to the peopling of the whole earth, it involves a manifest absurdity, to suppose, that a certain abundance of the funds for the maintenance of labour, which, wherever it has been found to exist, depends upon the land bearing a very great proportion to the people, should experience no change, while this proportion was gradually altering, so as ultimately to become the opposite of what it was at first.

From this slight survey of what has certainly taken place, and is actually taking place, with respect to the funds for the maintenance of labour in different countries, we conceive that the three following propositions may be stated as among the *facts* least capable of being controverted.

1. That man, like all other animals, multiplies in proportion to the means of subsistence which, under the actual circumstances in which he lives, are placed within his reach.

2. That there is a power of increase in the human race, much greater than is generally exercised, always ready to exert itself as soon as it finds an opening; and appearing continually in sudden starts of population, whenever the funds for the maintenance of labour have experienced an increase, in whatever way this may have been occasioned.

3. That this power of increase is so great, and, in its nature, necessarily so different from any increase which can result from adding together different portions of a limited quantity of land, or gradually improving the cultivation of the whole, that the funds for the maintenance of labour cannot, under any system the most favourable to human industry, be made permanently to keep pace with such an increase of population as has been observed to take place for short periods in particular countries; and consequently, as man cannot live without food, that the superior power of population cannot be kept on a level with the funds which are to support it, without the almost constant operation of considerable *checks*, of some kind or other.

What these checks are, is the next important question; and, keeping in mind, that it is strictly and purely a question of mere *fact*, and not of reasoning or hypothesis, let us first hear Dr Smith. In speaking of the dependence of man, like other animals, on the means of subsistence, and of the impossibility of his increasing beyond them, he observes, 'But, in civilized society, it is only among the inferior ranks of people, that the scantiness of subsistence can set limits to the further multiplication of the species; and it can do so in no other way, than by destroying a great part of the children which their fruitful marriages produce.'

As the poverty and misery which would destroy a considerable portion of children, must necessarily be most severely felt, not only by the human beings thus suffering, but by their parents and survivors, it must be acknowledged, that such a premature mortality is a very harsh leveller; and it is fortunate for the human race, that there are other ways besides this, by which population may proportion itself to the means of subsistence. Mr Malthus shows clearly, that the effects of the difficulty of providing for a family, do not appear merely in premature mortality, but in the delay of engaging in a connexion which is likely to be attended with such a consequence. And this view of the subject not only accords better with our ideas of a being who possessed the distinctive faculty of reason, but is completely confirmed by what is taking place in all the countries with which we are acquainted, where we find, that when the funds for the maintenance of labour become comparatively scanty, the marriages generally become later and less frequent.

It appears, then, without entering into any argument or detail, that the checks to population may be divided into two general classes – those which operate in *preventing the birth* of a population which cannot be supported, and those which *destroy it* after it has been brought into being; or, as Mr Malthus has called them, the *preventive* checks and the *positive checks*.

The necessary and constant operation of some checks to population, in almost all the societies with which we are acquainted, being fully established, and these checks being most clearly divisible into the two before mentioned classes, we can scarcely hesitate in determining which of them we should wish to see put in operation.

It is observed, in most countries, that in years of scarcity and dearness, the marriages are fewer than usual; and if, under all the great variations to which the increase of the means of subsistence is necessarily exposed from a variety of causes; from a plenty or scarcity of land; from a good or a bad government; from the general prevalence of intelligence and industry, or of ignorance and indolence; from the opening of new channels of commerce, or the closing of old ones, &c. &c., the population were proportioned to the actual means of subsistence, more by the prudence of the labouring classes in delaying marriage, than by the misery which produces premature mortality among their children, – it can hardly be doubted that the happiness of the mass of mankind would be decidedly improved.

It is further certain, that, under a given increase of the funds for the maintenance of labour, it is physically impossible to give to each labourer a larger share of these funds, or materially to improve his condition, without some increase of the preventive check; and consequently, that all efforts to improve the condition of the poor, that have no tendency to produce a more favourable proportion between the means of subsistence and the population which is to consume them, can only be partial or temporary, and must ultimately defeat their own object.

It follows, therefore, as a natural and necessary conclusion, that in order to improve the condition of the lower classes of society, to make them suffer less under any diminution of the funds for the maintenance of labour, and enjoy more under any actual state of these funds, it should be the great business to discourage helpless and improvident habits, and to raise them as much as possible to the condition of being who 'look before and after.' The causes which principally tend to foster helpless, indolent and improvident habits among the lower classes of society, seem to be despotism and ignorance, and every plan of conduct towards them which increases their dependence, and weakens the motives to personal exertion. The causes, again, which principally tend to promote habits of industry and prudence, seem to be, good government and good education, and every circumstance which tends to increase their independence and respectability. Wherever the registers of a country, under no particular disadvantages of situation, indicate a great mortality, and the general prevalence of the check arising from disease and death, over the check arising from prudential habits, there we almost invariably find the people debased by oppression, and sunk in ignorance and indolence. Wherever, on the contrary, in a country without peculiar advantages of situation, or peculiar capability of increase, the registers indicate a small mortality, and the prevalence of the check from prudential habits above that from premature mortality; there, we as constantly find security of property established, and some degree of intelligence and knowledge, with a taste for cleanliness and comforts, pretty generally diffused.

Nor does experience seem to justify the fears of those who think, that one vice at least will increase in proportion to the increase of the preventive check to population. Norway, Switzerland, England and Scotland, which are most distinguished for the smallness of their mortality, and the operation of the prudential restraint on marriage, may be compared to advantage with other countries, not only with regard to the general moral worth and respectability of their inhabitants, but with regard to the virtues which relate to the intercourse of the sexes. We cannot, as Mr Malthus observes, estimate with tolerable accuracy the degree in which chastity in the single state prevails. Our general conclusions must be founded on general results; and these are clearly in our favour.

We appear, therefore, to be all along borne out by experience and observation, both in our premises and conclusions. From what we see and know, indeed, we cannot rationally expect that the passions of man will ever to so completely subjected to his reason, as to enable him to avoid all the moral and physical evils which depend upon his own conduct. But this is merely saying, that perfect virtue is not to be expected on earth; an assertion by no means new, or peculiarly applicable to the present discussion. The differences observable in different nations, in the pressure of the evils resulting from the tendency of the human race to increase faster than the means of subsistence, entitle us fairly to conclude, that those which are in the best state are still susceptible of considerable improvement; and that the worst may at least be made equal to the best. This is surely sufficient both to animate and to direct our exertions in the cause of human happiness; and the direction which our efforts will receive, from thus turning our attention to the laws that relate to the increase and decrease of mankind, and seeing their effects exemplified in the state of the different nations around us, will not be into any new and suspicious path, but into the plain, beaten track of morality. It will be our duty to exert ourselves to procure the establishment of just and equal laws, which protect and give respectability to the lowest subject, and secure to each member of the community the fruits of his industry; to extend the benefits of education as widely as possible, that, to the long list of errors from passion, may not be added the still longer list of errors from ignorance; and, in general, to discourage indolence, improvidence, and a blind indulgence of appetite, without regard to consequences; and to encourage industry, prudence, and the subjection of the passions to the dictates of reason. The only change, if change it can be called, which the study of the laws of population can make in our duties, is, that it will lead us to apply, more steadily than we have hitherto done, the great rules of morality to the case of marriage, and the direction of our charity; but the rules themselves, and the foundations on which they rest, of course remain exactly where they were before.

This appears to us to be the substance of what Mr Malthus has said. Yet this theory, and these conclusions, simple and consistent as they appear to be, and resting, as they do all along, upon the most obvious and undeniable facts, are rejected by a pretty large class of religious and respectable people, because they think, that the acknowledgement of a law of increase in the human race greater than any possible increase of the means of subsistence, is an impeachment of the power or benevolence of the Deity. Mr Ingram says, 'that upon the first perusal of the sentiments contained in the Essay, the religious mind revolts at the apparent want of intelligence and contrivance in the Author of the creation, in infusing a principle into the nature of man, which it required the utmost exertion of human prudence and ingenuity to counteract.'

In answer to this, and to all similar objections, we should observe, first, that we are not permitted to reject truths, of which our senses and experience give us the firmest assurance, because they do not accord with our preconceived notions respecting the attributes of the Deity. All our evidence for the prevailing benevolence of the works of creation – all our evidence for the power of the Creator – is derived from these sources. This evidence we must not, and cannot refuse to hear, in the first instance; and it is an after concern, to reconcile the undeniable state of the fact to the attributes which we assign to the Divinity.

But to such persons as Mr Ingram, and the class who often urge this objection, we have a further answer. We should observe, that from those who do not believe in revelation, we might expect such an objection; but that it appears to come with peculiar inconsistency from Christians. We do not pretend to be deep theologians; but we have always understood that the highest authorities, both in the English and Scotish church, have uniformly represented this world as a state of discipline and preparation for another; and indeed, that this doctrine is almost universally considered as the characteristic doctrine of the New Testament.

Now, we will venture to say, that, in the whole compass of the laws of nature, not one can be pointed out, which, in so peculiar and marked a manner, accords with this view of the state of man on earth. The purpose of the earthquake, the hurricane, or the drought, by which thousands and even millions of the human race are at once overwhelmed, or left to perish in lingering want – it must be owned, is inscrutable; particularly as we have been expressly cautioned, in scripture, not to be too ready to consider such events in the light of judgments for the offences of the persons thus suffering. Yet that these events, which are of obvious and acknowledged recurrence, should be passed over without difficulty by the Christian, and that he should be staggered by a law of nature, which eminently illustrates and confirms one of the main doctrines of his religion, is, we own, to us, quite unaccountable; and affords a very curious instance of the inconsistency of human reason. If it be really true, as we believe it is, that this life is a state of discipline and preparation for another, is it possible that we should find any difficulty in believing that a law of nature exists peculiarly calculated to rouse the faculties, and direct the exertions of the human race, which, by its varying pressure, and the various difficulties to which it gives rise, exercises and enlarges the powers of the mind, and calls into action all the great moral virtues which dignify and adorn human nature, as necessary to human happiness; which, above all, is constantly inculcating the necessity of the subjection of the passions to the dictates of reason and religion, and which, even if vice and misery were almost banished from the earth by the efforts of human virtue, would occasion the necessity of constant watchfulness and attention to maintain and secure the happiness which had been obtained?

On the other hand, if this law does exist, as we cannot for a moment doubt, from the evidence of incontestable facts, it merely affords a striking illustration and confirmation of that view of human life which is held out to us in the Scriptures; and, instead of being objected to by the Christian, it ought to be hailed as a powerful ally; as, to us at least, it appears to be one of those natural laws discovered by human experience, which may be urged with considerable force in favour of revealed religion.

The next class of objectors consists of worldly statesmen and politicians, who, at the slightest mention of checks to population, immediately conceive that our armies will want soldiers, and our manufactures hands. To such persons, it would of course be in vain to urge, that defence is better than conquest, and that the happiness of a society is a consideration paramount to the extent of its exports. If we had no other arguments than these, we know full well that it would be useless to urge them against such objectors. But, even these persons, we think, must allow, that the power of a country, both in war and in commerce, must depend upon that part of its population which is active and efficient, not upon that which is helpless and inefficient. If it has been found by experience that one country, which has, we will say, 200,000 births in each year, does not rear so many to puberty as another country which has only 100,000, must it not be allowed, that the first is the weaker of the two? And if, in addition to the question of numerical force, we take into consideration the state of misery and depression in the first country, which must have occasioned the premature mortality, we cannot doubt that the second would be infinitely superior in the industry and energy, as well as the happiness of its inhabitants. Not only would a country, where the checks to population arise from the prudential habits of the lower classes, rather than from premature mortality, possess a greater military and manufacturing population, with the same means of subsistence, but, from the very circumstance of the country's containing this large proportion of persons in the active periods of life, the means of subsistence would stand a much fairer chance of being increased with rapidity. This is, in fact, confirmed by experience. England, Scotland, Switzerland and Norway, where the premature checks to population are observed to prevail with the greatest force, increase faster in the funds for the maintenance of labour and, of course, in the population supported by them, than most of the countries of Europe that have a larger proportion of births.

So far, therefore, is it from being true, that the increased prudence of the poor, with regard to marriage, would be attended with a falling off in the military and commercial population of a country, or by any obstructions to its further increase, as far as our experience has hitherto gone, it must be acknowledged that its effects have been just the reverse.

We have heard it, however, asked, whether, if the advice which inculcates an increased prudence with regard to marriage, were really attended to, it might not be carried too far, and materially diminish the population of a country, or prevent its increase? In answer to this, we should readily allow, that the event, however improbable, was within the range of possibility; but should add, that if such possibilities were to preclude similar precepts, the range of moral instruction would be limited indeed. It will hardly be admitted, that we should be deterred from enforcing, with all our power, the precepts of benevolence in opposition to selfishness, because, if we really made men quite regardless of their own interests, we should do much more harm than good. There is, in such cases, a mean point of perfection, which it is our duty to be constantly aiming at; and the circumstance of this point being surrounded on all sides with dangers, is only according to the analogy of all ethical experience. The fact undoubtedly is, that, in that past history of the world and in its actual condition, we see countless examples of the misery produced by the neglect of this prudential abstinence; and no instance, even of the slightest inconvenience, from its excessive influence. As there is, in reality no danger of ever making the mass of mankind too generous or too compassionate, so there is just as little of our depopulating the world by making them too much the creatures of reason, and giving prudence too great a mastery over the natural passions and affections. The prevailing error in the game of life is, not that we miss the prizes through excess of timidity, but that we overlook the true state of the chances in our eager and sanguine expectations of winning them. Of all the objections that ever were made to a moralist who offered to arm men against the passions that are everywhere seducing them into misery, the most flattering, but, undoubtedly, the most chimerical, is, that his reasons are so strong, that if he were allowed to diffuse them, passion would be extinguished altogether, and the activity, as well as the enjoyments of man, annihilated along with his vices.

What we have now stated is as much, we suppose, as the indolent students, for whose benefit it is chiefly intended, will be well able to digest at a meal. We shall stop here, therefore, for the present; and, if any of them are induced, by what we have said, to venture on the perusal of Mr Malthus's entire book, we engage, for their encouragement, to help them over the startling passages of it, by a short examination of the other objections which have been urged against it.

# APPENDIX 1817
## [T. R. Malthus]

Since the publication of the last edition of this Essay in 1807, two works have appeared, the avowed object of which are directly to oppose its principles and conclusions. These are *the Principles of Population and Production*, by Mr. Weyland; and *an Inquiry into the Principle of Population*, by Mr. James Grahame.

I would willingly leave the question, as it at present stands, to the judgment of the public, without any attempt on my part to influence it further by a more particular reply; but as I professed my readiness to enter into the discussion of any serious objections to my principles and conclusions, which were brought forward in a spirit of candour and truth; and as one at least of the publications above mentioned may be so characterized, and the other is by no means deficient in personal respect, I am induced shortly to notice them.

I should not, however, have thought it necessary to advert to Mr. Grahame's publication, which is a slight work without any very distinct object in view, if it did not afford some strange specimens of misrepresentation, which it may be useful to point out.

Mr. Grahame in his second chapter, speaking of the tendency exhibited by the law of human increase to a redundance of population, observes that some philosophers have considered this tendency as a mark of the foresight of nature, which has thus provided a ready supply for the waste of life occasioned by human vices and passions; while 'others, of whom Mr. Malthus is the leader, regard the vices and follies of human nature, and their various products, famine, disease and war, as *benevolent remedies* by which nature has enabled human beings to correct the disorders that would arise from that redundance of population which the unrestrained operation of her laws would create'.[1]

[1] P. 100.

These are the opinions imputed to me and the philosophers with whom I am associated. If the imputation were just, we have certainly on many accounts great reason to be ashamed of ourselves. For what are we made to say? In the first place, we are stated to assert that *famine* is a benevolent remedy for *want of food*, as redundance of population admits of no other interpretation than that of a people ill supplied with the means of subsistence, and consequently the benevolent remedy of famine here noticed can only apply to the disorders arising from scarcity of food.

Secondly, we are said to affirm that nature enables human beings by means of diseases to correct the disorders that would arise from a redundance of population – that is, that mankind willingly and purposely create diseases, with a view to prevent those diseases which are the necessary consequence of a redundant population, and are not worse or more mortal than the means of prevention.

And thirdly, it is imputed to us generally, that we consider the vices and follies of mankind as benevolent remedies for the disorders arising from a redundant population; and it follows as a matter of course that these vices ought to be encouraged rather than reprobated.

It would not be easy to compress in so small a compass a greater quantity of absurdity, inconsistency, and unfounded assertion.

The two first imputations may perhaps be peculiar to Mr. Grahame; and protection from them may be found in their gross absurdity and inconsistency. With regard to the third, it must be allowed that it has not the merit of novelty. Although it is scarcely less absurd than the two others, and has been shown to be an opinion not to be inferred from any part of it, it has been continually repeated in various quarters for fourteen years, and now appears in the pages of Mr. Grahame. For the last time I will now notice it; and should it still continue to be brought forward, I think I may be fairly excused from paying the slightest further attention either to the imputation itself, or to those who advance it.

If I had merely stated that the tendency of the human race to increase faster than the means of subsistence was kept to a level with these means by some or other of the forms of vice and misery, and that these evils were absolutely unavoidable, and incapable of being diminished by any human efforts; still I could not with any semblance of justice be accused of considering vice and misery as the remedies of these evils, instead of the very evils themselves. As well nearly might I be open to Mr. Grahame's imputations of considering the famine and disease necessarily arising from a scarcity of food as a benevolent remedy for the evils which this scarcity occasions.

But I have not so stated the proposition. I have not considered the evils of vice and misery arising from a redundant population as unavoidable, and incapable of being diminished. On the contrary, I have pointed out a mode by which these evils may be removed or mitigated by removing or mitigating their cause. I have endeavoured to show that this may be done consistently with human virtue and happiness. I have never considered any possible increase of population as an evil, except as far as it might increase the proportion of vice and misery. Vice and misery, and these alone, are the evils which it has been my great object to contend against. I have expressly proposed moral restraint as their rational and proper remedy; and whether the remedy be good or bad, adequate or inadequate, the proposal itself, and the stress which I have laid upon it, is an incontrovertible proof that I never can have considered vice and misery as themselves remedies.

But not only does the general tenour of my work, and the specific object of the latter part of it, clearly show that I do not consider vice and misery as remedies; but particular passages in various parts of it are so distinct on the subject, as not to admit of being misunderstood but by the most perverse blindness.

It is therefore quite inconceivable that any writer with the slightest pretension to respectability should venture to bring forward such imputations; and it must be allowed to show either such a degree of ignorance, or such a total want of candour, as utterly to disqualify him for the discussion of such subjects.

But Mr. Grahame's misrepresentations are not confined to the passage above referred to. In his Introduction he observes that, in order to check a redundant population, the evils of which I consider as much nearer than Mr. Wallace, I 'recommend immediate recourse to human efforts, to the restraints prescribed by Condorcet, for the correction or mitigation of the evil'.[2] This is an assertion entirely without

[2] P. 18.

foundation. I have never adverted to the check suggested by Condorcet without the most marked disapprobation. Indeed I should always particularly reprobate any artificial and unnatural modes of checking population, both on account of their immorality and their tendency to remove a necessary stimulus to industry. If it were possible for each married couple to limit by a wish the number of their children, there is certainly reason to fear that the indolence of the human race would be very greatly increased; and that neither the population of individual countries, nor of the whole earth, would ever reach its natural and proper extent. But the restraints which I have recommended are quite of a different character. They are not only pointed out by reason and sanctioned by religion, but tend in the most marked manner to stimulate industry. It is not easy to conceive a more powerful encouragement to exertion and good conduct than the looking forward to marriage as a state peculiarly desirable; but only to be enjoyed in comfort by the acquisition of habits of industry, economy and prudence. And it is in this light that I have always wished to place it.

In speaking of the poor-laws in this country, and of the tendency (particularly as they have been lately administered) to eradicate all remaining spirit of independence among our peasantry, I observe that 'hard as it may appear in individual instances, dependent poverty ought to be held disgraceful'; by which of course I only mean that such a proper degree of pride as will induce a labouring man to make great exertions, as in Scotland, in order to prevent himself or his nearest relations from falling upon the parish, is very desirable, with a view to the happiness of the lower classes of society. The interpretation which Mr. Grahame gives to this passage is that the rich 'are so to embitter the pressure of indigence by the stings of contumely, that men may be driven by their pride to prefer even the refuge of despair to the condition of dependence!!'[3] – a curious specimen of misrepresentation and exaggeration.

I have written a chapter expressly on the practical direction of our charity; and in detached passages elsewhere have paid a just tribute to the exalted virtue of benevolence. To those who have read these parts of my work, and have attended to the general tone and spirit of the whole, I willingly appeal, if they are but tolerably candid, against these charges of Mr. Graham,

[3] P. 236.

which intimate that I would root out the virtues of charity and benevolence, without regard to the exaltation which they bestow on the moral dignity of our nature; and that in my view the 'rich are required only to harden their hearts against calamity, and to prevent the charitable visitings of their nature from keeping alive in them that virtue which is often the only moral link between them and their fellow-mortals'.[4] It is not indeed easy to suppose that Mr. Graham can have read the chapter to which I allude, as both the letter and spirit of it contradict, in the most express and remarkable manner, the imputations conveyed in the above passages.

These are a few specimens of Mr. Grahame's misrepresentations, which might easily be multiplied; but on this subject I will only further remark that it shows no inconsiderable want of candour to continue attacking the dwelling upon passages which have ceased to form a part of the work controverted. And this Mr. Grahame has done in more instances than one, although he could hardly fail to know that he was combating expressions and passages which I have seen reason to alter or expunge.

I really should not have thought it worth while to notice these misrepresentations of Mr. Grahame if, in spite of them, the style and tone of his publication had not appeared to me to be entitled to more respect than most of my opponents.

With regard to the substance and aim of Mr. Graham's Work, it seems to be intended to show that emigration is the remedy provided by nature for a redundant population; and that if this remedy cannot be adequately applied, there is no other that can be proposed which will not lead to consequences worse than the evil itself. These are two points which I have considered at length in the Essay; and it cannot be necessary to repeat any of the arguments here. Emigration, if it could be freely used, has been shown to be a resource which could not be of long duration. It cannot therefore under any circumstances be considered as an adequate remedy. The latter position is a matter of opinion, and may rationally be held by any person who sees reason to think it well founded. It appears to me, I confess, that experience most decidedly contradicts it; but to those who think otherwise, there is nothing more to be said, than that they are bound in consistency to acquiesce in the

[4] *Ibid.*

necessary consequences of their opinion. These consequences are that the poverty and wretchedness arising from a redundant population or, in other words, from very low wages and want of employment, are absolutely irremediable, and must be continually increasing as the population of the earth proceeds; and that all the efforts of legislative wisdom and private charity, though they may afford a wholesome and beneficial exercise of human virtue, and may occasionally alter the distribution and vary the pressure of human misery, can do absolutely nothing towards diminishing the general amount or checking the increasing weight of this pressure.

Mr. Weyland's work is of a much more elaborate description than that of Mr. Grahame. It has also a very definite object in view: and although, when he enters into the details of his subject, he is compelled entirely to agree with me respecting the checks which practically keep down population to the level of the means of subsistence, and has not in fact given a single reason for the slow progress of population, in the advanced stages of society, that does not clearly and incontrovertibly come under the heads of moral restraint, vice or misery; yet it must be allowed that he sets out with a bold and distinct denial of my premises, and finishes, as he ought to do from such a beginning, by drawing the most opposite conclusions.

After stating fairly my main propositions, and adverting to the conclusion which I have drawn from them, Mr. Weyland says: 'Granting the premises, it is indeed obvious that this conclusion is undeniable.'[5]

I desire no other concession than this; and if my premises can be shown to rest on unsolid foundations, I will most readily give up the inferences I have drawn from them.

To determine the point here at issue it cannot be necessary for me to repeat the proofs of these premises derived both from theory and experience, which have already so fully been brought forward. It has been allowed that they have been stated with tolerable clearness; and it is known that many persons have considered them as unassailable, who still refuse to admit the consequences to which they appear to lead. All that can be required on the present occasion is to examine the validity of the objections to these premises brought forward by Mr. Weyland.

[5] *Principles of Population and Production*, p. 15.

Mr. Weyland observes, 'that the origin of what are conceived to be the mistakes and false reasonings, with respect to the principle of population, appears to be the assumption of a tendency to increase in the human species, the quickest that can be proved possible in any particular state of society, as that which is natural and theoretically possible in all; and the characterizing of every cause which tends to prevent such quickest possible rate as checks to the natural and spontaneous tendency of population to increase; but as checks evidently insufficient to stem the progress of an overwhelming torrent. This seems as eligible a mode of reasoning, as if one were to assume the height of the Irish giant as the natural standard of the stature of man, and to call every reason, which may be suggested as likely to prevent the generality of men from reaching it, checks to their growth.'[6]

Mr. Weyland has here most unhappily chosen his illustration, as it is in no respect applicable to the case. In order to illustrate the different rates at which population increases in different countries, by the different heights of men, the following comparison and inference would be much more to the purpose.

If in a particular country we observed that all the people had weights of different sizes upon their heads, and that invariably each individual was tall or short in proportion to the smallness or greatness of the pressure upon him; that every person was observed to grow when the weight be carried was either removed or diminished, and that the few among the whole people, who were exempted from this burden, were very decidedly taller than the rest; would it not be quite justifiable to infer that the weights which the people carried were the cause of their being in general so short; and that the height of those without weights might fairly be considered as the standard to which it might be expected that the great mass would arrive, if their growth were unrestricted?

For what is it, in fact, which we really observe with regard to the different rates of increase in different countries? Do we not see that, in almost every state to which we can direct our attention, the natural tendency to increase is repressed by the difficulty which the mass of the people find in procuring an ample portion of the necessaries of life, which shows itself

---

[6] P. 17.

more immediately in some or other of the forms of moral restraint, vice and misery? Do we not see that invariably the rates of increase are fast or slow, according as the pressure of these checks is light or heavy; and that in consequence Spain increases at one rate, France at another, England at a third, Ireland at a fourth, parts of Russia at a fifth, parts of Spanish America at a sixth, and the United States of North America at a seventh? Do we not see that, whenever the resources of any country increase, so as to create a great demand for labour and give the lower classes of society a greater command over the necessaries of life, the population of such country, though it might before have been stationary or proceeding very slowly, begins immediately to make a start forwards? And do we not see that in those few countries, or districts of countries, where the pressure arising from the difficulty of procuring the necessaries and conveniences of life is almost entirely removed, and where in consequence the checks to early marriages are very few, and large families are maintained with perfect facility, the rate at which the population increases is always the greatest?

And when to these broad and glaring facts we add, that neither theory nor experience will justify us in believing, either that the passion between the sexes, or the natural prolificness of women, diminishes in the progress of society; when we further consider that the climate of the United States of America is not particularly healthy, and that the qualities which mainly distinguish it from other countries are its rapid production and distribution of the means of subsistence – is not the induction as legitimate and correct as possible, that the varying weight of the difficulties attending the maintenance of families, and the moral restraint, vice and misery which these difficulties necessarily generate, are the causes of the varying rates of increase observable in different countries; and that, so far from having any reason to consider the American rate of increase as peculiar, unnatural and gigantic, we are bound by every law of induction and analogy to conclude that there is scarcely a state in Europe where, if the marriages were as early, the means of maintaining large families as ample, and the employment of the labouring classes as healthy, the rate of increase would not be as rapid, and in some cases I have no doubt, even more rapid, that in the United States of America?

Another of Mr. Weyland's curious illustrations is the following: He says that the *physical tendency* of a people in a commercial and manufacturing state to double their number in twenty-five years is 'as absolutely gone as the tendency of a bean to shoot up further into the air, after it has arrived at its full growth'; and that to assume such a *tendency* is to build a theory upon a mere shadow, 'which, when brought to the test, is directly at variance with experience of the fact; and as unsafe to act upon, as would be that of a general who should assume the force of a musket-shot to be double its actual range, and then should calculate upon the death of all his enemies as soon as he had drawn up his own men for battle within this line of assumed efficiency'.[7]

Now I am not in the least aware who it is that has assumed the *actual* range of the shot, or the actual progress of population in different countries, as very different from what it is observed to be; and therefore cannot see how the illustration, as brought forward by Mr. Weyland, applies, or how I can be said to resemble his miscalculating general. What I have really done is this (if he will allow me the use of his own metaphor): having observed that the range of musket-balls, projected from similar barrels and with the same quantity of powder of the same strength, was, under different circumstances, very different, I applied myself to consider what these circumstances were; and, having found that the range of each ball was greater or less in proportion to the smaller or greater number of the obstacles which it met with in its course, or the rarity or density of the medium through which it passed, I was led to infer that the variety of range observed was owing to these obstacles; and I consequently thought it a more correct and legitimate conclusion, and one more consonant both to theory and experience, to say that the *natural tendency* to a range of a certain extent, or the force impressed upon the ball, was always the same, and the actual range, whether long or short, only altered by external resistance; than to conclude that the different distances to which the balls reached must proceed from some mysterious change in the *natural tendency* of each bullet at different times, although no observable difference could be noticed either in the barrel or the charge.

I leave Mr. Weyland to determine which would be the conclusion of the natural philosopher, who was observing the different velocities and ranges of projectiles passing through

[7] P. 126.

resisting media; and I do not see why the moral and political philosopher should proceed upon principles so totally opposite.

But the only arguments of Mr. Weyland against the *natural tendency* of the human race to increase faster than the means of subsistence are a few of these illustrations which he has so unhappily applied, together with the acknowledged fact, that countries under different circumstances and in different stages of their progress, do really increase at very different rates.

Without dwelling therefore longer on such illustrations, it may be observed, with regard to the fact of the different rates of increase in different countries, that as long as it is a law of our nature that man cannot live without food, these different rates are as absolutely and strictly *necessary* as the differences in the power of producing food in countries more or less exhausted; and that to infer from these different rates of increase, as they are actually found to take place, that 'population has a *natural tendency* to keep within the powers of the soil to afford it subsistence in every gradation through which society passes', is just as rational as to infer that every man has a *natural tendency* to remain in prison who is necessarily confined to it by four strong walls; or that the pine of the crowded Norwegian forest has no *natural* tendency to shoot out lateral branches, because there is no room for their growth. And yet this is Mr. Weyland's first and grand proposition, on which the whole of his work turns!!!

But though Mr. Weyland has not proved, or approached towards proving, that the *natural* tendency of population to increase is not unlimited; though he has not advanced a single reason to make it appear probable that a thousand millions would not be doubled in twenty-five years just as easily as a thousand, if moral restraint, vice and misery, were equally removed in both cases; yet there is one part of his argument which undoubtedly might, under certain circumstances, be true; and if true, though it would in no respect impeach the premises of the Essay, it would essentially affect some of its conclusions.

The argument may be stated shortly thus – that the natural division of labour arising from a very advanced state of society, particularly in countries where the land is rich, and great improvements have taken place in agriculture, might throw so large a portion of the people into towns, and engage so many in unhealthy occupations, that the immediate checks to population might be too powerful to be overcome even by an abundance of food.

It is admitted that this is a possible case; and, foreseeing this possibility, I provided for it in the terms in which the second proposition of the Essay was enunciated.

The only practical question then worth attending to, between me and Mr. Weyland, is whether cases of the kind above stated are to be considered in the light in which I have considered them in the Essay, as exceptions of very rare occurrence, or in the light in which Mr. Weyland has considered them, as a state of things naturally accompanying every stage in the progress of improvement. On either supposition, population would still be repressed by some or other of the forms of moral restraint, vice or misery; but the moral and political conclusions, in the actual state of almost all countries, would be essentially different. On the one supposition moral restraint would, except in a few cases of the rarest occurrence, be one of the most useful and necessary of virtues; and on the other, it would be one of the most useless and unnecessary.

This question can only be determined by an appeal to experience. Mr. Weyland is always ready to refer to the state of this country; and, in fact, may be said almost to have built his system upon the peculiar policy of a single state. But the reference in this case will entirely contradict his theory. He has brought forward some elaborate calculations to show the extreme difficulty with which the births of the country supply the demands of the towns and manufactories. In looking over them the reader, without other information, would be disposed to feel considerable alarm at the prospect of depopulation impending over the country; or at least he would be convinced that we were within a hair's breadth of that formidable point of *non-reproduction*, at which, according to Mr. Weyland, the population *naturally* comes to a full stop before the means of subsistence cease to be progressive.

These calculations were certainly as applicable twenty years ago as they are now; and indeed they are chiefly founded on observations which were made at a greater distance of time than the period here noticed. But what has happened since? In spite of the enlargement of all our towns; in spite of the most rapid increase of manufactories, and of the proportion of people employed in them; in spite of the most extraordinary and unusual demands for the army and navy; in short, in spite of a state of things which, according to Mr. Weyland's theory, ought to have brought us long since to the point of *non-reproduction*, the population of the country has advanced at a rate more rapid than was ever known at any period of its history. During the ten years from 1800 to 1811, as I have mentioned in a former part of this work, the population of this country (even after making an allowance for the presumed deficiency of the returns in the first enumeration) increased at a rate which would double its numbers in fifty-five years.

This fact appears to me at once a full and complete refutation of the doctrine that, as society advances, the increased indisposition to marriage and increased mortality in great towns and manufactories always overcome the principle of increase; and that, in the language of Mr. Weyland, 'population, so far from having an inconvenient tendency uniformly to press against the means of subsistence, becomes by degrees very slow in overtaking those means.'

With this acknowledged and glaring fact before him, and with the most striking evidences staring him in the face that, even during this period of rapid increase, thousands both in the country and in towns were prevented from marrying so early as they would have done, if they had possessed sufficient means of supporting a family independently of parish relief, it is quite inconceivable how a man of sense could bewilder himself in such a maze of futile calculations, and come to a conclusion so diametrically opposite to experience.

The fact already noticed, as it applies to the most advanced stage of society known in Europe, and proves incontrovertibly that the actual checks to population, even in the most improved countries, arise principally from an insufficiency of subsistence, and soon yield to increased resources, notwithstanding the increase of towns and manufactories, may I think fairly be considered as quite decisive of the question at issue.

But in treating of so general and extensive a subject as the Principle of Population, it would surely not be just to take our examples and illustrations only from a single state. And in looking at the other countries Mr. Weyland's doctrine on population is, if possible, still more completely contradicted. Where, I would ask, are the great towns and manufactories in Switzerland, Norway and Sweden, which are to act as *the graves of mankind*, and to prevent the possibility of a redundant population? In Sweden the proportion of the people living in the country is to those who live in towns as 13 to 1; in England this proportion is about 2 to 1; and yet England increases much faster than Sweden. How is this to be reconciled with the doctrine that the progress of civilization and improvement is always accompanied by a correspondent abatement in the natural tendency of population to increase? Norway, Sweden and Switzerland have not on the whole been ill governed; but where are the necessary 'anticipating alterations', which, according to Mr. Weyland, arise in every society as the powers of the soil diminish, and 'render so many persons unwilling to marry, and so many more, who do marry, incapable of reproducing their own numbers, and of replacing the deficiency in the remainder'?[8] What is it that in these countries indisposes people to marry, but the absolute hopelessness of being able to support their families? What is it that renders many more who do marry incapable of reproducing their own numbers, but the diseases generated by excessive poverty – by an insufficient supply of the necessaries of life? Can any man of reflection look at these and many of the other countries of Europe, and then venture to state that there is no moral reason for repressing the inclination to early marriages; when it cannot be denied that the alternative of not repressing it must necessarily and unavoidably be premature mortality from excessive poverty? And is it possible to know that in few or none of the countries of Europe the wages of labour, determined in the common way by the supply and the demand, can support in health large families; and yet assert that population does not press against the means of subsistence, and that 'the evils of a redundant population can never be necessarily felt by a country till it is actually peopled up to the full capacity of its resources'?[9]

Mr. Weyland really appears to have dictated his book with his eyes blindfolded and his ears stopped. I have a great respect for his character and intentions; but I must say that it has never been my fortune to meet with a theory so uniformly contradicted by experience. The very slightest glance at the different countries of Europe shows, with a force amounting to

[8] P. 124.
[9] P. 123.

demonstration, that to all practical purposes the *natural tendency* of population to increase may be considered as a given quantity; and that the actual increase is regulated by the varying resources of each country for the employment and maintenance of labour, in whatever stage of its progress it may be, whether it is agricultural or manufacturing, whether it has few or many towns. Of course this actual increase, or the actual limits of population, must always be far short of the utmost powers of the earth to produce food; first, because we can never rationally suppose that the human skill and industry actually exerted are directed in the best *possible* manner towards the production of food; and secondly because, as I have stated more particularly in a former part of this work, the greatest production of food which the powers of the earth would admit cannot possibly take place under a system of private property. But this acknowledged truth obviously affects only the actual quantity of food and the actual number of people, and has not the most distant relation to the question respecting the *natural tendency* of population to increase beyond the powers of the earth to produce food for it.

The observations already made are sufficient to show that the four main propositions of Mr. Weyland, which depend upon the first, are quite unsupported by any appearances in the state of human society, as it is known to us in the countries with which we are acquainted. The last of these four propositions is the following: 'This tendency' (meaning the natural tendency of population to keep within the powers of the soil to afford it subsistence) 'will have its complete operation so as constantly to maintain the people in comfort and plenty in proportion as religion, morality, rational liberty and security of person and property approach the attainment of a perfect influence.'[10]

In the morality here noticed, moral or prudential restraint from marriage is not included: and so understood, I have no hesitation in saying that this proposition appears to me more directly to contradict the observed laws of nature than to assert that Norway might easily grow food for a thousand millions of inhabitants. I trust that I am disposed to attach as much importance to the effects of morality and religion on the happiness of society, even as Mr. Weyland; but among the

[10] C. iii. p. 21.

moral duties I certainly include a restraint upon the inclination to an early marriage when there is no reasonable prospect of maintenance for a family; and unless this species of virtuous self-denial be included in morality, I am quite at issue with Mr. Weyland; and so distinctly deny his proposition as to say that no degree of religion and morality, no degree of rational liberty and security of person and property, can under the existing laws of nature place the lower classes of society in a state of comfort and plenty.

With regard to Mr. Weyland's fifth and last proposition;[11] I have already answered it in a note which I have added, in the present edition, to the last chapter of the third book,[12] and will only observe here that an illustration to show the precedence of population to food, which I believe was first brought forward by an anonymous writer, appears so to have pleased Mr. Grahame as to induce him to repeat it twice, is one which I would willingly take to prove the very opposite doctrine to that which it was meant to support. The apprehension that an increasing population would starve[13] unless a previous increase of food were procured for it, has been ridiculed by comparing it with the apprehension that increasing numbers would be obliged to go naked unless a previous increase of clothes should precede their births. Now however well or ill-founded may be our apprehensions in the former case, they are certainly quite justifiable in the latter; at least society has always acted as if it thought so. In the course of the next twenty-four hours there will be about 800 children born in England and Wales; and I will venture to say that there are not ten out of the whole number, that come at the expected time, for whom clothes are not prepared before their births. It is said to be dangerous to meddle with edged tools which we do not know how to handle; and it is equally dangerous to meddle with illustrations which we do not know how to apply, and which may tend to prove exactly the reverse of what we wish.

On Mr. Weyland's theory it will not be necessary further to enlarge. With regard to the practical conclusions which he has drawn from it in our own country, they are such as might be

[11] C. iii. p. 22.

[12] Pp. 205-6.

[13] This I have never said; I have only said that their condition would be deteriorated, which is strictly true.

expected from the nature of the premises. If population, instead of having a tendency to press against the means of subsistence, becomes by degrees very slow in overtaking them, Mr. Weyland's inference, that we ought to encourage the increase of the labouring classes by abundant parochial assistance to families, might perhaps be maintained. But if his premises be entirely wrong, while his conclusions are still acted upon, the consequence must be that universal system of unnecessary pauperism and dependence which we now so much deplore. Already above one-fourth of the population of England and Wales are regularly dependent upon parish relief; and if the system which Mr. Weyland recommends, and which has been so generally adopted in the midland counties, should extend itself over the whole kingdom, there is really no saying to what height the level of pauperism may rise. While the system of making an allowance from the parish for every child above two is confined to the labourers in agriculture, whom Mr. Weyland considers as the breeders of the country, it is essentially unjust, as it lowers without compensation the wages of the manufacturer and artificer: and when it shall become just by including the whole of the working classes, what a dreadful picture does it present! What a scene of equality, indolence, rags and dependence, among one-half or three-fourths of the society! Under such a system to expect any essential benefit from *saving banks* or any other institutions to promote industry and economy is perfectly preposterous. When the wages of labour are reduced to the level to which this system tends, there will be neither power nor motive to save.

Mr. Weyland strangely attributes much of the wealth and prosperity of England to the cheap population which it raises by means of the poor-laws; and seems to think that, if labour had been allowed to settle at its natural rate, and all workmen had been paid in proportion to their skill and industry, whether with or without families, we should never have attained that commercial and manufacturing ascendance by which we have been so eminently distinguished.

A practical refutation of so ill-founded an opinion may be seen in the state of Scotland, which in proportion to its natural resources had certainly increased in agriculture, manufactures and commerce, during the last fifty years, still more rapidly than England, although it may fairly be said to have been essentially without poor-laws.

It is not easy to determine what is the price of labour most favourable to the progress of wealth. It is certainly conceivable that it may be too high for the prosperity of foreign commerce. But I believe it is much more frequently too low; and I doubt if there has ever been an instance in any country of very great prosperity in foreign commerce, where the working classes have not had good money wages. It is impossible to sell very largely without being able to buy very largely; and no country can buy very largely in which the working classes are not in such a state as to be able to purchase foreign commodities.

But nothing tends to place the lower classes of society in this state so much as a demand for labour which is allowed to take its natural course, and which therefore pays the unmarried man and the man with a family at the same rate; and consequently gives at once to a very large mass of the working classes the power of purchasing foreign articles of consumption, and of paying taxes on luxuries to no inconsiderable extent. While, on the other hand, nothing would tend so effectively to destroy the power of the working classes of society to purchase either home manufactures or foreign articles of consumption, or to pay taxes on luxuries, as the practice of doling out to each member of a family an allowance, in the shape of wages and parish relief combined, just sufficient, or only a very little more than to furnish them with the mere food necessary for their maintenance.

To show that, in looking forward to such an increased operation of prudential restraint as would greatly improve the condition of the poor, it is not necessary to suppose extravagant and impossible wages, as Mr. Weyland seems to think, I will refer to the proposition of a practical man on the subject of the price of labour; and certainly much would be done, if this proposition could be realized, though it must be effected in a very different way from that which he has proposed.

It has been recommended by Mr. Arthur Young so as to adjust the wages of day-labour as to make them at all times equivalent to the purchase of a peck of wheat. This quantity, he says, was earned by country labourers during a considerable period of the last century, when the poor-rates were low, and not granted to assist in the maintenance of those who were able to work. And he goes on to observe that 'as the labourer would (in this case) receive 70 bushels of wheat for 47 weeks' labour, exclusive of five weeks for harvest; and as a family of six persons consumes in a year no more than 48 bushels; it is clear that such wages of labour would cut off every pretence of parochial assistance; and of necessity the conclusion would follow, that all right to it in men thus paid should be annihilated for ever'.[14]

An adjustment of this kind, either enforced by law, or used as a guide in the distribution of parish assistance, as suggested by Mr. Young, would be open to insuperable objections. At particular times it might be the means of converting a dearth into a famine. And in its general operation, and supposing no change of habits among the labouring classes, it would be tantamount to saying that, under all circumstances, whether the affairs of the country were prosperous or adverse; whether its resources in land were still great, or nearly exhausted; the population ought to increase exactly at the same rate − a conclusion which involves an impossibility.

If, however, this adjustment, instead of being enforced by law, were produced by the increasing operation of the prudential check to marriage, the effect would be totally different, and in the highest degree beneficial to society. A gradual change in the habits of the labouring classes would then effect the necessary retardation in the rate of increase, and would proportion the supply of labour to the effective demand, as society continued to advance, not only without the pressure of a diminishing quantity of food, but under the enjoyment of an increased quantity of conveniences and comforts; and in the progress of cultivation and wealth the condition of the lower classes of society would be in a state of constant improvement.

A peck of wheat a day cannot be considered in any light as excessive wages. In the early periods of cultivation, indeed, when corn is low in exchangeable value, much more is frequently earned; but in such a country as England, where the price of corn, compared with manufactures and foreign commodities, is high, it would do much towards placing the great mass of the labouring classes in a state of comparative comfort and independence; and it would be extremely desirable, with a view to the virtue and happiness of human society, that no land should be taken into cultivation that could not pay the labourers employed upon it to this amount.

With these wages as the average minimum, all those who

---

[14] *Annals of Agriculture*, No. 270, p. 91, note.

were unmarried, or, being married, had small families, would be extremely well off; while those who had large families, though they would unquestionably be subjected sometimes to a severe pressure, would in general be able, by the sacrifice of conveniences and comforts, to support themselves without parish assistance. And not only would the amount and distribution of the wages of labour greatly increase the stimulus to industry and economy throughout all the working classes of the society, and place the great body of them in a very superior situation, but it would furnish them with the means of making an effectual demand for a great amount of foreign commodities and domestic manufactures, and thus, at the same time that it would promote individual and general happiness, would advance the mercantile and manufacturing prosperity of the country.[15]

Mr. Weyland, however, finds it utterly impossible to reconcile the necessity of moral restraint either with the nature of man, or the plain dictates of religion on the subject of marriage. Whether the check to population, which he would substitute for it, is more consistent with the nature of a rational being, the precepts of revelation, and the benevolence of the Deity, must be left to the judgment of the reader. This check, it is already known, is no other than the unhealthiness and mortality of towns and manufacturies.[16] And though I have never felt any difficulty in reconciling to the goodness of the Deity the necessity of practising the virtue of moral restraint in a state allowed to be a state of discipline and trial; yet I confess that I could make no attempt to reason on the subject, if I were obliged to believe, with Mr. Weyland, that a large proportion of the human race was doomed by the inscrutable ordinations of Providence to a premature death in large towns.

---

[15] The merchants and manufacturers who so loudly clamour for cheap corn and low money wages, think only of selling their commodities abroad, and often forget that they have to find a market for their returns at home, which they can never do to any great extent, when the money wages of the working classes, and monied incomes in general, are low. One of the principal causes of this check which foreign commerce has experienced during the last two or three years, has been the great diminution of the home market for foreign produce.

[16] With regard to the indisposition to marriage in towns, I do not believe that it is greater than in the country, except as far as it arises from the greater expense of maintaining a family, and the greater facility of illicit intercourse.

If indeed such peculiar unhealthiness and mortality were the proper and natural check to the progress of population in the advanced stages of society, we should justly have reason to apprehend that, by improving the healthiness of our towns and manufactories, as we have done in England during the last twenty years, we might really defeat the designs of Providence. And though I have too much respect for Mr. Weyland to suppose that he would deprecate all attempts to diminish the mortality of towns, and render manufactories less destructive to the health of the children employed in them; yet certainly his principles lead to this conclusion, since his theory has been completely destroyed by those laudable efforts which have made the mortality of England – a country abounding in towns and manufactories, less than the mortality of Sweden – a country in a state almost purely agricultural.

It was my object in the two chapters on *Moral Restraint*, and its *Effects on Society*, to show that the evils arising from the principle of population were exactly of the same nature as the evils arising from the excessive or irregular gratification of the human passions in general; and that from the existence of these evils we had no more reason to conclude that the principle of increase was too strong for the purpose intended by the Creator, than to infer, from the existence of the vices arising from the human passions, that these passions required diminution or extinction, instead of regulation and direction.

If this view of the subject be allowed to be correct, it will naturally follow that, notwithstanding the acknowledged evils occasioned by the principle of population, the advantages derived from it under the present constitution of things may very greatly overbalance them.

A slight sketch of the nature of these advantages, as far as the main object of the Essay would allow, was given in the two chapters to which I have alluded; but the subject has lately been pursued with considerable ability in the Work of Mr. Sumner on the Records of the Creation; and I am happy to refer to it as containing a masterly development and completion of views of which only an intimation could be given in the Essay.

I fully agree with Mr. Sumner as to the beneficial effects which result from the principle of population, and feel entirely convinced that the natural tendency of the human race, to increase faster than the possible increase of the means of subsistence, could not be either destroyed, or essentially diminished, without diminishing that hope of rising and fear of falling in society, so necessary to the improvement of the human faculties and the advancement of human happiness. But with this conviction on my mind, I feel no wish to alter the view which I have given of the evils arising from the principle of population. These evils do not lose their name or nature because they are overbalanced by good: and to consider them in a different light on this account, and cease to call them evils, would be as irrational as the objecting to call the irregular indulgences of passion vicious, and to affirm that they lead to misery, because our passions are the main sources of human virtue and happiness.

I have always considered the principle of population as a law peculiarly suited to a state of discipline and trial. Indeed I believe that, in the whole range of the laws of nature with which we are acquainted, not one can be pointed out which in so remarkable a manner tends to strengthen and confirm this scriptural view of the state of man on earth. And as each individual has the power of avoiding the evil consequences to himself and society resulting from the principle of population by the practice of a virtue clearly dictated to him by the light of nature, and sanctioned by revealed religion, it must be allowed that the ways of God to man with regard to this great law of nature are completely vindicated.

I have, therefore, certainly felt surprise as well as regret that no inconsiderable part of the objections which have been made from the principles and conclusions of the Essay on Population have come from persons for whose moral and religious character I have so high a respect, that it would have been particularly gratifying to me to obtain their approbation and sanction. This effect has been attributed to some expressions used in the course of the work which have been thought too harsh, and not sufficiently indulgent to the weaknesses of human nature and the feelings of Christian charity.

It is probable that, having found the bow bent too much one way, I was induced to bend it too much the other, in order to make it straight. But I shall always be quite ready to blot out any part of the work which is considered by a competent tribunal as having a tendency to prevent the bow from becoming finally straight, and to impede the progress of truth. In deference to this tribunal I have already expunged the passages which have been most objected to, and I have made some few further corrections of the same kind in the present edition. By these alterations I hope and believe that the work has been improved without impairing its principles. But I still trust that whether it is read with or without these alterations, every reader of candour must acknowledge that the practical design uppermost in the mind of the writer, with whatever want of judgment it may have been executed, is to improve the condition and increase the happiness of the lower classes of society.

*Note 1825*

Since the last edition of this work was published an answer from Mr. Godwin has appeared, but the character of it both as to matter and manner is such that I am quite sure every candid and competent inquirer after truth will agree with me in thinking that it does not require a reply. To return abusive declamation in kind would be as unedifying to the reader as it would be disagreeable to me, and to argue seriously with one who denies the most glaring and best attested facts respecting the progress of America, Ireland, England, and other states,[1] and brings forward Sweden, one of the most barren and worst supplied countries of Europe, as a specimen of what would be the natural increase of population under the greatest abundance of food, would evidently be quite vain with regard to the writer himself, and must be totally uncalled for by any of his readers whose authority could avail in the establishment of truth.

---

[1] See article *Population* in the Supplement to the 'Encyclopaedia Britannica'.

THE QUARTERLY REVIEW
Vol. XVII, July 1817
[J. B. Sumner]

Art. IV. – *An Essay on the Principle of Population; or, a View of its past and present Effects on Human Happiness; with an Inquiry into our prospects respecting the future Removal or Mitigation of the Evils which is occasions.* By R. T. Malthus, A.M. late Fellow of Jesus College, Cambridge, and Professor of History and Political Economy in the East India College, Hertfordshire. The Fifth Edition, with important Additions. Three Vols. 8vo, London. 1817.

That preposterous course which is a fatal error in morals, is indispensable in political science; mankind must act first, and reason afterwards. The axioms of political economy, like those of natural philosophy, can only result from experience and repeated observation: thus it happens that the progress of civilization, as it increases the variety of relations and combinations in which men are placed with respect to each other, and multiplies the transactions in which they are involved, has the collateral effect of introducing a new set of intellectual pursuits, and engaging mankind in the study of fresh sciences as it gradually advances. There is not a wider difference between the simple barter of wine or oxen for arms or slaves, and the bills of exchange which form the medium of modern commerce, than between the comparative knowledge of the principles by which national and individual transfers of property are regulated, as exhibited in the crude and contradictory 'Politics' of Aristotle, and in the scientific conclusions of the 'Wealth of Nations.' Aristotle was as well calculated as any man to build up a scientific system: but a sufficient series of experiments to found it upon, was wanting. Hence it was naturally to be expected that in the progress of civilization and political economy, the last subject studied and explained should be the facts relating to POPULATION, because this branch of political science requires a collection of statistic details which can only be furnished by an advanced state of society: and because it is little likely to attract attention till men are generally placed in circumstances like those in which we find them in modern Europe. In ancient times, the density of population was limited by the facility, and still more by the habit of emigration, which, after all, while the distance is short, and climate similar, and artificial wants comparatively few, is a much milder process than expatriation from Europe to America, or from England to the shores of the Euxine. The universal habits of slavery, moreover, among the Greeks and Romans, and such a systematic demoralization as is betrayed by the enactment of a lex Julia, to say nothing of perpetual and murderous wars, would naturally tend to keep the subject out of view. During the middle ages, population had a regular preventive check in feudal habits, and a regular positive check in civil wars: and though famines were no less frequent than severe, it was quite evident that they did not originate in the redundancy of people, but in the want of channels for distributing produce, and in the total ignorance and neglect of agriculture. It was not, therefore, till the security of property and the tranquil state of things which followed the establishment of a settled government, made it the first desire of every man to sit down, if not under his own vine, at least by his own fire-side and in the circle of a family; it was not till avenues were gradually opened to industry and enterprise, and allowed that desire to be generally gratified; it was not till these prosperous circumstances gave an impulse to the power of population, that the inhabitants of the various countries of Europe encroached rapidly upon the productive soil, and have made it at last a matter of speculation how far the territory itself may be able to support the numbers existing in it; and what proportion there is between the natural powers of the earth, and those of unrestrained population.

Unquestionably the details which we now possess from registers and statistical tables and other authentic sources, are of a nature to invite the curiosity and ensure the attention of all those who have a taste for researches into the history of their fellow creatures, even apart from all practical consequences. The first survey of the subject affords a striking problem. It presents us with a view of men essentially the same in their passions, constitutions, and physical powers, yet, in different countries, or in the same country at different times, varying in the rate in which they increase their numbers through every degree of a very extensive scale: in some cases requiring no more than twenty-five years, and in others perhaps no less than a thousand, to double them. There is no occasion to travel far in search of instances. Our own dominions exhibit the following variations.

| | | |
|---|---|---|
| In Canada, the population doubles | in | 28 years. |
| In Ireland | in | 34 |
| In England and Wales (calculating the whole of the last century) | in | 100 |
| In Hindostan (perhaps) | in | 1000 |

Those who profess to see nothing remarkable in these variations, must have very different ideas from ours as to what is interesting in the history of the human race. Again, if we trace the subject back to the origin of the increase, we find in different countries a similar difference in the proportion which the number of annual marriages bears to the number of the existing population. Here, for the sake of wider illustration, we will extend our view beyond our own territories. In Russia, according to a table furnished by Mr. Tooke, it appears that among ninety-two persons one marriage is contracted, or of forty-six persons one marries annually: so that the proportion of marriages to the actual population is on average as one to ninety-two. Whereas in most countries the proportion is considerably smaller: being

| | | | |
|---|---|---|---|
| in Sweden | 1 | to | 110* |
| in England | 1 | to | 122[1] |
| in Norway | 1 | to | 130* |
| in the Pays de Vaud | 1 | to | 140* |

It is further remarkable that the annual proportion of marriages is by no means uniform even in the different counties of our native land. According to the curious table, prefixed to the returns for 1811, it varies from one in a hundred and five, which is the highest, (with the exception of Middlesex,) to one in a hundred and fifty-three. For example,

---

* Malthus, vol. i. p. 410.

[1] Preliminary Observations on the Population Abstract, by Mr. Rickman, p. xxix.

in Yorkshire (East Riding) the marriages are as

|  |  |  |  |
|---|---|---|---|
|  | 1 | to | 105 persons |
| in Warwickshire | 1 | to | 116 |
| in Essex | 1 | to | 128 |
| in Shropshire | 1 | to | 143 |
| in Monmouthshire | 1 | to | 153 |

How are we to account for these striking variations? Confessedly we have no ground to assume either any material difference in the prolific power, or in the instincts on which the increase of the species depends. The American race is but a branch of the European stock, and, had it remained on its parent soil, would have partaken of the same gradual increase, doubling itself in a century at the quickest: but the same branch, when rooted in Transatlantic ground, doubles in twenty-five years. Take any given number: say 10,000: these persons remaining in France or England, would in a hundred years have increased to 20,000: but transplanted to America, in a hundred years they become 160,000. Nay, even in the same country the rate of increase is very different in different periods, and periods too with only a trifling interval between them. England, during the first half of the last century, only gained a million of inhabitants; increasing from 5,475,000 to 6,467,000: but during the last half, increased nearly three times as fast, having reached 9,163,000 at the census of 1801. At that period the rate of doubling was about eighty-three years; but the increase from 1801 to 1811 was in still greater proportion, and should it continue, would double the whole population in fifty-five years.

At this point, then, Mr. Malthus takes up the question. Why it is, that in America the numbers increase so fast, in Hindostan so slow? Why faster in Ireland than in England? Why is it, that in England the population increases at different rates in different periods? or that in those counties which either extensive marshes or crowded manufacturing towns render comparatively unhealthy, marriages are earlier and more general than in the more salubrious and agricultural districts? Are the natural inclinations colder in Shropshire than in Warwickshire, or in Monmouthshire than in either? or is it more reasonable to suppose that the natural inclinations are generally uniform, but that they are necessarily repressed in some situations by the difficulty of providing for a family, more than in the mining and manufacturing districts, where the average duration of life is shorter, and the resources of labour more extensive? Is it not that the power of increase in the human race is much greater than the power of adding to the supply of food, by which last, however, their increase must inevitably be regulated? Is it any thing but the impossibility of procuring a proportionate augmentation of subsistence which prevents mankind, in all healthy countries, from making an annual addition to their numbers as great as that which takes place in America or in some parts of the Russian territory?

So at least argues Mr. Malthus; and the returns of the annual marriages, which were not in existence at the publication of his Essay, afford a clear illustration of his original remark.

> 'It is evident that in every country where the resources are any way limited the *preventive* and *positive* checks to population must vary inversely as each other; that is, in countries either naturally unhealthy or subject to a great mortality, from whatever cause it may arise, the preventive check will prevail very little. In those countries, on the contrary, which are naturally healthy, and where the preventive check is found to prevail with considerable force, the positive check will prevail very little or the mortality be very small.' – p. 24.

Our readers will probably remember that we have not been hasty in adopting Mr. Malthus's conclusions; and that we have condemned without hesitation the unqualified severity and harshness with which they were originally accompanied and introduced to public notice. Whoever casts his eyes around him, and surveys the labour, the distress, the penury, and the ignorance in which a great part of the human race, even in the most favoured countries, are more or less immersed, must want all the finer feelings and most amiable charities of our nature, if he does not spontaneously give way to the benevolent desire of correcting so much vice and relieving so much misery. Under the influence of these feelings, even the chimerical visions of Mr. Owen have attracted attention; and for some time his violation of practical experience and defiance of common sense, appeared to find excuse, in consideration of the amiable sentiments to which they were sacrificed. Even when the rugged lessons of experience or the incontrovertible testimonies of evidence assure us of the utter hopelessness of realizing this amelioration to its desirable extent; still the hardest lesson to forget is that which was first imbibed in other schools than those of philosophy; and the hope of some effectual improvement in the condition of our species remains 'the last infirmity of noble minds.' Mr. Malthus himself, in the preface to his original edition, 'professes to have read some of the speculations on the future improvement of society in a temper very different from a wish to find them visionary; but he had not acquired that command over his understanding which would enable him to believe what he wishes, without evidence, or to refuse his assent to what might be unpleasing when accompanied with evidence.

Under circumstances thus confessedly disadvantageous, the author cannot have been surprized at the slow and reluctant assent which his principles have obtained. He has a prejudice to encounter at every step; and it must be owned that no pains were originally employed to win an easy way, and make the reader part readily with his prejudices. Every succeeding edition has improved in this respect; and in the present especially the author has equally gratified our self-complacency and displayed his own candour, by expunging those passages to which we had most pointedly objected, as liable to misrepresent the subject, and inflict an unnecessary violence on the feelings of the reader.[2] The existing state of our domestic

[2] The following quotations contain an account of the alterations and additions which have been made since the last edition was published.

'On account of the nature of the subject, which it must be allowed is one of permanent interest, as well as of the attention likely to be directed to it in future, I am bound to correct those errors of my work, of which subsequent experience and information may have convinced me, and to make such additions and alterations as appear calculated to improve it, and promote its utility.

'It would have been easy to have added many further historical illustrations of the first part of the subject; but as I was unable to supply the want I once alluded to, of accounts of sufficient accuracy to ascertain what part of the natural power of increase each particular check destroys, it appears to me that the conclusion, which I had before drawn from very ample evidence of the only kind that could be obtained, would hardly receive much additional force by the accumulation of more, precisely of the same description.

'In the first two books, therefore, the only additions are a new chapter on France, and one on England, chiefly in reference to facts which have occurred since the publication of the last edition.

'In the third book, I have given an additional chapter on the Poor-Laws; and as it appeared to me that the chapters on the Agricultural and Commercial Systems, and the Effects of encreasing Wealth on the Poor,

economy certainly renders the inquiry peculiarly interesting at this moment; and we enter upon it with no slight advantage after the discussions which this branch of political science (which when Mr. Malthus first published his essay was almost an untried field of speculation) has recently undergone. At all events, respecting a book which has taken such firm hold of the public attention, and which, in the judgment of its partisans, is likely to effect a greater change in the current of public opinion than any which has appeared since the 'Wealth of Nations,' we owe a duty to the author and to our readers, which we shall endeavour impartially to perform.

The essay opens with an inquiry into the natural rate of the increase of mankind, compared with that of the subsistence necessary for their support. It appears from some well known examples, that population, where there is no difficulty in procuring a proportionate addition to the supply of food, doubles itself every twenty-five years, or proceeds in a geometrical ratio. Subsistence however, in countries once settled and limited, cannot possibly be accumulated at the same rate. If we can suppose that the produce of England in 1817 should by great exertions be doubled by the year 1842, that is, should be so far and so long able to support the probable increase of an unrestrained population; yet we cannot possibly imagine that it could be again doubled in twenty-five years more, and enabled to meet the demand of forty-four millions in 1867. The most sanguine speculator could only expect the

were not either so well arranged, or so immediately applicable to the main subject, as they ought to be; and as I further wished to make some alterations in the chapter on Bounties upon Exportation, and add something on the subject of Restrictions upon Importation, I have recast and rewritten the chapters which stand the 8th, 9th, 10th, 11th, 12th, 13th, in the present edition; and given a new title, and added two or three passages to the 14th, and last chapter of the same book.

'In the fourth book I have added a new chapter to the one entitled *Effects of the Knowledge of the principal Cause of Poverty on Civil Liberty*; and another to the chapter on *the different Plans of employing the Poor*; and I have made a considerable addition to the Appendix, in reply to some writers on the Principles of Population, whose works have appeared since the last edition.

'These are the principal additions and alterations made in the present edition. They consist in a considerable degree of the application of the general principles of the Essay to the present state of things.

'For the accommodation of the purchasers of the former editions, these additions and alterations will be published in a separate volume.' – Preface, pp. 12–14.

produce to be increased in the same proportion as during the preceding period, or to proceed in the arithmetical ratio of 1, 2, 3; while population, as appears in America, has a natural tendency to increase in the geometrical ratio 1, 2, 4, &c.

'Taking the whole earth, instead of this island, emigration would of course be excluded; and, supposing the present population equal to a thousand millions, the human species would increase as the numbers 1, 2, 4, 8, 16, 32, 64, 128, 256, and subsistence as 1, 2, 3, 4, 5, 6, 7, 8, 9. In two centuries the population would be as the means of subsistence as 256 to 9; in three centuries as 4096 to 13, and in two thousand years the difference would be almost incalculable.' – vol. i. p. 15.

After reading this prefatory statement, we naturally expect to learn, in the subsequent chapters, that a part, at least, of mankind are placed in some of these different relations as to their food and numbers; or at any rate, that these two opposite forces can only be brought to a tolerable equality by some process totally inconsistent with virtue or happiness. We forget that this is only an abstract view of the subject; that these different relations never can really exist, being uniformly checked at the first step of their hostile progress: and that we are in much more actual danger from every comet that traverses our system, than from the risk that population should ever be to the means of subsistence even as 4 to 3. For this reason we have always regretted the place which these calculations hold in the head and front of the essay. Not because we demur to their justice as abstract truths; but because they seem to perplex the reasoning, by keeping out of sight the facts which it is the real object of the book to prove. The increase of population, no doubt, in favourable situations, is matter of historical notoriety, and may be ascertained on visible and undeniable evidence. But the degree of increase of which human subsistence is capable is necessarily in a great measure hypothetical. Here, therefore, is scope for argument and discussion; and it is for this purpose that the details which follow the author's leading statement are so practically valuable. But it must be observed, that according to the mode in which these details are introduced, they do not bear upon the original propositions, that subsistence increases according to one ratio, and population in another; but on a different set of propositions, which are enunciated in the second chapter, and which the various checks to population in different climates and stages of civilization are subsequently brought in to prove. The opening statements, therefore, are only made to be abandoned; and, if they were to be abandoned, had better not have been made, or at least not placed in so conspicuous a position.

It may be necessary, perhaps, to explain our objection more fully. The author's principle is this: that population has a natural tendency to increase much faster than food can be provided for it; and that the difference between these two ratios in the relative increase of subsistence and population has always occasioned a great deal of poverty and misery in the world. In order to establish his point, two separate courses of argument lay ready for his choice. First, to begin, as he has begun, with a statement of the geometrical and arithmetical ratio, taken as a probable assumption; and then to bring forward his statistical and historical details, in order to show the justice of that original proposition. For if there is this difference, or any such difference between the ratios in which population and subsistence naturally proceed, it follows that there must be in almost all countries a pressure of mankind against the existing supply of food. It must be obtained and increased with so much difficulty, that except in very particular situations, there must always remain some part of the people to whom the necessaries of life will be barely and scantily awarded. This would have given him occasion to appeal to the various records which we possess of the human race: and to prove, from history and experience, that notwithstanding the various drains on population occasioned in some countries by wars and outrages, in others by vicious customs, in others by epidemic disorders, and in others by unhealthy occupations, still there is a constant pressure against the available supply of subsistence; a pressure uniform in its operation though variable in its degree. Other accounts satisfactorily show, that wherever the means of subsistence have been suddenly increased, either by emigration, or by the addition of some new territory, or by the effects of war and pestilence sweeping off a portion of the original inhabitants, this facility of supply has immediately occasioned a start in the progress of population, which has quickly either filled up the chasm or covered the vacant surface. We possess, therefore, this further proof that the same power of natural increase which keeps population fully up to the level of subsistence, is constantly seeking opportunity to exert itself still more; and, like a stream forcibly dammed up, will rush onward as soon as the sluices are opened; or, like a tree whose roots are confined, is always pushing its fibres in every direction, and searching for room to spread and expand them.

Such is, in fact, the general outline of the course of evidence by which the leading principle of the book may be supported, and the superiority of the power of population to the power of producing subsistence maintained. But those who are familiar with the essay itself will be immediately aware that this is not the process of reasoning which the author has actually pursued. Leaving altogether, as we observed, his original statement, he undertakes to prove the following propositions:

'1. Population is necessarily limited by the means of subsistence. 2. Population invariably increases where the means of subsistence increase. 3. The checks which repress the superior power of population, and keep its effects on a level with the means of subsistence, are all resolvable into moral restraint, vice, and misery.' – p. 34.

Here we must remark, that these three propositions, considered as a chain of argument, are thus far defective, that the *superior power of population* is affirmed, not proved; which amounts to an assumption of the very point in question. Should it be thought that this superior power of population had been sufficiently exhibited by the comparative ratios contained in the preceding chapter, which is the opinion of the author himself;[3] still he must allow that it ought to have been affirmed in a separate proposition, in order to place the argument in a legitimate and logical form.

But although the arithmetical and geometrical ratios of subsistence and population respectively may satisfactorily and forcibly illustrate the superior power of population to those who are disposed to admit their justice, still it must be remembered, that the natural tendency to increase, and still more the comparative power of augmenting subsistence, are only and can only be fixed hypothetically. The population of America has increased geometrically for the last century; granted; but America is still supported from her own soil;

[3] See Note to Appendix, vol. iii. p. 344.

therefore in America subsistence has increased geometrically as well as population: has increased in the four periods of twenty-five years in the proportion of 1, 2, 4, 8. In our own country, on the other hand, produce has been very far from increasing even arithmetically in the same periods of twenty-five years; instead of proceeding at the rate of 1, 2, 3, 4, it has proceeded as 1, 1¼, 1½, 1¾, 2; and that barely; for our population, which in the course of the century has actually doubled, was not, at the end of it, independent of foreign supplies.

Without intended therefore to assert that Mr. Malthus's calculation is either too high in the one case or too low in the other, since he professes to consider the average state of the whole earth; the fact, we think, should always be kept in view, that the assumption of the comparative ratios is hypothetical, and necessarily must be so: and we may fairly object to its being propounded as a philosophical axiom no less indisputable than the principles of motion or gravitation, or any other of the ascertained and unerring laws of nature, that population increases in a geometrical, and subsistence in an arithmetical ratio. As long as it is understood that this is a mere assumption for the sake of argument or illustration, all is well. But when it is appealed to, as it commonly has been, and as we lately heard it at a public meeting, as a definite ordinance of the Creator; which is, to say the least of it, to place the laws of Providence under a very unprepossessing aspect; it is time to remember, that to prove this is neither the object nor the result of Mr. Malthus's essay. Though the power of population may not be rated too high, speaking of an unlimited state, nor of production too low, speaking of a limited; still, while the rate of population is taken from one state of society, and of subsistence from another, there will always remain a door of escape to a pertinacious adversary; who can only be chained down to the broad fact, that population has a tendency to increase beyond the means of subsistence.

The arrangement of which we complain has, without doubt, been injurious to the success and reception of the main principle of the Essay. Many persons, for instance, have mistaken in this way the leading object of the work; and Mr. Malthus had found reason to complain of its being said that he had written a quarto volume to prove that population increased in a geometrical, and food in an arithmetical ratio. App. p. 344. Others have caught hold of the belief, that such being the natural difference between the ratios of population and food – the details were introduced in order to show the necessity of misery to reconcile and bring them to a level. C'est la nécessité de misère qu'il s'agit de démontrer, says a French antagonist of Mr. Malthus; and then accuses him of uniformly arguing in a circle, and proving the necessity of misery by the existence of misery. Mr. Grahame, another adversary, asserts in still rounder terms, that some philosophers, 'of whom Mr. Malthus is the leader, regard the vices and follies of human nature, and their various products, famine, disease and war, as *benevolent remedies* by which nature has enabled human beings to correct the disorders that would arise from that redundance of population which the unrestrained operation of her laws would create.'

> 'These are the opinions,' replies Mr. Malthus, 'imputed to me and the philosophers with whom I am associated. If the imputation were just, we have certainly on many accounts great reason to be ashamed of ourselves. For what are we made to say? In the first place, we are stated to assert that *famine* is a benevolent remedy for *want of food*, as redundance of population admits of no other interpretation than that of a people ill supplied with the means of subsistence, and consequently the benevolent remedy of famine here noticed can only apply to the disorders arising from scarcity of food.
>
> 'Secondly, we are said to affirm that nature enables human beings by means of diseases to correct the disorders that would arise from a redundance of population; – that is, that mankind willingly and purposely create diseases, with a view to prevent those diseases which are the necessary consequence of a redundant population, and are not worse or more mortal than the means of prevention.
>
> 'And thirdly, it is imputed to us generally, that we consider the vices and follies of mankind as benevolent remedies for the disorders arising from a redundant population; and it follows as a matter of course that these vices ought to be encouraged rather than reprobated.
>
> 'It would not be easy to compress in so small a compass a greater quantity of absurdity, inconsistency, and unfounded assertion.
>
> 'The first two imputations may perhaps be peculiar to Mr.

Grahame; and protection from them may be found in their gross absurdity and inconsistency. With regard to the third, it must be allowed that it has not the merit of novelty. Although it is scarcely less absurd than the two others, and has been shown to be an opinion no where to be found in the Essay, nor legitimately to be inferred from any part of it, it has been continually repeated in various quarters for fourteen years, and now appears in the pages of Mr. Grahame. For the last time I will not notice it; and should it still continue to be brought forward, I think I may be fairly excused from paying the slightest further attention either to the imputation itself, or to those who advance it.

'If I had merely stated that the tendency of the human race to increase faster than the means of subsistence, was kept to a level with these means by some or other of the forms of vice and misery, and that these evils were absolutely unavoidable, and incapable of being diminished by any human efforts; still I could not with any semblance of justice be accused of considering vice and misery as the remedies of these evils, instead of the very evils themselves. As well nearly might I be open to Mr. Grahame's imputations of considering the famine and disease necessarily arising from a scarcity of food as a benevolent remedy for the evils which this scarcity occasions.

'But I have not so stated the proposition. I have not considered the evils of vice and misery arising from a redundant population as unavoidable, and incapable of being diminished. On the contrary, I have pointed out a mode by which these evils may be removed or mitigated by removing or mitigating their cause. I have endeavoured to show that this may be done consistently with human virtue and happiness. I have never considered any possible increase of population as an evil, except as far as it might increase the proportion of vice and misery. Vice and misery, and these alone, are the evils which it has been my great object to contend against. I have expressly proposed moral restraints as their rational and proper remedy; and whether the remedy be good or bad, adequate or inadequate, the proposal itself, and the stress which I have laid upon it, is an incontrovertible proof that I never can have considered vice and misery as themselves remedies.' - App. p. 389-392.

This answer is quite decisive. But still it might occur to Mr. Malthus that so great a misapprehension of his views could hardly have become so general, unless there had been something in the conduct and arrangement of his arguments which led to these erroneous conclusions, and counteracted the force of his frequent disclaimers. The explanation, we imagine, is to be found in the unaccommodating ratios of population and subsistence, and the commanding position assigned them in the outset of his book, while an equally formidable array of positive and preventive checks to population is drawn up on the other hand, with the apparent design of bringing them to a level. Whereas if the author had contented himself with beginning from the propositions which he really proves, his work would have had the same utility, and have exhibited the same practical truths, with the additional advantage of less outraging the feelings of his readers. Still the immense superiority of the power of unchecked population to that of production in a limited territory is so undeniable a fact, that it should by no means have been entirely omitted; and it might with great propriety have been brought forward as a corroboration of the general argument of the essay.

If, on the other hand, he had deemed it the most striking or philosophical mode of treating the subject to follow out his original statement, the different ratios of food and population, we think he would have pursued a clearer course of reason by adhering to it, instead of bringing forward a separate string of propositions: for as it is, an opponent may complain that he is required to assent to a different fact from that which is proved to his conviction; or he may find fault with the narrowness of the induction compared with the importance of the conclusion, and appeal to exceptions which different ages and states of society cannot fail to furnish, or resort to some of the various shifts by which it is always possible to block up the avenues of a reluctant understanding. In short, the question is incapable of demonstrative proof, or of determination à priori; and the evidence, the practical evidence, that the power of population is infinitely greater than the power of production, must ultimately rest on the actual pressure of population against produce. It is only after pointing out the existence of great and undeniable checks to population, and still proving the close pressure against subsistence, that the superiority of the power of population can be satisfactorily and incontrovertibly established.

If we are right in these strictures upon the conduct of our author's argument, it may account for the known fact, that many intelligent persons have declared themselves dissatisfied with Mr. Malthus's reasoning, though they were unable to deny his conclusions. But whether we are right or wrong, it may be convenient at all events to place the subject in a somewhat different point of view: and accordingly we propose, without hesitation, the following axioms on the subject of population, as unanswerably proved in the Essay before us:-

1. 'Population is necessarily limited by the means of subsistence.' This requires only to be stated.

2. There are various 'checks which repress' the natural 'power of population, and keep its effects on a level with the means of subsistence; which are all resolvable into moral restraint, vice, and misery.'

3. Notwithstanding the effect of these checks, 'population always increases as the means of subsistence increase:' or, as it might be affirmed with perfect justice, always increase so as to press against the available supply.

Our readers will observe how far these propositions deviate from the author's own terms, which we stated in a preceding page; and that we consider the superiority of the natural power of population over the power of production, to be proved by the existence of the checks alluded to in the second of our propositions: in spite of which, the pressure of mankind against the existing produce is matter of universal experience. To recapitulate the evidence of these facts, collected by Mr. Malthus, would be to transcribe the first and second books of his work: it is taken from every region of the world, and every period of history, and every stage of society; and largely shews that mankind have uniformly increased and multiplied, in conformity with the command of their Creator: and also that, agreeably to the same Creator's denunciation, they have always been condemned to acquire their subsistence by painful and continual labour.

The practical conclusion resulting from the book is this: that redundancy is not only a much greater evil than deficiency of population, but much more to be apprehended, much more likely to happen; that legislators therefore begin in the wrong place when they employ any adventitious means to give direct encouragment to population; since they have only to increase subsistence, or the power of commanding it, and population will invariably follow; and in fact does always exist, to the full amount of the available supply of food. This is a question of no slight interest every where; but comes particularly home to our own country; where we have now in regular operation a principle allowed even by its advocates to be a forcing principle, and which, especially during the last twenty years, has been so exercised, as to become an actual bounty on population. If Mr. Malthus is right, such a bounty is not only unnecessary, but must lead to consequences injurious, if not fatal to national happiness. If on the other hand he is wrong, we may still persist in providing at the public expense a subsistence for all who may be born, even if there should be no demand on the part of the community for their labour. As the question is of such important and immediate interest, we will consider in their turn the various objections which may be thought to invalidate Mr. Malthus's conclusions.

I. The first and most obvious of these is taken from the present state of many countries which are known to have been formerly populous, and are now comparatively deserts; as Northern Africa, and Persia, and the immense territories which compose the Turkish empire. When we measure these vast districts on the map, and compare the square miles of fertile territory with the actual number of their inhabitants, the natural impression which the mind receives is that the pressure of population is a vain terror; or, as the French opponent of Mr. Malthus terms it, un sophisme très habilement soutenu.

Mankind however, it is very plain, cannot be supported by the *possible* abundance of their soil, but must depend upon its actual produce. It is sufficiently notorious that Egypt and Greece, and Syria and Anatolia, were formerly as much more populous, than in the state of degradation to which a wretched tyranny has now reduced them, as they were more distinguished in arts and comparative civilization. History points out to us as many cities in those districts, as we can now find villages; and there is little doubt but in those ages less actual distress was felt from insufficient supply than now, when families occupy the place of provinces.

Insecurity of property is the great bane of all these countries. Mankind seem upon the whole to be well enough inclined to industry, if they can only reckon upon reaping its fruits; but no one labours for labour's sake, or sows without a prospect of gathering the harvest. Throughout the whole of these districts, however, the peasant is uniformly subject to plunder of one sort or other; either the legalized exactions of tyranny, or to the devastation of barbarous incursions. Throughout Turkey the system of oppressing and pillaging all who may have collected the most trifling property begins from the throne, and systematically descends through all the ramifications of government. Where all offices are notoriously bought, and bought at a competition; where all are held during pleasure, the pleasure of an insecure and arbitrary despot; do we require the details of travellers to fill up the outlines of such a country, and throw in its darker shades? or is it sufficient to refer to the principles of our common nature, in order to paint the picture in its true colours?

Under circumstances of this nature, it is certainly not surprising that the inhabitants of these countries should be few, either in proportion to their extent, or their possible fertility: the wonder is greater that the people should reach, nay press rudely against the limits of their supply. This fact however is as undeniable as the wretchedness of their political situation, and is authenticated by the testimony of every traveller, Volney, Thornton, Clarke, Morier, &c. who furnish abundant materials to prove, that in spite of the little inducement there is either to live, or to propagate life in these countries, still they are inhabited fully up to the limits of the available subsistence. The want of regular government, and the various political evils under which they labour, can effectually extinguish virtue, and public spirit, and literature, and industry: but population still keeps equal pace with the measure of the supply; still treads so closely upon it, that any deficiency in the seasons, any unexpected drought, or epidemic among the cattle, reduces them to severe distress, and even to absolute famine.

The mistakes on this head are not to be set to the account of our author, but of those among his readers, who because he has represented the lowest classes in these countries as subject to seasons of penury and want, have understood him to mean that over-population is the *cause* of their misery. The cause of their misery is the government and the habits it generates: and while these remain, neither the addition nor subtraction of millions of people would make any permanent difference in their situation. The addition, indeed, would cause an immediate famine and mortality; and the subtraction immediate plenty. If half their number were suddenly exterminated, the remaining half would of course enjoy abundance for a single season: but that season over, the effect would only be to sink the ratio of industry in proportion to the decreased demand, till the numbers gradually reproduced occasioned the necessity of again cultivating the desolated lands.

The just inference from these and all other ill governed or barbarous countries, relates to the tendency of population considered as a law of our nature, and no way bears upon the effects of that law on human happiness. The condition of people so circumstanced would not be one jot the better, though the power of population were diminished to any conceivable extent: indeed it is sufficiently abated by vicious customs and wide-wasting plagues, and probably at the present time is absolutely retrograde. We wish this point to be borne in mind; not only as being important to the question at issue, but as making part of a very general error with regard to the real conclusion deducible from Mr. Malthus's theory. The cause of the distress is moral and political vice; and the distress itself is only brought in as evidence to attest the uniform law which raises population up to the supply of food even under most unfavourable circumstances of natural or civil discouragement.

II. The pressure of population against supply in countries far advanced in civilization is more generally acknowledge by all who have paid attention to the subject. Still it is very possible that those who have not looked into the details of political economy, or accustomed themselves to its language, may not recognize the existence of the pressure so confidently and familiarly assumed. We read of distant times and distant countries in which multitudes have died by famine. There the want of subsistence is a palpable fact. But since the improvements in the circulation and distribution of produce from one country to another introduced by commerce, and from one part of the same country to another, facilitated by internal communication, the misery of *famine* is exchanged for the milder operation of *scarcity*, which only shews itself in an enhancement of the money-price of corn. Besides, a great quantity of human food is wasted in manufactures, is employed in distilleries, or is prodigally consumed in various forms of luxury. How does this agree with the alleged fact, that population presses against the actual supply? This, no doubt, is a very superficial objection, and is answered by the first elements of political science. But as we see every day that many persons, even of those whom they concern, have been very partially imbued with these first elements, we are unwilling to pass it over altogether.

It is evident that the man whose assistance is necessary to any master or employer of workmen must be supported by that employer, together with his family. For the precise purpose of obtaining this support, he consents to give his labour: and there are still many cases in which the recompense is actually made in the shape of provision. But one of the first and simplest operations of civilization, is to make all bargains through a common medium; and accordingly the return for labour, like other payments, is given in money. This money payment is very different in different countries, and in the same country at different times; but whatever it is, the quantity of subsistence it will procure, and not the nominal amount of the payment, is the standard by which the labour's return must be estimated. The only way therefore in which we can judge of the pressure of population, is by the rate of wages; and the only way in which we can estimate the rate of wages, is by the quantity of support which it will procure to the labourer, according to the customary mode of living in the country.

For this reason, from the time when the weekly labour is recompensed in money, the pressure of population is less directly visible to the eye of the common observer. Its operation in itself becomes a more complex concern; and it is moreover concealed from view by the quantity of machinery which is going on together. Its effect however is sufficiently discoverable in the diminished rate of wages, following the increased competition for employ. In countries like America, where there is plenty of fresh land ready to make an ample recompense to any capitalist who will take the pains of reclaiming it from the beasts of the forest, or the wandering savage of the plain, a labourer, in almost any department, may immediately meet with an employer. The competition there is among the masters, to find workmen; not among the workmen to find employ: but in most of the old countries of Europe the tide is commonly setting the other way; and especially in the lowest and simplest operations of industry, the competition is on the side of the labourer. The labourer is therefore in a much greater degree dependent upon his employer, and his remuneration is seldom larger than the support of his family absolutely demands.

To understand in practice what has been thus far stated in theory, our readers have only to look around them, and see the mode in which a great part of their countrymen are at this moment living; and then to answer, whether the human species in civilized countries does not increase up to the lowest quantity of support necessary to their preservation.

Beginning with the case of our peasants, the average wages in husbandry may be rated at 12s. per week: take the wife's earnings at two shillings, the total for the year will amount to £36:8s. With regard to the expenses, no one will place the consumption of a family throughout at less than a half-peck loaf per week to each individual. It is not reckoned lower even by overseers. At 1s. the quartern loaf the expense will stand thus, for a family with three children.

| | | |
|---|---|---|
| Bread for five persons, at 10s. per week, | £26 0 | per anu. |
| Soap and candles, at 8d.  do. | 1 16 | |
| Rent | 3 0 | |
| Clothing and furniture | 3 0 | |
| Fuel, 2s. in winter, 1s. in summer | 3 4 | |
| Total | £37 0 | |

This calculation carries us at once beyond the earnings, though no allowance has been made for medicine, loss of time, or any other article of food than wheaten bread. Whatever *luxuries* are claimed, must be saved out of the necessaries of life, or by substituting a cheaper and less nutritious article for the favourite food of the country; and if there be four children instead of three, under the working age, the additional child brings an expense of £5 per annum, and of course diminishes the chance of the workman's earnings. In estimating the bread too at 1s., we have taken rather a favourable average. Experience of the last twenty years has proved to us that we must not expect a stationary price. In the present year (1817) the average price would be about 3s. 4d. thus adding nine pounds to the annual expenditure, and bringing us so far beyond the actual wages. Yet the poor must be supported in dear years as well as cheap; and the whole statement justifies us in asserting that our agricultural poor are brought by the competition of labourers to as low a rate of wages, both nominal and real, as will enable them to rear a family.

Whoever has travelled in a manufacturing district will not have found things wearing a brighter aspect, or venture to affirm that the population seem better fed, better clothed, or better lodged than nature requires in order to keep up their number. At times indeed there is more variation in their rate of wages than among the peasantry, owing to an unusual demand for some particular manufacture, or to some temporary speculation. But these demands are followed by a decline no less rapid, and the average wages of the year do not exceed a moderate pittance. These facts, gleaned from the very surface of our own country, are domestic proofs of a population reaching the average supply; and it is well known that the effect of the picture would not be altered for the better, if Scotland and Ireland were added to the view. But if we stop here, we shall stop, after all, short of the population. As a population cannot be supported without food, it can never, of course, materially exceed the average supply. Still the tendency to increase is so strong, that in a civilized or fully peopled country it never rests on this side, it always encroaches a little beyond it. How is this possible? or if possible, how can it be proved? – Too easily. We have seen that labour is the only claim to support which the poorer classes can offer; to be without labour, therefore, is to be without support; and to multiply beyond the demand for labour, is to multiply beyond the available supply of food. But it is matter of experience that in all the departments of national industry there are always more claimants for employ than can obtain it; and though the excess, for obvious reasons, is at different periods very different in degree, the fact is undeniable, that there are always more workmen, than can find employers in manufactures; always more journeymen mechanics, than can be supplied with work; always more agricultural labourers, than, taking the year throughout, can be employed in useful husbandry. Every individual of these superfluous labourers is evidence of a population exceeding the supply of food.

This argument cannot be set aside by urging that if there is an excess of labourers in one department of manufacture, there is a deficiency in another; or that if there is a want of work in one part of the country, there is a want of workmen in another. We must argue of these things as we practically find them; and it is unnecessary to enter upon the question, whether if a central board for labour could be established, as Mr.

Colquhoun proposes, the demand upon the whole would not, after a certain time, be just as much above the supply of work that could be furnished, as it is now. Neither is it any sufficient contradiction of the statement, to say that, after all, the number of unemployed workmen is comparatively trifling. In the first place, we feel by too sensible experience that this is not always true. But not to argue on a general fact of our nature from accidental periods of distress, we must remember that in England the law authorises the poor to demand support, whether they can or cannot find employ: and accordingly many of them are set to sift gravel or level mole hills, or something equally profitable, and receive perhaps ten shillings per week for work which does not return a farthing to the employer. In manufacturing towns also, the benevolent sympathy of the masters often keeps a larger number of hands on the list, than they can employ with advantage to themselves; but the support of these superfluous hands must in fairness be set down to the score of charity, and not to an effectual demand for labour. Extensive charities, public subscriptions, and speculative enterprise in this country tend at all times to conceal from public observation the competition of labourers; but we have no doubt that the testimony of every parish in the kingdom, town and country taken together, would agree with the evidence actually laid before the Parliamentary Committees, and prove the population to be uniformly beyond the demand for labour, though it might be dangerous to assess the actual amount of the excess. Whether one in ten, or one in fifty labourers who are able and willing to work, are unable to provide a field for their industry, is not very material – it is evident that the redundance is on the side of the labourer: and somewhere between these two points, we imagine, the experience of different places and periods of time would justify us in fixing the degree of that redundance.

If this statement is correct, and a just result of what is continually passing before our eyes; then it becomes clear that there is no sufficient foundation for the opinion of an author whose principles we highly respect, and who argues that the collection of a larger part of the people into towns, and their engagement in unhealthy occupations in advanced states of society, so far increases the natural mortality and diminishes the average duration of life, as to equalize the acknowledged disproportion between the powers of population and production. Mr. Malthus, in his Appendix to the present edition, has considered this objection at some length. He admits the possibility of the case, which is provided for in the cautious terms in which his second proposition was enunciated; but he appeals to the state of the various countries in Europe, to shew that there is no appearance of any of them approaching that condition, when moral restraint may become a useless and unnecessary virtue; or when those who are disposed to marry, need employ no previous foresight as to their means of supporting a family.

'The question,' he says, 'can only be determined by an appeal to experience. Mr. Weyland is always ready to refer to the state of this country; and, in fact, may be said almost to have built his system upon the peculiar policy of a single state. But the reference in this case will entirely contradict his theory. He has brought forward some elaborate calculations to shew the extreme difficulty with which the births of the country supply the demands of the towns and manufactories. In looking over them, the reader, without other information, would be disposed to feel considerable alarm at the prospect of depopulation impending over the country; or at least he would be convinced that we were within a hair's breadth of that formidable point of *non-reproduction*, at which, according to Mr. Weyland, the population *naturally* comes to a full stop before the means of subsistence cease to be progressive.

'These calculations were certainly as applicable twenty years ago as they are now; and indeed they are chiefly founded on observations which were made at a greater distance of time than the period here noticed. But what has happened since? In spite of the enlargement of all our towns; in spite of the most rapid increase of manufactories, and of the proportion of people employed in them; in spite of the most extraordinary and unusual demands for the army and navy; in short, in spite of a state of things which, according to Mr. Weyland's theory, ought to have brought us long since to the point of *non-reproduction*, the population of the country has advanced at a rate more rapid than was ever known at any period of its history. During the ten years from 1800 to 1811, as I have mentioned in a former part of this work, the population of this country (even after making an allowance for the presumed deficiency of the returns in the first enumeration) increased at a rate which would double its numbers in fifty-five years.

'This fact appears to me at once a full and complete refutation of the doctrine, that, as society advances, the increased indisposition to marriage and the increased mortality in great towns and manufactures always overcome the principle of increase; and that, in the language of Mr. Weyland, "population, so far from having an inconvenient tendency uniformly to press against the means of subsistence, becomes by degrees very low in overtaking those means."

'With this acknowledged and glaring fact before him, and with the most striking evidences staring him in the face, that even, during this period of rapid increase, thousands both in the country and in towns were prevented from marrying so early as they would have done, if they had possessed sufficient means of supporting a family independently of parish relief, it is quite inconceivable how a man of sense could bewilder himself in such a maze of futile calculations, and come to a conclusion so diametrically opposite to experience.

'The fact already noticed, as it applies to the most advanced stage of society known in Europe, and proves incontrovertibly that the actual checks to population, even in the most improved countries, arise principally from an insufficiency of subsistence, and soon yield to increased resources, notwithstanding the increase of towns and manufactories, may I think fairly be considered as quite decisive of the question at issue.

'But in treating of so general and extensive a subject as the Principle of Population, it would surely not be just to take our examples and illustrations only from a single state. And in looking at the other countries Mr. Weyland's doctrine on population is, if possible, still more completely contradicted. Where, I would ask, are the great towns and manufactories in Switzerland, Norway, and Sweden, which are to act as *the graves of mankind*, and to prevent the possibility of a redundant population? In Sweden the proportion of the people living in the country is to those who live in town as thirteen to one; in England this proportion is about two to one; and yet England increases much faster than Sweden.

How is this to be reconciled with the doctrine that the progress of civilization and improvement is always accompanied by a correspondent abatement in the natural tendency of population to increase? Norway, Sweden and Switzerland have not on the whole been ill-governed; but where are the necessary "anticipating alterations," which, according to Mr. Weyland, arise in every society as the powers of the soil diminish, and "render so many persons unwilling to marry, and so many more, who do marry, incapable of reproducing their own numbers, and of replacing the deficiency in the remainder?" What is it that in these countries indisposes people to marry, but the absolute hopelessness of being able to support their families? What is it that renders many more who do marry incapable of reproducing their own numbers, but the diseases generated by excessive poverty – by an insufficient supply of the necessaries of life? Can any man of reflection look at these and many of the other countries of Europe, and then venture to state that there is no moral reason for repressing the inclination to early marriages; when it cannot be denied that the alternative of not repressing it must necessarily and unavoidably be premature mortality from excessive poverty? And is it possible to know that in few or none of the countries of Europe the wages of labour, determined in the common way by the supply and the demand, can support in health large families; and yet assert that population does not press against the means of subsistence, and that "the evils of a redundant population can never be necessarily felt by a country till it is actually peopled up to the full capacity of its resources?" – vol. iii. pp. 407–412.

The fact is, and Mr. Weyland as a sincere friend to humanity will rejoice at it notwithstanding its effect upon his argument, that the same progressive stage of civilization in which mankind are collected together in large towns, and subjected to the evils and diseases belonging to such a situation, brings also the antidote together with the malady; and by applying more general and more skilful attention to the means of prevention and cure, checks that premature mortality which unhealthy occupations and crowded streets would otherwise occasion. We have been at pains to verify this observation; and it is a satisfactory result of the inquiry to find, that those closely-peopled seats of manufactories and trade which were once emphatically called the graves of mankind, and in which Mr. Weyland's argument would bury so large a proportion of his countrymen, are now comparatively the abodes of health and longevity; so humane, so successfully and indisputably humane have been the improvements in the management of prisons, and hospitals, and work-houses; the establishment of fever-wards, and the various rules for ventilating, and purifying, and fumigating crowded manufactories.

By a calculation which Mr. Weyland has taken from Price's Reversionary Payments, it appeared that the annual deaths even in the small town of Newbury were to the whole population as 1 in 28 or 29, at the time when that calculation was made. Whereas the register of that town for the last ten years shews that the average duration of life is now exactly double. The annual deaths, at the present period, are as 1 in 56 of the whole; the average number for the last ten years amounting to 87, on a population which the last census states at 4900.

Thus it was formerly calculated that in Manchester, containing 34,000 souls, half the number born died under two years of age; in Northampton, containing 7000, under ten; and Mr. Weyland makes these calculations the hinges of his argument. We cannot put in so precise an answer to these particular cases; but common observation, and the judgment of the best-informed persons in those and similar situations concur in persuading us that matters are very different now; not to mention, that as the deaths in the whole of Lancashire are but as 1 in 48, and half the population of that county is contained in the two immense towns of Manchester and Liverpool, it is impossible to doubt the annual births must greatly exceed the annual deaths even in those unfavourable situations; and the population be progressive, instead of requiring continued supplies from the country to replace the domestic waste.

In fact, if this is true of Birmingham, no one will hesitate about Manchester. We have been favoured with an abstract of the baptisms and burials in Birmingham for thirteen years from the beginning of this century, out of which there have been only three, viz. 1801, 1802, and 1810, in which the former have not very considerably exceeded; and in the whole period the births have gained about one-seventh on the deaths, the baptisms averaging 2120 per annum, the burials 1979; or 1 in 43 of the whole population, taken at 85,753 in 1811. The register of the largest parish in the unhealthy city of Coventry gives nearly a similar result. So that the average duration of life in a town of 80,000 persons is fifteen years longer at the present time, than it was in a population of 4,000 fifty years ago. This increased healthiness of the community assists in accounting for the extraordinary increase of population within the last ten years, and in some degree for the pressure which has been lately experienced; as also for the flourishing state of Assurance Societies, and all other institutions which calculate upon the Swedish and other tables of fifty years date; and which ought no longer to be considered as authority for the general average of life in this country.

At all events it is very clear that we cannot depend on the mortality of towns, for ridding us of any superfluous population; and we own it is more gratifying to our minds to conclude that the advancement of civilization should counter-balance the unhealthiness which attends some of its occupations by the improvements of medical skill, than that there should be a constant and necessary waste of human life from premature mortality.

'If indeed such peculiar unhealthiness and mortality were the proper and natural check to the progress of population in the advanced stages of society, we should justly have reason to apprehend that, by improving the healthiness of our towns and manufactories, as we have done in England during the last twenty years, we might really defeat the designs of Providence. And though I have too much respect for Mr. Weyland to suppose that he would deprecate all attempts to diminish the mortality of towns, and render manufactories less destructive to the health of the children employed in them; yet certainly his principles lead to this conclusion, since his theory has been completely destroyed by those laudable efforts which have made the mortality of England – a country abounding in towns and manufactures, less than the mortality of Sweden – a country in a state almost purely agricultural.' – vol. iii. p. 424.

The conclusion is, therefore, that the natural progress of civilization does not so far retard the natural progress of population, as to counteract its universal tendency to surpass the limits of subsistence: though it is no doubt true that where any such causes of comparative unhealthiness exist, population could never increase in its greatest possible or even its greatest known ratio.

In a country of limited resources, this comparative shortness of life has no other effect than to accelerate the period or increase the chances of marriage. We have before alluded to the different averages exhibited by the table of marriages in the different counties of England. In Warwickshire, 1 takes place annually among 116 persons; in Worcestershire, 1 among 132; in Dorsetshire, 1 in 135; in Monmouthshire, 1 in 153; in all England, 1 in 120; in Wales, 1 in 130. From which it would appear that Monmouthshire, notwithstanding its picturesque beauty, is the very worst place to be born in, and Warwickshire, notwithstanding the smoke of its collieries and steam engines, the very best; and so it is, for all who have learnt from circulating libraries that life without love is not worth the having; but if we proceed to the next column, it appears that the value of love is fairly placed in the scale against the value of life, and that the average expectation of life varies with tolerable exactness according to the average expectation of marriage; the annual burials being to the whole population in Warwickshire, 1 in 42; in Worcestershire, 1 in 52; in Dorsetshire, 1 in 57; in Monmouthshire, 1 in 64; in all England, 1 in 49; in Wales, 1 in 60. This proves, if any thing can prove, the great restraint which prudence imposes in this country upon the power of population; and yet notwithstanding both the prudential restraint and the unhealthiness of many districts, population has proceeded to a length and swelled to an amount which we now find inconvenient, and are obliged to meet by growing demands on public and private charity, and glad to remedy by extensive emigration.

III. The objection which next occurs affords a more plausible argument against the general position. This is the case of agricultural countries, from which provisions of various kinds are regularly exported to supply the deficiency of those in a different state of civilization. The exportation of surplus produce conveys the idea that plenty is to be had at home for little or nothing: and there is no doubt but the country where labour is best rewarded in subsistence at least, if not in general comforts, is a country in this agricultural state, where a large family is a treasure, and where no apprehensions as to the difficulty of supporting one retard the progress of population.

Still, however, the general law asserts its power even here. Population pushes itself fully up to the means of subsistence, if by subsistence we speak of that which is available to their use; though the production power of the land being as yet commensurate with the activity of the population, the one has not outstripped the other. The case therefore which was considered under the last head, of labourers without labour, rarely occurs; but still those who look, even here, for gratuitous supply, will be bitterly disappointed. Those who from accident or misfortune cannot offer the return of labour for what they demand, or who from idleness will not, have much less chance of being maintained without than in a closely-peopled society like ours; while the surplus returns of those who do labour, instead of feeding an idle population, are bartered for artificial luxuries, or for foreign manufactures of necessity, or ornament, or utility. This is even the best state of an exporting country. But in ill-regulated societies, exportation may habitually take place while the mass of the people, or the very labourers who produce the surplus provision, are reduced to a degree of poverty and privation comparatively unknown in the countries which are dependent on them, and receiving the annual supply. Ireland and Poland have long exported; yet no one who knows the situation of their inhabitants will deny that there is more habitual distress, more squalid poverty endured there, than in their customers England and Holland. The actual supply of Ireland consists of the finest pork and beef; but what does this avail the cotter, who is supported on milk and potatoes? The actual supply of Poland consists of the finest wheat, to the growth of which the soil is more favourable than any in Europe; but what does this benefit the peasant, whose ordinary subsistence is obtained from rye bread and an inferior kind of pulse? It is true if the actual quantity of food in any given country could be equally divided amongst the members of it even in a year of the greatest want, and were consumed by them in the most frugal manner, there could seldom be an absolute scarcity, supposing the transaction to be extraordinary, and the division unexpected. But in the nature of things we know this is practically impossible; and that must be taken as the supply of a country, which its inhabitants in their several classes are able to command by the labour which in return they are able to offer.

It would therefore be an error to suppose that when we have found a country which, like Poland or America, or that part of Russia which borders on the Black Sea, regularly exports a quantity of human sustenance, we have found a country where mankind do not increase up to the supply. We have found a place, at least America and Russia are instances of it, where a man in possession of a certain capital may say, Here I will fix my standard, here my principal will find an easy employment, and here my labour will secure an ample support to any family which may be sent me. But we have not found a place where a man may say, here is a vacant space and quantity of superfluous produce which will support me gratuitously at my ease. There is no superfluous food in the world; no where any thing to spare, or to be had without return.

This assertion, if necessary, might receive additional confirmation from inquiring what, after all, is the boasted export of these abundant countries, and what proportion it bears to their own population. The whole of the exports of corn from the United States to all parts of the world in 1805, amounted to

777,543 barrels of flour,
55,400 bushels of oats,
861,501 of Indian corn,
56,836 tierces of rice;

with an inconsiderable growth of rye, wheat, and barley;[4] all which would furnish, according to the average consumption of England, a year's subsistence to about 200,000 persons; i.e. would support an addition of one thirtieth to the domestic population, rated at that period at six millions. Poland, which has also been inconsiderately treated as an inexhaustible granary, could never supply, during the excessive demand of the late war, more than 500,000 quarters, and on an average not more than half that quantity, i.e. according to our average consumption, at the highest, food for 400,000 persons, at the lowest for 200,000, which probably bears about the same proportion to the Polish population as the exportation from the

[4] See Mr. Jacob's pamphlet on the 'Protection of British Agriculture,' p. 56, &c. If some theorists in political economy would consider these facts and calculations, we should hardly be harassed with their speculations for supporting a manufacturing population by foreign agriculture.

United States. Yet these are the countries which send abroad by far the greatest quantity of corn, taken in comparison with their population: and when we estimate the dependence of America upon foreign countries for many necessaries of civilized life, and most of its luxuries; when we remember that the extensive land proprietors in Poland depend altogether on their exports for the means of a most lavish profusion; when we consider the immense exertions to procure corn which continued from 1795 to 1812, and the enormous price, both actual and relative, which it bore, and that the demand, being in a great measure regular, must have materially increased the cultivation; when we take all these elements into the calculation, we shall be rather struck with the near approach of the inhabitants to the produce, than with the amount of the surplus. The exportation, when reduced to figures, rather tends to show the pressure, than to furnish an exception against it; when we reflect that if the whole of the exported produce had been retained at home, it would not have supported the existing population above ten days beyond the year, or maintained an addition of more than a thirtieth part to the whole. We are inclined to doubt whether all the human subsistence which is exported from all the countries of the world, and is not balanced by a return of equivalent imports, if it could be exactly computed, would be found to exceed what might suffice for a year's supply of a million of persons, i.e. for a thousandth part of the probable population of the world. If this calculation comes any where near the truth, it will powerfully demonstrate the strength of population, with which even the extent and fertility of America or the southern departments of the Russian territory can only just keep pace; and which even the slack demand for labour in Ireland and the wretched vassalage of Poland cannot effectually restrain.

IV. The next objection which we shall briefly notice is of a more delicate nature, and connected with our feelings of natural and revealed religion. Upon this point there is something which well deserves remark in the first reception experienced by our author. He who referred the greatest evils of human life to a strong natural principle, might have looked for popular applause and gratitude, while he seemed to take the blame off our own shoulders, and throw it upon the constitution of things in which we have no active share; while he endeavoured to exonerate human laws or regulations, and to prove that the disease which preyed upon social happiness was more radical and inveterate than the wisest legislation could cure.

It might have been imagined that the discovery would be hailed as flattering our pride, and accepted as a satisfactory solution of many of those natural and civil evils, which, in spite of all our attempts to eradicate them, have always sprung up in every state of society, which are not only rankly luxuriant under bad administration, but have never been altogether extirpated even by the most careful culture.

On the contrary, the great majority of the public shut their eyes against the facts, and their ears against the conclusion; those who could not help acknowledging the force of both, took all possible pains to discard them from their minds, and to forget the assent which they could not entirely withhold; and those who were neither able to judge of premises nor inference, proclaimed by a general outcry their weakness and their fears, and started at the name of Malthus as an enemy of God and man. They preferred, it seems, that any imputation should lie against the institutions of society, rather than that they should be forced to give up the flattering prospect of a general amelioration in the condition of the human race. We have always thought this fact not a little remarkable; as furnishing a curious proof of the strong conviction inherent in mankind, that notwithstanding the distresses they see around them and the calamities they are subject to, they are still under the protecting dominion of a merciful as well as a powerful Creator; a conviction so deeply rooted that when they meet with a course of argument which appears to them (whether rightly or not) to end in a contrary conclusion, they at once infer the fallacy of the premises, and had rather mistrust the logic of their heads, than resign the consolatory feeling of their hearts.

Still it was soon found a much easier matter to disbelieve Mr. Malthus than to refute him. This ought earlier to have admonished his opponents, as it has at last taught them, to examine whether his premises, or their conclusions were really in the wrong; whether the fault were in his arguments, or in their impressions; whether, in short, the great features of the country, as he had represented them, were not correctly drawn, though the medium through which they were accidentally viewed had thrown a harsh and disagreeable tone of colouring over the picture; just as the state of mind, in Crabbe's ingenious tale of the Lover's Journey, gives to the same objects the tint of a March east wind, or of a glowing autumnal evening. It is not difficult to trace a similar effect in the work before us, arising naturally from the leading principle in the author's view when he sat down to the composition. A visionary notion of theoretical perfectibility could only be met by a practical statement of the evils, moral and physical, which beset human nature. Society has no greater enemy than the man who would substitute theory for experience; and no sincerer friend than the man who appeals to experience to refute him. To the chimerical reformer of the political and moral world, Mr. Malthus justly answers, such hopes are illusory and such schemes impracticable, while mankind exist as they are; there is a principle inherent in their very constitution, which will uniformly bring them, as in all ages and countries as it has already brought them, into a situation in which there will be labour, indigence, distress, and disease.

Here we have at once a key to the peculiar turn which the argument takes, which is certainly, at first sight, not a little unprepossessing. The principle which the Essay undertakes to explain, is uniformly treated in the light of an EVIL. The very title-page announces 'an inquiry into our prospects respecting the future removal or mitigation of *the evil* which it occasions.' Speaking of moral restraint, the author says, 'if this restraint do not produce vice, it is undoubtedly the *least evil* that can arise from the principle of population.' He elsewhere argues that 'we must submit to the action of a great check to population in some form or other, as an inevitable law of nature; and the only inquiry that remains is, how it may take place with the *least possible prejudice* to the virtue and happiness of society.' Even that habitual prudence, which leads mankind, or ought to lead them, to consider the means of providing for a family before they incur the responsibility of supporting one, is uniformly entitled the *'fear of misery.'*

It is well known what gave the argument this peculiar direction, and brought it into the notice of the world, with a more forbidding aspect than was likely to meet with a welcome reception. Had Mr. Godwin and his party followed another of the various mazes of error, and instead of attacking social institutions, directed their censures against the Creator of the world, who had interwoven with the constitution of mankind a principle which could not fail to render vice and misery universal; then we should have felt the advantage of the same enlightened understanding ready to meet the enemy on different grounds; shifting the line of his argument to encounter the opposite movements of his adversary, and prompt to take up another and an equally strong position. The merest sciolist in the book of nature, he might have argued, knows that he ought to search for good, and not evil, as the final object of any extensive principle in our constitution. The writer whom I oppose impeaches the wisdom of the Creator's measures because he is blind to His designs. Thales might as justly have blamed His arrangement, in revolving the larger round the smaller body, or Ptolemy have censured the want of a continent to balance Africa or Asia. It is not evident how this pressure of population against the actual subsistence, is uniformly exciting the industry of mankind to render more subsistence available? how the necessities it occasions improve the human faculties by exercise, and invigorate virtue? how it thus furnishes the best opportunities of strengthening those powers which want of exertion uniformly impairs, and of exhibiting those virtues which most conspicuously adorn the moral nature of man? It is for the censurer of the providential arrangement of things to show how the same purposes might have been answered by other and better means. Above all, can we fail to observe that this principle, imposed as it is by a Creator whom we see and feel to be benevolent, is a strong corroboration of the truth of that revelation which declares mankind to be placed here in a preparatory state? Have we not every reason from analogy to believe, that, if He had intended this for their final destination, He would have rendered perfection attainable; and that, as he has not placed perfection within their reach, he designs this world as a state of discipline?

That such would have been the general strain of our author's reasoning, had be been called upon by circumstances to refute one error instead of another, we never doubted, and the present edition confirms our previous conviction.

> 'It was my object,' says Mr. Malthus, 'in the two chapters on *Moral Restraint*, and its *Effects on Society*, to shew that the evils arising from the principle of population were exactly of the same nature as the evils arising from the excessive or irregular gratification of the human passions in general; and

that from the existence of these evils we had no more reason to conclude that the principle of increase was too strong for the purpose intended by the Creator, than to infer, from the existence of the vices arising from the human passions, that these passions required diminution or extinction, instead of regulation and direction.

'If this view of the subject be allowed to be correct, it will naturally follow that, notwithstanding the acknowledged evils occasioned by the principle of population, the advantages derived from it under the present constitution of things may very greatly overbalance them.

'A slight sketch of the nature of these advantages, as far as the main object of the Essay would allow, was given in the two chapters to which I have alluded; but the subject has lately been pursued with considerable ability in the Work of Mr. Sumner on the Records of the Creation; and I am happy to refer to it as containing a masterly developement and completion of views, of which only an intimation could be given in the Essay.

'I fully agree with Mr. Sumner as to the beneficial effects which result from the principle of population, and feel entirely convinced that the natural tendency of the human race to increase faster than the possible increase of the means of subsistence could not be either destroyed or essentially diminished without diminishing that hope of rising and fear of falling in society, so necessary to the improvement of the human faculties and the advancement of human happiness. But with this conviction on my mind, I feel no wish to alter the view which I have given of the evils arising from the principle of population. These evils do not lose their name or nature because they are overbalanced by good: and to consider them in a different light on this account, and cease to call them evils, would be as irrational as the objecting to call the irregular indulgences of passion vicious, and to affirm that they lead to misery, because our passions are the main sources of human virtue and happiness.

'I have always considered the principle of population as a law peculiarly suited to a state of discipline and trial. Indeed I believe that, in the whole range of the laws of nature with which we are acquainted, not one can be pointed out, which in so remarkable a manner tends to strengthen and confirm this scriptural view of the state of man on earth. And as each individual has the power of avoiding the evil consequence to himself and society resulting from the principle of population by the practice of a virtue clearly dictated to him by the light of nature, and sanctioned by revealed religion, it must be allowed that the ways of God to man with regard to this great law of nature are completely vindicated.

'I have, therefore, certainly felt surprise as well as regret that no inconsiderable part of the objections which have been made to the principles and conclusions of the Essay on Population has come from persons for whose moral and religious character I have so high a respect, that it would have been particularly gratifying to me to obtain their approbation and sanction. This effect has been attributed to some expressions used in the course of the work which have been thought too harsh, and not sufficiently indulgent to the weakness of human nature, and the feelings of Christian charity.

'It is probable, that having found the bow bent too much one way, I was induced to bend it too much the other, in order to make it straight. But I shall always be quite ready to blot out any part of the work which is considered by a competent tribunal as having a tendency to prevent the bow from becoming finally straight, and to impede the progress of truth. In deference to this tribunal I have already expunged the passages which have been most objected to, and I have made some few further corrections of the same kind in the present edition. By these alterations I hope and believe that the work has been improved without impairing its principles. But I still trust that whether it is read with or without these alterations, every reader of candour must acknowledge that the practical design uppermost in the mind of the writer, with whatever want of judgment it may have been executed, is to improve the condition and increase the happiness of the lower classes of society.' – vol. iii. pp. 424–428.

We introduce this passage, partly as furnishing the best reply to the objection under consideration, and partly to account for the different impression which the Essay itself formerly conveyed; but chiefly as an instructive example of that candour which always attends true philosophy. While the ignorant or bigoted writer is only rendered pertinacious by confutation, the philosophic reasoner gives its due weight to his adversary's argument, and is either more firmly settled in his own opinion by impotent attempts to subvert it, or ready to modify his statements where he sees occasion. Truth being his object, he would consent to gain his object even if he were obliged to forego the honours of victory; and, therefore, if the victory finally rest with him, he enjoys the splendour of conquest, and not the mere credit of obstinate resistance.

V. The last objection we shall notice relates to the value of the whole subject, and of the conclusion to which it brings us. What after all is gained towards that important end, the regulation of private conduct, by these general views? How would it suit the gallantry of one sex, or the delicacy of the other, that public expedience should take place of individual attachment, or the ardour of love be graduated according to the current rate of population?

With respect to this, we know very well that men will marry, as they ought to marry, and as they always have married, on other considerations than those of philosophy or the general good. The high encomium passed upon Cato, *Urbi* pater est, *urbique* maritus, is not likely to be often claimed in our times, nor are we anxious that it should. Such qualities may be very grand, but they are very unamiable. There is little fear, however, lest men should begin to consult in these private matters any other rule than that which they have hitherto consulted, their own private interest. Can they support the probable expense of the married state, in that sphere of life in which they were born and educated; or into which they may be contented to descend, in order to gratify one passion at the expense of another? This is the only question they have to ask, and the answer to it will indicate their duty, and ought to direct their conduct. The wages of labour in every profession and vocation not only afford the only practicable rule of individual interest, but are, in fact, a general index of the proportion which the means of subsistence bear to the existing population.

But laying aside individual cases, we entirely concur with the author in the importance of general rules, and therefore in the practical value of that fact which he has added to our stock of universal truths, viz. the tendency of mankind to pass the limit of their subsistence. In all advanced societies mankind exist in a very artificial state, and laws, as we know, are enacted with the intent of directing the habits of the community into those channels which appear most beneficial in the view of the legislator. The question, then, is, what sort of laws are we to promulgate? are we to discourage celibacy? to accelerate the increase of population, and give a bounty on large families? Nor is this only an abstract question, such as Harrington or Sir Thomas More, or any other framer of an ideal commonwealth might have asked; but one that comes particularly home to our English interests. Our poor laws, as now administered, are neither more nor less than a standing bounty on increase, on redundant increase, by supporting at the public expense those fathers of families, who could not support themselves, even whilst single, by labour: and though formerly Mr. Malthus expressed a doubt whether they had really enlarged population so much as they had extended misery, while the redundant (i.e. the unemployed) poor were crowded into workhouses or farmed out in manufactories, there can now be no question upon the subject, when public money is either added to the regular wages of labour, or supplied in its stead.

When the expediency of such a practice becomes matter of discussion, a general rule of reference is of the utmost importance; and is furnished at once by the universal truth, that mankind have a tendency in all cases to multiply beyond the regular supply of food, or regular demand of labour. This determines the point, and shows that the impulse is to be first applied to labour, which will spontaneously increase population, and not to population, which may not so certainly obtain subsistence by finding labour: and even if it finally succeeds, there is an intermediate risk, and a certainty of distress and discontent.

The importance of having such a rule established may be best appreciated by reflecting on the consequences of wanting, or neglecting it. These were predicted by Mr. Malthus at a period when there was an extraordinary demand for men, and very little disposition to suppose the possibility of any evil arising out of the redundancy of population. But his remarks on the nature and effects of the poor laws have been in the most striking manner confirmed by the experience of the years 1815, 1816, and 1817.

> 'During these years, two points of the very highest importance have been established, so as no longer to admit of a doubt in the mind of any rational man.

'The first is, that the country does not in point of fact fulfil the promise which it makes to the poor in the poor-laws, to maintain and find in employment, by means of parish assessments, those who are unable to support themselves or their families, either from want of work or any other cause.

'And secondly, that with a very great increase of legal parish assessments, aided by the most liberal and praiseworthy contributions of voluntary charity, the country has been wholly unable to find adequate employment for the numerous labourers and artificers who were able as well as willing to work.

'It can no longer surely be contended that the poor-laws really perform what they promise, when it is known that many almost starving families have been found in London and other great towns, who are deterred from going on the parish by the crowded, unhealthy and horrible state of the workhouses into which they would be received, if indeed they could be received at all; when it is known that many parishes have been absolutely unable to raise the necessary assessments, the increase of which, according to the existing laws, have tended only to bring more and more persons upon the parish, and to make what was collected less and less effectual; and when it is known that there has been an almost universal cry from one end of the kingdom to the other for voluntary charity to come in aid of the parochial assessments.' – vol. ii. pp. 351, 352.

This evil, which we cannot help referring to the existing habit of interference with the wages of labour, and with the ordinary progress of population, can only be remedied by a return to the natural course; and the easiest mode of accomplishing this object is really the single question for Parliament to consider; the extent as well as the cause of the evil itself being alike established by the evidence which they have so laboriously collected. But we must not digress into another wide and difficult field of discussion.

Secondly, it is no slight advantage to be provided with an incontrovertible answer to all sweeping reformers; and to know on positive grounds that the face of civilized society must always remain uniform in its principal lineaments, and be distinguished by the same features which it has hitherto borne; that our business therefore is to lessen or remove its blemishes, and to prevent their growing into deformities: but that we can no more organize a community without poverty, and its consequence, severe labour, than we can organize a body without natural infirmities, or add a limb to the human frame. Some perhaps may think it a misfortune to know thus much – and certainly if ignorance in this case would lead to bliss, it were folly to be wise; but it can only conduct to inevitable misery. In fact, the present year has shewn the practical value of this advancement in our knowledge. The Spenceans, it is true, who coolly talk of dividing the land among the people and establishing an Agrarian Republic, are not of a sort to be addressed by reason. But it is always satisfactory to have reason on the side of law; and to be prepared to prove, if any will listen, that these new sons of the earth, these ΣΠΑΡΤΟΙ of modern sedition or modern ignorance, after having devoured all the property of the country, would soon be reduced, like their predecessors of old, to the necessity of devouring one another. And that their leaders, however ill-informed, have sense enough to discover the barrier which the Principle of Population opposes against their schemes, is evident from the rancorous hostility with which Evans, the Cadmus of the tribe, has attacked Mr. Malthus in what he is pleased to entitle his 'Christian Policy.'

With this general view of the bearings on the subject upon our internal economy, we shall close our remarks upon the important addition to political science contained in Mr. Malthus's Essay. Upon the book itself, which has already reached a fifth edition, it would now be superfluous to pronounce an elaborate opinion. The author, as we have often intimated, might have clothed his principles in a more attractive garb, and have introduced them to the public under a more favourable aspect: and we cannot help regretting that the same masterly hand, which first pointed out why equality, and plenty, and community of goods were unattainable to beings constituted like mankind, had not also proceeded to show that they were no less undesirable; that the same powerful guide, who first checked, in her untried course, the frail bark of universal happiness, sailing as she was 'with youth at the prow and pleasure at the helm,' and pointed out the unforeseen bank on which she could not fail to split, had not also taken the pains to prove that the course human nature was forced to pursue is also the best it could pursue, when the object and end of the voyage are added to the consideration.

# LONDON MAGAZINE 1823
[Thomas de Quincey]

## I – Malthus[1]

"Go, my son," – said a Swedish chancellor to his son, – "go and see with how little cost of wisdom this world is governed." "Go," might a scholar, in like manner say, after a thoughtful review of literature, "go and see – how little logic is required to the composition of most books." Of the many attestations to this fact, furnished by the history of opinions in our hasty and unmeditative age, I know of none more striking than the case of Mr. Malthus, both as regards himself and his critics. About a quarter of a century ago Mr. Malthus wrote his Essay on Population, which soon rose into great reputation. And why? not for the truth it contained; *that* is but imperfectly understood even at present; but for the false semblance of systematic form with which he had invested the truth. Without any necessity he placed his whole doctrine on the following basis: man increases in a geometrical ratio – the food of man in an arithmetical ratio. This proposition, though not the main error of his work, is *one*; and therefore I shall spend a few lines in exposing it. I say then that the distinction is totally groundless: both tend to increase in a geometric ratio; both have this tendency checked and counteracted in the same way. In every thing which serves for the food of man, no less than in man himself, there is a *positive* ground of increase by geometrical ratios; but in order that this positive ground may go on to its effect, there must in each case be present a certain *negative* condition (i.e. *conditio sine qua non*)[2]: for the food, as

---

1 [This forms the second note as originally published, the first being "Walking Stewart," already printed in vol. vii. of the Works]

2 Once for all let me say to the readers of these memoranda, that I use the term *negative condition* as equivalent to the term *conditio sine qua non*, and both in the scholastic sense. The negative condition of X is that which being absent X can*not* exist; but which being present X will not *therefore* exist, unless a positive ground of X be co-present. Briefly, – If not, not: if yes, not therefore yes.

suppose for wheat, the negative condition is soil on which it may grow, and exert its virtue of self-multiplication; for man the negative condition is food; *i.e.* in both cases the negative condition is the same – *mutatis mutandis*: for the soil is to the wheat what the wheat is to man. Where this negative condition is present, both will increase geometrically; where it is absent, neither. And so far is it from being true that man has the advantage of the wheat, or increases according to any other law, as Mr. Malthus affirms, that, on the contrary, the wheat has greatly the advantage of man (though both increase according to the same law.) But, says Mr. Malthus, you would find it impossible to increase the annual supply of wheat in England by so much as the continual addition even of the existing quantity; whereas man might, on a certain supposition, go on increasing his species in a geometric ratio. What is that supposition? Why this – that the negative condition of increase, the absence of which is the actual resistance in both cases to the realization of a geometric increase, is here by supposition restored to man but *not* restored to the wheat. It is certainly true that wheat in England increases only by an arithmetic ratio; but then so does man: and the inference thus far would be, that both alike were restricted to this law of increase. "Aye, but then man," says Malthus, "will increase by another ratio, if you allow him an unlimited supply of food." Well, I answer, and so will the wheat: to suppose this negative condition (an unlimited supply of food) concurring with the positive principle of increase in man, and to refuse to suppose it in the wheat, is not only contrary to all laws of disputing – but is also on this account the more monstrous, because the possibility and impossibility of the negative concurring with this positive ground of increase is equal, and (what is still more to the purpose) is identical for both: wheresoever the concurrence is realised for man, there of necessity it is realised for the wheat. And, therefore, you have not only a right to demand the same concession for the wheat as for the man, but the one concession is actually involved in the other. As the soil (S) is to the wheat (W), so is the wheat (W) to man (M); *i.e.* $S : W :: W : M$. You cannot even by way of hypothesis assume any cause as multiplying the third term, which will not also pre-suppose the multiplication of the first: else you suffer W as the third term to be multiplied, and the very same W as the second term not to be multiplied. In fact, the coincidence of the negative with the positive ground of increase must of necessity take place in all countries during the early stages of society for the food of man no less than for man: this coincidence must exist and gradually cease to exist for both simultaneously. The negative condition, without which the positive principle of increase in man and in the food of man is equally inefficient, is withdrawn *in fact* as a country grows populous: for the sake of argument, and as the basis of a chain of reasoning, it may be restored *in idea* to either; but not more to one than to the other. That proposition of Mr. Malthus, therefore, which ascribes a different law of increase to man and to the food of man (which proposition is advanced by Mr. Malthus and considered by most of his readers as the fundamental one of his system) is false and groundless. Where the positive principle of increase meets with its complement the negative ground, there the increase proceeds in a geometrical ratio – alike in man and in his food: where it fails of meeting this complement, it proceeds in an arithmetical ratio, alike in both. And I say that wherever the geometrical ratio of increase exists for man, it exists of necessity for the food of man: and I say that whenever the arithmetical ratio exists for the food of man, it exists of necessity for man.

Lastly, – I repeat that, even where the food of man and man himself increase in the same *ratio* – (viz. a geometrical ratio), yet that the food has greatly the advantage in the *rate* of increase. For assume any cycle of years (suppose 25) as the period of a human generation and as corresponding to the annual generations of wheat, then I say that, if a bushel of wheat and a human couple (man and woman) be turned out upon Salisbury plain – or, to give them more area and a better soil for experiment, on the stage of Canada and the uncolonized countries adjacent, – the bushel of wheat shall have produced its cube – its 4th – 10th – Mth power in a number of years which shall always be fewer than the number of periods of 25 years in which the human pair shall have produced its cube – its 4th – 10th – Mth power, etc. And this assertion may be easily verified by consulting any record of the average produce from a given quantity of seed corn.

II. The famous proposition therefore about the geometrical and arithmetical ratios as applied to man and his food – is a radical blunder. I come now to a still more remarkable blunder, which I verily believe is the greatest logical oversight that has ever escaped any author of respectability. This oversight lies in Mr. Malthus's view of population considered not with reference to its own internal coherency but as an answer to Mr. Godwin. That gentleman, in common with some other philosophers, – no matter upon what arguments, – had maintained the doctrine of the 'perfectibility' of man. Now, says Mr. Malthus, without needing any philosophic investigation of this doctrine, I will overthrow it by a simple statement drawn from the political economy of the human race: I will suppose that state of perfection, towards which the human species is represented as tending, to be actually established: and I will show that it must melt away before the principle which governs population. How is this accomplished? briefly thus:– In every country the food of man either goes on increasing simply in an arithmetical ratio, or (in proportion as it becomes better peopled) is rapidly tending to such a ratio. Let us suppose this ratio everywhere established, as it must of necessity be as soon as no acre of land remains untilled which is susceptible of tillage; since no revolutions in the mere science of agriculture can be supposed capable of transmuting an arithmetic into a geometric ratio of increase. Food then increasing under this law can never go on *pari passu* with any population which should increase in a geometric ratio? Now what is it that prevents population from increasing in such a ratio? Simply the want of food. But how? Not directly, but through the instrumentality of vice and misery in some[3] shape or other. These are the repressing forces which everywhere keep down the increase of man to the same ratio as that of his food – viz. to an arithmetic ratio. But vice and misery can have no existence in a state of perfection; so much is evident ex vi termini. If then these are the only repressing forces, it follows that in a state of perfection there can be none at all. If none at all, then the geometric ratio of increase will take place. But, as the arithmetic ratio must still be the law for the increase of food, the population will be constantly getting ahead of the food. Famine, disease, and every mode of wretchedness will

---

[3] What is the particular shape which they put on in most parts of the earth – furnishes matter for the commentary of Mr. Malthus on his own doctrine, and occupies the greater part of his work. The materials are of course drawn from voyages and travels; but from so slender a reading in that department of literature, that the whole should undoubtedly be re-written and more learnedly supported by authorities.

return; and thus out of its own bosom will the state of perfection have regenerated the worst form of imperfection by necessarily bringing back the geometric ratio of human increase unsupported by the same ratio of increase amongst the food. This is the way in which Mr. Malthus applies his doctrine of population to the overthrow of Mr. Godwin. Upon which I put this question to Mr. Malthus. In what condition must the human will be supposed, if with the clear view of this fatal result (such a view as must be ascribed to it in a state of perfection), it could nevertheless bring its own acts into no harmony with reason and conscience? Manifestly it must be in a most diseased state. Ay, says Mr. Malthus, but "I take it for granted" that no important change will ever take place in that part of human nature. Be it so, I answer: but the question here is not concerning the *absolute* truth, - Is there any hope that the will of man can ever raise itself from its present condition of weakness and disorder? The question is concerning the formal or logical truth - concerning the truth *relatively* to a specific concession previously made. Mr. Malthus had consented to argue with Mr. Godwin on the supposition that a state of perfection might be and actually was attained. How comes he then to "take for granted" what in a moment makes his own concession void? He agrees to suppose a perfect state; and at the same time he includes in this supposition the main imperfection of this world - viz. the diseased will of man. This is to concede and to retract in the same breath; explicitly to give, and implicitly to refuse. Mr. Godwin may justly retort upon Mr. Malthus - you promised to show that the state of perfection should generate out of itself an inevitable relapse into that state of imperfection: but *your* state of perfection already includes imperfection, and imperfection of a sort which is the principal parent of almost all other imperfection. Eve, after her fall, was capable of a higher resolution than is here ascribed to the children of perfection; for she is represented by Milton as saying to Adam

>              - miserable it is
> To be to others cause of misery,
> - Our own begotten; and of our loins to bring
> Into this cursed world a woeful race,
> That after wretched life must be at last
> Food for so foul a monster: in thy power

It lies yet, ere conception, to prevent
The race unblest – to being yet unbegot.
Childless thou art, childless remain: –
P.L. Book X.

What an imperfect creature could meditate, a perfect one should execute. And it is evident that if ever the condition of man were brought to so desirable a point as that, simply be replacing itself, the existing generation could preserve unviolated a state of perfection, it would become the duty (and, if the duty, *therefore* the inclination of perfect beings) to comply with that ordinance of the reason.[4]

III. Thus far on the errors of Mr. Malthus: – now let me add a word or two on the errors of his critics. But first it ought in candour to be acknowledged that Mr. Malthus's own errors, however important separately considered, are venial as regards his system; for they leave it unaffected, and might be extirpated by the knife without drawing on any consequent extirpations or even any alterations. That sacrifice once made to truth and to logic, – I shall join with Mr. Ricardo (Pol. Econ. p. 498, 2d ed.) in expressing my persuasion "that the just reputation of the Essay on Population will spread with the cultivation of that science of which it is so eminent an ornament." With these feelings upon Mr. Malthus's merits, it may be supposed that I do not regard his critics with much sympathy; taking them generally, they seem to have been somewhat captious, and in a thick mist as to the true meaning and tendency of the doctrine. Indeed I question whether any man amongst them could have begun his own work by presenting a just analysis of that which he was assailing; which, however, ought always to be demanded peremptorily of him who assails a

[4] Mr. Malthus has been charged with a libel of human nature for denying its ability, even in its present imperfect condition, to practise the abstinence here alluded to – provided an adequate motive to such abstinence existed. But this charge I request the reader to observe that I do not enter into. Neither do I enter into the question – whether any great change for the better in the moral nature of the man is reasonably to be anticipated. What I insist on is simply the *logical* error of Mr. Malthus in introducing into the hypothesis which he consents to assume one element which is a contradiction *in terminis* to that hypothesis. Admit that Mr. Malthus is right in denying the possibility of a perfect state of man on this earth; he cannot be right in assuming an enormous imperfection (disorder of the will) as one constituent of that perfect state.

systematic work, for the same reason that in the old schools of disputation the respondent was expected to repeat the syllogism of his opponent before he undertook to answer it. Amongst others Mr. Coleridge, who probably contented himself *more suo* with reading the first and last pages of the work, has asserted that Mr. Malthus had written a 4to. volume (in which shape the second edition appeared) to prove that man could not live without eating. If this were the purpose and amount of the Malthusian doctrine, doubtless an infra-duodecimo would have been a more becoming size for his speculations. But I, who have read the 4to. must assure Mr. Coleridge that there is something more in it than *that*. I shall also remind him that if a man produces a body of original and eminently useful truths, in that case the more simple – the more elementary – the more self-evident is the proposition on which he suspends the chain of those truths, – the greater is his merit. Many systems of truth which have a sufficient internal consistency, have yet been withheld from the world, or have lost their effect, simply because the author has been unable to bridge over the gulph between his own clear perceptions and the universal knowledge of mankind – has been unable to deduce the new truths from the old *precognita*. I say therefore that our obligations to Mr. Malthus are the greater for having hung upon a postulate, so simple as that which Mr. Coleridge alleges, so much valuable instruction both theoretic and practical as his work contains. Is it nothing for our theoretic knowledge that Mr. Malthus has taught us to judge more wisely of the pretended depopulations from battle, pestilence, and famine, with which all history has hitherto teemed? Is it nothing for our practical knowledge that Mr. Malthus has taught the lawgivers and the governors of the world to treat with contempt the pernicious counsels of political economists from Athenian days down to our own – clamouring for direct encouragements to population? Is it nothing for England that he first has exposed the fundamental[5] vice of our Poor Laws – (viz. that they act as a bounty on population), and placed a light-house upon the

---

[5] Fundamental, I mean, for the political economist: otherwise for the philosopher they have a still profounder vice, in their obvious tendency to degrade the moral character of their objects in their best elements of civil respectability.

rocks to which our course was rapidly carrying us in darkness? Is it nothing for science and the whole world that, by unfolding the laws which govern population, he has given to political economy its complement and sole desideratum; which wanting, all its movements were insecure and liable to error; which added, political economy (however imperfect as to its development) has now become, as to the *idea* of its parts, perfect and orbicular? – Is this, and more that might be alleged, nothing? I say, Mr. Coleridge,

> – Is this nothing?
> Why then the world, and all that's in't, is nothing:
> The covering sky is nothing, Bohemia nothing.
> *Winter's Tale.*

Others, who have been more just to Mr. Malthus than Mr. Coleridge, and have admitted the value of the truths brought forward, have disputed his title to the first discovery. A fuller development and a more extensive application of these truths they concede to him: but they fancy that in the works of many others before him they find the outlines of the same truths more or less distinctly expressed. And doubtless in some passages of former economists, especially of Sir James Steuart, and in one work of Wallace (Views of Providence, etc.) there is so near an approach made to the Malthusian doctrine – that at this day, when we are in possession of that doctrine, we feel inclined to exclaim in the children's language of blind-man's-buff – Lord! how he *burns*! – But the best evidence that none of these writers did actually touch the central point of the doctrine, is this: that none of them deduced from it those corollaries as to the English poor law – foundling-hospitals – endowments of cottages with land – and generally of all artificial devices for stimulating population, which could not have escaped a writer of ability who had once possessed himself of the entire truth. In fact, such is the anarchy of thought in most writers on subjects which they have never been led to treat systematically – that it is nothing uncommon to meet with a passage written apparently under Malthusian views in one page of a writer who in the next will possibly propose a tax on celibacy – a prize for early marriages – or some other absurdity not less outrageously hostile to those views. – No! let the merit of Mr. Malthus be otherwise what it may, his originality is incontestable –

unless an earlier writer can be adduced who has made the same oblique applications of the doctrine, and in general who has shown with what consequences that doctrine is pregnant; separate from which consequences the mere naked doctrine, in and for itself, is but a meagre truth.

# THE VALLEY OF THE AVON
From *Rural Rides* (1826)
[William Cobbett]

*Down the Valley of the Avon in Wiltshire*
'Thou shalt not muzzle the ox when he treadeth out the corn.'  Deuteronomy, ch. xxv. ver. 4.

## Milton, Monday 28th August

I came off this morning on the Marlborough road about two miles, or three, and then turned off, over the downs, in a north-westerly direction, in search of the source of the AVON RIVER, which goes down to Salisbury. I had once been at NETHER-AVON, a village in this valley; but, I had often heard this valley described as one of the finest pieces of land in all England; I knew that there were about *thirty parish churches*, standing in a length of about *thirty miles*, and in an average width of *hardly a mile*; and, I was resolved to see a little into the *reasons* that could have induced our fathers to build all these churches, especially if, as the Scotch would have us believe, there were but a mere handful of people in England *until of late years*.

The first part of my ride this morning was by the side of SIR JOHN ASTLEY'S park. This man is one of the *members of the county* (gallon-loaf BENNETT being the other): they say that he is good to the labouring people; and he ought to be good for *something*, being a member of Parliament of the Lethbridge and Dickinson stamp. However he has got a thumping estate; though, be it borne in mind, the *working people* and the *fund-holders* and the *dead-weight* have each their *separate mortgage* upon it; of which this Baronet has, I dare say, too much justice to complain, seeing that the amount of these mortgages was absolutely necessary to carry on PITT and PERCEVAL and CASTLEREAGH WARS; to support *Hanoverian soldiers in England*; to fight and beat the Americans on the *Serpentine River*; to give *Wellington a kingly estate*; and to defray *the expenses of Manchester and other yeomanry cavalry*;

besides all the various charges of *Power-of-Imprisonment Bills* and of *Six-Acts*. These being the cause of the mortgages, the 'worthy Baronet' has, I will engage, too much justice to complain of them.

In steering across the down, I came to a large farm, which a shepherd told me was MILTON HILL FARM. This was upon high land, and before I came to the edge of this *Valley of Avon* which was my land of promise; or, at least, of great expectation; for I could not imagine that thirty churches had been built *for nothing* by the side of a brook (for it is no more during the greater part of the way) thirty miles long. The shepherd showed me the way towards MILTON; and at the end of about a mile, from the top of a very high part of the down, with a steep slope towards the valley, I first saw this *Valley of Avon*; and a most beautiful sight it was! Villages, hamlets, large farms, towers, steeples, fields, meadows, orchards, and very fine timber-trees, scattered all over the valley. The shape of the thing is this: on each side *downs*, very lofty and steep in some places, and sloping miles back in other places; but each *out-side* of the valley are downs. From the edge of the downs begin capital *arable fields* generally of very great dimensions, and, in some places, running a mile or two back into little *cross valleys*, formed by hills of downs. After the corn-fields come *meadows*, on each side, down to the *brook*, or *river*. The farm-houses, mansions, villages, and hamlets, are generally situated in that part of the arable land which comes nearest the meadows.

Great as my expectations had been, they were more than fulfilled. I delight in this sort of country; and I had frequently seen the vale of the *Itchen*, that of the *Bourne*, and also that of the *Teste*, in Hampshire; I had seen the vales amongst the *South Downs*, but I never before saw any thing to please me like this valley of the Avon. I sat upon my horse, and looked over Milton and Easton and Pewsey for half an hour, though I had not breakfasted. The hill was very steep. A road, going slanting down it, was still so steep, and washed so very deep, by the rains of ages, that I did not attempt to *ride* down it, and I did not like to lead my horse, the path was so narrow. So seeing a boy with a drove of pigs, going out to the stubbles, I beckoned him to come up to me; and he came and led my horse down for me. But now before I begin to ride down this beautiful vale, let me give as well as my means will enable me, a

# THE VALLEY OF THE AVON

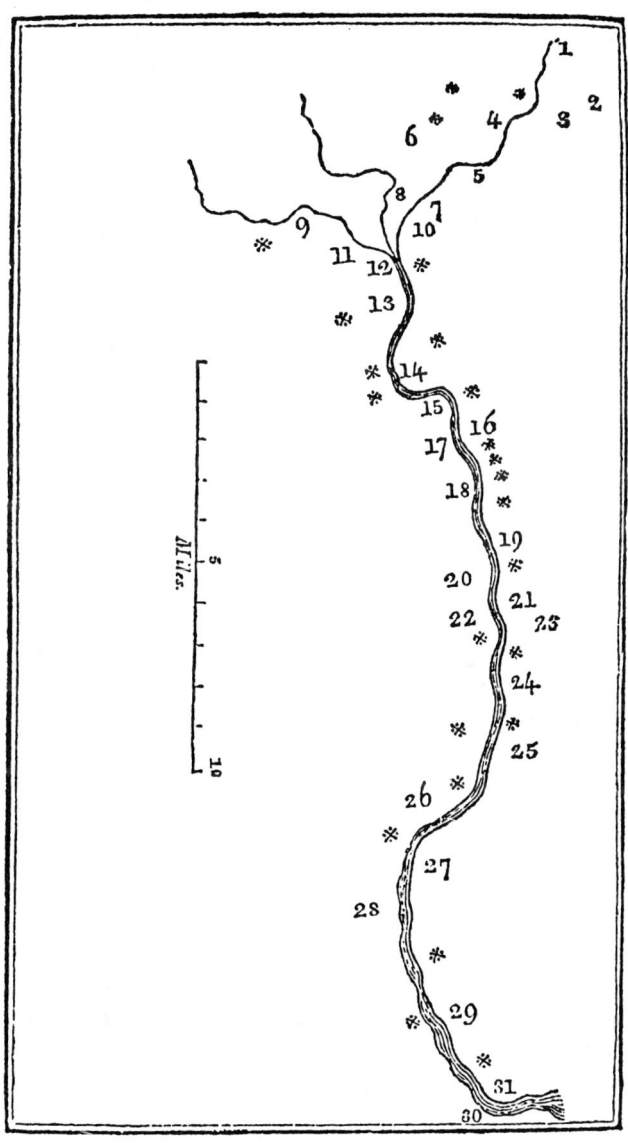

plan or map of it, which I have made in this way: a friend has lent me a *very old* map of Wiltshire describing the spots where all the *churches* stand, and also all the spots where *Manor-houses*, or *Mansion-houses* stood. I laid a piece of very thin paper upon the map, and thus traced the river upon my paper, putting *figures* to represent the spots where the churches stand, and putting *stars* to represent the spots where Manor-houses, or Mansion houses formerly stood. Endless is the variety in the shape of the high lands which form this valley. Sometimes the slope is very gentle, and the arable lands go back very far. At others, the downs come out into the valley almost like piers into the sea, being very steep in their sides, as well as their ends towards the valley. They have no slope at their other ends: indeed they have no *back ends*, but run into the main high land. There is also great variety in the *width* of the valley; great variety in the width of the meadows; but the land appears all to be of the very best; and it must be so, *for the farmers confess it.*

It seemed to me, that one way, and that not, perhaps, the least striking, of exposing the folly, the stupidity, the inanity, the presumption, the insufferable emptiness and insolence and barbarity, of those numerous wretches, who have now the audacity to propose to *transport* the people of England, upon the principle of the monster MALTHUS, who has furnished the unfeeling oligarchs and their toad-eaters with the pretence, that *man has a natural propensity to breed faster than food can be raised for the increase*; it seemed to me, that one way of exposing this mixture of madness and of blasphemy was, to take a look, now that the harvest is in, at the *produce*, the *mouths*, the *condition*, and *the changes that have taken place*, in a spot like this, which God has favoured with every good that he has had to bestow upon man.

From the top of the hill I was not a little surprised to see, in every part of the valley that my eye could reach, a due, a large, portion of fields of *Swedish turnips*, all looking extremely well. I had found the turnips, of both sorts, by no means bad, from Salt Hill to Newbury; but from Newbury through Burghclere, Highclere, Uphusband, and Tangley, I had seen but few. At and about Ludgarshall and Everley, I had seen hardly any. But, when I came, this morning, to Milton Hill farm, I saw a very large field of what appeared to me to be fine Swedish Turnips. In the *valley*, however, I found them much finer, and the fields were very beautiful objects, forming, as their colour did, so great a contrast with that of the fallows and the stubbles, which latter are, this year, singularly clean and bright.

Having gotten to the bottom of the hill, I proceeded on to the village of MILTON, the church of which is, in the map, represented by the figure 3. I left EASTON (2) away at my right, and I did not go up to WATTON RIVERS (1) where the river AVON rises, and which lies just close to the south-west corner of Marlborough Forest, and at about 5 or 6 miles from the town of Marlborough. Lower down the river, as I thought, there lived a friend, who was a great farmer, and whom I intended to call on. It being my way, however, always to begin making enquiries soon enough, I asked the pig-driver where this friend lived; and, to my surprise, I found that he lived in the parish of Milton. After riding up to the church, as being the centre of the village, I went on towards the house of my friend, which lay on my road down the valley. I have many, many times witnessed *agreeable surprise*; but I do not know, that I ever in the whole course of my life, saw people so much surprised and pleased as this farmer and his family were at seeing me. People often *tell* you, that they are *glad to see* you; and in general they speak truth. I take pretty good care not to approach any house, with the smallest appearance of a design to eat or drink in it, unless I be *quite sure* of a cordial reception; but my friend at FIFIELD (it is in Milton parish) and all his family really seemed to be delighted beyond all expression.

When I set out this morning, I intended to go all the way down to the city of Salisbury (31) *to-day*; but, I soon found, that to refuse to sleep at FIFIELD would cost me a great deal more trouble than a day was worth. So that I made my mind up to say in this farm-house, which has one of the nicest gardens, and it contains some of the finest flowers, that I ever saw, and all is disposed with as much good taste as I have ever witnessed. Here I am, then, just going to bed after having spent as pleasant a day as I ever spent in my life. I have heard to-day, that BIRKBECK lost his life by attempting to cross a river on horseback; but if what I have heard besides be true, that life must have been hardly worth preserving; for, they say, that he was reduced to a very deplorable state; and I have heard, from what I deem unquestionable authority, that his two beautiful and accomplished daughters are married to *two common labourers*, one a *Yankee* and the other an *Irishman*, neither of whom has, probably, a second shirt to his back, or a single pair of shoes to put his feet into! These poor girls owe their ruin and misery (if my information be correct), and, at any rate, hundreds besides BIRKBECK himself, owe their utter ruin, the most scandalous degradation, together with great bodily suffering, to the vanity, the conceit, the presumption of BIRKBECK who, observe, richly merited all that he suffered, not excepting his death; for, he sinned with his eyes open; he rejected all advice; he *persevered after he saw his error*; he dragged thousands into ruin along with him; and he most vilely calumniated the man, who, after having most disinterestedly, but in vain, endeavoured to preserve him from ruin, endeavoured to preserve those who were in danger of being deluded by him. When in 1817, before he set out for America, I was, in Catherine Street, Strand, London, so earnestly *pressing him not to go to the back countries*, he had one of these daughters with him. After talking to him for some time, and describing the risks and disadvantages of the back countries, I turned towards the daughter, and, in a sort of joking way, said: 'Miss Birkbeck, take my advice: don't let any body get *you* more than *twenty miles* from Boston, New York, Philadelphia, or Baltimore.' Upon which he gave me a most *dignified* look, and, observed: 'Miss Birkbeck has *a father*, Sir, whom she knows it to be her duty to obey.' This snap was enough for me. I saw, that this was a man so full of self-conceit, that it was impossible to do any thing with him. He seemed to me to be bent upon his own destruction. I thought it my duty to warn *others* of their danger: some took the warning; others did not; but he and his brother adventurer, FLOWER, never forgave me, and they resorted to all the means in their power to do me injury. They did me no injury, no thanks to them; and I have seen them most severely, but, most justly, punished.

*Amesbury, Tuesday, 29th August*
I set off from FIFIELD this morning, and got here (25 on the map) about one o'clock, with my *clothes wet*. While they are drying, and while a mutton chop is getting ready, I sit down to make some notes of what I have seen since I left ENFORD ... but, here comes my dinner: and I must put off my notes till I have dined.

*Salisbury, Wednesday 30th August*
My ride yesterday, from MILTON to this city of SALISBURY, was, without any exception, the most pleasant; it brought before me

the greatest number of, to me, interesting objects, and it gave rise to more interesting reflections, than I remember ever to have had brought before my eyes, or into my mind, in any one day of my life; and therefore, this ride was, without any exception, the *most pleasant* that I ever had in my life, as far as my recollection serves me. I got a little *wet* in the middle of the day; but, I got dry again, and I arrived here in very good time, though I went over the ACCURSED HILL (Old Sarum), and went across to LAVERSTOKE, before I came to Salisbury.

Let us now, then, look back over this part of Wiltshire, and see whether the inhabitants ought to be '*transported*' by order of the '*Emigration Committee*,' of which we shall see and say more by-and-by. I have before described this valley *generally*; let me now speak of it a little more in detail. The farms are all large, and, generally speaking, they were always large, I dare say; because *sheep* is one of the great things here; and sheep, in a country like this, must be kept in *flocks*, to be of any profit. The sheep principally manure the land. This is to be done only by *folding*; and, to fold, you must have a *flock*. Every farm has its portion of *down*, *arable*, and *meadow*; and, in many places, the latter are *watered meadows*, which is a great resource where sheep are kept in flocks; because these meadows furnish grass for the suckling ewes, early in the spring; and, indeed, because they have always food in them for sheep and cattle of all sorts. These meadows have had no part of the suffering from the drought, this year. They fed the ewes and lambs in the spring, and they are now yielding a heavy crop of hay; for, I saw men mowing in them, in several places, particularly about NETHERAVON (18 on the map), though it was raining at the time.

The turnips look pretty well all the way down the valley; but, I see very few, except *Swedish turnips*. The early common turnips very nearly all failed, I believe. But, the stubbles are beautifully bright; and the *rick-yards* tell us, that the crops are good, especially of *wheat*. This is not a country of *pease* and *beans*, nor of *oats*, except for home consumption. The crops are *wheat*, *barley*, *wool* and *lambs*, and these latter not to be sold to butchers, but to be sold, at the great fairs, to those who are going to keep them for some time, whether to breed from, or, finally to fat for the butcher. It is the *pulse* and the *oats* that appear to have failed most this year; and, therefore, this Valley has not suffered. I do not perceive that they have many *potatoes*; but, what they have of this base root seem to look well enough. It was one of the greatest villains on earth (Sir WALTER RALEIGH), who (they say) first brought this root into England. He was hanged at last! What a pity, since he was to be hanged, the hanging did not take place before he became such a mischievous devil as he was in the latter two-thirds of his life!

The stack-yards down this Valley are beautiful to behold. They contain from *five* to *fifteen* banging *wheat-ricks*, besides *barley-ricks*, and *hay-ricks*, and also besides the *contents of the barns*, many of which exceed *a hundred*, some *two hundred*, and I saw one at PEWSEY (4 in map), and another at FITTLETON (16 in map), each of which exceeded *two hundred and fifty* feet in length. At a farm, which, in the old maps, is called *Chissenbury Priory* (14 in map), I think I counted twenty-seven ricks of one sort and another, and sixteen or eighteen of them *wheat-ricks*. I could not conveniently get to the yard, without longer delay than I wished to make; but, I could not be much out in my counting. A very fine sight this was, and it could not meet the eye without making one look round (and in vain) *to see the people who were to eat all this food*; and without making one reflect on the horrible, the unnatural, the base and infamous state, in which we must be, when projects are on foot, and are openly avowed, for *transporting* those who raise this food, *because they want to eat enough of it to keep them alive*; and when no project is on foot for *transporting* the idlers who live in luxury upon this same food; when no project is on foot for transporting pensioners, parsons, or dead-weight people!

A little while before I came to this farm-yard, I saw, *in one piece*, about *four hundred acres* of wheat-stubble, and I saw a sheep-fold, which, I thought, contained *an acre of ground*, and had in it about *four thousand sheep and lambs*. The fold was divided into three separate flocks; but the piece of ground was one and the same; and I thought it contained about an acre. At one farm, between PEWSEY and UPAVON, I counted more than 300 hogs in one stubble. This is certainly the most delightful farming in the world. No *ditches*, no *water-furrows*, no *drains*, hardly any *hedges*, no *dirt* and *mire*, even in the wettest seasons of the year; and though the *downs* are *naked* and *cold*, the valleys are snugness itself. They are, as to the downs, what *ah-ahs* are, in parks or lawns. When you are going over the downs, you look *over* the valleys, as in the case of the *ah-ah*; and, if you be not acquainted with the country, your surprise, when you come to the edge of the hill, is very great. The *shelter*, in these valleys, and particularly where the downs are *steep* and *lofty* on the sides, is very complete. Then, the trees, are every where *lofty*. They are generally *elms*, with some *ashes*, which delight in the soil that they find here. There are, almost always, two or three large clumps of trees in every parish, and a rookery or two (not *rag*-rookery) to every parish. By the water's edge there are *willows*; and to almost every farm, there is a fine *orchard*, the trees being, in general, very fine, and, this year, they are, in general, well loaded with fruit. So that, all taken together, it seems impossible to find a more beautiful and pleasant country than this, or to imagine any life more easy and happy than men might here lead, if they were untormented by an accursed system that takes the food from those that raise it, and gives it to those that do nothing that is useful to man.

Here the farmer has always an *abundance of straw*. His farm-yard is never without it. Cattle and horses are bedded up to their eyes. The yards are put close under the shelter of a hill, or are protected by lofty and thick-set trees. Every animal seems comfortably situated; and, in the dreariest days of winter, these are, perhaps, the happiest scenes in the world; or, rather, they would be such, if those, whose labour makes it all, trees, corn, sheep and every thing, had but *their fair share* of the produce of that labour. What share they really have of it one cannot exactly say; but, I should suppose, that every labouring *man* in this valley raises as much food as would suffice for *fifty*, or *a hundred persons*, fed like himself.!

At a farm at MILTON there were, *according to my calculation*, 600 quarters of wheat and 1200 quarters of barley of the present year's crop. The farm keeps, on an average, 1400 sheep, it breeds and rears an usual proportion of pigs, fats the usual proportion of hogs, and, I suppose, rears and fats the usual proportion of poultry. Upon inquiry, I found that this farm, was, in point of produce, about *one-fifth* of the parish. Therefore, the land of this parish produces annually about 3000 quarters of wheat, 6000 quarters of barley, the wool of 7000 sheep, together with the pigs and poultry. Now, then, leaving green, or moist, vegetables out of the question, as being things that human creatures, and especially *labouring* human creatures ought never to use *as sustenance*, and saying nothing, at present, about milk and butter; leaving these wholly out of the question, let us see how many people the produce of this parish would keep, supposing the people to live all alike, and to have plenty of food and clothing. In order to come at the fact here, let us see what would be the consumption of *one family*; let it be a family of *five persons*; a man, wife, and three children, one child big enough to work, one big enough to eat heartily, and one a baby; and this is a pretty fair average of the state of people in the country. Such a family would want 5lb. of bread a-day; they would want a pound of mutton a-day; they would want two pounds of bacon a-day; they would want, on an average, winter and summer, a gallon and a half of beer a-day; for, I mean that they should live without the aid of the Eastern or the Western slave-drivers. If *sweets* were absolutely necessary for the baby, there would be quite *honey* enough in the parish. Now, then, to begin with the bread, a pound of good *wheat* makes a pound of good bread; for, though the *offal* be taken out, the *water* is put in; and, indeed, the fact is, that a pound of wheat will make a pound of bread, leaving the offal of the wheat to feed pigs, or other animals, and to produce other human food in this way. The family would, then, use 1825lb. of wheat in the year, which, at 60lb. a bushel, would be (leaving out a fraction) 30 bushels, or three quarters and six bushels, *for the year*.

Next comes the *mutton*, 365lb. for the year. Next the bacon, 730lb. As to the *quantity of mutton produced*; the sheep are *bred* here, and not fatted in general; but we may fairly suppose that each of the sheep *kept* here, each of the *standing-stock*, makes, first or last, *half a fat sheep*; so that a farm that *keeps*, on an average, 100 sheep, produces annually 50 fat sheep. Suppose the mutton to be 15lb. a quarter, then the family will want, within a trifle of, seven sheep a year. Of bacon or pork, 36 *score* will be wanted. Hogs differ so much in their propensity to fat, that it is difficult to calculate about them: but this is a very good rule: when you see a fat hog, and know how many *scores* he will weigh, set down to his account *a sack* (half a quarter) of barley for *every score* of his weight; for, let him have been *educated* (as the French call it) as he may, this will be about the real cost of him when he is fat. A sack of barley will make a score of bacon, and it will not make more. Therefore, the family would want 18 quarters of barley in the year for bacon.

As to the *beer*, 18 gallons to the bushel of malt is very good; but, as we allow of no spirits, no wine, and none of the slave-produce, we will suppose that a *sixth* part of the beer is *strong stuff*. This would require two bushels of malt to the 18 gallons. The whole would, therefore, take 35 bushels of malt; and a bushel of barley makes a bushel of malt, and, by the *increase* pays the expense of malting. Here, then, the family would want, for beer, four quarters and three bushels of barley. The annual consumption of the family, in victuals and drink, would then be as follows:

|        | Qrs. | Bush. |
|--------|------|-------|
| Wheat  | 3    | 6     |
| Barley | 22   | 3     |
| Sheep  | 7    |       |

This being the case, the 3000 quarters of wheat, which the parish annually produces, would suffice for 800 families. The 6000 quarters of barley, would suffice for 207 families. The 3500 fat sheep, being half the number kept, would suffice for 500 families. So that here is, produced in the parish of MILTON, *bread* for 800, *mutton* for 500, and *bacon and beer* for 207 families. Besides victuals and drink, there are clothes, fuel, tools and household goods wanting; but, there are milk, butter, eggs, poultry, rabbits, hares, and partridges, which I have not noticed, and these are all *eatables*, and are all *eaten* too. And as to clothing, and, indeed, fuel and all other wants beyond eating and drinking, are there not 7000 *fleeces* of South-down wool, weighing, all together, 21,000lb., and capable of being made into 8,400 yards of broad cloth, at two pounds and a half of wool to the yard? Setting, therefore, the wool, the milk, butter, eggs, poultry, and game against all the wants beyond the *solid food and drink*, we see that the parish of Milton, that we have under our eye, would give bread to 800 families, mutton to 580, and bacon and beer to 207. The reason why wheat and mutton are produced in a proportion so much greater than the materials for making bacon and beer, is, that the wheat and the mutton are more loudly demanded *from a distance*, and are much more cheaply conveyed away in proportion to their value. For instance, the wheat and mutton are wanted for the infernal WEN, and *some* barley is wanted there in the shape of *malt*; but hogs are not fatted in the WEN, and a larger proportion of the barley is used where it is grown.

Here is, then, bread for 800 families, mutton for 500, and bacon and beer for 207. Let us take the average of the three, and then we have 502 families, for the keeping of whom, and in this good manner too, the parish of Milton yields a sufficiency. In the wool, the milk, butter, eggs, poultry, and game, we have seen ample, and much more than ample, provision for *all wants*, other than those of mere *food and drink*. What I have allowed in food and drink is by no means excessive. It is but a pound of bread, and a little more than half-a-pound of meat a day to each person on an average; and the beer is not a drop too much. There are no green and moist vegetables included in my account; but, there would be some, and they would not do any harm; but, no man can say, or, at least, none but a base usurer, who would grind money out of the bones of his own father; no other man can, or will, say, that I have been *too liberal to this family*; and yet, good God! what *extravagance* is here, if the labourers of England *be now treated justly*!

Is there a family, even amongst those who live the hardest, in the WEN, that would not shudder at the thought of living upon what I have allowed to this family? Yet what do *labourers' families get*, compared to this? The answer to that question ought to make us shudder indeed. The amount of my allowance, compared with the amount of the allowance that labourers now have, is necessary to be stated here, before I proceed further. The wheat 3 qrs. and 6 bushels at present price (56s. the quarter) amounts to 10l. 10s. The barley (for bacon and beer) 22 qrs. 3 bushels, at present price (34s. the quarter), amounts to 37l. 16s. 8d. The seven sheep, at 40s. each, amount to 14l. The total is 62l. 6s. 8d; and this, observe, for *bare victuals and drink*; just food and drink enough to keep people in working condition.

What then *do* the labourers get? To what fare has this wretched and most infamous system brought them? Why such a family as I have described is allowed to have, *at the utmost*, only about 9s. a week. The parish allowance is only about 7s. 6d. for the five people, including clothing, fuel, bedding and every thing! Monstrous state of things! But, let us suppose it to be *nine shillings*. Even that makes only 23l. 8s. a year, for food, drink, clothing, fuel and every thing, whereas I allow

62*l*. 6s. 8d. a year for the *bare eating and drinking*; and that is little enough. Monstrous, barbarous, horrible as this appears, we do not, however, see it in half its horrors; our indignation and rage against this infernal system is not half roused, till we see the *small number of labourers* who raise all the food and the drink, and, of course, the mere trifling portion of it that they are suffered to retain for their own use.

The parish of MILTON does, as we have seen, produce food, drink, clothing, and all other things, enough for 502 families, or 2510 persons upon *my allowance*, which is a great deal more than *three times* the present allowance, because the present allowance includes clothing, fuel, tools and every thing. Now, then, according to the 'POPULATION RETURN,' laid before Parliament, this parish contains 500 persons, or, according to my division, *one hundred families*. So that here are about *one hundred* families to raise food and drink enough, and to raise wool and other things to pay for all other necessaries, for *five hundred* and *two* families! Aye, and five hundred and two families fed and lodged, too, *on my liberal scale*. Fed and lodged according to *the present scale*, this one hundred families raise enough to supply more, and many more, than *fifteen hundred* families; or *seven thousand five hundred* persons! And yet *those who do the work are half starved*! In the 100 families there are, we will suppose, 80 able working men, and as many boys, sometimes assisted by the women and stout girls. What a handful of people to raise such a quantity of food! What injustice, what a hellish system it must be, to make those who raise it *skin and bone and nakedness*, while the food and drink and wool are almost all carried away to be heaped on the fund-holders, pensioners, soldiers, dead-weight, and other swarms of tax-eaters! If such an operation do not need putting an end to, then the devil himself is a saint.

Thus it must be, or much about thus, all the way down this fine and beautiful and interesting valley. There are 29 agricultural parishes, the two last (30 and 31) being in *town*; being FISHERTON and SALISBURY. Now according to the 'POPULATION RETURN,' the whole of these 29 parishes contain 9116 persons; or, according to my division 1823 families. There is no reason to believe, that the proportion that we have seen in the case of MILTON does not hold good all the way through; that is, there is no reason to suppose, that the *produce* does not exceed the *consumption* in every other case in the same degree that it does in the case of MILTON. And, indeed if I were to judge from the number of *houses* and the number of *ricks of corn*, I should suppose, that the excess was still greater in several of the other parishes. But, supposing it to be no greater; supposing the same proportion to continue all the way from WATTON RIVERS (1 in map) to STRATFORD DEAN (29 in map), then here are 9116 persons raising food and raiment sufficient for 45,580 persons, fed and lodged according to my scale; and sufficient for 136,740, persons according to the scale on which the unhappy labourers of this fine valley are now fed and lodged!

And yet there is an *'Emigration Committee'* sitting to devise the means of getting *rid*, not of the *idlers*, not of the *pensioners*, not of the *dead-weight* not of the *parsons*, (to *'relieve'* whom we have seen the poor labourers taxed to the tune of a million and a half of money) not of the soldiers; but to devise means of getting rid of *these working people*, who are grudged even the miserable morsel that they get! There is in the men calling themselves 'English country gentlemen' something superlatively base. They are I *sincerely believe*, the most cruel, the most unfeeling, the most brutally insolent: but I *know*, I can *prove*, I can *safely take my oath*, that they are the MOST BASE of all the creatures that God ever suffered to disgrace the human shape. The base wretches know well, that the *taxes* amount to more than *sixty millions* a year, and that the *poor-rates* amount to about *seven millions*; yet, while the cowardly reptiles never utter a word against the taxes, they are incessantly railing against the poor-rates, though it is, (and they know it) the taxes that make the paupers. The base wretches know well, that the sum of money given, even to the *fellows that gather* the taxes, is greater in amount than the poor-rates; the base wretches know well, that the money, given to the *dead-weight* (who ought not to have a single farthing), amounts to more than the poor receive out of the rates; the base wretches know well, that the common foot-soldier now receives more pay per week (7s. 7d.) exclusive of *clothing, firing, candle*, and *lodging*; the base wretches know, that the common foot-soldier receives more *to go down his own single throat*, than the overseers and magistrates allow to *a working man, his wife* and *three children*; the base wretches know all this well; and yet their railings are confined to the *poor* and the *poor-rates*; and it is expected that they will, next session, urge the Parliament to pass a law to enable overseers and vestries and magistrates *to transport paupers beyond the seas*! They are base enough for this, or for any thing; but the whole system will go to the devil long before they will get such an act passed; long before they will see perfected this consummation of their infamous tyranny.

It is manifest enough, that the *population* of this valley was, at one time, many times over what it is now; for, in the first place, what were the *twenty-nine* churches built *for*? The population of the 29 parishes is *now* but little more than *one-half* of that of the single parish of Kensington; and there are several of the churches bigger than the church at Kensington. What, then, should all these churches have been built FOR? And besides, where did the *hands* come from? And where did the *money* come from? These twenty-nine churches would now not only hold all the inhabitants, men, women, and children, but all the household goods, and tools, and implements, of the whole of them, farmers and all, if you leave out the wagons and carts. In three instances, FIFIELD, MILSTON, and ROACH-FEN (17, 23, and 24), the *church-porches* will hold all the inhabitants, even down to the bed-ridden and the babies. What then, will any man believe that these churches were built for such little knots of people? We are told about the *great superstition* of our fathers, and of their readiness to *gratify the priests* by building altars and other religious edifices. But, we must think those priests to have been most devout creatures indeed, if we believe, that they chose to have the money laid out in *useless* churches, rather than have it put into their own pockets! At any rate, we all know that *Protestant Priests* have no whims of *this sort*; and that they never lay out upon churches any money that they can, by any means, get hold of.

But, suppose that we were to believe that the Priests had, in old times, this unaccountable taste; and suppose we were to believe that a knot of people, who might be crammed into a church-porch, were seized, and very frequently too, with the desire of having a big church to go to; we must, after all this, believe that this knot of people were more than *giants*, or that they had surprising *riches*, else we cannot believe that they had *the means* of gratifying the strange wishes of their Priests and their own not less strange *piety* and *devotion*. Even if we could believe that they thought that they were paving their way to heaven, by building churches which were a hundred times too large for the population, still we cannot believe, that the building could have been effected without *bodily force*; and, where was this force to *come from*, if the people were not more numerous than they now are? What, again, I ask, were these twenty-nine churches stuck up, *not a mile from each other*; what were twenty-nine churches made FOR, if the population had been no greater than it is now?

But, in fact, you plainly see all the traces of a great ancient population. The churches are almost all large, and built in the best manner. Many of them are *very fine* edifices; very costly in the building; and, in the cases where the body of the church has been altered in the repairing of it, so as to make it smaller, the *tower*, which every where defies the hostility of time, shows you what the church must formerly have been. This is the case in several instances; and there are two or three of these villages which must formerly have been *market-towns*, and particularly PEWSY and UPAVON (4 and 13). There are now no less than *nine* of the parishes, out of twenty-nine that have either *no parsonage-houses*, or have such as are in such a state that a Parson will not, or cannot, live in them. Three of them are without any parsonage-houses at all, and the rest are become poor, mean, falling-down places. This latter is the case at UPAVON, which was formerly a very considerable place. Nothing can more clearly show, than this, that all, as far as buildings and population are concerned, has been long upon the decline and decay. Dilapidation after dilapidation have, at last, almost effaced even the parsonage-houses, and that too in *defiance of the law*, ecclesiastical as well as civil. The *land* remains; and the crops and the sheep come as abundantly as ever; but they are now *sent almost wholly away*, instead of remaining as formerly, to be, in great part, consumed in these twenty-nine parishes.

The *stars*, in my map, mark the spots where *manor-houses*, or *gentlemen's mansions*, formerly stood, and stood, too, only about *sixty years ago*. Every *parish* had its manor house in the first place; and then there were, down this Valley, *twenty-one others*; so that, in this distance of about *thirty miles*, there stood FIFTY MANSION HOUSES. Where are they *now*? I believe there are but EIGHT, that are at all worthy of the name of *mansion houses*; and even these are but poorly kept up, and, except in two or three instances, are of no benefit to the labouring people; they employ but few persons; and, in short, do not half supply the place of *any eight* of the old mansions. All these mansions, all these parsonages, aye, and their goods and furniture, together with the clocks, the brass-kettles, the brewing-vessels, the good bedding and good clothes and good furniture, and the stock in pigs, or in money, of the inferior classes, in this series of once populous and gay villages and hamlets; all these have been by the accursed system of taxing and funding and paper-money, by the well-known exactions of the state, and by the not less real, though less generally understood, extortions of the *monopolies* arising out of paper-money; all these have been, by these accursed means, conveyed away, out of this Valley, to the haunts of the tax-eaters and the monopolizers. There are many of the *mansion houses*, the ruins of which you yet behold. At MILTON (3 in my map) there are two mansion houses, the walls and the *roofs* of which yet remain, but which are falling gradually to pieces, and the garden walls are crumbling down. At ENFORD (15 in my map) BENNET the Member for the county, had a large mansion house, the *stables* of which are yet standing. In several places, I saw, still remaining, indubitable traces of an ancient manor house, namely a *dove-cote* or *pigeon-house*. The poor pigeons have kept possession of their heritage, from generation to generation, and so have the *rooks*, in their several rookeries, while the paper-system has swept away, or, rather *swallowed-up*, the owners of the dove-cotes and of the lofty trees, about forty families of which owners have been ousted in this one Valley, and have become dead-weight creatures, tax-gatherers, barrack-fellows, thief-takers, or, perhaps, paupers or thieves.

Senator SNIP congratulated, some years ago, that preciously honourable 'Collective *Wisdom*' of which he is a most worthy Member; SNIP congratulated it on the *success of the late war* in *creating capital*! SNIP is, you must know a great *feelosofer*, and a not less great *feenanceer*. SNIP cited, as a proof of the great and glorious effects of paper-money, the *new and fine houses in London*, the *new streets and squares*, the *new roads, new canals* and *bridges*. SNIP was not, I dare say, aware, that this same paper-money had destroyed forty mansion houses in this Vale of Avon, and had taken away all the goods, all the substance, of the little gentry and of the labouring class. SNIP was not, I dare say, aware, that this same paper-money had, in this one Vale of only thirty miles long, dilapidated, and in some cases, wholly demolished, *nine* out of *twenty-nine* even of the parsonage houses. I told SNIP at the time (1821), that paper-money could *create no valuable thing*. I begged SNIP to bear this in mind. I besought all my readers, and particularly Mr MATHIAS ATWOOD (one of the members for *Lowther-town*), not to believe that paper-money ever did, or ever could, CREATE any thing of any value. I besought him to look well into the matter, and assured him, that he would find that though paper-money could CREATE nothing of value, it was able to TRANSFER every thing of value; able to strip a little gentry; able to dilapidate even parsonage houses; able to rob gentlemen of their estates, and labourers of their Sunday-coats and their barrels of beer; able to snatch the dinner from the board of the reaper or the mower, and to convey it to the barrack-table, of the Hessian or Hanoverian grenadier; able to take away the wool, that ought to give warmth to the bodies of those who rear the sheep, and put it on the backs of those who carry arms to keep the poor, half-famished shepherds in order.

I have never been able clearly to comprehend what the beastly Scotch *feelosofers* mean by their '*national wealth*;' but, as far as I can understand them, this is their meaning: that national wealth means, that which is *left* of the products of the country over and above what is *consumed*, or *used*, by those whose labour causes the products to be. This being the notion, it follows, of course, that the *fewer* poor devils you can screw the products out of, the *richer* the nation is. This is, too, the notion of BURDETT as expressed in his silly and most nasty, musty aristocratic speech of last session. What, then, is to be done with this *over-produce*? Who is to have it? Is it to go to pensioners, placemen, tax-gatherers, dead-weight people, soldiers, gendarmerie, police-people, and, in short, to whole millions *who do no work at all*? Is this a cause of '*national wealth*'? Is a nation made *rich* by taking the food and clothing from those who create them, and giving them to those who do nothing of any use? Aye, but, this *over-produce* may be given to *manufacturers*, and to those who supply the food-raisers with what they want besides food. Oh! but this is merely an *exchange* of one valuable thing for another valuable thing; it is an exchange of labour in Wiltshire for labour in Lancashire; and, upon the whole, here is no *over-production*. If the produce be *exported*, it is the same thing: it is an *exchange* of one sort of labour for another. But, *our course* is, that there is not an *exchange*; that those who labour, no matter in what way, have a large part of the fruit of their labour *taken away*, and receive nothing *in exchange*. If the over-produce of this Valley of Avon were given, by the farmers, to the weavers in Lancashire, to the iron and steel chaps of Warwickshire, and to other makers or sellers of useful things, there would come an abundance of all these useful things into this valley from Lancashire and other parts; but if, as is the case, the over-produce goes to the fund-holders, the dead-weight, the soldiers, the lord and lady and master and miss pensioners and sinecure people; if the over-produce go to them, as a very great part of it does, nothing not even the parings of one's nails, *can come back to the valley in exchange*. And, can this operation, then, add to the '*national wealth*'? It adds to the '*wealth*' of those who carry on the affairs of state; it fills their pockets, those of their relatives and dependants; it fattens all tax-eaters; but, it can give no *wealth* to the 'nation,' which means, *the whole of the people*. National Wealth means, the *Commonwealth* or *Commonweal*; and these mean, the general *good*, or *happiness*, of the people, and the *safety* and *honour of the state*; and, these are not to be secured by robbing those who labour, in order to support a large part of the community in *idleness*. DEVIZES is the market-town to which the corn goes from the greater part of this Valley. If, when a wagon-load of wheat goes off in the morning, the wagon came back at night loaded with cloth, salt, or something or other, *equal in value to the wheat*, except what might be necessary to leave with the shopkeeper as his profit; then, indeed, the people might see the wagon go off without tears in their eyes. But, now, they see it go *to carry away*, and to bring *next to nothing in return*.

What a *twist* a head must have before it can come to the conclusion, that the *nation* gains in *wealth* by the government being able to cause the work to be done by those who have hardly any share in the fruit of the labour! What a *twist* such a head must have! The Scotch *feelosofers*, who seem all to have been, by nature, formed for negro-drivers, have an insuperable objection to all those establishments and customs which occasion *holidays*. They call them a *great hinderance*, a great *bar to industry*, a great *draw-back from 'national wealth.'* I wish each of these unfeeling fellows had a spade put into his hand for ten days, only ten days, and that he were compelled to dig only just as much as one of the common labourers at Fulham. The metaphysical gentleman would, I believe, soon discover the *use of holidays*! But *why* should men, why should *any* men, work *hard*? Why, I ask, should they work *incessantly*, if working part of the days of the week be sufficient? Why should the people at MILTON, for instance, work incessantly, when they now raise food and clothing and fuel and every necessary *to maintain well five times their number*? Why should they not have some holidays? And, pray, say, thou conceited Scotch feelosofer, how the '*national wealth*' can be increased by making these people work *incessantly*, that they may raise food and clothing, to go to feed and clothe *people who do not work at all*?

The state of this Valley seems to illustrate the infamous and really diabolical assertion of MALTHUS, which is, that the human kind have a NATURAL TENDENCY, *to increase beyond the means of sustenance for them*. Hence, all the schemes of this and the other Scotch writers for what they call *checking population*. Hence all the *beastly*, the *nasty*, the abominable writings, put forth to teach labouring people *how to avoid having children*. Now, look at this Valley of AVON. Here the people raise nearly *twenty times as much food and clothing as they consume*. They raise five times as much, even according to my scale of living. They have been doing this for many, many years. They have been doing it *for several generations*. Where, then, is their NATURAL TENDENCY *to increase beyond the means of sustenance for them*? Beyond, indeed, the means of that sustenance *which a system like this will leave them*. Say that, Sawneys, and I agree with you. Far beyond the means that the taxing and monopolizing system will leave in their hands: that is very true; for it leaves them nothing but the scale of the poor-book: they must cease to breed at all, or they must exceed this mark; but, the *earth*, give them their fair share of its products, will always give sustenance in sufficiency to those who apply to it by skilful and diligent labour.

The villages down this Valley of Avon, and, indeed, it was the same in almost every part of this county, and in the North and West of Hampshire also, used to have great employment for the women and children *in the carding and spinning of wool for the making of broad-cloth*. This was a very general employment for the women and girls; but, it is *now wholly gone*; and this has made a vast change in the condition of the people, and in the state of property and of manners and morals. In 1816, I wrote and published a *Letter to the*

*Luddites*, the object of which was *to combat their hostility to the use of machinery*. The arguments I there made use of were general. I took the matter in the abstract. The *principles* were all correct enough; but their application *cannot be universal*; and, we have a case here before us, at this moment, which, in my opinion, shows, that the mechanic inventions, pushed to the extent that they have been, have been productive of great calamity to this country, and that they will be productive of still greater calamity; unless, indeed, it be their brilliant destiny to be the immediate cause of *putting an end to the present system*.

The greater part of manufactures consists of *clothing* and *bedding*. Now, if by using a machine, we can get our coat with less labour than we got it before, the machine is a desirable thing. But, then, mind, we must have the machine *at home* and we *ourselves* must have *the profit* of it; for, if the machine be *elsewhere*; if it be worked *by other hands*; if *other persons* have the *profit* of it; and if, in consequence of the existence of the machine, we have hands at home, who have *nothing to do*, and whom we must keep, then the machine is an injury to us, however advantageous it may be to those who use it, and whatever traffic it may occasion with foreign States.

Such is the case with regard to this cloth-making. The machines are at *Upton-Level*, *Warminster*, *Bradford*, *Westbury*, and *Trowbridge*, and here are some of the hands in the Valley of Avon. This Valley raises food and clothing; but, in order to raise them, it must have *labourers*. These are absolutely necessary; for, without them this rich and beautiful Valley becomes worth nothing except to wild animals and their pursuers. The labourers are *men* and *boys*. Women and girls occasionally; but the men and the boys are as necessary as the light of day, or as the air and the water. Now, if beastly MALTHUS, or any of his nasty disciples, can discover a mode of having men and boys *without having women and girls*, then, certainly, the *machine* must be a good thing; but, if this Valley *must absolutely have the women and the girls*, then the machine, by leaving them with *nothing to do*, is a mischievous thing; and a producer of most dreadful misery. What, with regard to the poor, is the great complaint now? Why, that the *single man* does not receive the same, or any thing like the same, wages as the *married* man. Aye, it is the *wife* and girls that are the burden; and to be sure a burden they must be, under a system of taxation like the present, and with *no work to do*. Therefore, whatever may be *saved* in labour by the *machine* is no benefit, but an injury to the mass of the people. For, in fact, all that the women and children earned was so much *clear addition* to what the family earns now. The greatest part of the clothing in the United States of America *is made by the farm women and girls*. They do almost the whole of it; and all that they do is done *at home*. To be sure, they might buy *cheap*; but they must buy for *less than nothing*, if it would not answer their purpose to *make* the things.

The survey of this Valley is, I think, the finest answer in the world to the 'EMIGRATION COMMITTEE' fellows, and to JERRY CURTEIS (one of the Members for Sussex), who has been giving '*evidence*' before it. I shall find out, when I can get to see the *report*, what this 'EMIGRATION COMMITTEE' would be *after*. I remember, that, last winter, a young woman complained to one of the Police Justices, that the *Overseers* of some parish were going to *transport her orphan brother to Canada*, because he became chargeable to their parish! I remember also, that the Justice said, that the intention of the Overseers was '*premature*'; for that 'the BILL *had not yet passed*'! This was rather an ugly story; and I do think, that we shall find, that there have been, and are, some pretty propositions before this 'COMMITTEE.' We shall see all about the matter, however, by-and-by; and, when we get the *transporting* project fairly before us, shall we not then loudly proclaim 'the *envy* of surrounding nations and *admiration* of the world'!

But, what ignorance, impudence and insolence must those base wretches have, who propose to *transport* the labouring people, as being *too numerous*, while the produce, which is obtained by their labour, is more than sufficient for three, four, or five, or even ten times their numbers! JERRY CURTEIS, who has, it seems, been a famous witness on this occasion, says that the *poor-rates*, in many cases, amount to as much as the *rent*. Well; and what then, JERRY? The rent may be high enough too, and the farmer *may afford to pay them both*; for, a very large part of what you call *poor-rates* ought to be called *wages*. But, at any rate, what has all this to do with the *necessity of emigration*? To make out such necessity, you must make out that you have *more mouths than the produce of the parish will feed*? Do then, JERRY, tell us, another time, a little about *the quantity of food* annually raised in four or five adjoining parishes; for, is it not something rather damnable, JERRY, to talk of *transporting* Englishmen, on account of the *excess of their numbers*, when the fact is notorious, that their labour produces five or ten times as much food and raiment as they and their families consume!

However, to drop JERRY, for the present, the baseness, the foul, the stinking, the carrion baseness, of the fellows that call themselves '*country gentlemen*' is, that the wretches, while railing against the poor and the poor-rates; while affecting to believe, that the poor are wicked and lazy; while complaining that the poor, the working people, are *too numerous*, and that the country villages are too populous: the carrion baseness of these wretches, is, that, while they are thus *bold* with regard to the working and poor people, they never even whisper a word against pensioners, placemen, soldiers, parsons, fund-holders, tax-gatherers, or tax-eaters! They say not a word against the prolific *dead-weight*, to whom they GIVE A PREMIUM FOR BREEDING, while they want to check the population of labourers! They never say a word about the too great populousness of the WEN; nor about that of Liverpool, Manchester, Cheltenham, and the like! Oh! they are the most cowardly, the very basest, the most scandalously base reptiles that ever were warmed into life by the rays of the sun!

In taking my leave of this beautiful vale I have to express my deep shame, as an Englishman, at beholding the general *extreme poverty* of those who cause this vale to produce such quantities of food and raiment. This is, I verily believe it, the *worst used labouring people upon the face of the earth*. Dogs and hogs and horses are treated with *more civility*; and as to food and lodging, how gladly would the labourers change with them! This state of things never can continue many years! *By some means or other* there must be an end to it; and my firm belief is, that that end will be dreadful. In the mean while I see, and I see it with pleasure, that the common people *know that they are ill used*; and that they cordially, most cordially, hate those who ill-treat them.

During the day I crossed the river about fifteen or sixteen times; and in such hot weather it was very pleasant to be so much amongst meadows and water. I had been at NETHER-AVON (18) about eighteen years ago, where I had seen a great quantity of hares. It is a place belonging to Mr HICKS BEACH, or BEECH, who was once a member of parliament. I found the place *altered* a good deal; out of repair; the gates rather rotten: and (a very bad sign!) the *roof of the dog-kennel falling in*! There is a church, at this village of NETHERAVON, large enough to hold *a thousand or two* of people, and the whole parish contains only 350 souls, men, women and children. This Netheravon was formerly a great lordship, and in the parish there were three considerable mansion-houses, besides the one near the church. These mansions are all down now; and it is curious enough to see the former *walled gardens* become *orchards*, together with other changes, all tending to prove the gradual decay in all except what appertains merely to *the land* as a thing of production for the distant market. But, indeed, the people and the means of enjoyment *must go away*. They are *drawn* away by the taxes and the paper-money. How are *twenty thousand new houses* to be, all at once, building in the WEN, without people and food and raiment going from this valley towards the WEN? It must be so; and this unnatural, this dilapidating, this ruining and debasing work must go on, until that which produces it be destroyed.

When I came down to STRATFORD DEAN (29 in map), I wanted to go across to LAVERSTOKE, which lay to my left of Salisbury; but just on the side of the road here, at Stratford Dean, rises the ACCURSED HILL. It is very lofty. It was originally a hill in an irregular sort of sugar-loaf shape: but, it was so altered by the Romans, or by somebody, that the upper three-quarter parts of the hill now, when seen from a distance, somewhat resemble *three cheeses*, laid one upon another; the bottom one a great deal broader than the next, and the top one like a Stilton cheese, in proportion to a Gloucester one. I resolved to rise over this ACCURSED HILL. As I was going up a field towards it, I met a man going home from work. I asked how he *got on*. He said, very badly. I asked him what was the cause of it. He said the *hard times*. 'What *times*,' said I; 'was there ever a finer summer, a finer harvest, and is there not an *old* wheat-rick in every farm-yard?' 'Ah!' said he, '*they* make it bad for poor people, for all that.' '*They*?' said I, 'who is *they*?' He was silent. 'Oh, no no! my friend,' said I, 'it is not *they*; it is that ACCURSED HILL that has robbed you of the supper that you ought to find smoking on the table when you get home.' I gave him the price of a pot of beer, and on I went, leaving the poor dejected assemblage of skin and bone to wonder at my words.

The hill is very steep, and I dismounted and led my horse up.

Being as near to the top as I could conveniently get, I stood a little while reflecting, not so much on the changes which that hill had seen, as on the changes, the terrible changes, which, in all human probability, it had *yet to see*, and which it would have greatly *helped to produce*. It was impossible to stand on this accursed spot, without swelling with indignation against the base and plundering and murderous sons of corruption. I have often wished, and I, speaking out loud, expressed the wish now: 'May that man perish for ever and ever, who, having the power, neglects to bring to justice the perjured, the suborning, the insolent and perfidious miscreants, who openly sell their country's rights and their own souls.'

From the ACCURSED HILL I went to LAVERSTOKE where 'JEMMY BOROUGH' (as they call him here), the Judge, lives. I have not heard much about 'JEMMY' since he tried and condemned the two young men who had wounded the gamekeepers of ASSHETON SMITH and LORD PALMERSTON. His Lordship (Palmerston) is, I see, making a tolerable figure in the newspapers as a *share-man*! I got into Salisbury about half-past seven o'clock, less tired than I recollect ever to have been after so long a ride; for, including my several crossings of the river and my deviations to look at churches and farm-yards, and rick-yards, I think I must have ridden nearly forty miles.